EMPLOYMENT LAW FOR THE PARALEGAL

The West Legal Studies Series

Your options keep growing with West Legal Studies

Each year our list continues to offer you more options for every area of the law to meet your course or on-the-job reference requirements. We now have over 140 titles from which to choose in the following areas:

Administrative Law	Family Law
Alternative Dispute Resolution	Federal Taxation
Bankruptcy	Intellectual Property
Business Organizations/Corporations	Introduction to Law
Civil Litigation and Procedure	Introduction to Paralegalism
CLA Exam Preparation	Law Office Management
Client Accounting	Law Office Procedures
Computer in the Law Office	Legal Research, Writing, and Analysis
Constitutional Law	Legal Terminology
Contract Law	Paralegal Employment
Criminal Law and Procedure	Real Estate Law
Document Preparation	Reference Materials
Environmental Law	Torts and Personal Injury Law
Ethics	Will, Trusts, and Estate Administration

You will find unparalleled, practical support

Each book is augmented by instructor and student supplements to ensure the best learning experience possible. We also offer custom publishing and other benefits such as West's Student Achievement Award. In addition, our sales representatives are ready to provide you with dependable service.

We want to hear from you

Our best contributions for improving the quality of our books and instructional materials is feedback from the people who use them. If you have a question, concern, or observation about any of our materials, or you have a product proposal or manuscript, we want to hear from you. Please contact your local representative or write us at the following address:

West Legal Studies, 3 Columbia Circle, P.O. Box 15015, Albany, NY 12212-5015

For additional information point your browser at
www.westlegalstudies.com

WEST
THOMSON LEARNING

EMPLOYMENT LAW FOR THE PARALEGAL

OCLC Record

Peggy N. Kerley

WEST
THOMSON LEARNING

Australia   Canada   Mexico   Singapore   Spain   United Kingdom   United States

WEST
THOMSON LEARNING™

WEST LEGAL STUDIES

Employment Law for the Paralegal
by Peggy N. Kerley

Business Unit Director:
Susan L. Simpfenderfer

Executive Editor:
Marlene McHugh Pratt

Senior Acquisitions Editor:
Joan M. Gill

Developmental Editor:
Andrea Edwards

Editorial Assistant:
Lisa Flatley

Executive Production Manager:
Wendy A. Troeger

Production Manager:
Carolyn Miller

Production Coordinator:
Matthew J. Williams

Executive Marketing Manager:
Donna J. Lewis

Channel Manager:
Nigar Hale

Cover Image:
Photodisc

Cover Designs:
TBD Publishing Services

For permission to use material from this text or product, contact us by
Tel (800) 730-2214
Fax (800) 730-2215
www.thomsonrights.com

Library of Congress Cataloging-in-Publication Data

Kerley, Peggy N.
    Employment law for the paralegal / Peggy Kerley.
       p.   cm.
    "West Legal Studies Series."
    Includes index.
    ISBN 0-7668-1533-1
    1. Labor laws and legislation—United States.   2. Legal assistants—United States—Handbooks, manuals, etc.   I. Title.

KF3319.6.K47 2001
344.7301—dc21

2001046669

Notice to the Reader

Publisher does not warrant or guarantee any of the products described herein or perform any independent analysis in connection with any of the product information contained herein. Publisher does not assume, and expressly disclaims, any obligation to obtain and include information other than that provided by the manufacturer.

The reader is expressly warned to consider and adopt all safety precautions that might be indicated by the activities herein and to avoid all potential hazards. By following the instructions contained herein, the reader willingly assumes all risks in connection with such instructions.

The publisher makes no representation or warranties of any kind, including but not limited to, the warranties of fitness for particular purpose of merchantability, nor are any such representations implied with respect to the material set forth herein, and the publisher takes no responsibility with respect to such material. The publisher shall not be liable for any special, consequential, or exemplary damages resulting, in whole or part, from the readers' use of, or reliance upon, this material.

CONTENTS

CHAPTER 7—OVERVIEW OF DISCRIMINATION IN EMPLOYMENT LAW

CHAPTER 8—THE AMERICANS WITH DISABILITIES ACT

PREFACE

As a paralegal educator, you are aware of the need to skillfully blend the principles of the law with its practical application. The employment law paralegal meets new and different challenges on the job every day. These daily challenges require that, from the first day on the job, the employment law paralegal must be prepared to understand what needs to be done in a specific legal and factual situation and why it must be done. The paralegal must be able to recognize the most efficient, effective, and economical way to accomplish each task. *Employment Law for the Paralegal* was planned and written with those specific goals in mind.

To successfully acquaint the paralegal student with the intricate blend of legal theory and practical legal skills required for the area of employment law, the author has recognized the fact that many students will take this course early in their paralegal education, while others will not be introduced to the subject until the latter part of their curriculum. Consequently, the author has been careful to present this often-complicated and difficult area of the law in a simple, straightforward fashion that can be understood by the newest paralegal student but will, hopefully, present a challenge to the "seasoned" paralegal student.

ORGANIZATION OF THE TEXTBOOK

For clarity, the text proceeds in a chronological order through the employment relationship. Chapter 1 introduces the student to the background of employment law and discusses the master-servant and principal-agent relationships. It includes material on the rapidly developing area of independent contractor and differentiates between an independent contractor and an employee. The text discusses new categories of employees—the leased or temporary employee, in addition to the concept of "joint employer." This chapter also extensively reviews the doctrine of employment at will before turning to a detailed discussion of one exception to that doctrine, the employment contract. Chapter 2 introduces the student to the establishment of the employment relationship, including affirmative action, advertising for a job vacancy, the interview process, pre-employment testing, and a breakdown of provisions of the written employment contract. Chapters 3 and 4 discuss employment compensation and employee benefits, and Chapter 5 reviews methods of employee evaluation. Chapter 6 presents the issue of proper and improper terminations and the potential damages arising from improper terminations.

Chapters 7 through 14 provide an in-depth view of the volatile issue of employment discrimination in light of such landmark legislation as Title VII, the Americans with Disabilities Act, the Age Discrimination in Employment Act, the Equal Pay Act, and the Family Medical Leave Act. Legislators, attorneys, and even courts often find the issue of discrimination difficult to understand and even more difficult to apply equitably in the area of employment. Volumes have been written on the subject matter covered in this section of the text. Each day courts are rendering decisions that affect or possibly drastically change prior legal holdings in critical areas such as disability, sexual harassment, and religious discrimination. Care has been taken to include landmark cases in these areas at the time the text was published. However, as always, students are reminded that an important duty of a paralegal in any legal specialty is to make certain that any case relied upon is still "good law." Paralegal students are given useful forms and charts in these eight chapters to assist with their work in the area of employment discrimination.

Chapter 15 explores the controversial subject of the employer's rights versus the employee's right to privacy in such areas as drug testing, polygraph testing, workplace searches, the employee's credit history, and the employer's access to electronic mail and telephone messages sent and received by its employees. Also included in this chapter are examples of drug testing policies, polygraph procedures, and other means of implementing the employer's perceived right to monitor its employees' behavior in the workplace.

The immigration law practice is a veritable Mecca for employment paralegals. Newspapers, Internet job banks, and paralegal organization newsletters are filled with job opportunities in this employment specialty area. Chapter 16 gives an overview of immigration. The increasing flow of individuals from other countries into the United States makes knowledge of at least basic immigration principles a necessity for the employment paralegal.

Finally, Chapter 17 provides an introduction to safety requirements in employment law, particularly through OSHA, and the state-specific area of employment law-workers' compensation. The student is provided with information on the location and telephone numbers of state workers' compensation agencies and OSHA offices.

FEATURES OF THE TEXTBOOK

Cases. A majority of the chapters contain a landmark case on the chapter material, including the judicial history of the case, facts of the case, pertinent sections of the court's actual opinion, and the disposition of the case.

Terms. Each chapter contains a list of all legal terms in chapter material. The terms appear in boldface within the chapter. These terms and their definitions are also compiled in a Glossary at the end of the book.

Review Questions. Each chapter contains questions for review and discussion to provide students with a sense of continuity with the learning objectives and to guarantee that students understand the chapter material.

Chapter Projects. The Chapter Projects offer the paralegal students an opportunity to perform a major paralegal task outlined in the chapter. Chapter projects include such activities as writing memos and letters and drafting pleadings, motions, and discovery.

Appendices. The Appendices contain valuable forms, charts, agency directories, and Internet listings that correlate with the text material.

SUPPLEMENTAL MATERIALS

- **Instructor's Manual with Test Bank** Written by the author of the text, the Instructor's Manual contains chapter outlines, teaching suggestions, answers to review questions, transparency masters and a test bank. The Instructor's Manual can also be found on-line at **www.westlegalstudies.com**. Please click on Resources, then go into the Instructor's Lounge.
- **Web Page** Come visit our Web site at **www.westlegalstudies.com** where you will find valuable information specific to this book such as hot links and sample materials to download, as well as other West Legal Studies products.
- **WESTLAW®** West's on-line computerized legal research system offers students "hands-on" experience with a system commonly used in law offices. Qualified adopters can receive ten free hours of WESTLAW®. WESTLAW® can be accessed with Macintosh and IBM PC and compatibles. A modem is required.
- **Court TV Videos** West Legal Studies is pleased to offer the following videos from Court TV. Available for a minimal fee:
    - New York v. Ferguson—Murder on the 5:33: The Trial of Colin Ferguson
      ISBN 0-7668-1098-4
    - Ohio v. Alfieri—Road Rage
      ISBN 0-7668-1099-2

- Flynn v. Goldman Sachs—Fired on Wall Street: A Case of Sex Discrimination?
  ISBN 0-7668-1096-8
- Dodd v. Dodd: Religion and Child Custody in Conflict
  ISBN 0-7668-1094-1
- Fentress v. Eli Lilly & Co. et al.—Prozac on Trial
  ISBN 0-7668-1095-X
- In Re Custody of Baby Girl Clausen—Child of Mine: The Fight for Baby Jessica
  ISBN 0-7668-1097-6
- Northside Partners v. Page and New Kids on the Block (Intellectual Property)
  ISBN 0-7668-0426-7
- Maglica v. Maglica (Contract law)
  ISBN 0-7668-0867-X
- Hall v. Hall (Family Law)
  ISBN 0-7668-0196-9
- Berring Legal Research Videos

- **West's Paralegal Video Library** includes:

  - The Drama of the Law II: Paralegal Issues Video
    ISBN 0-314-07088-5
  - *I Never Said I Was a Lawyer* Paralegal Issues Video
    ISBN 0-314-08049-X
  - The Making of a Case Video
    ISBN 0-314-07300-0
  - Mock Trial Video—Anatomy of a Trial: A Contracts Case—Business Litigation
    ISBN 0-314-07343-4
  - Mock Trial Video—Trial Techniques: A Products Liability Case
    ISBN 0-314-07342-6
  - Arguments to the United States Supreme Court
    ISBN 0-314-07070-2

These videos are available at no charge to qualified adopters.

Please note the Internet resources are of a time sensitive nature and URL addresses may often change or be deleted.

Contact us at westlegalstudies@delmar.com

ACKNOWLEDGMENTS

My thanks and acknowledgment go to all those who reviewed the book and provided meaningful feedback, suggestions, and insights.

Michelle Wales
Samford University

Bernard Behrend
Duquesne University

Decateur Reed
Arapahoe Community College

Ana M. Otero
Center for Advanced Legal Studies

Howard Schwager
Madonna University

Anita Tebbe
Johnson County Community College

Angela L. Ekker
Arapahoe Community College

Eli C. Bortman
Suffolk University

Deborah L. Chesi
Pueblo Community College

Ronald C. Goldfarb
Middlesex County College

CHAPTER 1

The Employment Relationship

OVERVIEW

Virtually every relationship in life is established and governed by law. The initiation and dissolution of marriage, the purchase or disposition of real estate, the establishment of a new business, and the employment process are examples of such legal relationships.

The earliest employment relationship was totally controlled by the employer, who had the ability to select an employee, control the hours and rates of pay for the employee, and discharge the employee with or without cause, known as **employment at will**. In the past several decades, the doctrine of employment at will has been further defined and modified by statutes and judicial interpretation.

This chapter analyzes the parties to the employment relationship, how such a relationship is created and maintained, and the types of employment relationships that may be established.

The determination of the parties to an employment relationship, particularly whether an individual is an employee or independent contractor (IC), is often controversial due to conflicting definitions of an employee in federal statutes and regulations. However, employment relationships may initially be defined in two broad categories: master-servant or principal-agent.

MASTER-SERVANT RELATIONSHIP

The master-servant relationship exists when one person, referred to as the **servant**, is employed by another person, the **master**, and is subject to that person's control as to *what* work is done and *how* it is done. An essential element for a judicial finding of a master-servant relationship is the extent of control exercised by the master.

An example of a master-servant relationship is the paralegal-attorney relationship. *Oran's Law Dictionary, Third Edition*, offers the following definition of a paralegal: "The American Bar Association restricts the term 'paralegal' to legal assistants . . . who work under a lawyer's 'ultimate' supervision on 'substantive' legal work that the lawyer would otherwise do." The reference to "ultimate" supervision is simply another term for the attorney's "control" of *what* work a paralegal performs and *how* the work is performed.

In addition to the obligations that the master and servant have to each other, the master is liable for any **tort**, a civil (as opposed to a criminal) wrong, other than a breach of contract, which results in injury to another person. The doctrine of the master's liability for a servant's action within the scope of employment is commonly referred to as *respondeat superior*, a Latin phrase meaning "Let the master answer." If a servant commits a tort while pursuing his or her own interest, the master is not liable, and any relief or damage award to a third party will generally come from the servant individually. If an employee is injured at work because of the master's own negligence, the employer is legally responsible for those injuries.

Additionally, if a third party is injured by a servant who is not fit to do the job for which he or she has been hired, the master might be liable under the concept of **negligent hiring**, defined as the master's careless hiring of someone who was likely to injure third parties.

PRINCIPAL-AGENT RELATIONSHIP

A **principal** is an employer or anyone else who has another person (an agent) do things for her or him. The **agent** has the legal authority to act on behalf of the principal and to bind the principal to third persons by contract. The majority of such relationships include consideration for the agent, in which case the agent becomes an employee of the principal. An agent is specifically prohibited from acting outside of or beyond the scope of his or her authority in this type of relationship.

An agent is a **fiduciary** (acting for another in a position of trust) to the principal. Thus, the agent owes the principal a high duty of loyalty and is prohibited from acting on behalf of himself or herself in any transaction for the principal.

The principal-agent relationship differs substantially from the master-servant relationship in the area of control. An agent has discretion for the method by which he or she carries out the agency. The principal does not control the agent's actions, whereas a master controls the servant's actions.

A principal is held liable for all contracts that the agent enters into on the principal's behalf because the purpose of the agency relationship is to contractually bind the principal to third persons. Unlike in the case of the master-servant relationship, only the agent is liable for his or her negligent injury of a third person.

An agency relationship is created by one of the following three methods:

Agreement

If two individuals agree that one should act as the other's agent, the agency relationship is created. No consideration is required for an agency, but consideration *is* necessary to create an employment relationship.

Estoppel

Under the theory of **estoppel**, an individual is stopped by his or her own prior acts from claiming a right against another person who has legitimately relied on those acts. An example in agency law would be an individual who intentionally or negligently allows a third party to believe that another individual is his or her agent, and the third person relies on this belief that the "presumed" agent has authority, to the detriment of the third party. In such an instance, the law will "estop" or bar the principal from claiming that no agency existed.

Example   A home owner suggests that a prospective purchaser tour his or her home with the home owner's nephew. In the presence of the home owner, the nephew discusses the home's features, sales price, and potential financing with the prospective purchaser. Based upon representations from the nephew, the prospective purchaser applies for a home loan. After expending several hundred dollars in the financing effort, the home owner advises the mortgage company that he or she never agreed to the sales price, and that the nephew never had the authority to offer the home for the quoted price. In this case, the home owner would be estopped from claiming that the nephew was his or her agent.

Ratification

Ratification is the confirmation and acceptance of a previous act done by another person. In an incident where there was no agency when a contract was entered into, but the "unofficial" principal agrees to the contract, the agency relationship is created retroactively.

Example   Assume that in the example above, the home owner and nephew had no agency agreement permitting the nephew to act as the home owner's agent. In addition, the home owner was not present when the nephew showed the property and discussed the sales price and financing with the prospective purchaser. However, if the home owner subsequently signed a purchase and sales agreement with the prospect for the price represented by the nephew, these actions would constitute the home owner's ratification of the nephew's acts.

WHO IS AN EMPLOYER?

Courts and regulatory agencies have generally defined an **employer** as someone who hires another to perform work on his or her behalf, and who has the right to control the details of how the work is performed. Most statutes specifically include in this definition entities such as employment agencies and labor organizations. A difficult issue employers often face is the number of employees required in order to subject the employer to a particular statute, as listed below.

The Civil Rights Act (CRA) of 1866 regulates the actions of all individuals or entities that enter into a contract to employ another. An employer under the CRA of 1866 is any entity with 15 or more employees.

Title VII of the Civil Rights Act of 1964 applies to all firms or the firms' agents engaged in an industry affecting commerce that employ 15 or more employees for each working day in each of 20 or more weeks in the current or preceding calendar year. Entities exempt from Title VII include government-owned corporations, Indian tribes, and bona fide private membership clubs.

The Age Discrimination in Employment Act (ADEA) of 1967 applies to all entities or their agents that employ 20 or more employees on each working day for 20 or more weeks during the current or preceding calendar year. The ADEA does not exempt Indian tribes or private membership clubs, as does Title VII.

The Americans with Disabilities Act (ADA) of 1990 applies to all employers who have 15 or more employees for each working day in each of 20 or more calendar weeks in the current or preceding calendar year, and any agent of such person.

The Family Medical Leave Act (FMLA) of 1993 covers all public employers and all private employers that employ 50 or more people for at least 20 weeks in the current or previous calendar year.

The Pregnancy Discrimination Act (PDA) of 1978 is an amendment to Title VII that applies to all firms or the firms' agents engaged in an industry affecting commerce that employ 15 or more employees for each working day in each of 20 or more weeks in the current or preceding calendar year. Entities exempt from the PDA include government-owned corporations, Indian tribes, and bona fide private membership clubs.

COMMON LAW DUTIES OF THE EMPLOYER

An employer's duties to the employer, as described in the RESTATEMENT (SECOND) OF AGENCY, include the following:

1. contractual duties;
2. duty not to unreasonably interfere with the employee's work;
3. duty to provide information (for example, risks involved with the job and information necessary to perform the job duties);
4. duty to keep and render accounts (regarding the employee's wages);
5. duty of good conduct;
6. duty to provide a safe workplace; and
7. duty to indemnify the employee (for example, the employer has a common law duty to compensate the employee for expenditures incurred upon behalf of the employer).

WHO IS AN EMPLOYEE?

An **employee** is a person in the service of another under any contract of hire, express or implied, oral or written, where the employer has the power or right to control and direct the employee in the material details of how the work is to be performed.

The issue of whether an individual is considered to be an employee or an independent contractor is both critical and confusing, as the courts, federal government, and employers are unable to agree on a single definition of "employee." The distinction between employee and independent contractor, discussed subsequently in this chapter, is significant for tax law compliance, benefit plans, cost reduction plans, and discrimination claims. An employer's responsibilities and liabilities generally are greater when a worker is an employee.

DISTINGUISHING EMPLOYEES FROM INDEPENDENT CONTRACTORS

Overview

In recent years, the answer to the question of "Who is an employee?" has become more elusive. Any office or plant staff might include both **independent contractors** (persons who contract with an "employer" to do a particular piece of work by their own methods and under their own control) and employees, working side by side. The manner in which the employer classifies these two groups has major ramifications in terms of employer liability and tax responsibility.

A company owes an independent contractor fewer rights than an employee. Both federal and state statutes protect employees from discrimination. However, an independent contractor receives no such protection. Employees receive benefits from an employer. The independent contractor must provide his or her own benefits, such as health insurance, life insurance, and retirement fund; must pay his or her own taxes; and must provide his or her own workers' compensation coverage.

In recent years, many employers have sought to classify their workers as independent contractors because of their belief that this classification would reduce their tax liability and benefit cost. Because the Fair Labor Standards Act (FLSA), as discussed in Chapter 3, generally favors classification of a worker as an employee, not as an independent contractor, employers have frequently found themselves accused of a violation of the FLSA or Internal Revenue Service (IRS) regulations.

Legal Tests for Determining IC or Employee Status

The tests for determining whether a worker is an employee or independent contractor can be quite subjective and may vary, depending on which of the following enforcement agencies of the government applies the test.

- the IRS
- state unemployment compensation insurance agencies
- state workers' compensation insurance agencies
- state tax departments
- U.S. Department of Labor (DOL)
- the National Labor Relations Board (NLRB)

Because each of these agencies is concerned with worker classification for different reasons, each has its own classification practices. One agency need not consider other agencies' decisions in classifying a particular worker. As a result, it is possible for one agency to determine that a worker is an IC and for another agency to determine that he or she is an employee.

Example   The DOL might classify a paralegal working a temporary position at a law firm as an employee, and the IRS might determine that, for purposes of enforcing its regulations, the paralegal is an independent contractor.

Common Law Right to Control Test

The **right to control test** is sometimes also referred to as the **agency test**. If the employer has the right to control the details of the work, the manner in which the individual works, and the progress of the work, the individual is considered to be an employee. The operative phrase in this test is the "right to control." An employer's failure to control is irrelevant. If no other person or entity has the right to control the details of an individual's work, then that individual is considered to be an independent contractor under this common law test. Examples of control that are normally exercised by an employer over an employee include determining the beginning and ending of the hours worked, providing the tools used to perform the work, and determining the amount of time spent on particular aspects of the job.

- If the worker is engaged in a distinct occupation, particularly as a professional, this normally reflects an independent contractor relationship.
- The more highly skilled the occupation, the greater indication there is of an independent contractor relationship.
- Payment by the job, as opposed to the hours worked, reflects an independent contractor relationship.
- If the worker is in business for himself or herself and performs work for others, that indicates an independent contractor relationship.

The existence of an employment agreement reflecting that an individual is an independent contractor is insufficient to establish independent contractor status. Courts will apply the right to control or other tests, and will examine the employment agreement, to determine the individual's employment status.

Common Law Economic Realities Test

The **economic realities test** focuses upon whether the alleged employee is dependent upon the business for which he or she is working. Factors in the test include:

1. Whether the services rendered are an integral part of the employer's business.
2. The permanency of the relationship. Longer-term relationships are found to indicate employee status, with a one-year term as the guide.
3. Whether the employer provides facilities and equipment. For example, does the worker provide all of the equipment used on the job? If so, that worker is an independent contractor.

4. The extent of the opportunity for profit or loss.
5. The independent business operation of the individual. If the individual advertises his or her services in the community or provides work for others, this will lead to a finding of independent contractor status.
6. The employer's only control of the individual's work is the *result* to be obtained. In this case, an independent contractor status exists.
7. The individual exercises independent initiative and judgment. Again, in this case, the individual will be classified as an independent contractor.

Common Law Hybrid Test

Some courts have applied a common law **hybrid test** that combines the right to control and economic realities tests to determine whether an individual is an employee or independent contractor.

Because the common law right to control test excludes so many persons from Title VII coverage, many courts have applied a more liberal, modified common law test, that considers not only the degree of control, but the "economic realities," as discussed in the case below.

Sprides v. Reinhardt, 613 F.2d 826, 20 FEP 141 (D.C. Cir. 1979)

Facts:

The plaintiff was a female broadcaster who had worked intermittently for four years as a foreign language broadcaster for a division of the Voice of America. During most of this period, she had worked pursuant to purchase order vendor (POV) contracts. After her supervisor refused to renew her contract, stating that "he could no longer justify the expenditure of POV funds for a female voice," Sprides filed suit, alleging sex discrimination in her termination. The district court dismissed her complaint on the ground that Title VII applies only to "employees" of the federal government, and Sprides was, according to her contract, an independent contractor. The court of appeals reversed, holding that the determination of employee or independent contractor status must be based on a consideration of all the circumstances surrounding the working relationship.

Opinion by Judge McGowan:

Nevertheless, the extent of the employer's right to control the "means and manner" of the worker's performance is the most important factor to review here. . . . If an employer has the right to control and direct the work of an individual, not only as to the result to be achieved, but also as to the details by which that result is achieved, an employer/employee relationship is likely to exist.

Additional matters of fact that an agency or reviewing court must consider, among others, (1) the kind of occupation, with reference to whether the work usually is done under the direction of a supervisor, or is done by a specialist, without supervision; (2) the skill required in the particular occupation; (3) whether the "employer" or the individual in question furnishes the equipment used and the place of work; (4) the length of time during which the individual has worked; (5) the method of payment, whether by time or by the job; (6) the manner in which the work relationship is terminated; *i.e.*, by one or both parties, with or without notice and explanation; (7) whether annual leave is afforded; (8) whether the work is an integral part of the business of the "employer"; (9) whether the worker accumulates retirement benefits; (10) whether the "employer" pays social security taxes; and (11) the intention of the parties.

The court in the *Sprides* case noted that the characterization that the parties assign to a relationship—in this case, that of an independent contractor—is one of the factors to be considered, but is not controlling.

Some courts have concluded that this involved, hybrid test is essentially the same as the common law agency test.

IRS Test

The IRS applies 20 factors in its analysis of whether an individual is an employee or an independent contractor. Figure 1-1 is a test that can be administered to determine a worker's status for IRS purposes.

An individual worker or employer may request a determination from the IRS of the worker's employment status for purposes of tax withholding by completing an IRS Form SS-8 (see Figure 1-2).

In 1996, the IRS issued Final Workers Classification Training Materials for its agents in connection with the determination of independent contractor status. Under the Training Materials, the 20 factors listed in Figure 1–1 are referred to as an "analytical tool and not the legal test used for determining worker status." The determinative legal test is whether the person receiving the services has the right to direct and control the means and details of the work. In addition, the Training Materials point out that some of the 20 factors are not as relevant in the test as they once were.

Safe Haven Provision—Section 530 of the Revenue Act of 1978

Congress recognized the controversies surrounding the independent contractor versus employee determination as early as 1978, and enacted a temporary provision which, in certain circumstances, does not permit the status of the worker as an independent

Factor	Yes Or No
Must comply with the employer's instructions about when, where, and how to work	
Receives training from or at the direction of the employer (includes working with other experienced employees or attending meetings)	
Provides services that are integrated into the business (i.e., the success or continuation of the employer's business significantly depends upon the performance of certain services that the worker provides)	
Performs the work personally	
Hires, supervises, and pays assistants for the employer	
Has a continuing relationship with the employer (typically exists in situations where the worker performs work on a frequently recurring, although irregular, interval)	
Follows set hours of work	
Works full-time for the employer	
Performs work on the employer's premises	
Must perform the work in a sequence set by the employer	
Submits regular oral or written reports to the employer	
Receives payments of regular amounts at set intervals	
Receives payment for business and/or traveling expenses	
Relies on the employer for tools and/or materials	
Lacks a significant investment in facilities used to perform services	
Cannot make a profit or suffer a loss from services	
Works for one employer at a time	
Does not offer services to the general public	
Can be fired by the employer	
May quit work at any time without liability	
Total Yes Responses	

Note: No one factor in the checklist nor group of factors is more indicative of employee status than another. Although the existence of a high number of "yes" answers will most likely indicate the presence of an employment relationship, a correspondingly lower number may or may not. Employers should err on the side of caution or elect to pursue an IRS ruling when in doubt about whether a worker is an employee or independent contractor.

Figure 1-1
Internal Revenue Service 20-factor Test For Determining Employee Status

Form SS-8

(Rev. June 1997)

Department of the Treasury
Internal Revenue Service

Determination of Employee Work Status
for Purposes of Federal Employment Taxes
and Income Tax Withholding

OMB No. 1545-0004

Paperwork Reduction Act Notice

We ask for the information on this form to carry out the Internal Revenue laws of the United States. You are required to give us the information. We need it to ensure that you are complying with these laws and to allow us to figure and collect the right amount of tax.

You are not required to provide the information requested on a form that is subject to the Paperwork Reduction Act unless the form displays a valid OMB control number. Books or records relating to a form or its instructions must be retained as long as their contents may become material in the administration of any Internal Revenue law. Generally, tax returns and return information are confidential, as required by Code section 6103.

The time needed to complete and file this form will vary depending on individual circumstances. The estimated average time is: **Recordkeeping,** 34 hr., 55 min.; **Learning about the law or the form,**12 min.; and **Preparing and sending the form to the IRS,** 46 min. If you have comments concerning the accuracy of these time estimates or suggestions for making this form simpler, we would be happy to hear from you. You can write to the Tax Forms Committee, Western Area Distribution Center, Rancho Cordova, CA 95743-0001. **DO NOT** send the tax form to this address. Instead, see **General Information** for where to file.

Purpose

Employers and workers file Form SS-8 to get a determination as to whether a worker is an employee for purposes of Federal employment taxes and income tax withholding.

General Information

Complete this form carefully. If the firm is completing the form, complete it for **ONE** individual who is representative of the class of workers whose status is in question. If you want a written determination for more than one class of workers, complete a separate Form SS-8 for one worker

from each class whose status is typical of that class. A written determination for any worker will apply to other workers of the same class if the facts are not materially different from those of the worker whose status was ruled upon.

*Caution: Form SS-8 is **not** a claim for refund of social security and Medicare taxes or Federal income tax withholding. Also, a determination that an individual is an employee does not necessarily reduce any current or prior tax liability. A worker must file his or her income tax return even if a determination has not been made by the due date of the return.*

Where to file.—In the list below, find the state where your legal residence, principal place of business, office, or agency is located. Send Form SS-8 to the address listed for your location.

Location:	Send to:
Alaska, Arizona, Arkansas, California, Colorado, Hawaii, Idaho, Illinois, Iowa, Kansas, Minnesota, Missouri, Montana, Nebraska, Nevada, New Mexico, North Dakota, Oklahoma, Oregon, South Dakota, Texas, Utah, Washington, Wisconsin, Wyoming	Internal Revenue Service SS-8 Determinations P.O. Box 1231, Stop 4106 AUSC Austin, TX 78767
Alabama, Connecticut, Delaware, District of Columbia, Florida, Georgia, Indiana, Kentucky, Louisiana, Maine, Maryland, Massachusetts, Michigan, Mississippi, New Hampshire, New Jersey, New York, North Carolina, Ohio, Pennsylvania, Rhode Island, South Carolina, Tennessee, Vermont, Virginia, West Virginia, All other locations not listed	Internal Revenue Service SS-8 Determinations Two Lakemont Road Newport, VT 05855-1555
American Samoa, Guam, Puerto Rico, U.S. Virgin Islands	Internal Revenue Service Mercantile Plaza 2 Avenue Ponce de Leon San Juan, Puerto Rico 00918

Name of firm (or person) for whom the worker performed services	Name of worker
Address of firm (include street address, apt. or suite no., city, state, and ZIP code)	Address of worker (include street address, apt. or suite no., city, state, and ZIP code)

Trade name	Telephone number (include area code) ( )	Worker's social security number

Telephone number (include area code) ( )	Firm's employer identification number

Check type of firm for which the work relationship is in question:

☐ **Individual**   ☐ **Partnership**   ☐ **Corporation**   ☐ **Other** (specify) ▶ ....

Important Information Needed To Process Your Request

This form is being completed by: ☐ Firm   ☐ Worker

If this form is being completed by the worker, the IRS **must** have your permission to disclose your name to the firm.

Do you object to disclosing your name and the information on this form to the firm? . . . . ☐ **Yes**   ☐ **No**

If you answer "Yes," the IRS cannot act on your request. **Do not complete the rest of this form unless the IRS asks for it.**

Under section 6110 of the Internal Revenue Code, the information on this form and related file documents will be open to the public if any ruling or determination is made. However, names, addresses, and taxpayer identification numbers will be removed before the information is made public.

Is there any other information you want removed? . . . . ☐ **Yes**   ☐ **No**

If you check "Yes," we cannot process your request unless you submit a copy of this form and copies of all supporting documents showing, in brackets, the information you want removed. Attach a separate statement showing which specific exemption of section 6110(c) applies to each bracketed part.

Form **SS-8** (Rev. 6-97)

Figure 1-2

IRS Form SS-8. Determination of Employee Work Status.

This form is designed to cover many work activities, so some of the questions may not apply to you. **You must answer ALL items or mark them "Unknown" or "Does not apply."** *If you need more space, attach another sheet.*

Total number of workers in this class. (Attach names and addresses. If more than 10 workers, list only 10.) ▶ _____

This information is about services performed by the worker from _____ to _____
(month, day, year) (month, day, year)

Is the worker still performing services for the firm? . . . . □ **Yes** □ **No**

● If "No," what was the date of termination? ▶ _____
(month, day, year)

1a Describe the firm's business ....
 b Describe the work done by the worker ....
....

2a If the work is done under a written agreement between the firm and the worker, attach a copy.
 b If the agreement is not in writing, describe the terms and conditions of the work arrangement ....
....

 c If the actual working arrangement differs in any way from the agreement, explain the differences and why they occur ......
....

3a Is the worker given training by the firm? . . . . □ **Yes** □ **No**
 ● If "Yes," what kind? ....
 ● How often? ....
 b Is the worker given instructions in the way the work is to be done (exclusive of actual training in 3a)? . □ **Yes** □ **No**
 ● If "Yes," give specific examples ....
 c Attach samples of any written instructions or procedures.
 d Does the firm have the right to change the methods used by the worker or direct that person on how to
 do the work? . . . . □ **Yes** □ **No**
 ● Explain your answer ....
....

 e Does the operation of the firm's business require that the worker be supervised or controlled in the
 performance of the service? . . . . □ **Yes** □ **No**
 ● Explain your answer ....
....

4a The firm engages the worker:
 □ To perform and complete a particular job only
 □ To work at a job for an indefinite period of time
 □ Other (explain) ....
 b Is the worker required to follow a routine or a schedule established by the firm? . . . . □ **Yes** □ **No**
 ● If "Yes," what is the routine or schedule? ....
....
....

 c Does the worker report to the firm or its representative?. . . . . □ **Yes** □ **No**
 ● If "Yes," how often? ....
 ● For what purpose? ....
 ● In what manner (in person, in writing, by telephone, etc.)? ....
 ● Attach copies of any report forms used in reporting to the firm.
 d Does the worker furnish a time record to the firm? . . . . □ **Yes** □ **No**
 ● If "Yes," attach copies of time records.
5a State the kind and value of tools, equipment, supplies, and materials furnished by:
 ● The firm ....
....
 ● The worker ....
....

 b What expenses are incurred by the worker in the performance of services for the firm? ....
....

 c Does the firm reimburse the worker for any expenses? . . . . □ **Yes** □ **No**
 ● If "Yes," specify the reimbursed expenses ....

Figure 1-2 (*continued*)

6a Will the worker perform the services personally? . . . . ☐ Yes ☐ No

b Does the worker have helpers? . . . . ☐ Yes ☐ No

- If "Yes," who hires the helpers? ☐ Firm ☐ Worker
- If the helpers are hired by the worker, is the firm's approval necessary? . . . . ☐ Yes ☐ No
- Who pays the helpers?   ☐ Firm ☐ Worker
- If the worker pays the helpers, does the firm repay the worker? . . . . ☐ Yes ☐ No
- Are social security and Medicare taxes and Federal income tax withheld from the helpers' pay? . . ☐ Yes ☐ No
- If "Yes," who reports and pays these taxes?   ☐ Firm   ☐ Worker
- Who reports the helpers' earnings to the Internal Revenue Service? ☐ Firm ☐ Worker
- What services do the helpers perform? ....

7 At what location are the services performed? ☐ Firm's ☐ Worker's ☐ Other (specify) ....

8a Type of pay worker receives:
☐ Salary   ☐ Commission ☐ Hourly wage   ☐ Piecework ☐ Lump sum   ☐ Other (specify) ....

b Does the firm guarantee a minimum amount of pay to the worker? . . . . ☐ Yes ☐ No

c Does the firm allow the worker a drawing account or advances against pay? . . . . ☐ Yes ☐ No

- If "Yes," is the worker paid such advances on a regular basis? . . . . ☐ Yes ☐ No

d How does the worker repay such advances? ....

9a Is the worker eligible for a pension, bonus, paid vacations, sick pay, etc.? . . . . ☐ Yes ☐ No

- If "Yes," specify ....

b Does the firm carry worker's compensation insurance on the worker? . . . . ☐ Yes ☐ No

c Does the firm withhold social security and Medicare taxes from amounts paid the worker? . . . . . ☐ Yes ☐ No

d Does the firm withhold Federal income tax from amounts paid the worker? . . . . ☐ Yes ☐ No

e How does the firm report the worker's earnings to the Internal Revenue Service?
☐ Form W-2 ☐ Form 1099-MISC ☐ Does not report ☐ Other (specify) ....

- Attach a copy.

f Does the firm bond the worker? . . . . ☐ Yes ☐ No

10a Approximately how many hours a day does the worker perform services for the firm? ....

b Does the firm set hours of work for the worker? . . . . ☐ Yes ☐ No

- If "Yes," what are the worker's set hours? _____ a.m./p.m. to _____ a.m./p.m. (Circle whether a.m. or p.m.)

c Does the worker perform similar services for others? . . . . ☐ Yes ☐ No ☐ Unknown

- If "Yes," are these services performed on a daily basis for other firms? . . . . . ☐ Yes ☐ No ☐ Unknown
- Percentage of time spent in performing these services for:
  This firm .... % Other firms .... % ☐ Unknown
- Does the firm have priority on the worker's time? . . . . ☐ Yes ☐ No
- If "No," explain ....

d Is the worker prohibited from competing with the firm either while performing services or during any later period? . . . . ☐ Yes ☐ No

11a Can the firm discharge the worker at any time without incurring a liability? . . . . ☐ Yes ☐ No

- If "No," explain ....

b Can the worker terminate the services at any time without incurring a liability? . . . . ☐ Yes ☐ No

- If "No," explain ....

12a Does the worker perform services for the firm under:
☐ The firm's business name   ☐ The worker's own business name   ☐ Other (specify) ....

b Does the worker advertise or maintain a business listing in the telephone directory, a trade journal, etc.? . . . . ☐ Yes ☐ No ☐ Unknown

- If "Yes," specify ....

c Does the worker represent himself or herself to the public as being in business to perform the same or similar services? . . . . ☐ Yes ☐ No ☐ Unknown

- If "Yes," how? ....

d Does the worker have his or her own shop or office? . . . . ☐ Yes ☐ No ☐ Unknown

- If "Yes," where? ....

e Does the firm represent the worker as an employee of the firm to its customers? . . . . ☐ Yes ☐ No

- If "No," how is the worker represented? ....

f How did the firm learn of the worker's services? ....

13 Is a license necessary for the work? . . . . ☐ Yes ☐ No ☐ Unknown

- If "Yes," what kind of license is required? ....
- Who issues the license? ....
- Who pays the license fee?

Figure 1-2 (*continued*)

14 Does the worker have a financial investment in a business related to the services performed?. . . . . ☐ **Yes** ☐ **No** ☐ **Unknown**
  • If "Yes," specify and give amount of the investment ....

15 Can the worker incur a loss in the performance of the service for the firm? . . . . ☐ **Yes** ☐ **No**
  • If "Yes," how? ....

16a Has any other government agency ruled on the status of the firm's workers? . . . . ☐ **Yes** ☐ **No**
  • If "Yes," attach a copy of the ruling.

  b Is the same issue being considered by any IRS office in connection with the audit of the worker's tax return or the firm's tax return, or has it been considered recently? . . . . ☐ **Yes** ☐ **No**
  • If "Yes," for which year(s)? ....

17 Does the worker assemble or process a product at home or away from the firm's place of business? ☐ **Yes** ☐ **No**
  • If "Yes," who furnishes materials or goods used by the worker? ☐ **Firm**　　☐ **Worker**　　☐ **Other**
  • Is the worker furnished a pattern or given instructions to follow in making the product? . . . . ☐ **Yes** ☐ **No**
  • Is the worker required to return the finished product to the firm or to someone designated by the firm? ☐ **Yes** ☐ **No**

18 Attach a detailed explanation of any other reason why you believe the worker is an employee or an independent contractor.

Answer items 19a through o only if the worker is a salesperson or provides a service directly to customers.

19a Are leads to prospective customers furnished by the firm?. . . . . ☐ **Yes** ☐ **No** ☐ **Does not apply**
  b Is the worker required to pursue or report on leads? . . . . ☐ **Yes** ☐ **No** ☐ **Does not apply**
  c Is the worker required to adhere to prices, terms, and conditions of sale established by the firm? . . ☐ **Yes** ☐ **No**
  d Are orders submitted to and subject to approval by the firm? . . . . ☐ **Yes** ☐ **No**
  e Is the worker expected to attend sales meetings?. ☐ **Yes** ☐ **No**
  • If "Yes," is the worker subject to any kind of penalty for failing to attend?. . . . . ☐ **Yes** ☐ **No**
  f Does the firm assign a specific territory to the worker? . . . . ☐ **Yes** ☐ **No**
  g Whom does the customer pay?　　☐ **Firm**　　☐ **Worker**
  • If worker, does the worker remit the total amount to the firm? . . . . ☐ **Yes** ☐ **No**
  h Does the worker sell a consumer product in a home or establishment other than a permanent retail establishment? . . . . ☐ **Yes** ☐ **No**
  i List the products and/or services distributed by the worker, such as meat, vegetables, fruit, bakery products, beverages (other than milk), or laundry or dry cleaning services. If more than one type of product and/or service is distributed, specify the principal one ....
  j Did the firm or another person assign the route or territory and a list of customers to the worker? . . ☐ **Yes** ☐ **No**
  • If "Yes," enter the name and job title of the person who made the assignment ....
  k Did the worker pay the firm or person for the privilege of serving customers on the route or in the territory? ☐ **Yes** ☐ **No**
  • If "Yes," how much did the worker pay (not including any amount paid for a truck or racks, etc.)? $ ....
  • What factors were considered in determining the value of the route or territory? ....
  l How are new customers obtained by the worker? Explain fully, showing whether the new customers called the firm for service, were solicited by the worker, or both ....
  m Does the worker sell life insurance? . . . . ☐ **Yes** ☐ **No**
  • If "Yes," is the selling of life insurance or annuity contracts for the firm the worker's entire business activity? . . . . ☐ **Yes** ☐ **No**
  • If "No," list the other business activities and the amount of time spent on them ....
  n Does the worker sell other types of insurance for the firm? . . . . ☐ **Yes** ☐ **No**
  • If "Yes," state the percentage of the worker's total working time spent in selling other types of insurance .... %
  • At the time the contract was entered into between the firm and the worker, was it their intention that the worker sell life insurance for the firm:　　☐ on a full-time basis　　☐ on a part-time basis
  • State the manner in which the intention was expressed ....
  o Is the worker a traveling or city salesperson? . . . . ☐ **Yes** ☐ **No**
  • If "Yes," from whom does the worker principally solicit orders for the firm? ....
  • If the worker solicits orders from wholesalers, retailers, contractors, or operators of hotels, restaurants, or other similar establishments, specify the percentage of the worker's time spent in the solicitation .... %
  • Is the merchandise purchased by the customers for resale or for use in their business operations? If used by the customers in their business operations, describe the merchandise and state whether it is equipment installed on their premises or a consumable supply

Under penalties of perjury, I declare that I have examined this request, including accompanying documents, and to the best of my knowledge and belief, the facts presented are true, correct, and complete.

Signature ▶　　　　　　　　　　　　Title ▶　　　　　　　　　　　　Date ▶

If the firm is completing this form, an officer or member of the firm must sign it. If the worker is completing this form, the worker must sign it. If the worker wants a written determination about services performed for two or more firms, a separate form must be completed and signed for each firm. Additional copies of this form may be obtained by calling 1-800-TAX-FORM (1-800-829-3676).

Figure 1-2 (*continued*)

contractor to be challenged by the IRS, even though the IRS may believe the worker to be an employee. The safe haven provisions were originally set to expire in 1980, but have been extended indefinitely.

An employer cannot be penalized for classifying a particular worker as an independent contractor if the following three requirements are met:

1. The employer has treated the worker for federal tax purposes as an independent contractor, and has filed all required federal tax returns in a manner that is consistent with the treatment of the individual as an independent contractor; and
2. The employer has consistently treated all persons holding substantially similar positions as independent contractors for federal tax filing purposes; and
3. The employer has a "reasonable basis" for treating the worker as an independent contractor.

Benefits of Hiring Independent Contractors

Companies usually save money by utilizing an IC in lieu of an employee. In addition to salaries or other types of compensation, employers generally must pay on behalf of its employees all or a portion of the following:

- federal payroll taxes, including a 7.65% Social Security tax and a small (0.08%) federal unemployment tax
- state unemployment insurance premiums
- workers' compensation insurance premiums
- employee benefits, such as paid vacations, health insurance, sick leave, retirement benefits, or disability insurance; and
- office space and equipment.

These expenses often account for 20% to 30% of employment costs. A business incurs none of these expenses (with the possible exception of office space and equipment) when it utilizes an IC. Even though an IC might be paid more per hour than an employee who is doing the same work, the IC will still cost the company less.

A company's exposure to certain types of lawsuits, such as employment discrimination or wrongful termination (discussed in Chapter 6), is reduced when an IC is utilized instead of an employee.

Another important benefit to many companies is that the IC provides a level of flexibility that cannot be obtained through the use of employees. An IC is paid to accomplish only a specific task. Training time and expense is avoided with an IC who is already experienced in his or her field.

Risks of Hiring Independent Contractors

Despite the extensive benefits listed above, many businesses are justifiably reluctant to use an IC because of the consequences of incorrectly classifying an employee as an IC.

Audits by state agencies occur even more often than IRS audits because many workers classified as ICs apply for unemployment compensation after the workers' services are terminated.

Example   A law firm enlists the services of 30 paralegals for a temporary assignment in its litigation section. When the assignment ends after 11 months, several of the paralegals file for unemployment compensation, claiming that they were employees of the law firm. If the law firm denies the unemployment compensation claims on the basis that it believes the paralegals were working as ICs, the state unemployment compensation commission might perform an audit of the law firm's classification of ICs.

In the example above, the law firm could be subject to fines and penalties if the state agency determines that the workers should have been classified as employees for unemployment compensation purposes.

Reporting Requirements for Independent Contractors—Form 1099

Any company that utilizes an independent contractor must report annual payments to the IC of $600 or more on a Form 1099. This form, like the W-2 Form for an employee, must be distributed to the IC by January 31 of the following year, and a transmittal form, Form 1096, must be filed with the IRS no later than February 28 of the next year.

Written IC Agreements

Companies utilizing an IC should do so under the terms of a written IC agreement (see Figure 1-3). Use of such an agreement avoids possible disputes later by providing a written description of the services that the IC is to perform, when and where the services are to be performed, and how much the IC will be paid.

Although a written IC agreement will never officially make a worker an IC, it will help to show the IRS and other agencies that both parties intended to create a company-IC relationship, and not an employer-employee relationship.

This contract is made on this _____ day of _____, _____, between
_____, herein referred to as Owner, doing business at
_____, City of _____, State of
_____, and , hereinafter referred to as Contractor, doing business
at _____, City of _____, State of
_____.

RECITALS

1. Owner operates a business at the address set forth above and desires to have the
   following services performed at Owner's place of business:

   _____

   _____

   _____

2. Contractor agrees to perform these services for Owner under the terms and
   conditions set forth inthis contract.

   In consideration of the mutual promises contained herein, it is agreed:

   A. **Description of Work:** The Contractor shall perform all services gener-
      ally related to Contractor's usual line of business, including, but not lim-
      ited to those listed in "1" above.

   B. **Payment:** Owner will pay Contractor the sum of $ _____ Dollars
      ($ _____) for the work performed under this contract, under
      the following schedule:

      _____

      _____

      _____

   C. **Relationship of Parties:** This contract creates an independent contrac-
      tor-employer relationship. Owner is interested only in the results to be
      achieved. Contractor is solely responsible for the conduct and control of
      the work. Contractor is not an agent or employee of Owner for any pur-
      pose. Employees of Contractor are not entitled to any benefits that
      Owner provides Owner's employees. This is not an exclusive agreement.
      Both parties are free to contract with other parties for similar services.

Figure 1-3
Independent Contractor's Agreement

       D. **Liability:** Contractor assumes all risks connected with work to be performed.

          Contractor also accepts all responsibility for the condition of tools and equipment used in the performance of this contract and will carry for the duration of this contract public liability insurance in an amount acceptable to Owner. Contractor agrees to indemnify Owner for any and all liability or loss arising from the performance of this contract.

       E. **Duration:** Either party may cancel this contract with 30 days' written notice to the other party; otherwise, the contract shall remain in force for a term of one year from the date hereof.

IN WITNESS WHEREOF, the parties have executed this agreement in the City of _____, State of _____, the day and year first above written.

_____   _____
     (Signature of Owner)   (Signature of Contractor)

Figure 1-3 (*continued*)

An IC agreement must be followed to be beneficial. If a company treats a worker as an employee instead of as an IC, the agreement will have been a wasted exercise.

Intellectual Property Issues with the IC

When a company retains an IC to create a work of authorship, such as artworks, musical works, computer programs, brochures, photographs, or multimedia, the company should be concerned with copyright ownership.

The copyright laws provide that unless the work an IC creates falls into one of nine categories, the hiring company will not own the copyright to the IC's work unless it obtains a written assignment of copyright ownership. Such an assignment should be obtained before an IC begins work—preferably through an IC agreement.

Certain commissioned works by an IC, including a contribution to a collective work, a motion picture screenplay, a test, answers to a test, and electronic databases, are considered to be works for hire, to which the hiring company automatically owns all rights under copyright law. However, both the company and the IC must sign a written agreement stating that the work is made for hire. This agreement should be incorporated into the IC agreement or prepared as a separate agreement.

In *Community for Creative Non-Violence v. Reid*, 490 U.S. 730 (1989), the Supreme

Court decided a dispute between a sculptor and a non-profit group where each party claimed copyright ownership in a statue. The ultimate question in that case, discussed below, was whether the statue was "prepared by an employee within the scope of his or her employment."

Community for Creative Non-Violence v. Reid, 490 U.S. 730 (1989)

Facts:

In the fall of 1985, the Community for Creative Non-Violence (CCNV), a Washington, D.C. organization dedicated to eliminating homelessness, and one of its trustees, entered into an oral argument with Reid, a sculptor, to produce a statue dramatizing the plight of the homeless for display at a 1985 Christmas pageant in Washington.

The parties subsequently were involved in a copyright ownership lawsuit. The district court ruled for CCNV in its suit, holding that the statue was a "work made for hire" as defined in the Copyright Act of 1976, and was therefore owned exclusively by CCNV. The court of appeals reversed, holding that the sculpture was not a "work made for hire," since it was not "prepared by an employee within the scope of his or her employment" in light of Reid's status as an independent contractor under agency law.

Opinion by Justice Marshall:

Reid was an independent contractor rather than a §101 (1) "employee," since, although CCNV members directed enough of the work to ensure that the statue met their specifications, all other relevant circumstances weigh heavily against finding an employment relationship. Reid engaged in a skilled occupation; supplied his own tools; worked in Baltimore without daily supervision from Washington; was retained for a relatively short period of time; had absolute freedom to decide when and how long to work in order to meet his deadline; and had total discretion in hiring and paying assistants. Moreover, CCNV had no right to assign additional projects to Reid; paid him in a manner in which independent contractors are often compensated; did not engage regularly in the business of creating sculpture or, in fact, in any business; and did not pay payroll or Social Security taxes, provide any employee benefits, or contribute to unemployment insurance or workers' compensation funds.

For the aforestated reasons, we affirm the judgment of the Court of Appeals for the District of Columbia Circuit.

Noting the absence of a meaningful definition of "employee" or "employment," the Court in *Community for Creative Non-Violence v. Reid* held:

[W]here Congress uses terms that have accumulated settled meaning under . . . the common law, a court must infer, unless a statute otherwise dictates, that Congress means to incorporate the established meaning of these terms . . . in the past, when Congress has used the term "employee" without defining it we have concluded that Congress intended to describe the conventional master-servant relationship as understood by common law agency doctrine. (490 U.S. at 739–740)

A Recent Court Decision Distinguishing "Independent Contractor"

The following case is considered to be a significant decision relating to a determination of independent contractor status:

Vizcaino v. Microsoft Corp., 120 F. 3d 1006 (9th Cir. 1997)

Facts:

Like many software companies, Microsoft added to its regular roster of permanent employees a number of workers that it classified as independent "freelancers." Microsoft paid these individuals cash compensation (often more than it paid its employees), but none of the fringe benefits. These workers were purportedly brought onboard to perform specific projects in areas such as proofreading, formatting, indexing, production editing, and software testing.

Microsoft had these "freelancers" sign agreements that provided that they were independent contractors and were not entitled to participate in Microsoft's employee benefit plans. In addition, Microsoft did not withhold or pay any Social Security or other payroll taxes for these individuals.

There was one major problem with Microsoft's designation of these workers as ICs: Microsoft did not treat them as ICs. Instead, Microsoft integrated these workers into its workforce. Often an alleged IC worked alongside a regular employee, shared the same supervisor, performed identical functions, and worked the same hours. In addition, Microsoft furnished the ICs admittance card keys, office equipment, and company supplies. Microsoft's treatment of these individuals was clearly treatment granted to an employee, not an IC.

When the IRS audited Microsoft's payroll tax accounts in 1989 and 1990, it determined that since Microsoft treated these individuals as employees, they had to be treated as employees for purposes of Federal Insurance Contributions Act (FICA), FUTA, and withholding taxes. Microsoft agreed and admitted that they should have been classified as employees *for tax purposes*. Following the IRS's ruling, Microsoft paid back payroll taxes and overtime for the workers, and even moved some of the workers to a permanent employee status. Others were offered the choice of termination or working for Microsoft as employees of a new temporary employee agency. The agency would treat the workers as its own employees, and would pay the workers, withhold income taxes, and pay the employer's portion of FICA.

The IRS decision was not the end of Microsoft's legal troubles. Eight of the workers who had been formerly incorrectly classified demanded full employee benefits for the period they had worked as independent contractors. Those benefits included participation in the 401(k) and discount stock purchase plans offered to regular employees. When Microsoft refused this request, these workers filed suit.

The federal district court dismissed the workers' lawsuit, but the Ninth Circuit Court of Appeals ruled that the workers could not be excluded from Microsoft's benefit plans because they were common law employees, not ICs. Later, a 15-judge panel of the Ninth Circuit decided to rehear this case. Their decision in the spring of 1999 largely affirmed the prior decision.

Opinion by Judge Fernandez:

Microsoft, like other advanced employers, makes certain benefits available to all of its employees who meet minimum conditions of eligibility. For some time, it did not believe that the workers could partake of certain of these benefits because it thought that they were independent contractors. In that it was mistaken, as it now knows and concedes.

The mistake brought Microsoft difficulties with the IRS, but it has resolved those difficulties by making certain payments and by taking other actions. The mistake has also brought it difficulties with the workers, and the time has come to resolve those.

Therefore, we now determine that the reasons for rejecting the Workers' participation in the SPP and the ESPP were invalid. Any remaining issues regarding the rights of a particular worker in the ESPP and his available remedies must be decided by the district court upon remand. However, any remaining issues regarding the right of any or all of the workers to participate in the SPP must be decided by the plan administrator upon remand.

REVERSED and REMANDED to the district court as to the ESPP, REVERSED and REMANDED to the district court for further remand to the plan administrator as to the SPP.

Employers and independent contractors can learn a lot from the *Vizcaino* decision. First, merely having a worker sign an agreement that he or she is an IC will not automatically and legally make the individual an IC. The worker must be treated like an IC on the job.

Incorrectly classifying workers as ICs has always been expensive, but the *Vizcaino* case makes it even more expensive in the case of companies that offer generous employee benefit programs. Companies who hire even one IC should promptly add provisions to all employee benefit plans, including stock options, vacation, sick leave, health insurance, and retirement plans, specifically excluding coverage for contingent workers.

A worker who believes that he or she has been incorrectly classified as an IC instead of an employee may complain directly to the IRS by filing Form SS-8 (see Figure 1–2).

THE EMERGENCE OF TEMPORARY OR LEASED WORKERS/EMPLOYEES

In addition to using independent contractors, employers have attempted to avoid increased labor costs while at the same time adding necessary skills and flexibility to their workforce through the use of "temporary" or "leased" employees. **Temporary employees** are workers of one employer who are assigned to relatively short projects of another employer, the "client company." **Leased employees** are workers who are assigned to projects of relatively longer duration, which require greater technical expertise and may, in some cases, involve relatively less direct control and supervision by the employer who is leasing the employee.

Regardless of the designation given, the main legal issue for employers is whether or not a particular temporary or leased worker is an "employee" for purposes of various employment laws. Determining the employer of the temporary or leased worker is not a simple task. Courts tend to look at the right of control over the employee's daily activities to make that determination.

In *Amarnare v. Merrill Lynch, Pierce, Fenner & Smith, Inc.*, 611 F. Supp. 344 (S.D.N.Y. 1984) and *Magnuson v. Peak Technical Services*, 808 F. Supp. 500 (E.D. Va. 1992), the courts developed a test for determining whether or not an employer is subject to Title VII liability for temporary employees.

Amarnare v. Merrill Lynch, Pierce, Fenner & Smith, Inc.,
611 F. Supp. 344 (S.D.N.Y. 1984)

Facts:

Amarnare alleged that Merrill Lynch was her "joint employer" with Mature Temps, and that Merrill Lynch violated Title VII by discharging her from her temporary job of two weeks as an administrative assistant at Merrill Lynch because of her sex (female), race (black), and national origin (Afro-American). Additionally, she alleged that during the two-week period that she worked at Merrill Lynch, she applied for a permanent position at Merrill Lynch and was turned down because of the company's discriminatory policy against women and blacks. The plaintiff admitted that Mature Temps paid her salary during the brief period of her services to Merrill Lynch. However, she claimed that Merrill Lynch controlled her work hours, workplace, and work assignments; hired, trained, and supervised her; and ultimately discharged her. She also alleged that no white male or white female was terminated in the manner she was terminated.

Merrill Lynch filed a motion to dismiss the plaintiff's claims, alleging that no relationship of employer and employee existed between Merrill Lynch and the plaintiff as she was employed by Mature Temps. Merrill Lynch admitted that it engaged her services from Mature Temps, but claimed that it discharged her after two weeks because her services were unsatisfactory. Merrill Lynch argued that because Amarnare was an independent contractor, and not its employee, Amarnare's claims were not covered by Title VII.

Opinion by Judge Weinfeld:

Title VII forbids an "employer" to engage in an "unlawful employment practice." An "employer is a person engaged in commerce who has employed fifteen or more persons during a specified period. Merrill Lynch does not deny that it qualifies as an employer under this definition. As such, Merrill Lynch is forbidden by Title VII "to fail or refuse to hire or to discharge any individual, or *otherwise to discriminate against any individual with respect to his compensation, term, conditions, or privileges of employment*, because of such individual's race, color, religion, sex or national origin." By its terms, this prohibition is not limited to employers who discriminate against their own employees. Indeed, it is significant that in providing a private right of action against a statutory employer Title VII does not refer to "employee" but to "the person aggrieved," a term that has been construed "as comprehending individuals who do not stand in a direct employment relationship with an employer." Amarnare alleges that Merrill Lynch and Mature Temps were her joint employers. This conclusion, if warranted, is sufficient to bring her action within the ambit of Title VII, though it is not necessary to do so. Even if Amarnare were an employee only of Mature Temps, she may invoke the statute on the ground that Merrill Lynch interfered with her employment opportunities with Mature Temps.

When an employer has the right to control the means and manner of an individual's performance, as Merrill Lynch allegedly had with regard to Amarnare, an employer-employee relationship is likely to exist. Factors other than control are then of marginal importance. In this case, the only other factor Amarnare alleges is that she was paid directly by Mature Temps rather than Merrill Lynch. This factor by itself is an insufficient basis on which to characterize plaintiff as an independent contractor.

That she was subject to the direction of Merrill Lynch in her work assignments, hours of service, and other usual aspects of employee-employer relationship permits an inference that she was an employee of both Mature Temps and Merrill Lynch during the two-week period in question.

Federal courts have . . . held that a person whose salary is paid by one entity while his services are engaged on a temporary basis by another is an employee of both entities.

Merrill Lynch allegedly has blocked plaintiff's access to temporary employment through Mature Temps, and the Ninth Circuit has held that Title VII applies in this situation.

Even if she remains an employee of Mature Temps and continues to receive temporary assignments at other companies, she asserts a claim for loss of opportunity to work for Mature Temps as an administrative assistant at Merrill Lynch.

Amarnare has alleged that her work at Merrill Lynch was praised by two of her supervisors, that one of these supervisors later discharged her on the ground that her work was unsatisfactory, and that no other white employee, male or female, had been discharged by Merrill Lynch in the manner that she was discharged.

The allegation that Merrill Lynch denied the plaintiff's application for permanent employment also states a Title VII claim in view of the allegations supporting her claim of unlawful discharge. If Amarnare could prove facts that show she was discharged from her temporary position because of her race and national origin, it could be inferred that race and national origin were also factors in the defendant's alleged decision to deny her application for permanent employment, provided she made such application.

The defendant's motion to dismiss the amended complaint is denied with regard to the claims that Merrill Lynch discharged Amarnare from her temporary job and refused to hire her for a permanent job because of her race and national origin. The motion is granted however, insofar as those claims are based upon allegations of sex discrimination.

DOCTRINE OF JOINT EMPLOYMENT

Overview

The origins of the doctrine of **joint employment**, a job in which the essential terms and conditions of the employee's work are controlled by two or more entities, are traceable to labor law. This doctrine is normally applied in the context of determining a party's employer for purposes of collective bargaining agreements between unions and businesses. Joint employment is analyzed in a similar fashion to cases analyzed under the FLSA, discussed in Chapter 3. While joint employment is not normally a doctrine associated with Title VII cases, the increasing number of litigation matters involving temporary employees, temporary agencies, and on-site employers have required the courts to analyze the relationships in the context of more than one employer for an employee.

Tests for Determining Joint Employment

Courts generally utilize two main tests to determine the existence of a joint employment relationship: the "mutual control" or "labor relations" test and a test referred to as an "integration test," as discussed in the case below.

Magnuson v. Peak Technical Services, 808 F. Supp. 500 (E.D. Va. 1992)

Facts:

Magnuson was a temporary employee who was sexually harassed by her on-site supervisor, Blaylock, general manager of Fairfax. Magnuson brought an action against the temporary agency that employed her, Peak Technical Services, the on-site employer, Fairfax, Blaylock, and Volkswagen, the corporation for whom her on-site employer was a dealer. Magnuson's understanding of her employment arrangement was that she would receive her salary and benefits from Peak, but that her work would relate solely to the marketing and sales of Volkswagen automobiles. She also understood that Volkswagen would continue to provide direct training and supervision for her work as a field marketing specialist. Several months later, Magnuson became a manufacturer's representative.

Opinion by Judge Ellis:

Analysis properly begins with the threshold determination of whether each of the four defendants can be held liable as an "employer" for purposes of Title VII.

The conclusion that all of the defendants satisfy the statutory definition of "employer" does not end the inquiry. Put another way, the question is whether any or all of the defendants have a relationship with plaintiff whereby they exercise the requisite control over her employment situation so as to be deemed *her* employer under Title VII. Most Title VII cases involve the conventional single employer situation and the typical employer-employee relationship, where this control is obvious.

As the sparse authority reflects, the term "employer" under Title VII should be "construed in a functional sense to encompass persons who are not employers in conventional terms, but who nevertheless control some aspect of an individual's compensation, terms, conditions, or privileges of employment." *Bostik v. Rappleyea*, 629 F. Supp. 1328, 1334 (N.D.N.Y. 1985).

Most Title VII lawsuits, as noted above, typically present a scenario where an employee-plaintiff maintains a cause of action against her single, contractual employer. But this case is not so straightforward. Magnuson's employment situation is more complicated because there does not seem to be just a single employer. Rather, each of the defendants in this case appears to have exercised some amount of control over her employment as a manufacturer's representative. An individual may be the employee of more than one "employer" for purposes of Title VII. As a result, Magnuson's relationship to each defendant must be examined in order to ascertain whether that defendant may be held liable as Magnuson's "employer" because it exercised the requisite control over the compensation, terms, conditions, or privileges of her employment.

None of the parties dispute that Peak is plaintiff's employer for purposes of Title VII. Magnuson received her paychecks and benefits from Peak, entered into a written employment agreement with Peak, and reported to supervisors at Peak. Magnuson and Peak clearly had the type of direct employer-employee relationship that is typically the subject of Title VII lawsuits.

No contractual employment relationship existed between Magnuson and Volkswagen. It appears, however, that Volkswagen exercised significant control over the terms and conditions of Magnuson's employment as a manufacturer's representative. The record also supports Magnuson's claims that Volkswagen exercised control over her actual work performance. Volkswagen apparently defined many of Magnuson's job duties and responsibilities, provided all of her initial job training, sent her additional training materials on a weekly basis, and received reports on her work performance. Magnuson also appears to have been under the supervision of a Volkswagen manager, John Swisher.

Indeed, the terms of Magnuson's written contract provide that Volkswagen, as "the client," would retain some measure of control over Magnuson's employment situation. It states that Magnuson i) would adhere to the client's normal work schedule; ii) have a client supervisor sign a weekly timeslip; and iii) report to both her client supervisor and a Peak supervisor if she missed work for any reason. Thus, since a fact-finder could conclude that Volkswagen retained control over Magnuson's employment as a manufacturer's representative, Volkswagen may be treated as Magnuson's "joint employer" for purposes of Title VII.

Fairfax, like Volkswagen, does not have a direct employer-employee relationship with Magnuson. The realities of Magnuson's position as a manufacturer's representative, however, arguably brought her under Fairfax's control as a *de facto* employee. Magnuson's job duties and responsibilities required her to work on the premises of Fairfax Volkswagen, work with Fairfax personnel, attend sales meetings, and to submit to the apparent authority of Fairfax's general manager, Richard Blaylock. If it is established at trial that Fairfax exercised substantial control over Magnuson's work performance, then it may be held independently liable as an "employer" for purposes of Title VII.

Blaylock's potential liability as an employer for purposes of Title VII necessarily depends on whether Magnuson establishes that Fairfax is her employer under Title VII. An employee of a Title VII employer may be liable himself if, as the employer's agent, he exercised supervisory authority over the alleged victim. Evidence in the record supports Magnuson's claim that she submitted to Blaylock's supervisory authority. The supervisory employee need not have ultimate authority to hire or fire to qualify as an employer as long as he or she has significant input into such personnel decisions. Indeed, so long as Blaylock exerted authority and as a supervisor over the terms and conditions of Magnuson's employment, he may be an employer of hers under Title VII.

The *Magnuson* court first held that the employer must meet the statutory definition of an employer under Title VII. Second, the court held that the employer-employee relationship must meet the criteria established in the *Amarnare* case. Under the *Magnuson* test, both the temporary agency and the dealership were found to be employers for purposes of Title VII. In addition, the court found that, based on the statutory definition of employer, the dealership and Volkswagen were also employers.

The court then analyzed the relationships based on the *Amarnare* criteria and found that the relationship between the plaintiff and her temporary agency was clearly that of employer-employee. The court further held that because many of the functions of the dealership went to the means of control and manner of performance, the dealership was an employer for Title VII purposes. In reaching this decision, the court considered such things as defining job duties, setting the work schedule, signing the employee's time slip, and having the temporary employee report to an on-site supervisor as controlling the means of work. On-site interviewing and training were viewed as controlling the manner of the plaintiff's performance.

The holdings of two Supreme Court cases, *Boire v. Greyhound Corp.*, 376 U.S.

473 (1964) and *Falk v. Brennan*, 414 U.S. 190 (1973), indicate that under both the NLRB and the FLSA, an employee can have more than one legal employer.

To determine whether two or more related entities are proper defendants in a Title VII claim, the courts have used the four-part "NLRB test," as reflected in the case discussed below.

Swallows v. Barnes & Noble Book Stores, Inc., 128 F.3d 990, 75 FEP 346 (6th Cir. 1997)

Facts:

Barnes & Noble was a private corporation under contract to manage and operate a Tennessee state university's bookstores. The plaintiffs in this case, bookstore employees, filed suit under the ADEA and ADA against both Barnes & Noble and the State of Tennessee. Tennessee asked the court to dismiss the complaint against it, arguing that Barnes & Noble, not the university, was the plaintiffs' employer. The court rejected the plaintiffs' reliance on the single or integrated enterprise doctrine, absent the following: (1) interrelated operations; (2) common management, directors, and boards; (3) centralized control of labor relations and personnel; and (4) common ownership and financial control. There was no evidence that Barnes & Noble made employment decisions as the state's agent. The Sixth Circuit affirmed the dismissal of all claims against the State of Tennessee.

Opinion by Judge Aldrich:

Prior to June 15, 1994, Charles Swallows, Teresia Walker and Vickie Heidel were employed by TTU in its bookstore, "The University Store." On or about June 15, 1994, TTU entered into an agreement with Barnes & Noble, whereby Barnes & Noble was to act as an independent contractor responsible for the operation and management of the bookstore for a period of at least three years.

TTU and Barnes & Noble were not "highly integrated with respect to ownership and operations." Nor did TTU maintain "an amount of participation [that] is sufficient and necessary to the total employment process, even absent total control or ultimate authority over hiring decisions." In short, there is nothing to indicate that TTU and Barnes & Noble functioned under anything other than an arm's length relationship. Thus, the district court properly found that TTU and Barnes & Noble cannot be treated as a single employer or integrated enterprise.

There is no evidence supporting plaintiffs' theory that Barnes & Noble acted as TTU's agent. TTU did not delegate to Barnes & Noble the authority to make employment decisions on its behalf, nor did it exercise the requisite control over Barnes & Noble's employment decisions. Therefore, the district court properly concluded that TTU cannot be considered plaintiffs' "employer" under the ADEA and/or the ADA on the basis that Barnes & Noble was acting as its agent.

For the foregoing reasons the judgment of the district court is AFFIRMED.

Mutual Control Test

Another test used to ascertain the existence of a joint employer relationship is the **mutual control test**. This test is based on the joint control over labor relations or working conditions of the employee. The Fifth Circuit examined the elements of this test in *Wirtz v. Lone Star Steel Co.*, 405 F.2d 668 (5th Cir. 1968). Wirtz brought an NLRB case against a trucking company that hauled exclusively for a mining concern. In determining whether or not a joint employment relationship existed, the Fifth Circuit asked the following five questions:

(a) Did the employment take place on the premises of the company?

In almost every case, a temporary employee will work at the on-site employer's business location. A temporary employee who works out of his or her home would have a more difficult time proving that a joint employment relationship exists than would a temporary employee who works at the on-site employer's location.

(b) How much control did the company exert over the employee?

If the on-site employer has the ability to control the daily activities of the contract employer, the courts will likely rule that a joint employment relationship exists.

(c) Did the company have the power to fire, hire, or modify the employment condition of the employees?

On-site employers have the ultimate say as to whether or not a temporary employee remains on the job. However, it is common for those decisions to be made in consultation with temporary agencies.

(d) Did the employees perform a "specialty job" within the production line?

Jobs performed by temporary employees vary greatly. The type of work performed will affect the length and substance of a temporary employee's relationship with an on-site employer. Temporary assignments for "professionals" such as lawyers, engineers, and accountants, will often be longer in duration and require a greater commitment on the part of the temporary worker. The greater the commitment to the on-site employer by the employee, the greater the possibility that this relationship would rise to the level of an employer-employee relationship.

(e) Could the employee refuse to work for the company?

Temporary employees often find a particular job or company too difficult or too unpleasant, and leave an assignment early or refuse to return to that job or company for subsequent assignments.

Integration Test

The **integration test** for joint employment requires that the employment relationship not only meet the standards for the mutual control test, but that a certain degree of integration must exist between the two employers.

Potential integration factors that courts have considered include:

1. the interrelationship between the two companies;
2. whether or not the two companies had common management;
3. the extent of centralization of labor relations; and
4. common ownership of the two companies.

COMMON LAW DUTIES OF THE EMPLOYEE

An employee owes a **fiduciary duty**, a duty to act with the highest degree of honesty and loyalty toward another person and in the best interests of the other person, to the employer.

The categories of an employee's duties are also described in the restatement (second) of agency, and include the following:

contractual duties;

duty of good conduct;

duty to exercise reasonable care in the performance of his or her duties;

duty to act only as authorized;

duty of loyalty;

duty to keep and render accounts regarding money or tangible items received from the employer in the performance of his or her duties or money belonging to the employer that the employee has received from a customer;

duty not to compete with the employer; and

duty not to utilize confidential information.

DOCTRINE OF EMPLOYMENT AT WILL

Employment at will is employment that is usually undertaken without a contract and may be terminated at any time, by either the employer or the employee, without cause.

Although this doctrine applies to both the employer and the employee, the employer generally exercises its options to terminate an employment relationship more often than does the employee. However, the employer's right to discharge an at-will employee is not an unlimited right.

Each state dictates whether employment at will is recognized, and some states have severely limited or eliminated this employment doctrine.

EXCEPTIONS TO EMPLOYMENT AT WILL DOCTRINE

Employment at will does not apply in certain cases, including the following:

1. employment contracts;
2. civil servants; and
3. collective bargaining.

Employment Contracts

Employment contracts are often used by employers for professional or executive positions in order to define terms and conditions of employment. These agreements may or may not modify the presumptive employment at will relationship discussed above. Any negotiation of an employment contract should ensure that the agreement is both enforceable and that it does not create contractual rights and obligations that the employer is either unwilling or unable to meet. A poorly drafted employment contract may create more problems for the employer than no contract at all.

From the perspective of the employee, an employment contract offers clarification of compensation and employee benefits. Additionally, employment contracts often provide an increased amount of job security by limiting an employer's right to terminate an employee at will. In summary, an employment contract provides certainty in an employee's terms and condition of employment.

The types of employment contracts commonly include the following:

Employment Contracts—Express Written

The employment at will doctrine does not apply in the case of a written contract that provides for a definite period of employment. A presumption of employment at will does not disappear, however, if the written employment contract is indefinite as to the term of the employment, or if the contract limits the employer's rights to terminate an employee at will. (Chapter 2 contains an extensive discussion of the role of the written employment contract in the employment relationship.)

Express Oral Employment Contracts

States generally permit the enforcement of express contracts or specific promises to employees, even if the promises are informal and oral.

Oral employment contracts that limit an employer's right to discharge an at-will employee are as enforceable as written employment contracts, provided that all of the requisite elements of a valid contract are present, and that the oral employment contract doesn't violate the Statute of Frauds. The **Statute of Frauds** provides that any contract that cannot be performed within one year is not enforceable unless it is in writing and signed by the person against whom the agreement is to be enforced.

To be an enforceable oral contract, the oral promise must contain a contract term to specifically limit the employer's right to terminate the employee at will. The courts have generally held that a promise of employment for a period of time "as long as the work is satisfactory" does not violate the one-year Statute of Fraud provision, because such a contract is considered to be performable within one year.

The employee must show that the oral promises were legally attributable to the employer or an agent of the employer acting within the scope of his or her authority.

Courts have normally found that broad, general comments by an employer, such as, "Employee X will not be discharged," are insufficient to alter at-will employment.

Implied Contracts of Employment (based on handbook or policy manual)

Although no express or written agreement regarding the duration of employment exists, courts may infer an implied contract of employment. The standard contract principles are necessary to provide the existence of an implied agreement, offer, acceptance, consideration, and meeting of the minds.

In cases where no specific promises were made, courts have determined that there was an implied contract that an employee would not be discharged except for "good cause."

Instances of implied contracts include:

- language in employee handbooks that states employees will be given an initial probationary period;
- language in disciplinary policies that sets out particular offenses for which an employee will be terminated;
- progressive disciplinary policies that permit an employee the chance to improve his or her performance, but the employee was not given such a chance; and
- the employee's outstanding work history of regular merit raises and good performance, evaluations, and/or promotions.

Many courts have held that handbooks and employee manuals are simply policy statements, not a contract, and do not limit the employer's right under the employment at will doctrine. Exceptions have occurred in cases where the employer stipulated that the handbook was a contract or adopted a statement in the handbook that an employee could only be discharged on the basis of good cause.

An effective method of avoiding the formation of an implied contract through the contents of a handbook or employee manual is the inclusion of an express disclaimer of the intent to form a contractual relationship. The employee has effective notice of the disclaimer when the employee signs an acknowledgment of receipt for the handbook and disclaimer. Appendix A is an example of an acknowledgment of receipt for an employee handbook or manual.

Implied Contracts of Employment (based on documents, words, actions, or a combination thereof)

Plaintiffs often allege that application forms, evaluation documents, or business plans imply a promise of job security. Courts, however, have generally held that such documents do not modify an employee's at-will status, unless the documents contain an express agreement permitting the modification of the at-will status.

Civil Service Employment

Government employment at the local, state, and federal levels is regulated by statute. Government employees, commonly referred to as **civil servants**, work under the authority of civil service commissions. The rights and obligations of civil servants are derived from a specific statute regulating a particular agency or department.

Collective Bargaining Agreements

The relationship between unions and union workers is statutorily regulated. Thus, no employment at will defense may be asserted by either of these parties. A **collective bargaining agreement**, a contract between a union and an employer's union members, serves as a specialized employment agreement for unions and union workers.

Public Policy Exception to Employment at Will

Public policy is defined as "broadly, principles and standards regarded by the legislature or by the courts as being of fundamental concern to the state and the whole of society," and "more narrowly, the principle that a person should not be allowed to do anything that would tend to injure the public at large."

"Public policy" is a term commonly used in determining the validity of contracts. Individual states determine whether the public policy exception applies. Some states, Alabama, for example, do not recognize this limitation.

An employer may defend a claim of discharge in violation of public policy by arguing that the discharge was based upon a "legitimate business reason," or that there was no causal connection between the plaintiff's discharge and his or her alleged refusal to commit an illegal act. Examples of a violation of public policy include discrimination and retaliation by the employer. As of January 2001, 44 states recognized public policy as an exception to employment at will.

Good Faith and Fair Dealing Exception to Employment at Will

Some courts have ruled that even under an employment at will relationship the parties must act in **good faith and fair dealing**, honest dealing, but the majority of courts do not apply this standard unless the employer discharged an employee for a reason that violated public policy. As of January 2001, 13 states recognized this exception to employment at will.

Wrongful Discharge Exception to Employment at Will

Wrongful discharge is a theory under which an employee is wrongfully dismissed. This theory is discussed extensively in Chapter 6.

TERMS

actual authority
agent
apparent authority
civil servants
collective bargaining agreement
economic realities test
employee
employer
employment at will
estoppel
estoppel authority
express authority
fiduciary
fiduciary duty

good faith and fair dealing
hybrid test
implied authority
independent contractors
integration test
joint employment
leased employees
master
mutual control
negligent hiring
principal
pubic policy
ratification
respondeat superior
servant
statute of frauds
temporary employees
tort
wrongful discharge

REVIEW QUESTIONS

1. Shortly after a law firm courier delivers documents for filing at the county courthouse, he receives a call from his teenage son, asking that he pick him up immediately from the local high school because his car won't start. The courier decides to take the time to help his son. However, while talking to his son by cell phone, he fails to stop at a stop sign and hits a truck in the intersection, causing extensive damage to the truck and injuries to its driver. Is the law firm liable for the damages caused by its courier? Explain the theory behind your answer.

2. A manufacturing company has been aware for several weeks that bolts securing a heavy frame are defective, but has taken no action to replace the bolts. An employee is seriously injured when the bolts pull away from the frame and the 50-pound frame falls on his arm. Under the theory of master-servant, would the manufacturing company be responsible to the employee for the injuries sustained?

3. The owner of an automotive repair shop hires a mechanic who has a record of mental problems that often result in sudden episodes of rage and physical vio-

lence. Two weeks after he is hired, the new mechanic suffers such an episode following his delivery of an automobile to an elderly female customer. He attacks the customer with such a force that she suffers a concussion and several broken bones. Was the owner of the repair shop liable for negligent hiring?

4. The plaintiff, Stetka, was given office space, scheduled for floor time, and required to attend sales meetings and to spend two to four hours a week in the office. With those exceptions, her work schedule was generally unstructured. Stetka set up her own meetings, brought in her own business, and marketed herself independently. Did the real estate company exercise sufficient control over Stetka to classify her as an employee, or is she an independent contractor? *Stetka v. Hunt Real Estate Corp.*, 859 F. Supp 661, 65 FEP 1311 (W.D.N.Y. 1994.)

5. Assume that Joseph Jackson performs interior decorator services for a local homebuilder under an employment contract that reflects his services are provided as an independent contractor. Following the termination of his relationship with the homebuilder, Jackson files suit, alleging age discrimination. The homebuilder denies its liability, on the basis that Jackson's contract states that he is an independent contractor, not an employee. Will the homebuilder be successful in this defense, and, if not, why not?

6. A terminated female factory worker files suit against her former employer, claiming that she had an "employment contract" for life through her employment application. Will the worker succeed in her lawsuit if her state recognizes employment at will? Why or why not?

7. George Miller files a lawsuit against his former employer, alleging that his immediate supervisor, a line manager, had assured him that he had a job for life with Wilson Electronics. Would the oral assurance of a line manager be sufficient to bind the employer? Explain why or why not.

8. An oil refinery, operating under a collective bargaining agreement, terminates a worker, claiming that the employee works under employment at will. Will the worker be successful in defeating a claim for termination under employment at will? Explain the legal theory for your answer.

9. Explain the mutual control test used to determine joint employment status.

10. How can an employer avoid creating an employment contract when it provides employees with an employee handbook?

PROJECTS

1. Search the Internet for the latest statistics and articles on leased employees. Identify potential Internet cites for this type of information. Summarize the key points of this research for presentation to your attorney prior to his meeting with a potential client—an agency that provides leased employees.

2. Research your federal circuit court's decisions since the *Vizcaino v. Microsoft Corp.*, 120 F. 3d 1006 (9th Cir. 1997) to locate subsequent decisions on the definition of "independent contractor." Read those cases and determine whether your circuit court has followed the Ninth Circuit's ruling. Prepare a case brief on the latest decision by your circuit court on this subject.

CHAPTER 2

Establishing the Employment Relationship

OVERVIEW

The employment relationship begins with recruitment. Locating, hiring and, ultimately, retaining qualified, skilled workers is of significant importance to employers. High costs associated with employee turnover and an increased legal liability for negligent hiring practices and wrongful termination are valid concerns of employers.

The next stage in the employment relationship after recruitment is the information gathering and actual employment selection from the pool of applicants. This second stage includes the application process, the interview, background and reference checks, and testing.

Two of the techniques utilized in the initial employment process include inquiry and examination. Preemployment inquiries in the application form or interview questions reveal basic background information about an applicant. Examinations or tests, however, are designed to gather more specific and probing information. The tests can be utilized to predict future job performance on the basis of aptitude, intelligence, skill level, physical capabilities, and honesty.

Example   Paralegals are often required to submit a writing sample prior to employment.

Many employers administer at least one type of formal preemployment test or examination of applicants, often including drug testing. Background and reference checks are critical to avoid potential claims of negligent hiring, as discussed in Chapter 1.

This chapter will investigate all facets involved in establishing an employment relationship, from recruiting through testing. Chapter contents will include references to requisite nondiscriminatory practices for each part of the employment relationship.

RECRUITMENT

Employee recruitment options include:

- newspaper advertisements;
- Internet postings;
- employee referrals;
- walk-ins;
- educational institutions; and
- professional search firms in a particular specialty.

Employers should consider whether the recruitment method chosen could discourage diversity among its workforce, or whether the recruitment method could have a discriminatory impact upon applicants. Recruitment, like every phase of the employment process, is subject to government regulation, including:

- Title VII of the Civil Rights Act of 1964;
- The Rehabilitation Act of 1973 (if a federal agency, employer, or contractor);
- The Americans with Disabilities Act of 1990 (in the case of a private sector employer);
- The Age Discrimination in Employment Act of 1967;
- The Immigration Reform and Control Act of 1986,
- The Pregnancy Discrimination Act and
- Numerous state laws relating to employment practices.

One method by which an employer might avoid potential discrimination claims in recruitment is the utilization of more than one recruitment method, including advertising in newspapers or other forms of media that are more likely to produce an applicant pool from diverse demographic groups.

Advertising

When advertising for employees, an employer should ensure that the language in the advertisement clearly describes both the position available and the necessary qualifications for the position. The inclusion of a statement in the advertisement that the employer is an "Equal Opportunity Employer" might also be considered. The advertisement should avoid language that might be construed as discriminatory, for example, an advertisement for "Recent college graduates," geared toward recruiting younger employees, or an advertisement for "Female wait staff," placed by a national restaurant chain known for hiring buxom, young females.

Internet Postings

The Internet offers a vast applicant pool for virtually all types of businesses. Many Internet placement listings are general in nature; however, specialized placement listings are also available. Governmental entities, private employers, educational institutions, and trade associations are examples of Internet placement listings. Sites are also available for general resume postings.

Employee Referral

Many companies offer a referral bonus to employees who recommend a friend or family member for an open position. Employee referrals are often thought of as a safe and inexpensive recruitment method because the employer is obtaining an applicant who is not an "unknown." However, if a company's workforce consists of primarily white males, the employer might face a charge of discrimination for failure to advertise for and recruit minorities.

Educational Institutions

College and technical schools offer vast resources for employees in a particular area, such as accounting, nursing, or computers. Most educational institutions provide a placement office and job bank for graduates. Again, this recruitment source has the potential for discrimination. A large portion of recent graduates may be young people who entered the institution straight from high school. In addition, recruiting from an expensive, private college could indirectly result in the exclusion or limitation of minority applicants.

Employment Agencies

Many companies use employment agencies—particularly specialized agencies, such as those placing only medical or legal personnel—to recruit applicants. The search firm often performs a screening and testing service for applicants prior to sending an applicant to an employer for interview. Employers should avoid placing "oral" changes to a job order. For example, an employer might suggest to an employment agency that the company is not interested in hiring young female applicants because of a belief that these applicants are not as dependable as older applicants. Compliance with such an order places the employment agency in a precarious position because employment agencies are subject to the same laws regarding discrimination as are employers!

Walk-in Applicants

Active recruiting may not be necessary if a company receives a large number of unsolicited applications. For example, many paralegals send unsolicited resumes to a number of law firms with the hope that one or more might have an opening. The danger facing a company that relies on walk-in applications is the possibility that not all types of employees will be attracted. For example, some minority paralegals might be hesitant to send in an unsolicited resume to a large national law firm because of intimidation resulting from the size and prestige associated with the firm.

EMPLOYMENT APPLICATIONS

The actual hiring process normally begins with an employment application. This form requests information that will serve to screen out applicants on the basis of education or experience requirements. However, questions on the form requesting date of birth, nationality, religion, marital status, number and ages of children, or ethnicity are not permitted by Title VII, because an employer is not permitted to make an employment decision based on those factors. Even if the employer does not base its employment decision on responses to these questions, the mere presence of the questions on the application is often sufficient to raise an inference of a disparate impact against the protected group to which the applicant belongs. Avoid any inquiry on the employment application that is not ESSENTIAL for effective evaluation of an applicant's qualifications for a particular position.

An employment application should contain the following statements or inquiries, with modifications for a particular position:

- A statement that the employer is an "Equal Opportunity Employer" and will not discriminate in any phase of the employment process.
- A statement that the application is neither an offer of employment or contract, along with a statement that employment with the company is on an at-will basis.
- A certification by the applicant that all information and answers provided by the applicant on the form and during the interview process are true and accurate, accompanied by an acknowledgment by the applicant that denial of employment or, in the event the applicant is hired, termination of employment may occur in the event of falsification of any information provided on the application or during the interview process.
- General information, including name, address, telephone number, position

sought, and availability. I-9 statement regarding proof of legal authorization to work in the United States.

- Work experience, including previous employers' names, addresses and telephone numbers, dates of employment, last pay rate, job titles and duties, supervisors' names and titles, and reasons for leaving the previous positions.
- Educational background, including high school and colleges attended, number of years completed (without the dates attended); whether the applicant graduated, and any degrees obtained; and any specialized licensing or vocational school certificate obtained.
- Military experience APPLICABLE TO THE JOB SOUGHT, including branch of service, rank, and special skills or training.
- Questions about whether the applicant was dishonorably discharged from other employment, with a statement that the facts of the discharge will be considered.
- Special questions relating to experience or certificates relevant to the position sought, including license or certification required, typing or word-processing skills, computer skills, languages, and professional affiliations.
- Personal and professional references.

THE INTERVIEW PROCESS

Strengthening the interview process and minimizing potential legal exposure for actions that might occur in the interview process can only be accomplished by extensive preparation in advance. Employers should use the job description for the vacancy and the applicant's resume or application form to develop specific questions for the applicant prior to the interview. These questions must be carefully designed to elicit only information regarding the skills, experience, and other qualifications necessary for the position.

Whenever possible, the applicant should meet with more than one interviewer, either in multiple interviews or by meeting with two interviewers simultaneously. Multiple interviewers often ensure objectivity in the employment selection process. In addition, one interviewer might pick up on one area in the interview dialog that another misses.

Personal small talk between the interviewer and the interviewee may jeopardize the integrity of the interview by veering into discriminatory topics.

Example   An interviewer's constant reference to a particular religion or political beliefs could be construed by an applicant to be intimidation or harassment.

Example   An applicant might be drawn into discussion of child care arrangements as a pretext for establishing a basis for discrimination.

Figure 2-1 lists proper and potentially improper inquiries relating to the most typically asked interview and employment application questions.

An objective evaluation and ranking of applicants' qualifications are useful for rating relevant factors such as communication skills, work experience, and specific job skills for the open position. This type of ranking system for job candidates provides the employer with specific evidence upon which to make and, if necessary, defend its hiring practices and decisions.

PREEMPLOYMENT TESTING

Preemployment testing occurs before hiring, or sometimes after hiring, but before employment, in connection with such qualities as integrity, honesty, drug and alcohol use, HIV status, or other such characteristics. This type of testing began in the 1950s as a response to the needs of American businesses. Since that time, preemployment testing has continued to be viewed as the answer to a myriad of employment problems, including personnel problems, ineffective hiring programs, and appropriate job placement for applicants.

Employers often cite two reasons for preemployment testing, including finding the best qualified individual for a position and to ensure that the applicant is free of personality or similar types of difficulties. Such testing may appear to be neutral. However, it may have a **disparate impact** (discrimination based on race, color, religion, sex, national origin, age, or disability that results from a practice that does not seem to be discriminatory and was not intended to be so), as discussed in depth in Chapter 7.

The second reason for preemployment testing is to search for impairments, such as drug and alcohol abuse, that may limit an applicant's ability to perform a job. Highly-publicized drug-related accidents in the rail and shipping industries (for example, the *Exxon Valdez* incident), among other areas, have added to concerns about the necessity for preemployment testing for impairments.

Courts perform a balancing test to determine the legality of preemployment testing for impairments, weighing the conflicting interest of the employer in securing a substance-free workplace against the privacy rights of the applicant. Chapter 15 provides an in-depth discussion of the issue of privacy in employment matters, including preemployment testing referred to as **ineligibility testing** for disqualifying factors that include drug and alcohol tests, HIV testing, and polygraphs.

Employers may conduct workplace testing for ineligibility in order to reduce

Subject	Proper Inquiry	Improper Inquiry
Age	"Can you show proof of age upon hire?" "Are you over 18 years of age?"	What is your age? What is your birth date? What are the dates you attended high school? What is your graduation date? What dates were you in the military?
Anti-nepotism	Note-need statement of company's anti-nepotism policy.	"Can you identify any relative or close friends who work for our company?"
Arrest	"Have you had a prior criminal conviction?" Note-must include a statement that it will not absolutely prohibit employment. Information will only be taken into consideration if conviction relates to specific job requirements.	"Have you ever been arrested?"
Bonding	Statement that a fidelity bond is an employment requirement.	"Have you ever been denied a fidelity bond?" "Have you ever had a fidelity bond cancelled?"
Citizenship or Birthplace	"Are you legally authorized to work in the U.S.? Note-must include statement that proof of that legal right to work will only be required after the applicant is hired.	"Are you a U.S. citizen?" "What country were you born in?" "What country were your parents born in?"
Education	"What is the highest grade attended?" "What high schools and/or colleges did you attend?" Note-these questions may be asked ONLY if such educational require-ments are job-related.	"What dates did you attend high school?" "What date did you graduate from high school?"
Height or weight	Note-questions may be asked, but ONLY if height or weight is a bona fide occupational qualification, and only should be asked with approval of attorney.	"What is your height?" "What is your weight?"
Hours of work	"Are you available to work overtime?" "Are you able to work 9-5?" (or other hours, as applicable)	"Did you work overtime as required at your former employment?"
Military service	"Did you gain your electronic experience in the military?" (or other job-related experience)	"What type of discharge did you receive?" "Do you have reserve duty obligations that would require you to miss work?"
Name	"Have you ever used another name?" "Have you ever used an assumed name?"	"What is your maiden name?" "Have you had your name changed legally?"

Figure 2-1
Guideline for Preemployment Inquiries

Subject	Proper Inquiry	Improper Inquiry
National origin	"What languages do you speak, read or write?" Note-ask only if relevant to job opening.	"What is your national origin or nationality?" "What is your native language?"
Organizations	"List all job-related organizations, clubs or professional organizations to which you belong?"	"What is your political affiliation?" "Are you a union member?"
Physical or Mental Disabilities	"Can you perform the functions of the job for which you are applying, with or without reasonable accommodation?" Note-ask question ONLY after explaining job functions. "Do you need reasonable accommodation to perform the job, and, if so, what type?" Note-ask only when you reasonably believe that the applicant will need reasonable accommodation because of an obvious disability or the applicant's voluntary disclosure of a disability.	"Do you have any physical or mental condition or disability that might affect your ability to perform the job for which you are applying?" "Are you in good health?" "Have you received disability or workers' compensation benefits in the past?"
Qualifications or or previous work work experience	"What are the names and addresses of your former employers?" "What are the dates of your previous employment?" "What was the reason for your leaving your previous employer(s)?" "What is your prior accounting (or other skills related to job opening) experience?"	"Do you type at least 80 words per minute?" for example – unless that is an actual job requirement.
Race	None-any data for affirmative action compliance or EEO recordkeeping should be recorded and maintained separately from the application.	"What is your race?" "What is your skin, hair or eyes color?
Religion	"Are you able to work the hours, days or shifts that I have outlined as our regular work schedule?"	"What is your religion?"
Residence	'What is your address?"	"Do you own or rent your home?" "How long have you lived at your present address?"
Sex	Ask ONLY if sex is a bona fide occupational qualification related to job performance and only after obtaining legal advice on existence of BFOQ.	"What is your sex?" "How many children do you have? What are their ages?" "What plans do you have for child care?"

Figure 2-1 (*continued*)

workplace injury or to provide a safer working environment. Drug testing, for example, has been shown to drastically reduce the number of workplace injuries and personal injury claims related to employment. Additionally, an employer may use ineligibility testing to predict employee performance. Personnel costs related to workplace crimes, personality conflicts, and drug use result in increased costs to the employer, thus serving as an impetus for ineligibility testing.

Eligibility testing is used to ensure that the applicant is capable of performing in and qualified for the position. These tests often include intelligence tests, eye exams, tests of physical stamina, aptitude tests, or tests for the existence of certain personality traits.

Example   Potential bus drivers may be required to undergo eye and hearing exams.

Title VII does not prohibit the use of a test that has been validated according to strict validation standards, even if a disparate impact results. Legal validation for eligibility tests must reflect that the test is a **business necessity** (a character trait that is necessary for the essence of the business.) The test must also predict job performance.

Example   A test for intelligence must test intelligence, and intelligence must be necessary for adequate performance of the position that the applicant seeks.

In 1978, the EEOC, assisted by several other government agencies, developed the Uniform Guidelines on Employee Selection Procedures. These guidelines allow employers to determine the proper use of tests and other employment selection procedures. Under these guidelines, if a selection test is shown to have an adverse impact on a protected class (selection rate for any one group of less than 80% of the selection rate of the group with the highest rate), the test must be **validated**—that is, there must be evidence that the test evaluates what it says it evaluates.

The EEOC guidelines list three forms of test validation. **Criterion-related validation** is the most traditional type of test validation. Such a test must accurately predict job performance as evidenced by the applicant's ability to do the job. This validation consists of collecting data relating to job performance from a simulated exercise, then creating statistical relationships between measures of job performance and test scores. The criterion is the performance score received. **Content validation** is a test that specifically examines applicants for the skills required by the specific position that the applicant seeks. Such a test should closely approximate an observable work behavior or observable work product. The third type of validation is **construct validation**. This type of test considers the psychological makeup of the applicant and compares it with the traits necessary for adequate job performance.

The Civil Rights Act of 1991 added a provision to Title VII that prohibits employers from adjusting or altering test scores on the basis of membership in a protected class, or from using different test cutoff scores on that basis. EEOC guidelines also mandate that employers of 100 or more employers must maintain specific records to ascertain the validity of tests and their impact on various populations where an adverse impact has been evidenced.

An employer must show, in addition to test validation, that the specific trait for which an applicant is being tested is a **bona fide occupational qualification (BFOQ)**, defined by *Oran's Dictionary of the Law* as "an employer's legitimate need to discriminate in hiring based on race, sex, age, etc." (See *Griggs*, discussed below.)

Griggs v. Duke Power Co., 91 S. Ct. 849 (1971)

Facts:

Thirteen African-Americans challenged the employer's requirement of either a high school diploma or a passing score on two separate intelligence tests as a condition of employment or job transfer. Neither test was intended to measure the ability to learn to perform a particular job or category of jobs at the plant. The testing requirement applied equally to blacks and whites, but the employer failed to show that the tests had a demonstrable relationship to successful performance of the jobs for which the tests were used. The testing requirement was not retroactive. Employees hired before the testing was required were performing satisfactorily and were being promoted. According to a company vice president, the company imposed the testing requirement to "improve the overall quality of the workforce."

The Court of Appeals relied on a subjective test of the employer's intent and found no showing of a discriminatory purpose in the diploma or test requirements and found no violation of Title VII. The Supreme Court disagreed, as reflected in the court's opinion below.

Opinion by Justice Burger:

The Act [Title VII] proscribes not only overt discrimination but also practices that are fair in form but discriminatory in operation. The touchstone is *business necessity*.

Good intent or absence of discriminatory intent does not redeem employment procedures or testing mechanisms that operate as 'built-in headwinds' for minority groups and are unrelated to measuring job capability. [The employer has the] burden of showing that any given requirement [has] a manifest relationship to the employment in question.

The judgment of the Court of Appeals is, as to that portion of the judgment appealed from, reversed.

Thousands of job applicants are required to take a **polygraph**, or lie detector test, each year. Ostensibly, the polygraph test is designed to detect dishonesty or deceitfulness in an applicant. In spite of the large number of applicants taking such tests, however, accuracy rates reflect that the test is far from reliable. Because of the large number of false positives resulting from the polygraph, the Federal Employee Polygraph Protection Act of 1988 was passed, as discussed in Chapter 15. This act has greatly reduced the use of the polygraph for employee selection.

The restricted use of polygraph tests has caused employers to resort to subjective tests that are intended to measure honesty or integrity through an analysis of written or oral answers to particular questions. The validity of such tests for obtaining useful information upon which to base employment decisions is questionable.

Drug and alcohol testing prior to employment is permitted by the Drug-Free Workplace Act of 1988, discussed extensively in Chapter 15.

Many employers require preemployment, post-offer medical tests to ensure that the applicant is physically capable of performing a particular position.

Example   A job requirement for an airline baggage handler might be the ability to lift 75 pounds. A medical examination would be required to verify that the applicant had no restrictions on lifting.

Such tests are prohibited prior to the job offer to protect against wrongful discrimination based upon a disability that was discovered during the test. The Americans with Disabilities Act and the Vocational Rehabilitation Act (VRA) require that all employees within the same job category must be subject to the medical examination requirement. Additionally, all information obtained through the medical examination process must be maintained in a confidential file, not in the general personnel file.

Genetic testing is a scientific development that uses laser and computer technology to evaluate an individual's biological predispositions based upon the presence of a specific disease-associated gene in an individual's DNA. This type of testing surfaced in the 1960s in connection with research relating to individuals who were "hypersusceptible" to certain chemicals utilized in a particular workplace. Many states prohibit the use of genetic testing as a condition of employment, because of the controversy surrounding such testing and the discrimination to which it might lead.

BACKGROUND REFERENCE CHECKS AND PREEMPLOYMENT INVESTIGATIONS

Prior to making a job offer, an employer should check an employee's personal and professional references. Depending upon the nature of the open position, employers may also want to consider a more extensive background check, possibly including a request for a credit report on the applicant.

Example   Bank teller applicants may be subject to credit checks.

Properly checking information obtained from the application and the interview is necessary for the employer to avoid a potential claim of negligent hiring. Failure to verify the applicant's statement that he or she has no prior criminal conviction could result in a negligent hiring claim, for example, when the applicant is subsequently arrested a third time for driving under the influence of alcohol while operating a public school bus.

UNIFORM GUIDELINES ON EMPLOYEE SELECTION PROCESS

In 1978 the Uniform Guidelines on Employee Selection Procedures were enacted in an effort to assist employers to comply with Title VII. These guidelines assist in determining the proper use of tests and other employee selection procedures. Under these guidelines, any selection procedure resulting in a disparate impact is discriminatory. **Disparate impact**—discrimination based on race, color, religion, sex, national origin, age, or disability that results from a practice that does not seem to be discriminatory and was not intended to be so—exists under the guidelines if the selection rate for any protected class is less than 80% of the rate for the group with the highest rate of selection (the four-fifths rule). There is no requirement under the guidelines to validate tests where no adverse impact results or has been shown.

In the event that the employer has two or more selection procedures available that are substantially equal for their stated purpose, the employer is directed by the guidelines to use the procedure that has been shown to have a lesser adverse impact.

OFFER LETTERS

Employers often provide a written offer of employment that verifies the terms agreed to by the employer and the prospective employee. The offer letter usually contains language stating that the individual has accepted the offer for a particular position and to begin work on a specific date. The offer letter also establishes the agreed-upon salary and benefits. Care should be taken to ensure that the offer letter does not offer a promise of continued employment that might affect the employer's ability to subsequently terminate the individual's employment.

No reference to a "permanent" position or a specified period of employment should be included in the offer letter. Because of the potential legal problems inherent in offer letters, the prior review of an offer letter by legal counsel and/or human resources professional is beneficial to the employer and the employee.

WRITTEN EMPLOYMENT CONTRACT

Employers often use written employment contracts, particularly for management, executive, and technical personnel. A carefully drafted employment contract insures that the agreement is enforceable and does not create obligations that the employer is not willing or able to meet. The written employment contract should contain the following provisions:

Description of the Employee's Position and Job Duties

This is an essential although elementary part of every employment contract. Courts are often called upon to determine whether the employer's unilaterally changing the employee's contractual job duties or transferring the employee to a different position from that stated in his or her employment contract constitutes a breach of contract. In the absence of those factors, the employer normally prevails in such litigation. However, that would not have been the case if the position and job duties had not been expressly described in the employment contract.

Compensation

Negotiating an acceptable compensation package is often the most difficult part of finalizing a written employment contract, for each party wants the more favorable position. Employee compensation in a written employment contract should address the following four areas: base pay, incentive compensation, employee benefits, and severance benefits.

The base pay is limited by the Fair Labor Standards Act (FLSA) discussed in Chapter 3. Incentive compensation is based upon performance-related criteria and is paid in addition to the base pay.

Most employers offer employee benefits as part of the compensation package. These benefits often include:

Insurance—health, life, disability, travel, accidental death and workers compensation;
Vacation;

Sick leave;

Pension, 401(k), profit sharing, deferred compensation plan, and stock
purchase plan;

Automobile or automobile allowance;

Paid parking;

Cellular telephone and/or pager;

Country club and/or health club membership; and

Tuition reimbursement.

Severance benefits are payments to an employee upon the termination of the employment relationship. These benefits are intended to compensate the employee for past services and to enable the employee to move into a new employment relationship. The employment agreement should contain a provision for circumstances under which severance benefits will not be payable.

Example   Severance benefits may not be due to an employee if the employee is terminated for good cause or voluntarily quits his or her employment.

Duration of Contract

Every written employment agreement should include a provision regarding the duration of the agreement. A **fixed-term agreement** ends at the expiration of the term stated in the agreement and is the simplest and most often utilized type of employment agreement. Such an agreement remains in effect for a stated time period—for example, one to five years. The term does not have to be expressed in months or years. It can be tied into some future event, such as the closing of the business. If the employee works beyond the fixed term, a court will generally find that the agreement was renewed for an additional term.

The employer cannot terminate an employee-at-will under a fixed-term employment agreement. Additionally, a majority of the courts and state statutes impose a "good cause" limitation on an employer's right to terminate a fixed-term employment agreement before the expiration of the term. An employer may relinquish its right to terminate at-will, or the parties may specify another option for termination prior to the expiration of the fixed-term employment agreement.

An **indefinite term employment agreement** is an agreement that does not specify a fixed term. This type of agreement is generally considered to be terminable at will, unless the parties limit the termination rights in the agreement. A **condition subsequent agreement** links a future event, such as the completion of a project, the sale of the business, or the employee's retirement, to the termination of the agreement. This type of agreement is quite similar to the indefinite-term agreement because the term of the agreement is not obvious from the language of the agreement. However, a condition subsequent agreement is different from an indefinite-term agreement because it is not intended to continue indefinitely, and it is not terminable at will. The **renewable employment agreement** includes a fixed-term, but provides for automatic renewal unless either party gives notice of its intent not to renew.

Termination

The termination clause is one of the most important provisions of an employment agreement. Absent such a clause, the possibility of litigation between the parties increases significantly. There are several types of terminations, and each has different legal consequences. Termination at will can be included in a written employment agreement. The agreement should specify the parties' rights to terminate the employment relationship.

"Good cause" is another type of termination clause. "Good cause" is generally defined as an employee's failure to perform the duties that a person in the industry would ordinarily perform under similar circumstances. The following are examples of acts that might be included in the **good cause termination** portion of the employment contract:

1. fraud, theft or embezzlement;
2. unauthorized disclosure of confidential company information or trade secrets;
3. breach of fiduciary duty;
4. failure to perform essential job functions;
5. disloyalty;
6. use of alcohol or controlled substances in the workplace;
7. carrying weapons into the workplace;
8. failure to follow safety regulations; and
9. failure to follow company policies.

Good faith dissatisfaction termination may be included in the employment agreement to allow an employer who is not satisfied with an employee's work performance to terminate the agreement before the expiration of the agreement's term. This clause cannot be used by an employer without justification, as the test in court is generally whether the acts that caused the termination would have induced a "reasonable employer" to take the same termination action.

The majority of employment agreements include a requirement that the employee be given notice prior to termination. If the employer does not choose to give a notice prior to terminating an employee, the employer has the option of paying the employee wages instead.

Protection of Trade Secrets

Theft of trade secrets has been the subject of an increased number of lawsuits in the past decade. Employers are justifiably concerned with protecting confidential information and with the ownership of work or products created by its employees. The importance of this clause is often tied into the employee's job position. For example, employment agreements covering engineering and research and development positions should normally contain a trade secrets protection clause.

Choice of State Law

Employment agreements, like other contracts, should contain a clause that specifies which state's law will be used to interpret the agreement. For example, the choice might be the state where the employee performs services, or the state where the company's corporate office is located. In the case of sales personnel, the services are often performed in multiple states. Absent a provision in the contract that specifies a choice of law, courts generally apply the law of the state that has the most significant relationship to the dispute, or the largest number of contacts with the employee and employer.

Successors and Assigns Provision

In an era of constant mergers and acquisitions, a successorship provision is needed to protect the parties' interest in the employment agreement. The employer is normally interested in being able to transfer any liabilities under the employment agreement to any company that purchases the employer's business. The employee will be more interested in a successorship provision that will ensure the employee a position with the successor in the event of a merger or acquisition.

Modification

Changes in the terms and conditions of the employment agreement are often necessary during the term of the agreement. Such a provision generally requires that any modification must be made in writing and signed by all parties to the agreement.

Severability

The **severability clause** provides that if any portion of the agreement is determined to be unenforceable, the other portions of the agreement continue to be effective. If there is no severability clause, the entire agreement might be unenforceable because of one unenforceable clause.

Arbitration

Employment law is an area in which arbitration has enjoyed a long and successful history. Reduced legal fees and swifter resolution of disagreements are two primary factors in the increased appeal of arbitration. Courts have generally found that an employer may legally require an employee to arbitrate an employment dispute.

Indemnification

Employment agreements for higher-level employees generally include indemnification provisions to cover actions by the executive employee.

Attorneys' Fees

The employment agreement should contain a provision stating which party will pay attorneys' fees in the event of litigation. In some cases, the agreement might contain a provision that each party will pay his or her own attorneys' fees.

Notices

The employment agreement should furnish an address where an employer can send an employee notice of certain events.

STATUTORY LIMITATIONS ON EMPLOYMENT CONTRACTS

Certain state and federal statutes limit or affect the terms of the employment relationship. For example: the Fair Labor Standards Act (FLSA), 29 U.S.C. §201, establishes the federal minimum wage and payment of overtime compensation. (See Chapter 3 for additional information on the FLSA.)

The Civil Rights Act of 1866, 42 U.S.C. §1981, prohibits race discrimination in the creation and enforcement of contracts, including employment contracts.

Title VII of the Civil Rights Act of 1964, 42 U.S.C. §1981, prohibits discrimination on the basis of race, color, religion, sex, and national origin in all terms and conditions of employment.

The Age Discrimination in Employment Act, 29 U.S.C. §621, prohibits age discrimination in all terms and conditions of employment.

The Americans with Disabilities Act, 42 U.S.C. §12101, prohibits disability discrimination in all aspects of employment and requires an employer to make reasonable accommodations to employ a disabled person.

The Family and Medical Leave Act, 29 U.S.C. §2601, requires unpaid leave in the event of birth, adoption, or serious illness.

AFFIRMATIVE ACTION AND THE EMPLOYMENT RELATIONSHIP

History of Affirmative Action

Affirmative action is defined as steps to remedy past discrimination in hiring or promotion—for example, by recruiting more minorities and women. Both employers and employees find this definition confusing at times. This confusion can lead to such statements as "I have to hire a black for the next opening" or "I lost my job to a woman because the government required that my company give my job to a less qualified woman." Nothing could be farther from the truth. The truth is generally found in a statement such as "The court found that my employer had discriminated against qualified blacks and/or women, and my employer was required to remedy the situation by hiring and promoting **qualified** blacks and/or women."

In its simplest form, affirmative action requires that the employer undertake an affirmative effort to bring qualified women or minorities, or others similarly statutorily mandated, into the workplace to make the workplace more reflective of the population from which the employee pool is drawn.

The initial affirmative action plan was signed by President Franklin D. Roosevelt on June 25, 1941, and was known as Executive Order 8802. That order applied only to defense contracts and was issued as a result of discrimination in national defense production during World War II. Following several changes, that executive order evolved into Executive Order 11246, which was signed into law by President Lyndon B. Johnson on September 24, 1965.

Executive Order 11246 prohibits employers who contract with the federal government to provide goods and services of $10,000 or more from discriminating "against any employee or applicant for employment because of race, color, religion, sex, or national origin." The order requires that the contractor take affirmative action to ensure that applicants are employed, and that employees are treated during employment, without regard to their race, color, religion, sex, or national origin. Affirmative action includes, but is not be limited to: employment, upgrading, demotion or transfer; recruitment or recruitment advertising; layoff or termination; rates of pay or other forms of compensation; and selection for training, including apprenticeship.

A contractor or subcontractor with 50 or more employees and a nonconstruction contract of $50,000 or more must develop a written **affirmative action plan** that is designed to remedy racially discriminatory practices suffered in the past by members of certain minority groups within 120 days of the beginning of the contract. Large contractors are also required to perform a **workplace assessment**, measuring the workplace for the representation of women and minorities in each of seven employment categories, ranging from unskilled workers to management employees. The employer is also required to compare the percentage of women and minority employees in those positions with the percentage of such employees available in the workforce from which the employer's workforce is drawn.

The Office of Federal Contract Compliance Programs (OFCCP) in the U.S. Department of Labor enforces Executive Order 11246. OFCCP's enforcement relates only to the employer's participation in federal government contracts. Executive Order 11246 contains no provision for private lawsuits by employees. As a result, remedies available to employees for affirmative action violations are limited to state fair employment practice laws, Title VII, or similar legislation. However, the Order provides that employees may file complaints with OFCCP, and may sue the Secretary of Labor to compel performance of executive order requirements.

OFCCP regulations define **underrepresentation** or **underutilization** as "having fewer minorities or women in a particular job group than would reasonably be expected by their availability." If the workplace assessment indicates that the employer has an underrepresentation in any given category, then the employer must develop a plan of corrective action, referred to as an affirmative action plan. The plan includes goals of the number of employees necessary to correct the underrepresentation and timetables for accomplishing the goals. Employers are required to submit annual reports of the affirmative action program results to the OFCCP.

The term "availability" with respect to women and minorities is not based on the number of each category in a given geographic area. It is based on the availability of women and minorities *qualified for the particular job*. For example, there may be a large number of women in a given geographic area, but only a small percentage might be qualified for such positions as petroleum geologist or master electrician.

Although the Civil Rights Act was enacted in 1964 to facilitate equal employment rights for all workers, no significant employment affirmative action case was decided by the U.S. Supreme Court until the case discussed below:

United Steelworkers of America, AFL-CIO v. Weber, 443 U.S. 193 (1979)

Facts:

In 1974, United Steelworkers of America and Kaiser Aluminum entered into a master collective-bargaining agreement. This agreement included an affirmative action plan designed to eliminate conspicuous racial imbalances in Kaiser's then almost exclusively white craft-work forces. The plan reserved 50% of the openings in the in-plant craft-training programs for blacks until the percentage of black craftworkers in a plant was commensurate with the percentage of blacks in the local labor force. In 1974, only 1.83% of the skilled craftworkers at one of Kaiser's plants were black, even though the local work force at the time was approximately 39% black. During the plan's first year, seven black and six white craft trainees were selected from the plant's production work force. The most senior black trainee had less seniority than several white production workers whose bids for admission were rejected. Thereafter, Weber, one of the white production workers, filed this class action in Federal District Court, alleging that the affirmative action program had resulted in junior black employees' receiving training in preference to senior white employees, causing discrimination in violation of Title VII. The District Court agreed that the affirmative action plan violated Title VII, entered judgment in favor of the plaintiff class, and granted injunctive relief. The Court of Appeals affirmed, holding that all employment preferences based upon race, including those preferences incidental to bona fide affirmative action plans, violated Title VII's prohibition against racial discrimination in employment.

Opinion by Justice Brennan:

Challenged here is the legality of an affirmative action plan-collectively bargained by an employer and a union-that reserves for black employees 50% of the openings in an in-plant craft-training program until the percentage of black craftworkers in the plant is commensurate with the percentage of blacks in the local labor force. The question for decision is whether Congress, in Title VII of the Civil Rights Act of 1964, left employers and unions in the private sector free to take such race-conscious steps to eliminate manifest racial imbalances in traditionally segregated job categories. We hold that Title VII does not prohibit such race-conscious affirmative action plans.

We need not today define in detail the line of demarcation between permissible and impermissible affirmative action plans. It suffices to hold that the challenged Kaiser-USWA affirmative action plan falls on the permissible side of the line. The purposes of the plan mirror those of the statute. Both were designed to break down old patterns of racial segregation and hierarchy. Both were structured to "open employment opportunities for Negroes in occupations which have been traditionally closed to them." 110 Cong. Rec. 6548 (1964) (remarks of Sen. Humphrey).

At the same time, the plan does not unnecessarily trammel the interests of the white employees. The plan does not require the discharge of white workers and their replacement with new black hires. Nor does the plan create an absolute bar to the advancement of white employees; half of those trained in the program will be white. Moreover, the plan is a temporary measure. It is not intended to maintain racial balance, but simply to eliminate a manifest racial imbalance. Preferential selection of craft trainees at the Gramercy plant will end as soon as the percentage of black skilled craftworkers in the Gramercy plant approximates the percentage of blacks in the local labor force.

We conclude, therefore, that the adoption of the Kaiser-USWA plan for the Gramercy plant falls within the area of discretion left by Title VII to the private sector voluntarily to adopt affirmative action plans designed to eliminate conspicuous racial imbalance in traditionally segregated job categories. Accordingly, the judgment of the Court of Appeals is REVERSED.

Quotas in Affirmative Action

Quotas are the strict numbers of women or minorities that must be hired to comply with affirmative action requirements. However, affirmative action and quotas are not synonymous. Affirmative action does not require hiring quotas for women or minorities to the exclusion of other qualified employees, regardless of whether the minorities or women are qualified for the job.

There is no quota requirement under either Executive Order 11246 or Title VII. The one time that hiring or promotion quotas is even permitted is when there has been a longstanding violation of the law and nothing else will accomplish the intent of the law. To the extent that established goals for affirmative action work, no quotas will be imposed as a remedy for underrepresentation.

Penalties for Noncompliance with Affirmative Action Regulations

A number of penalties may be imposed by the Secretary of Labor or the appropriate contracting agency, including:

1. Recommending to the EEOC or the Department of Justice that proceedings be instituted under Title VII;
2. Recommending to the Department of Justice that criminal proceedings be brought for furnishing false information to either a contracting agency or the Secretary of Labor;
3. Requesting the Attorney General to file suit to enforce the executive order in the event of actual or threatened substantial violations;
4. Publishing the names of nonconforming contractors or labor unions;
5. Canceling, terminating, or suspending all or portions of the contract; or

6. Debarring the noncomplying contractor from further government contracts until the contractor has satisfied the Secretary of Labor that it will abide by the order.

TERMS

affirmative action
affirmative action plan
bona fide occupational qualification (BFOQ)
construct validation
content validation
criterion-related validation
disparate impact
eligibility testing
ineligibility testing
polygraph
preemployment testing
quotas
underrepresentation
validated
workplace assessment

REVIEW QUESTIONS

1. The James Garcia Law Firm places an advertisement for a paralegal opening in only one newspaper—a Spanish newspaper. The position does not require a knowledge of Spanish. Mr. Garcia, Sr., the managing partner, defends the advertisement on the basis that he is more comfortable working with paralegals of a Hispanic background and doesn't want to bother with interviewing non-Hispanics who would respond to an advertisement in the town's major newspaper. Is Mr. Garcia's action a discriminatory employment action? What law does it violate? What are the potential penalties for Mr. Garcia's action?

2. A major cosmetics manufacturer requires a drug test of all applicants before a job offer is extended. Discuss why this would be a violation of employment law, and what laws might be violated.

3. The human resources manager of a law firm advises a white male paralegal applicant that he would like to hire the applicant but cannot. He explains that the law firm's affirmative action plan requires that the next three job openings be awarded to minority applicants, whether or not those applicants are qualified for the position. Is the human resources manager correct in the statement that he is "required" to hire minority applicants? Is the statement "whether or not those applicants are qualified for the position" a correct interpretation of affirmative action requirements?

4. A company places a job order with an employment agency to fill a paralegal vacancy. The personnel director orally advises the employment recruiter that the company prefers to hire only younger paralegals because it believes they have the energy and drive necessary for the seventy- to eighty-hour work weeks generally required at the firm. If the recruiter follows the employer's direction, would the recruiter, employer, or both, be guilty of violating the Age Discrimination in Employment Act?

5. If your human resources director makes a statement during a staff meeting that he believes that affirmative action is "passé," and the firm should no longer be concerned with affirmative action plans, what would be the possible basis for that statement? Is affirmative action a "dying breed," and, if so, why do you believe that to be true.

6. On her resume, Marsha Tennyson, an applicant for a paralegal position, states that she graduated from a particular paralegal program with honors. She signs a release so that the information on her resume can be verified. During the verification process, the law firm administrator learns that the applicant dropped out of the program before completion of the requisite courses, and that she had several failing grades for courses completed. Can the law firm survive a claim of discrimination filed by Ms. Tennyson once she is denied employment?

7. During the interview process, the senior partner of a prestigious metropolitan law firm asks a female applicant whether she has any children, why not, and if she plans on becoming pregnant. No such questions are asked of male applicants. Would the partner be guilty of sex discrimination, and, if so, under what anti-discrimination laws?

8. Discuss the basis for the Supreme Court's ruling that Kaiser's affirmative action plan did not "unnecessarily trammel the interests of the white employees" in *United Steelworkers of America, AFL-CIO v. Weber,* 443 U.S. 193 (1979).

9. In an offer letter, Miller Pharmaceuticals offers a paralegal applicant "a permanent position" with its corporate legal department. Explain why this offer does or does not constitute a contract.

10. Assume that a manufacturing plant in a rural East Texas location has openings for petroleum engineers. The company has an affirmative action plan in place that calls for future openings to be filled by minorities. There is a 38% female population in the area. Does that statistic require that the company hire unqualified females for the petroleum engineer openings? If not, why not?

PROJECTS

1. Search the Internet for job openings for paralegals in your state. List the categories of the Internet sites—for example, private placement agencies, state bar association, or educational institution. Prepare a summary of the qualifications for paralegals as listed in the ads. Include in the summary the specialty areas of the job openings, and the number of openings for employment law paralegals.

2. Prepare an employment contract for an employment paralegal that incorporates the written contract requirements discussed in this chapter.

CHAPTER 3

Compensation Regulations for Employers

OVERVIEW

Prior to 1938, no federal laws existed to regulate the minimum amount of wages that a worker could be paid, the rate that a worker should be paid for hours worked in excess of a particular number of hours, or a prohibition against pay differentials based solely on gender. In 1938, the **Fair Labor Standards Act** (FLSA) was enacted as part of the massive New Deal legislative program. The FLSA's purpose was the establishment of the federal minimum wage, maximum hours of work, overtime pay, and the regulation of child labor for employers engaged in interstate or foreign commerce and employees of state and local government (see 29 U.S.C. §201). FLSA is enforced by the Wage and Hour Division of the DOL. (Appendix B contains a listing of DOL regional offices.)

Although FLSA applies in all states, it permits states to regulate areas not covered by FLSA and to afford workers greater protections than those granted by the FLSA. Where state laws and the FLSA conflict, employers must allow the provision that is more favorable to the employee.

A second major piece of legislation regulating employment compensation was passed 25 years after the FLSA. The **Equal Pay Act** (EPA), discussed in this chapter, prohibits pay differentials based solely on gender.

FLSA DEFINITION OF THE EMPLOYER-EMPLOYEE RELATIONSHIP

In order for an employee to be covered by the FLSA, a bona fide employment relationship must be present. The terms "employer" and "employee" are broadly defined in the act. To determine whether an employment relationship exists, the language of the act must be considered.

Definition of Employer

The FLSA defines an **employer** as anyone directly or indirectly acting in the interest of an employer in relation to an employee.

Employers subject to FLSA include:

1. all enterprises engaged in interstate commerce or the production of goods for interstate commerce.
2. all hospitals, schools, and public agencies, regardless of size.

Small businesses that are not engaged in interstate commerce and have an annual gross volume under $500,000 are not covered by the FLSA.

Definition of Employee

Employee is defined in the Act as any individual employed by an employer. In 1992, the Supreme Court in *Nationwide Mutual Insurance Company v. Darden*, 503 U.S. 318 (1992), as discussed below, found that the FLSA "defines the verb 'employ' expansively to mean 'suffer or permit to work.'" This definition stretches the meaning of "employee" to cover some parties who might not otherwise have qualified as an employee.

Nationwide Mutual Insurance Company v. Darden, 503 U.S. 318 (1992)

Facts:

Contracts between Nationwide Mutual Insurance and Darden provided that Darden would sell only Nationwide policies, that Nationwide would enroll him in a company retirement plan for agents, and that he would forfeit his entitlement to plan benefits if, within a year of his termination and 25 miles of his prior business location, he sold insurance for Nationwide's competitors. After his termination, Darden began selling insurance for those competitors. Nationwide charged that Darden's new business activities disqualified him from receiving his retirement plan benefits, for which he then sued under the Employee Retirement Income Security Act (ERISA) of 1974.

The district court found that Darden was not a proper ERISA plaintiff because, under common law agency principles, he was an independent contractor rather than, as ERISA requires, an "employee," a term the Act defines as "any individual employed by an employer." The court of appeals reversed the district court, finding the traditional definition inconsistent with ERISA's policy and purposes, and holding that an ERISA plaintiff can qualify as an "employee" simply by showing (1) that he had a reasonable expectation that he would receive benefits, (2) that he relied on this expectation, and (3) that he lacked the economic bargaining power to contract out of benefit plan forfeiture provision.

Opinion by Justice Souter:

ERISA's nominal definition of "employee" as "any individual employed by an employer," is completely circular and explains nothing. Thus, we adopt a common-law test for determining who qualifies as an "employee" under ERISA, a test we most recently summarized in *Community for Creative Non-Violence v. Reid*, 490 U.S. 730, 109 S.Ct. 2166, 104 L.Ed. 2d 811 (1989):

"In determining whether a hired party is an employee under the general common law of agency, we consider the hiring party's right to control the manner and means by which the product is accomplished. Among the other factors relevant to this inquiry are the skill required; the source of the instrumentalities and tools; the location of the work; the duration of the relationship between the parties; whether the hiring party has the right to assign additional projects to the hired party; the extent of the hired party's discretion over when and how long to work; the method of payment; the hired party's role in hiring and paying assistants; whether the work is part of the regular business of the hiring party; whether the hiring party is in business; the provision of employee benefits; and the tax treatment of the hired party."

490 U.S. at 751–752, 109 S.Ct., at 2178–2179.

The FLSA . . . defines the verb "employ" expansively to mean "suffer or permit to work." This latter definition . . . stretches the meaning of "employee" to cover some parties who might not qualify as such under a strict application of traditional agency law principles. ERISA lacks any such provision, however, and the textual asymmetry between the two statutes precludes reliance on FLSA cases when construing ERISA's concept of "employee." While the Court of Appeals noted that "Darden most probably would not qualify as an "employee" under traditional agency principles, *Darden, supra,* at 70, it did not actually decide that issue. We therefore reverse the judgment and remand the case to that court for proceedings consistent with this opinion.

EMPLOYEE EXEMPTIONS UNDER FLSA

There are a number of exceptions to the FLSA, some of which are **total exemptions** (applying to both minimum wage and overtime requirements) and some of which are **partial exemptions** (applying only to overtime requirements). The major white-collar exemptions include executive, administrative, professional, and outside salespersons exemptions.

White-Collar Exemptions

There are four **white-collar exemptions** to the FLSA:

Executive

The executive's primary duty consists of management of the enterprise in which he or she is employed or of a recognized department or subdivision, regular and customary direction of the work of two or more full-time employees, and the authority to hire or fire other employees or whose input as to the hiring and firing, advancement and promotion, or any other change of status of other employees is given particular weight, and customary and regular exercise of discretionary powers. The **job duties**, not the **job title**, determine whether an employee is exempt.

Example   Executives include department director, plant manager or superintendent, production supervisor, and office manager or shift supervisor.

All executive employees must be paid on a salary basis. The salary level requirement of at least $250 per week for this classification has not changed in over 15 years. If the salary is between $155 and $249 per week, the employee must perform exempt work at least 80% of the time.

Administrative

The primary work of an administrative employee consists of:

a) the performance of office or nonmanual work directly related to management policies or general business operations of either the employer or the employer's customers, or the performance of functions in the administration of a school system, educational establishment, or institution, or of a department or subdivision there, in work directly relating to the academic instruction or training carried on therein;
b) customarily and regularly exercising discretion and independent judgment;
c) regularly and directly assisting an owner, manager, or an employee employed in a bona fide executive or administrative capacity or performing under only general supervision, working along specialized or technical lines requiring special training, experience, or knowledge, or executing under only general supervisor, special assignments and tasks.

Under the FLSA, the job duties, not the job title, determine whether an employee is exempt under the FLSA.

Example   Administrative positions include treasurer, comptroller, public relations director, marketing director, human resources or personnel director, or buyer.

The administrative employee must be paid on a salary basis, with the same requirements as those outlined for an "executive."

Professional

Primary duties of a professional include work requiring:

- advanced knowledge in a field of science or learning customarily acquired by a prolonged course of specialized intellectual instruction and study (four-year degree in relevant field is required except for diploma nurses and data processing personnel); or
- work that is original and creative in character in a recognized field of artistic endeavor, the result of which depends primarily on the invention, imagination, or talent of the employee; or
- teaching, tutoring, or lecturing by one who is employed as a teacher in the school system or educational institution, whose work requires the consistent exercise of discretion and judgment, and whose work is predominantly intellectual and varied in character and is of such character that the output produced or the result accomplished cannot be standardized in relation to a given period of time.

Once again, the job duties, and not the job title, determine whether an employee is exempt.

Example   Professionals include physician, registered nurse, attorney, engineer, psychologist, architect, artist, and chemist.

The salary requirement for a professional is at least $250 per week. If the employee is paid $170 to $249 per week, the employee must perform exempt work at least 80% of the time.

Certain computer system analysts, programmers, and software engineers are exempt from overtime if they are paid on a salary basis or are paid at an hourly rate of at least $27.63 per hour.

Outside Salespersons

This individual must regularly work away from the employer's place of business or away from an in-house office in making sales or obtaining orders for service for at least 80% of the time.

There is no salary basis for the outside salesperson category under the FLSA.

Total Exemptions (both overtime and minimum wage) under FLSA

Local retail and service establishments
Small agricultural operations

Small town newspapers with less than 4,000 subscribers

Recreational and amusement establishments and camps

Partial Exemptions (overtime) under FLSA

Interstate truck drivers, helpers, and mechanics

Rail and air common carrier employees

Auto dealer, salesperson, parts person, and mechanic

Taxicab driver

Domestic service employee in the household

Motion picture theater employees

Small town radio and television personnel (town of less than 100,000)

COMPENSATION FOR IRREGULAR HOURS—BELO CONTRACTS

Employers may offer a guaranteed weekly compensation to employees who work irregular hours (29 U.S.C. §207(f)). Such arrangements are often referred to as **Belo contracts** because of a Supreme Court case that decided the issue of fluctuating hours *Walling v. A.H. Belo Corp.*, 316 U.S. 624 (1942) is discussed below.

Walling v. A.H. Belo Corp., 316 U.S. 624 (1942)

Facts:

The administrator of the Wage and Hour Division of U.S. Department of Labor brought suit against A. H. Belo Corp., the publisher of the *Dallas Morning News* and other periodicals, and the owner and operator of radio station WFAA. The company had approximately 600 employees. Many of the employees, particularly those in the newspaper business, worked irregular hours. Prior to the effective date of the FLSA, October 24, 1938, Belo had been paying all but two or three of those employees more than the minimum wage required by the Act. They received two weeks of vacation each year, special bonuses at the end of the year amounting to approximately one week's earnings, and full pay during periods of illness. Employees were given time off to attend to personal affairs without deductions from pay. When the employees were required to work long hours in any week, they were given compensating time off in succeeding weeks.

After the enactment of the FLSA, but before its effective date, Belo endeavored to adjust its compensation system to meet the requirements of the Act by negotiating a contract with each of its employees except those in the mechanical department. These contracts were in the form of letters that stated the terms to which the employees had agreed.

The letters set out minimum wages and maximum hours of employment per week. The employees were guaranteed a certain sum per week, with the specified hourly rate fixed at 1/60th of the guaranteed weekly wage. When the employee worked enough hours at the contract rate to earn more than the guaranty, the surplus time was paid for at the rate of 150% of the hourly contract wage.

The purpose of Belo's arrangement with its employees was to permit as far as possible the payment of the same total weekly wage after the Act as before.

Requirements for a Belo contract include:

1. There must be a business necessity for the employee's irregular and fluctuating hours of work;
2. The contract between the employer and the employee must specify a regular pay rate that is not less than the statutory hourly minimum applicable to the employee;
3. The contract must provide for a weekly pay guarantee;
4. The contract must specify compensation at no less than one and one-half times the regular rate for all hours worked in excess of the maximum straight-line number in the statutory workweek applicable to the employee; and
5. The weekly guarantee, on the basis of the rates specified, must cover no more than 60 hours (29 U.S.C. §207(f)).

Opinion by Justice Byrnes:

When employer and employees have agreed upon an arrangement which has proven mutually satisfactory, we should not upset it and approve an inflexible and artificial interpretation of the Act which finds no support in its text and which as a practical matter eliminates the possibility of steady income to employees with irregular hours. Where the question is as close as this one, it is well to follow the Congressional lead and to afford the fullest possible scope to agreements among the individuals who are actually affected.

Many such employees value the security of a regular weekly income. They want to operate on a family budget, to make commitments for payments on homes and automobiles and insurance. Congress has said nothing to prevent this desirable objective. This Court should not.

Affirmed.

DUTIES IMPOSED ON NON-EXEMPT EMPLOYERS UNDER THE FLSA

The FLSA imposes five duties on non-exempt employers:

- to pay at least the minimum wage to employees;
- to pay overtime that is at least one and one-half times the average hourly pay;
- to pay men and women equally for equal work;
- to maintain certain child labor standards; and
- to maintain specified payroll records.

MINIMUM WAGE REQUIREMENTS UNDER THE FLSA

The **Minimum Wage Increase Act of 1996** (P.L. 104-188, Title II, 2104, 110 Stat. 1928 (August 20, 1996)), effective September 1, 1997, dictates that an employee covered by the FLSA must be paid a minimum hourly wage of $5.15. There are several exceptions to this requirement:

Full-Time Students and Handicapped Employees

A certificate of exemption from the DOL is required before an employer can pay an employee in these categories less than minimum wage.

Tipped Employees

An employer may pay "tipped employees" $2.13 per hour. This requirement applies only to employees who customarily earn more than $30 per month in tips and who actually receive tips equal to or greater than the amount of the credit.

Opportunity Wage

The FLSA was amended in 1996 to permit an employer to pay employees under the age of 20 a wage of not less than $4.25 per hour during the first 90 days of employment. However, the employer cannot discharge another employee or reduce the hours, wages, or employment benefits of a current employee to hire a qualified individual under the opportunity wage.

Trainees

A trainee is not covered by the FLSA. To avoid minimum wage requirements for the individual listed as a trainee, the employer must prove the following:

- The training is similar to that which would be provided in a vocational school;
- The training is for the benefit of the trainee;
- The training does not displace a regular employee;
- The employer does not receive any immediate advantage from the trainee's activities;
- The trainee is not necessarily entitled to a job upon completion of the training; and
- The employer and trainee both understand that the trainee is not entitled to wages for the time spent in training. (*Wage & Hour Manual (BNA)* 91:416 (1975))

COMPUTATION OF WAGES

The regular pay rate is defined as the hourly rate actually paid to the employee for the normal, non-overtime hours worked. The FLSA does not require that compensation be based on an hourly rate. Earnings may be determined on a commission, piece rate, or other basis. The Act only requires that the earnings be converted to an hourly rate to determine overtime pay.

An employer is prohibited from including certain items as part of an employee's wages if imposing that cost would cause the employee's net pay to fall below the minimum wage in any workweek.

Example   The cost and cleaning of uniforms when the nature of the business requires the employee to wear a uniform.

Example   The cost of tools or other materials involved in conducting the employer's business.

CALCULATING HOURS WORKED AND WORKWEEK

A workweek consists of seven consecutive 24-hour periods. It need not coincide with the calendar week, but may begin on any day and at any hour of the day (29 CFR Sec. 778.105).

Any activity that is controlled or required by the employer and is necessarily and primarily for the benefit of the employer's business constitutes hours worked. Examples of such activity include:

a) Rest and Meal Periods
   Short rest periods (generally five to 20 minutes) must be counted as hours worked, but meal periods are not normally counted if the employee is completely relieved of his or her job duties for the purpose of eating. If the employer is required to perform duties while eating, the meal period must be counted as hours worked.
b) Commuting Time
   The time spent commuting to and from the job site is not generally considered in the calculation of hours worked. However, time spent going from one job site to another during the workday or required travel to a conference or meeting place must be counted as hours worked. In the case of out-of-town overnight travel, all travel during normal work hours for all seven days is considered to be hours worked.

c) Waiting Time

Periods when an employee is on call may constitute hours worked, depending on whether the employee was "engaged to wait" or was "waiting to be engaged." When an employee is required to remain on call at the employer's premises or so close to the premises that the employee is unable to use that time for his or her own purposes, the employee is "engaged to wait" and such time is compensable. An employee who is on call during periods when the time can still be used for personal activities is "waiting to be engaged" and that time does not constitute hours worked.

Carrying a beeper or pager does not constitute hours worked if the employee is relatively free to come and go as he or she pleases.

d) Training Programs and Meetings

Attendance at meetings, training programs, and similar activities is not counted as work time in the following cases:

1. attendance is not within the employee's regular hours;
2. attendance is voluntary;
3. the event is not directly related to the employee's job; and
4. the employee performs no production work during such event.

e) Overtime

Overtime must be paid for all hours over 40 worked per week, unless there is a specific exception from overtime under the FLSA, as discussed earlier in this chapter. Hours that are paid but not worked, such as holidays, vacations, or sick days, do not count as hours worked under the FLSA.

The overtime rate is one and one-half times the employee's regular rate, which includes all forms of compensation, for each hour worked in excess of 40 hours in a workweek (or the maximum allowable in a given type of employment).

Employees who are paid a salary and whose hours vary from week to week receive an overtime premium calculated by adding one-half the rate per hour for each hour worked over 40. The rate per hour is the weekly salary divided by the actual number of hours worked in the workweek.

Example   A $400-a-week employee earns $8 per hour in a 50-hour week. Half that amount, $4, is the overtime premium per hour.

Overtime must be paid even if the time worked is not authorized. The employer's authorization of the overtime can be express or implied if an employer knows or has reason to believe that the employee is working and the employer permits the employee to work through lunch, work beyond his or her shift, or take work home. Employers cannot benefit from an employee's work without compensating the employee for the work.

Employees may neither waive their right to be compensated for overtime hours worked nor agree to a lower overtime rate than that required by the FLSA.

f) Compensatory Time

In 1985, Congress amended the FLSA to permit states and localities to compensate employees who work overtime with extra time off. Compensatory time off in lieu of overtime is not allowed in the private sector unless there is hour-for-hour compensatory time off in the same week, or time and one-half compensatory time off in the second week of a two-week pay period.

AREAS NOT REGULATED BY THE FLSA

The Act does not regulate the following areas:

overtime for weekend or holiday work;
vacation, holiday, severance, and sick pay;
rest periods, holiday off, and vacation time; and
pay raises and fringe benefits.

ADMINISTRATIVE ACTIONS REQUIRED OF EMPLOYERS UNDER FLSA

In addition to the substantive legal requirements of the FLSA, employers are required to comply with record keeping and posting requirements of the Act.

RECORD KEEPING

The FLSA requires that "[e]very employer subject to any provision of this Act . . . shall make, keep and preserve such records of the persons employed by him and of the wages, hours, and other conditions and practices of employment maintained by him" (29 U.S.C.A. §211(c)).

DOL regulations require an employer to retain certain categories of records pertaining to each employee for up to three years. Violation of the record keeping requirements subjects the employer to the penalties available under the Act.

RECORD RETENTION

Payroll records must be maintained for three years. Supplemental records such as time cards, work sheets, and so on, are to be maintained for two years. Appendix C identifies additional documents that an employer must maintain under FLSA regulations.

POSTING

All employers subject to the FLSA are required to post federally approved notices in conspicuous places to explain the minimum wage and overtime provisions. (Refer to Appendix D for specific posting requirements of the FLSA.)

RETALIATION

The FLSA provides that it is unlawful to:

discharge or in any other manner discriminate against any employee because such employee has filed any complaint or instituted or caused to be instituted any proceeding under or related to this chapter, or has testified or is about to testify in any such proceeding, or has served or is about to serve on an industry committee. (29 U.S.C. §215(a)(3)).

ENFORCEMENT OF THE FLSA

The Wage and Hour Division of the DOL interprets and enforces the provisions of the FLSA.

Broad investigative powers are granted to the DOL to enforce the FLSA, and include the right to inspect the employer's records and premises and to question employees.

An employee may also sue in any state or federal court on his or her own behalf and on behalf of other similarly situated employees.

BURDEN OF PROOF UNDER THE FLSA

The FLSA places the burden of proof on the defendant-employer, not the plaintiff-employee in FLSA claims. The employer, for example, has the burden of proving that an employee is exempt from the FLSA's overtime provisions, or that an individual is an independent contractor rather than an employee, as the plaintiff has alleged.

STATUTE OF LIMITATIONS IN FLSA CLAIMS

The Statute of Limitations in FLSA claims is two years from the date of the violation for ordinary damages, and three years from the date of the violation for willful violations of the Act.

PENALTIES FOR FLSA VIOLATIONS

Liquidated damages equal to back wages the court has ruled are due are available as a remedy for FLSA violations. In cases brought by the secretary of labor, an injunction against an employer is possible. Attorneys' fees can also be recovered. The DOL can assess civil money penalties up to $1,000 in the case of repeated or willful violations. Violations of the child labor provisions of the Act can result in a civil penalty of up to $10,000 for each employee who was the subject of such a violation.

If the violations are deliberate, voluntary, and intentional, the FLSA also authorizes the Department of Justice to bring criminal actions, subject to a five-year Statute of Limitations, which can result in fines up to $10,000, or, for a second violation, imprisonment for up to six months.

THE EQUAL PAY ACT

In 1963, Congress amended Section 6 of the FLSA by passing the EPA in response to the growing number of underpaid women in the workplace.

The stated purpose of the EPA is "to prohibit discrimination on account of sex in the payment of wages by employers engaged in commerce or in the production of goods for commerce." As set out in the purpose of the Act, the only protected class under the EPA is sex. Accordingly, an employer must pay female employees the same rate as male employees for the same work.

The EPA prohibits differentials in pay that are based primarily on gender. Employers covered by the EPA must ensure that male and female employees are paid equal wages for performing "substantially equal" jobs. This does not mean that the job titles and descriptions need to be identical for the EPA to apply. Job titles are *irrelevant* to an EPA analysis. If two jobs require equal skill, effort, and responsibility, and are performed under similar working conditions, they are equal for the purposes of the EPA. Minor differences in degree of skill required or in job responsibilities cannot justify a pay differential between men and women.

An employer may deviate from the equal pay requirements of the act only on the basis of:

1. seniority system;
2. merit system;
3. system based on quantity or quality of production; or
4. any differential factor other than sex.

The first three exceptions listed above are specific, but the last is general in nature and thus open to interpretation and disagreement. The secretary of labor has issued numerous interpretations of this exception, one of which expressly designates a bona fide training program as one factor "other than sex" that may validly produce a male-female wage difference. However, training programs that appear to be available only to employees of one sex will need to be carefully reviewed to determine whether such a program is bona fide.

Once the secretary of labor has carried his or her burden of showing that the employer pays workers of one sex more than workers of the opposite sex for equal work, the burden shifts to the employer to show that the differential is justified under one of the four exceptions listed above.

The following are examples of factors that have been found sufficient to justify pay differentials:

a. **Retention.** An employer may raise an employee's pay, regardless of the pay rates and gender of his or her counterparts, in order to retain the employee after he or she has been offered a higher-paying job. However, retention concerns cannot be used to justify permanent, across-the-board pay differentials between men and women.

b. **Red circle rates.** A permissible **red circle rate** occurs when a worker is temporarily paid at a higher-than-normal rate for a reason that is not based on gender. For example, when an employee with compromised health is temporarily reassigned to lighter duty but is paid his or her normal rate of pay, a red circle rate results. A red circle rate is permissible *only* if it is temporary. It may not be used for the purpose of maintaining a permanent wage differential between men and women.

c. **Different physical locations.** Typically, only jobs performed at the same physical location may be compared to one another. However, a pay differential between branch offices in order to adjust for cost of living is permissible.

d. **Different working conditions**. According to guidelines issued by the Equal Employment Opportunity Commission (EEOC), pay differentials may be justified by substantial differences in the surroundings and/or the hazards regularly encountered by two individuals performing the same job functions. "Surroundings" is defined as elements regularly encountered by a worker in the normal work environment (toxic fumes, inclement weather conditions, etc.). The term "hazards" refers to physical hazards regularly encountered, such as radiation exposure or the risk of injury from operating hazardous machinery. Slight or inconsequential differences in working conditions would not justify a differential in pay.

The EPA applies to employers with two or more employees, but is limited in application to certain types of companies (public agencies, companies engaged in the operation of schools, institutions of higher education, institutions involved in the care of the sick, aged, or the mentally ill or hospitals and, effective April 1, 1990, companies that have gross annual sales of at least $500,000 (29 US.C §203(s)).

The EPA, unlike the FLSA minimum wage and overtime pay provisions, has no exemption for executives, administrative or professional employees, or outside salespersons.

It is not necessary for *all* persons of one gender employed in a specific job classification to be discriminated against to establish an EPA violation—a single discrimination is sufficient for a violation of the Act.

EPA procedures and remedies are similar to those under the ADEA, which is also governed by the FLSA. However, the EPA has no administrative prerequisites to private enforcement, as do the other anti-discrimination statutes. An employee is not required to file a charge with the EEOC or state fair employment practices (FEP) agency, or to exhaust any administrative remedies in order to file an EPA action in federal court. However, the employee has the option of seeking relief by filing a charge with the EEOC, which has the authority to bring suit on the employee's behalf. If the EEOC files suit, the plaintiff is precluded from filing his or her personal suit.

Damages available under the EPA include back pay and an equal amount of the back pay award as liquidated damages, unless the court exercises its discretion to find that the employer had reasonable grounds to believe that its act or omission was not a violation of the statute (29 U.S.C. §§216, 260).

FEDERAL CHILD LABOR LAW

The minimum age for employment is 16 years under the **Federal Child Labor Law** (29 C.F.R. §779506). Employment of anyone between the ages of 16 and 18 in any occupation that the secretary of labor declares to be particularly hazardous for the employment of children between such ages is not permitted.

Example   Prohibited occupations for the 16- to 18-year-old employee age group include coal-mining, logging, roofing, and excavation.

Example   Acceptable occupations for children between the ages of 16 and 18 include retail, food service, and gasoline service.

TERMS

Belo contracts
economic realities test

employee
employer
Fair Labor Standards Act
Federal Child Labor Law
Minimum Wage Increase Act of 1996
red circle rate
white-collar exemptions

REVIEW QUESTIONS

1. The Alexander Law Firm's annual revenues are in excess of $25 million per year. Is the law firm required to pay overtime to its nonprofessional employees? Explain the reasoning behind your answer.

2. Nancy Swenson accepted a position as an eighth-grade teacher in the San Francisco school district. In addition to her teaching responsibilities, she was assigned the responsibility for the cheerleading squad. That responsibility included attending practices and all sporting events. While Nancy enjoyed teaching and her cheerleading squad duties, she began to resent the time that she was spending on the job. She complained to her principal about the long hours, and suggested that she should be given overtime pay for the extracurricular activities for which she was responsible. Explain the principal's response to Nancy's request, based on FLSA requirements.

3. In order to earn money for a new four-wheeler, Jeffrey Collins, a 14-year-old, has asked his parents for permission to work at a fast-food restaurant. His parents refuse his request, on the basis that he is not old enough to legally work in such an environment. Are his parents correct in the basis for their denial of his request? Why?

4. The Morton family has employed Sharon Evans to occasionally babysit for three small children while the parents travel for business purposes. Sharon Evans is thrilled to have the opportunity to earn extra money for college. However, her parents accuse the Mortons of unfair treatment because Sharon is paid less than minimum wage. Is there any relief available under the FLSA for this situation?

5. Janice Parker, a litigation paralegal, contacts the DOL to file a complaint against her law firm employer because of the 70-hour weeks she is expected to work. Jan-

ice's claim is based on her belief that the FLSA prohibits a mandatory work week in excess of 40 hours. Will she succeed in her claim?

6. Assume that the Alexander Law Firm in Exercise 1 was required to pay overtime to its nonprofessional employees, but failed to do so. Shortly after an accounting clerk filed a complaint with the DOL, the Alexander Law Firm terminated the clerk. Does the clerk have a claim against the law firm for wrongful termination? If so, what is the basis for that claim?

7. Jentzen Manufacturing Company assigns an employee who has suffered a workers' compensation accident to a position referred to as "light duty" for a period of time. Jentzen does not reduce the employee's salary while she is in the light duty position. Is this a violation of FLSA or EPA? Why or why not?

8. Assume that Jentzen Manufacturing Company employs 10 salespersons whose job is to travel specific geographic areas selling the company's products. The salespersons do not receive a salary but are paid by commission, a percentage of dollar volume of their sales. Jentzen considers these salespersons exempt employees. According to FLSA, is that a correct classification of the employees? Why or why not?

9. A paralegal in the Alexander Law Firm requests and receives a transfer from the firm's San Antonio, Texas office to the firm's Washington, D.C. office. Can the firm pay a location differential to the paralegal because of the higher cost of living for Washington, D.C.?

10. The Matlock Roofing Company received an employment application from the 17-year-old son of one of the owners. Would the company violate the Federal Child Labor Law if it agrees to hire the 17-year-old as a roofer? Would the answer be the same if the company employed him as an accounting clerk?

PROJECTS

1. Search the Internet to determine whether or not the paralegal position is normally recognized as an exempt position. What is the finding of your state courts in this area?

2. Search the Internet for salary studies conducted by paralegal associations, both locally and nationally. What are the categories of compensation listed? Is overtime included?

CHAPTER 4

Employee Benefits

OVERVIEW

The laws relating to employee benefits have undergone constant changes since the passage of the Employee Retirement Income Security Act of 1974 (ERISA). ERISA technically applies to **employee benefit plans**, defined in the Act as "any plan, fund or program established or maintained for the purpose of providing medical, surgical or hospital care or benefits, or benefits in the event of sickness, accident, disability, death or unemployment, or vacation benefits." Prior to ERISA, employees' benefits were largely unstructured and regulated by the employer.

Benefits are an important part of the employee's compensation package. Workers often elect to accept a position with a smaller salary but excellent benefits. For example, benefits for a single mother might be extremely important. Health insurance, life insurance, and before-tax child-care payments offer an emotional and financial security to a single mother. As workers age, the type of benefits they value the most often change. A recent college graduate with a young family might give little thought to investing in a 401(k) or other retirement fund. As that graduate moves up the corporate ladder or is recruited by another company, he or she will be acutely aware of the necessity to compare benefit programs. That employee will also need to be knowledgeable about COBRA benefits for the first time as he awaits eligibility for coverage with his new employer. However, as that graduate reaches middle age, life insurance and retirement benefits are of greater interest and importance.

Employers are unable to personally manage all of the benefit programs available for their employees. Thus, companies frequently seek the services of benefit specialists to administer their benefit programs. This chapter will review the types of employee benefits available and the penalties for violation of benefit regulations.

EMPLOYMENT RETIREMENT INCOME SECURITY ACT (ERISA) OF 1974

ERISA's enactment was largely a response to concerns relating to the protection of pension benefits of workers who had lost their jobs prior to reaching retirement age. Those concerns centered on companies that went bankrupt or simply discontinued business operations, leaving insufficient funds for the terminated employees when the employee reached retirement age.

Although ERISA is often viewed as a plan covering only retirement, the definition above reflects that it relates to much more than retirement. ERISA applies to any type of promised benefit to an employee. Employee benefits that go beyond pension plans discussed below are called "welfare benefits" and are reviewed later in this chapter.

Qualified Retirement Plans

A **qualified retirement plan** is a written plan established by an employer to provide retirement benefits for its employees. An employer contributes to a qualified retirement plan on behalf of the employee participants in the plan. Many employers offer a full-time employee, and in some cases part-time employees, the benefit of investing a portion of their salary in the company's pension or retirement plan. Upon the retirement of a participant, retirement benefits are then paid to the participant under the terms of the plan.

Qualified retirement plans are regulated by Section 401(a) of the Internal Revenue Code of 1986, as amended (Code) and Title I of ERISA. To be a qualified retirement plan, the plan must generally meet the requirements contained listed below:

- Funding through a trust that holds the plan's assets for the exclusive benefit of plan participants and their beneficiaries.
- Limit the maximum amount of annual contributions and benefits.
- Meet minimum participation, vesting and distribution requirements. (Effective January 1, 1997, only defined benefit plans are required to meet minimum participation requirements.)
- Set time limits on when benefits will be paid under the plan.
- Be nondiscriminatory as to contributions and benefits for employees who are not highly compensated.
- Prohibit the assignment or alienation of participants' interests in the plan, except through qualified domestic relations orders.

Effect of Qualification on Retirement Plans

The employer receives an income tax deduction for the amount of its annual contributions, subject to certain limitations set out in the Internal Revenue Code). Contributions and earnings on those contributions are tax-free in the plan until such as time as a distribution is made to the employee or the employee's beneficiaries. Generally, plan assets may not be distributed to a participant until the participant separates from the service of the employer or attains the retirement age stated in the plan. Qualified retirement plans offer distribution of benefits in a single sum, in installment payments, or through the purchase of an annuity, based upon the type of retirement plan.

Disqualification of Retirement Plans

The Internal Revenue Service may disqualify a retirement plan if an employer does not follow the requirements to maintain a qualified plan, as listed above. When a plan is disqualified, the employer may suffer numerous adverse tax consequences, including:

- The employer may lose its tax deduction for contributions the employer has made to the plan;
- The plan may be required to file tax returns and pay income taxes on its earnings, including both penalties and interest; and
- Distributions to participants may no longer be afforded favorable tax treatment.

Types of Qualified Retirement Plans

The two basic types of qualified retirement plans are defined contribution plans and defined benefit plans.

Defined Contribution Plans

Defined contribution plans are individual account plans. Each plan participant is assigned an account. Employer contributions on behalf of a participant are then allocated to the participant's individual account. At the time the participant separates from the service of the employer and requests a total distribution from the plan, the value of the distribution will be the **vested** (absolute, accrued, or complete) portion of the participant's account balance. That amount generally consists of the present market value of the total employer and employee contributions to the participant's account, plus earnings and gains in the account, and minus losses. Two common types of defined contribution plans include profit sharing 401(k) plans and money purchase plans.

PROFIT SHARING AND 401(K) PLANS

The most common forms of defined contribution plans are profit sharing and 401(k) plans. A **profit sharing plan** is an individual account plan that contains a contribution formula. An employer often provides a profit sharing plan as an incentive for employees to participate in the success of the company.

The formula for a profit sharing plan may be a fixed percentage of the participant's compensation (for example, 5% of compensation), or a discretionary amount that is determined by the employer each year. The profit sharing plan must also include a formula to allocate the contributions earnings and gains or losses to a participant's account, usually based upon the compensation of the participant compared to the total compensation for all participants in the plan year. Compensation in excess of $160,000 must be excluded when making contributions to a profit sharing plan, or when allocating the contributions to participants' individual accounts.

A **401(k) plan** is a profit sharing plan that permits employees to make salary deferral contributions to the profit sharing plan on a before-tax basis. The name is derived from the fact that such plans are governed by section 401(k) of the IRS Code. Employers often match participants' contributions to a 401(k) plan, thus encouraging employees to save for retirement. Effective as of 1998, employees may contribute up to $10,000, adjusted for cost of living increases from time to time by the IRS, to 401(k) plans.

MONEY PURCHASE OR PENSION PLANS

A **money purchase plan** is an individual account plan that requires that an employer commit to a specific contribution formula. This annual employer contribution, unlike with profit sharing plans, is not discretionary from year to year. Money purchase plans also have specific funding and distribution requirements that do not apply to profit sharing plans. Sometimes these plans are considered and referred to as "pension plans," but the Internal Revenue Code normally treats such plans as defined contribution plans. An employer may also be able to make a larger tax-deductible contribution to a money purchase plan than to a profit sharing plan.

Defined Benefit Pension Plans

A **defined benefit pension plan** is a plan established by an employer to systematically provide a pension to employees over a period of years after retirement, based on factors such as years of service, the participant's age, compensation, and possibly other variables.

The benefit from a defined benefit pension plan might consist of employer contributions, employee contributions, or a combination of both. This type of plan provides a fixed benefit to a participant. Plan earnings and gains or losses are not taken into consideration in determining a participant's benefit in a defined benefit pension plan. The employer's contribution to the defined benefit pension plan is based upon actuarial calculations that consider the amount of benefit, employee turnover, past investment experience, anticipated future employee compensation, and plan administrative expenses.

Defined benefit pension plans normally determine benefits by using one of the following methods of calculation:

- A fixed amount per month, with no consideration of the participant's rate of compensation or years of service. For example, a benefit of $450 per month.
- An amount based on the number of years of service. For example, a monthly benefit of $30 per month, multiplied by the number of years of service.
- A percentage of final compensation. For example, a monthly benefit of 35% of the final average monthly compensation.
- An amount based both upon final compensation and years of service. For example, a monthly benefit that equals 3% of the final average monthly compensation multiplied by the number of years of service.

Eligibility and Vesting Requirements of ERISA

All employees over 21 years of age who have completed one year of employment MUST be covered by the employer's pension plan under ERISA regulations. **Vesting** (absolute, accrued, complete right to benefits) occurs after five years of employment or gradually the employee's right to his or her pension benefit becomes non-forfeitable over seven years (20% per year, beginning in the third year). The employee's right to the pension benefit is vested after five years, but the employee is not able to obtain the money until retirement.

Fiduciary Duties of ERISA

ERISA established a **fiduciary duty** (a relationship in which a person who manages money or property for another person and in whom that other person has a right to place great trust) to prevent abuse by plan coordinators of the funds entrusted to them. All individuals who have the authority to make decisions about either the investment of the pension plan or who render plan investment advice are considered fiduciaries and are held to a higher standard of loyalty to those who have invested in the fund. Fiduciaries owe a duty to act in the best interest of those to whom they owe that fiduciary duty.

Disclosure Requirements of ERISA

Employers who maintain an employee benefit plan are required to provide a summary plan description (SPD) to plan participants. The SPD sets out information about the plan, including a description of the benefits provided by the plan, eligibility requirements, and the procedures by which eligible employees are able to file claims for benefits and appeal denials of claims.

Every five years after the distribution of the initial SPD, an employer must furnish an updated SPD to participants. In the event of no plan amendments during any five-year period, the updated SPD can be distributed every ten years rather than five years. When material changes to an employee benefit plan are made, the employer must prepare a summary of material modification (SMM) and provide all plan participants with the SMM. Additionally, ERISA requires that employers respond to all requests for plan information from participants.

Prior to August 5, 1997, employers were required to file SPDs and SMMs with the DOL. After that date, employers are only required to furnish those items to the DOL in response to a request by the DOL. A civil penalty of up to $100 per day or up to $1,000 per request may be assessed by the DOL if the requested documents are not provided within 30 days of the DOL request.

Reporting Requirements under ERISA

Employers must file annual reports (IRS Form 5500) with the IRS by the last day of the seventh month after the end of the plan year. Form 5500 requests information on the plan's financial condition, number of participants, funding arrangements, bonding, and insurance. The IRS then forwards a copy of Form 5500 to the DOL for its requisite review under Title I of ERISA.

All employee benefit plans that are funded other than through insurance contracts are required to provide participants with summary annual reports of the financial status of the plans within nine months after the end of the plan year.

Penalties for ERISA Violations

At a court's discretion, a plan administrator who refuses to comply with a plan participant's request for any information may be liable to the participant in an amount up to $110 a day or for other relief that the court deems proper.

If a fiduciary breaches his or her duties to an employee benefit plan or a plan participant, the fiduciary may be liable for damages to either the plan or the participant or for other relief as a court may determine. Additionally, the DOL must impose a civil penalty against a fiduciary that violates ERISA's fiduciary responsibility requirements equal to 20% of any amount that the plan recovers through either a settlement agreement or a judicial proceeding. It is within the DOL's sole discretion to waive or reduce the penalty under certain very limited circumstances. However, the DOL may be reluctant to waive or reduce penalties in view of its increased enforcement activity against plan administrators for employee benefit plans that fail to comply with either ERISA's reporting or disclosure requirements. The Internal Revenue Code provides for a penalty of $25 per day, up to $15,000, that may be imposed for not filing a required Form 5500 or for filing an incomplete Form 5500.

WELFARE BENEFIT PLANS

Employers offer a variety of welfare benefits to their employees, including some or all of the following types of benefits: medical, surgical, or hospital care, dental care, benefits in the case of accident, sickness, disability or death, dependent care, or severance pay.

Both federal and state laws govern welfare benefit plans. However, the law with the most impact on the provision of welfare benefits to employees is ERISA, as amended. ERISA defines an **employee welfare benefit plan** as a plan, fund, or program established by an employer for the purpose of providing the type of benefits discussed above through the purchase of insurance or other types of benefits for participants and their beneficiaries.

Title I of ERISA imposes a number of requirements on welfare benefit plans, discussed earlier in this chapter.

Health Care Benefits

Health care benefits are the most common types of welfare benefits. The cost of providing adequate health care benefits to employees has increased drastically in recent years. As a result, employers have undertaken a search for effective means to cut health care costs. This search has been impacted by increased regulation in recent years, in particular the Health Insurance Portability and Accountability Act (HIPAA) of 1996, as amended and the Consolidated Omnibus Budget Reconciliation Act (COBRA) of 1985, as amended.

Managed Care Programs

In an attempt to reduce both the cost of providing health care benefits to employees and to increase the effectiveness of the health care program, many employers have adopted a **managed care program.** In managed care, a purchaser of health care controls or influences the utilization of health care services in an attempt to achieve high-quality, cost-effective health care services. A growing number of employees are required to choose between in-network and out-of-network health care providers, obtain mandatory second opinions prior to elective surgery, and submit to a pre-admission review of any inpatient hospital services.

Managed care programs have been successful to the extent that they have generally provided the cost reductions desired by the employer. However, as evidenced by the written media and extensive television coverage, managed care programs have exposed employers to legal liability related to the medical care provider, quality of care rendered, as well as numerous other shortcomings perceived by the employee participants in managed care programs.

Cafeteria Plans

The Internal Revenue Code defines a **cafeteria plan** as a plan that offers the employee a choice between cash and certain statutory nontaxable benefits provided under either insured or self-funded plans. Available qualified benefits provided by the Internal Revenue Code include:

- Health benefits (medical, dental, and vision)
- Accidental death and dismemberment benefits
- Long-term disability benefits
- Paid vacation days

CONSOLIDATED OMNIBUS BUDGET RECONCILIATION ACT (COBRA)

COBRA is an acronym used to refer to the health care continuation coverage provisions contained in ERISA and the Internal Revenue Code. COBRA requires that employers offer **qualified beneficiaries**—those individuals who were actually covered under the plan on the day before the qualifying event, discussed below—an opportunity to purchase continued coverage under the plan at a cost of up to 102% of the group rate for periods up to 18 or 36 months. This required period of COBRA coverage is extended from 18 to 29 months for individuals who are entitled to the "disability extension" discussed below. Employers are normally permitted to charge individuals in that group 150% of the applicable group rate from the 19th through the 29th month of their COBRA coverage.

Plans Covered by COBRA

COBRA applies to all employer group health plans that provide medical, dental, vision, or prescription drug coverage, regardless of whether the benefits are paid by the employer or through the employer's insurance carriers. Benefits provided through HMOs and cafeteria plans, including medical expense flexible spending accounts, are subject to COBRA requirements.

Employers with 20 or more employees are covered by COBRA. Part-time employees are counted for COBRA purposes, whether or not they are participants in the plans. Even self-employed individuals may be considered employees, whether or not they are covered by the plan. Independent contractors, agents, and even company directors are also counted for the purposes of COBRA, but only if these individuals are ELIGIBLE to participate in the group health plan.

Qualifying Events

A **qualifying event** under COBRA regulations is any of the following that results in the loss of coverage of an employee, former employee, spouse, or dependent child under a group health plan subject to COBRA:

- The voluntary or involuntary termination of the employee's employment for any reason, including retirement, other than "gross misconduct."
- A reduction of the employee's work hours because of a layoff, change to part-time status, or strike.
- The employee's death.
- The employee's entitlement to Medicare.
- Divorce or legal separation of the employee and spouse.
- Loss of dependent-child status under the plan, due to age, marriage, or completion of education.
- Loss of coverage by a retiree within one year before or after the employer files for bankruptcy (limited to filings made on or after July 1, 1986.)

Qualified Beneficiaries

Qualified beneficiaries are individuals eligible for COBRA rights only if they were actually covered under the plan on the day before the qualifying event. Once a qualifying event occurs, the plan administrator is responsible for identifying the eligible individuals for COBRA rights. Only the participant (an employee or former employee), and the spouse and dependent children of that participant if they are covered by the plan, are potentially eligible for COBRA rights.

Effective January 1, 1997, the COBRA regulations were changed to include as a "qualified beneficiary" a child born to, adopted by or placed for adoption with a covered employee during the COBRA continuation coverage.

Notice Requirements under COBRA

An employer must notify the plan administrator in writing within 30 days after most qualifying events. If the qualifying event is a divorce, legal separation, or loss of dependent child status under the plan, the spouse, dependent child, or the participant on their behalf must notify the plan administrator of that qualifying event within 60 days after it occurs.

A qualified beneficiary who is determined by the Social Security Administration to have been disabled at any time during the first 60 days of COBRA continuation coverage is responsible for notifying the plan administrator within 60 days after the date the individual is determined to have been disabled, and must notify the plan administrator within 30 days after a final determination that he or she is no longer disabled.

The plan administrator has 14 days after receiving a timely notice in which to give written notice to each qualified beneficiary that the beneficiary may elect to continue coverage under COBRA.

At the time that group health plan coverage begins, the plan administrator must provide written notice to each covered employee and the covered spouse of the employee, if applicable, about their COBRA rights in general.

Election of COBRA Coverage

A qualified beneficiary may elect continued COBRA coverage only during the prescribed election period. This election period must begin whichever is later: the date the qualified beneficiary would lose coverage because of the qualifying or when notice of COBRA continuation rights is sent.

Duration of COBRA Coverage

Figure 4-1 is a summary of the date on which COBRA coverage ends, determined by the *earliest occurrence of those events* listed in the chart.

Penalties for COBRA Violations

Failure to comply with COBRA requirements may result in an excise tax penalty of $100 per day limited to $200 per day where the failure to comply involves more than one qualified beneficiary (with respect to the same qualifying event). This penalty accumulates for every day of non-compliance up to six months after the last day for which COBRA coverage would have been required for the qualified beneficiary.

GROUP HEALTH PLAN REFORM (HIPAA)

The **Health Insurance Portability and Accountability Act (HIPAA) of 1996** was signed into law on August 21, 1996 by President Clinton. HIPAA drastically changed federal law in the area of health care by making health care coverage more

"Qualifying Event"	"Qualified Beneficiary"	Length of COBRA Coverage
Termination or reduction in hours	Employee, spouse and dependent children	18 months*
Divorce/legal separation; death; Medicare entitlement of employee	Spouse and dependent children	36 months
Loss of dependent status under the plan	Dependent children	36 months

*An 11-month disability extension (from 18 months to 29 months of coverage) is available ot a "qualified beneficiary" who timely notifies the plan administrator that he or she has received a disability determination from the Social Security Administration.

Figure 4-1
Chart Of Cobra Coverage

widely available. Subsequent amendments added provisions for mental health parity and minimum hospital stays for mothers and newborns.

Summary of HIPAA Provisions

HIPAA applies to group health plans, including any employee welfare benefit plan maintained by employers with two or more participants. However, HIPAA does not require employers to maintain a group health plan or to provide any particular health care benefits. Recent revisions to HIPAA generally do not apply to such benefits as dental, vision, or long-term care.

Preexisting Condition Exclusion Limitations

HIPAA requires a group health plan to limit preexisting condition exclusions to 12 months (18 months for a late enrollee). The plan cannot consider prior medical conditions for more than six months to determine if an individual had a preexisting condition prior to enrollment in the plan.

Pregnancy cannot be excluded from HIPAA coverage as a preexisting condition. Preexisting condition exclusions cannot apply to newborns or adopted children who are covered under a group health plan within 30 days of birth or adoption.

"Portability" under HIPAA does not mean that employees and their dependents have the opportunity to take the same group health plan coverage from employer to employer. However, it does mean that a new employer's group health plan must offset, on a month for month basis, each month of a new employee and his or her dependents' prior "creditable coverage" against the new plan's preexisting condition exclusion.

The term **creditable coverage** includes health coverage arrangements that count toward reducing preexisting condition exclusion under a new employer's group health plan, and includes coverage under an employer-provided group health plan, an individual insurance policy, Medicare, or an HMO. A break of 63 days or more in an individual's health care coverage can result in a loss of creditable coverage. However, days counted toward such a break do not include any period of COBRA continuation coverage under a prior employer's group health plan or the waiting period required under a new employer's group health plan.

Notice Requirements of HIPAA

HIPAA places two notice requirements on group health plans with preexisting condition exclusions. A group health plan cannot impose such a preexisting condition exclusion on either a participant or participant's dependent before the plan notifies the participant in writing of the existence and terms of any preexisting condition exclusion under the plan, and the rights of participants to demonstrate creditable coverage.

A group health plan is required, upon receipt of certification of prior plan coverage, to determine an individual's period of creditable coverage. Before imposing any preexisting condition exclusion, a plan must give the individual a written determination of a preexisting condition exclusion period that applies and the basis for the determination. Additionally, in such a case the plan must provide the individual with a written explanation of any appeal procedures under the plan, and must afford a reasonable opportunity for the individual to submit additional evidence of creditable coverage. If an individual does not have a certification of prior plan coverage as discussed below, the individual has a right to demonstrate creditable coverage through other means, by presenting documents such as an explanation of benefit claims, pay stubs reflecting a payroll deduction for health coverage, a health insurance identification card, or a telephone call from the plan administrator to verify the individual's prior plan coverage.

Certification of Prior Plan Coverage

Any employee who terminates employment is entitled to a certificate of the employee's creditable coverage under the employer's group health plan. This certificate is simply a statement signed by an authorized representative of that group health plan of the employee's period of coverage under the plan. When the employee presents that certificate to a new employer, the new employer is then required to offset the employee's period of prior creditable coverage against the preexisting condition exclusion of the new employer's group health plan. That certificate must include any COBRA continuation coverage period.

The certificate must be provided at the time that an individual ceases to be covered under an employer's group health plan or otherwise becomes covered under

COBRA, at the time the individual ceases to be covered under COBRA, or at the request of an individual made within 24 months after the date coverage ended under the group health plan (including COBRA continuation coverage). Figure 4-2 is a model certificate for HIPAA. Both the group health plan and, if an insurance company is involved, that insurer, have an obligation to furnish a certificate.

Nondiscrimination Requirements under HIPAA

A group health plan cannot discriminate against employees or their dependents on the basis of certain health status factors, including:

- Medical condition
- Medical history
- Genetic information
- Claims history
- Disability

In return for adherence to a wellness program, a group health plan generally may establish discounts or rebates under HIPAA.

Special Enrollment Periods of HIPAA

HIPAA's special enrollment periods are quite controversial because they don't contain a specific limitation on a group health plan's waiting period, and do not preclude a group health plan from limiting enrollment opportunities for later enrollees—for example, to the annual open enrollment periods.

Under two circumstances, employees and their dependents may enroll in a group health plan at times other than immediately after the plan's waiting period or during the plan's open enrollment. HIPAA has special provisions to permit employees or dependents who lose other coverage to enroll in the plan, including:

- The employee or dependent had other coverage when the plan overage was previously offered, and
- The employee stated that the other overage was the reason for declining enrollment, and
- The other coverage was either COBRA continuation coverage that was concluded or overage that was terminated as a result of loss of eligibility (such as divorce, death, or termination of employment), or employer contributions toward such coverage were eliminated.

The employee must request such special enrollment no later than 30 days after the date of exhaustion or termination of the other coverage.

The second circumstance that permits a special enrollment period applies to

CERTIFICATE OF GROUP HEALTH PLAN COVERAGE

* IMPORTANT—This certificate provides evidence of your prior health coverage. You may need to furnish this certificate if you become eligible under a group health plan that excludes coverage for certain medical conditions that you have before you enroll. This certificate may need to be provided if medical advice, diagnosis, care, or treatment was recommended or received for the condition within the 6-month period prior to your enrollment in the new plan. If you become covered under another group health plan, check with the plan administrator to see if you need to provide this certificate. You may also need this certificate to buy, for yourself or you family, an insurance policy that does not exclude coverage for medical conditions that are present before you enroll.

1. Date of this certificate: _____

2. Name of group health plan: _____

3. Name of participant: _____

4. Identification number of participant: _____

5. Name of any dependents to whom this certificate applies: _____

6. Name, address, and telephone number of plan administrator or issuer responsible for providing this certificate:

   _____

   _____

   _____

7. For further information, call: _____

8. If the individual(s) identified in line 3 and line 5 has at least 18 months of creditable coverage (disregarding periods of coverage before a 63-day break), check here _____ and skip lines 9 to 10.

9. Date waiting period or affiliation period (if any) began: _____

10. Date coverage began: _____

11. Date coverage ended: _____ (or check if coverage is continuing as of the date of this certificate: _____).

Note: separate certificates will be furnished if information is not identical for the participant and each beneficiary.

Figure 4-2
Model Certificate

dependents. If an employee is enrolled in a group health plan, or was eligible to enroll in the plan but failed to enroll during a previous enrollment period, and that employee marries, or has a child, or adopts a child, several special enrollment options apply. In the event an employee marries, his or her new spouse may enroll in the plan, and so may the employee if he or she has not previously enrolled. Coverage in this situation is not later than the first day of the first month beginning after the date the completed request for enrollment is received. In the case the employee has a child or adopts a child, the child and the spouse may enroll in the plan if they were otherwise eligible for coverage but not already so enrolled, and so may the employee if he or she has not previously enrolled. In the case of a dependent's birth, coverage is effective as of the date of such birth. In the case of adoption, coverage begins on the date of adoption.

This dependent special enrollment period must not be less than 30 days, beginning on either the date that dependent coverage is made available or the date of the marriage, birth, or adoption, whichever is later.

HIPAA provides that an employee must be notified of these special enrollment rights on or before the time that the employee is offered the opportunity to enroll in the plan.

Disclosure to Participants

HIPAA amended ERISA to require a summary plan description for group health plans to participants and beneficiaries.

Parity in Mental Health Benefits

A group health plan of an employer with more than 50 employees that chooses to offer mental health coverage must set the same dollar caps for yearly and lifetime benefits for "mental health benefits" (which does not include benefits for treatment of either substance or chemical dependency) as allowed for medical or surgical benefits. This parity requirement ends for services furnished on or after September 30, 2001.

Newborns' and Mothers' Health Protection

A group health plan generally cannot restrict benefits for any hospital length of stay in connection with childbirth for the mother or newborn child, following a normal delivery, to less than 48 hours, and following a Caesarean section, to less than 96 hours.

Enforcement Provisions

HIPAA enforcement penalties are similar to COBRA's excise tax provisions. The amount of the tax is generally $100 per day per individual during which a failure occurs, until the time that the failure is corrected.

EXECUTIVE COMPENSATION

Employers typically negotiate executive compensation arrangements for key executives or management personnel. The qualified plan rules discussed above do not apply to executive compensation.

STOCK OPTIONS

Stock options are often granted to directors, employees, and other key personnel who contribute to the employer's success. Normally two types of options are offered: **incentive stock options (ISOs)** that are granted only to employees and that meet requirements of Section 422 of the Internal Revenue Code, and **nonqualified stock options (NSOs)**. If the requirements of Section 422 are met, and the optionee remains in the employment of the company until the time of the exercise of the stock options, the optionee generally will not have recognized income until the time of the sale of the option shares. If the optionee does not dispose of the option shares until the end of a statutory holding period, all income recognized in connection with the ISO will be considered a capital gain by the IRS. Normally, the holder of an NSO recognizes income at the time of the exercise of the option, and that income is ordinary income.

NONQUALIFIED DEFERRED COMPENSATION

Employers have frequently adopted **nonqualified deferred compensation plans** because of stringent limits on tax-qualified plan benefits that make it difficult to provide adequate benefits. Employees considering deferred compensation should consider the fact that an employee will be taxed on compensation, either when the compensation is received or **constructively received**, when the compensation is subject to the employee's control.

A certain amount of flexibility is given to employees to determine whether compensation is deferred, the manner in which it is invested while it is deferred, and when the compensation is distributed. The IRS requires that deferral and distribution elections must be made before the beginning of the period during which the compensation is earned (the calendar year), and an employee should not have any investment control over the deferred compensation.

GROUP TERM LIFE INSURANCE

The first $50,000 cost of term life insurance for the benefit of employees that the employer purchases is not included in the employee's gross income. Any group term life insurance policy must cover at least ten full-time employees, unless the employer has less than ten full-time employees; in that case all employees are covered.

SEVERANCE PAY BENEFITS

Severance pay is payment intended to provide financial security for employees whose jobs have been eliminated. Severance pay plans usually provide payments in a single lump sump or in installments to terminated employees.

Severance pay plans are considered to be welfare benefit plans, rather than pension plans, if the following three requirements are satisfied:

- The severance payments are not made for retirement reasons and do not hinge, either directly or indirectly, on the employee's retirement.
- The maximum benefit must not exceed the amount of two years of the employee's annual compensation rate prior to termination.
- The benefits must be paid within 24 months after the employee's separation from service.

Severance pay issues arise in the period before a plant closing or reduction in force. An employer may normally modify, amend, or terminate severance pay plans without violating ERISA requirements, if the plan provides for that right. However, employers should be cautious when addressing severance pay in either of the above two circumstances.

Caution must also be exercised to comply with rules under the Older Workers Benefit Protection Act (OWBPA), discussed in Chapter 9, in connection with either designing or carrying out severance pay plans.

TERMS

401(k) plan
cafeteria plan
COBRA
creditable coverage
defined benefit pension plan
employee benefit plans
employee welfare benefit plan
ERISA
fiduciary duty

Health Insurance Portability and Accountability Act (HIPAA) of 1996
incentive stock options (ISOs)
managed care program
money purchase plan
nonqualified deferred compensation plan
nonqualified stock options (NSOs)
profit sharing plan
qualified
qualified beneficiaries
qualified retirement plan
qualifying event
severance pay
vesting

REVIEW QUESTIONS

1. What is the difference between a defined contribution plan and a defined benefit plan?

2. Identify the two types of defined contribution plans.

3. Mary Ann worked for a law firm as a receptionist for slightly less than a year. When she resigned from the position, she was 20 years old. Would the firm have a duty to cover Mary Ann under its pension plan?

4. Wilkinson Office Products has ten employees. Is Wilkinson covered by COBRA?

5. Maritime Marina advises a new employee that preexisting conditions for the past two years will not be covered under its health coverage plan. Is that action permissible under HIPAA?

6. St. Luke's Hospital advised Melinda Morrison that she would be permitted to remain in the hospital for only 24 hours following the birth of her child. Does HIPAA allow that time restriction?

7. David Johnston questioned his employer's including $50,000 life insurance that it purchased on his behalf in his gross income. Will David be successful in his inquiry?

8. Identify five types of welfare plan benefits.

9. Name two types of stock options.

10. Jamie Carter is under the impression that HIPAA permits her to carry the same coverage from one employer to the other. Is her impression correct?

PROJECTS

1. Search the Internet listing of legal directories to determine the types and amounts of benefits provided to new associates by the law firms in your area.

2. Contact your local or state paralegal association to determine if recent salary surveys include information relating to benefits offered to paralegals in your area. Compare those benefits with those provided to new associates. Prepare a chart of the possible areas where paralegal benefits could be increased.

CHAPTER 5

Evaluating the Employee's Job Performance

OVERVIEW

There are significant business and legal reasons for employers to regularly evaluate an employee's job performance, from the "probationary" period of the job to the termination, whether voluntary or involuntary. Performance evaluations weigh heavily in human resource decisions, including compensation, promotion, transfer, and termination. In the event of employment litigation, courts often look first to performance appraisals during the period prior to termination.

The evaluation factor includes more than a review of job performance areas such as production or quality. Evaluation includes such diverse areas as adherence to company policies and the necessity for any disciplinary actions. One important measuring tool of an employee's performance is the employee's job description. The job description should have been utilized at the time of the interview, and the employee should consistently be reviewed with an eye to the categories contained in the job description. Performance appraisals keep employees regularly apprised of their standing with the employer and prevent surprises in the future. Overall, employee evaluations have a positive effect on the employment relationship. However, these appraisals have the potential for discriminatory effect. Discrimination may occur in diverse ways, from the way the appraisal is conducted to the way that the employer utilizes the evaluation. If the evaluations are well documented, they can either prevent discrimination claims or support a defense to subsequent discriminatory claims.

Often supervisors rate an employee as "satisfactory" or "good," without any thought as to whether the terms accurately reflect an employee's job performance. Many supervisors fear offending an employee by accurately evaluating his or her performance. Employees' expectations of an overall "satisfactory" evaluation tend to shade the evaluation process. Using the same rating for all employees renders the performance review virtually meaningless and unreliable, and opens up the employer for a lawsuit.

THE IMPORTANCE OF JOB DESCRIPTIONS IN EMPLOYEE EVALUATIONS

Job descriptions have traditionally been an important tool for defining jobs and measuring performance in those jobs. General categories within a job description usually include skills, education, licensing requirements, and the anticipated duties of the position. The job description should include general language, but must also be specific enough that the employee understands what the position entails. A caveat for all job descriptions might include the following language, "and other duties as assigned by the employer."

The Americans with Disabilities Act (ADA) of 1990 gives great importance to job descriptions. The ADA defines a qualified individual with a disability as "an individual with a disability who, with or without reasonable accommodation, can perform the *essential functions* of the employment position for which the individual holds or desires." (Emphasis added.) The ADA contains little guidance as to which job functions are considered "essential." However, EEOC regulations and guidelines distinguish between "fundamental job duties" and "marginal" functions of the position. An employer cannot disqualify an individual from a job if the disabled employee is unable to perform a "marginal" function. However, a disabled individual must be able to perform an "essential function" with or without reasonable accommodation. Otherwise, the individual is subject to being disqualified from the position.

A critical issue in establishing "essential" job functions is whether the employer actually requires employees in the position to perform those claimed "essential functions." The EEOC suggests that an employer should question "whether removing the function would fundamentally alter the position." In answering that question, the EEOC regulations require that the employer consider the following:

1. Whether the reason that the position exists is to perform the function.
2. The number of other employees available to perform that function or among whom the function could be distributed.
3. The degree of expertise or skill necessary to perform the function.

EEOC regulations list the following factors as relevant evidence for determining whether or not a job function is "essential."

- The employer's judgment as to what is essential for the position.
- The content of a written job description for the position.

- The work performance of former employees in the job and of current employees in similar jobs.
- The amount of time spent performing the function.
- The terms of a collective bargaining agreement.
- Any consequences of failing to require the employee to perform that function.

There is no requirement that an employer maintain job descriptions. However, written job descriptions carry more weight than an employer's unwritten, oral judgment of the essential elements of a job description.

THE ROLE OF EMPLOYEE HANDBOOKS IN EVALUATING EMPLOYEES

Evaluations measure more than the quantity or quality of an employee's production in the job. Such factors as absenteeism, adherence to dress codes, and compliance with safety policies are all components of satisfactory job performance.

A properly drafted employee handbook should disseminate information about the company and its policies, and penalties for violation of those policies. Whether or not an employer needs or wants an employee handbook is a personal decision. Once a decision is made to implement an employee handbook, the following guidelines apply to most employers:

1. **Avoid making contractual obligations within the handbook.**
   An attorney should review the handbook prior to its distribution to employees for problematic language that could create enforceable contract rights that the employer may not intend to create.
2. **Use clear and concise language.**
   The provisions of the handbook should avoid interpretations that the employer did not intend. Certain provisions in the handbook may not apply to all employees, and that must be clarified. For example, part-time employees might not be eligible for vacation or other benefits. Provisions relating to vacation and other benefits should clearly denote that part-time employees are not included.
3. **Allow for flexibility and modification.**
   Every employment contingency cannot be anticipated and covered in the employee handbook. The handbook must contain a statement that any or all provisions may be modified at the employer's discretion, in accordance with applicable law.
4. **Contain the following specific provisions:**
   a. Equal Employment Opportunity policy.
   b. No harassment policy.

This policy should define harassment and unacceptable conduct and establish procedures for reporting, investigating and resolving such claims.

c. **Employment at will policy (if applicable).**

This policy should be at the front of the handbook, and specifically state that the employment relationship is terminable at the will of either the employer or the employee at any time.

d. **Family and Medical Leave Act policy (if applicable).**

e. **Telephone and electronic communications systems policy.**

Employees should be notified that all such communications could be monitored in accordance with applicable laws. The policy should negate any privacy expectations regarding such communications. (See Chapter 15 for additional information to be included in this policy.)

f. **Handbook acknowledgment form.**

The employee should sign and return this form to the employer, acknowledging receipt of the handbook and that the employee has read and understood the handbook. A contract disclaimer and employment at will language are suggested for incorporation into the form. Appendix A is a sample handbook acknowledgment form.

Any reference to "permanent employment" or "permanent employee" should be avoided in the handbook, and the term "regular full-time employment" is suggested in lieu of those phrases. A statement that the "regular full-time employment" is for no definite period of time is also advisable. That language makes it more difficult for a court to conclude that an employment contract for a specific period of time exists, or that an employee has been hired on a permanent basis.

THE IMPORTANCE OF A PROBATIONARY PERIOD FOR EMPLOYEE EVALUATION PURPOSES

Many employers utilize probationary periods so they can evaluate an employee's work performance, and presumably terminate the employee without the need to follow lengthy, progressive disciplinary procedures. Careful wording is required for a probationary policy. At the end of the probationary period, an employee may claim that he or she cannot be terminated except for "just cause." The idea of a probationary period is inconsistent with the idea of an at-will employee.

Employers might consider changing the title of "probationary period" to "introductory period" or other language that does not implicitly promise additional rights upon completion of the prescribed period. It is also advisable to include a statement in the probationary policy that provides that, after the completion of probation, the employee's relationship with the employer is still one of employment-at-will.

DISCIPLINE POLICIES AND PERFORMANCE EVALUATIONS

Employee discipline is a sensitive component of the employment relationship. Regulation of employment decisions includes adoption and application of discipline policies. All discipline decisions must be nondiscriminatorily applied.

Discipline policies should include guidelines for administering discipline. Those guidelines must be clear to the employees and management to avoid attack by disgruntled employees in the form of complaints or even lawsuits.

It is important that disciplinary policies contain language that the policies are merely guidelines, and are not intended to cover every potential situation involving disciplinary action. The policies should also state that the guidelines are not meant to, and do not, change the employment at will relationship between the employee and employer.

Every disciplinary action must be factually documented. This process will often serve as a defense for the employer in the event of subsequent litigation for improper termination of the employee. The documentation should also include the corrective action taken by the employee following the disciplinary action. For example, if the employee has been disciplined for overcounting production, the documentation would consist of the daily production sheets prior to the discipline and immediately following the discipline.

Employee handbooks normally specify disciplinary procedures that must be followed before an employee is dismissed. Generally, disciplinary procedures are progressive in nature, for example:

1. **Oral Warnings**
   - Discuss the problem with the employee in private.
   - Reserve the oral warning for minor offenses. The supervisor should notify the employee that this discussion is in fact a warning and that the employee is being given the opportunity to correct the problem. The employee should be warned that if the behavior is not corrected within a specified time period, the employee will be subject to more severe disciplinary measures.
   - A notation of the oral warning that was given should be made both for the supervisor's records and placed in the employee's file. Some employers request that the employee sign the disciplinary action form to acknowledge

the warning. When an employee argues in an exit interview that he or she had no knowledge of any wrongdoing on their part, the signed discipline form might deter a subsequent legal action by the employee. Figure 5–1 is an example of a discipline report. If the employee refuses to sign the report, the supervisor or manager who was present during the disciplinary meeting should document the refusal.

2. **Written Warnings**

    -   This type of notice should be issued by the supervisor in a situation where an employee continues to disregard an oral warning, or in a case where the infraction is severe enough to warrant a written record immediately.

    -   The supervisor should set out in the written warning the nature of the infraction, dates of infractions if more than one, and sign the notice. He or she should discuss this warning with the employee and make certain that the employee understands the reasons for the disciplinary action.

    -   A copy of the warning notice should be given to the employee at the time of the discussion, and the employee should be asked to sign and date both the original and copy of the notice to acknowledge its receipt. The original of the notice should be placed in the employee's personnel file (see Figure 5-1).

3. **Suspensions**

    -   This form of discipline is normally reserved for the more severe infractions of rules, or for excessive violations for which the employee has already received a written warning and has not improved his or her performance or behavior during the allotted time for improvement. This is the most severe form of discipline short of termination. Such discipline should only be meted out after a thorough examination of the facts by the supervisor and his or her supervisors.

    -   The supervisor should provide a written summary of all facts leading up to the reason for the disciplinary suspension, the beginning date of the suspension, and the duration of the suspension. The supervisor should give the employee an opportunity to respond before implementing the suspension. The original copy of the disciplinary suspension notice should be placed in the employee's personnel file and a copy should be given to the employee.

    -   When the employee returns from a disciplinary suspension, the supervisor should make certain that the employee returns to his or her job with as little loss of self respect as possible.

4. **Meeting with Personnel Manager and Employee**

    If the undesirable behavior continues following the employee's suspension,

Employee's Name: _____ Social Security No. _____

Date of Hire: _____ Department: _____ Supervisor: _____

Date of DAR: _____ Date of Incident (Basis for DAR): _____

Summary of Incident: _____

_____

_____

_____

_____

_____

_____

Name(s) of Witness(es) to Incident: _____

_____

List any Prior Incidents for Same Infraction: _____

_____

Prior Verbal Warning: _____ Yes _____ No; Date of Verbal Warning: _____

Prior Written Warning: _____ Yes _____ No; Date of Prior Written Warning: _____

Prior Probation Period: _____ Yes _____ No; Beginning and Ending Dates of Probation:

_____

Employee's Statement Regarding Incident:

_____

_____

_____

_____

_____

_____

Figure 5-1
Disciplinary Action Report

Supervisor's Comments Regarding Conference with Employee: _____

_____

_____

_____

_____

_____

_____

_____   _____   _____

Employee   Supervisor   Date

Figure 5-1 (*continued*)

the supervisor should arrange for a meeting between the personnel manager and the employee. At that meeting, the employee should be advised in writing of each action that must be corrected. It is important that the employee understand that the failure to comply with these desired actions could result in termination.

TYPES OF EMPLOYMENT EVALUATIONS

Employers often utilize one of the three major types of evaluation: management by objective (MBO), the checklist system, and the summated scale. **Management by objective** measures an employee's performance on the basis of objectives set by the manger and employee to be met within a specified time period. The **checklist system** evaluates each employee through the use of a list of behaviors found to be related to job performance. The **summated scale** requires supervisors to indicate how often the employee satisfies each of several behavior-based statements, including desirable and undesirable performance.

GUIDELINES FOR EFFECTIVE PERFORMANCE EVALUATIONS

Supervisors and human resource personnel who are responsible for performance evaluations should be trained to ensure that evaluations are honest and accurate and evaluate both the strengths and weaknesses of the employee. Job-related evaluation forms are preferable, with the rating choices on the form specific to the area of performance being evaluated. Incorporating some constructive criticism in each evaluation has an advantage in the event of subsequent employment litigation. An employer must be able to document that all employees were given constructive criticism in evaluations in the event of a lawsuit in which a disgruntled employee claims that all employees were not held to the same standard of performance.

A review of the performance evaluation by another manager or supervisor who has no direct connection with the employee being evaluated adds another layer of honesty and lack of bias to the process.

Sitting through a performance evaluation is often uncomfortable for both the supervisor conducting the evaluation and the employee. An effort should be made to reduce the tension of the meeting, such as the supervisor's sitting on a sofa or comfortable chair, rather than sitting across the desk from the employee. The expression of positive areas in the beginning of the review is preferable. Once the employee has been verbally advised of the contents of the evaluation, an opportunity must be afforded the employee to respond, comment, or even object to the evaluation.

An employee should sign an acknowledgment on the evaluation form that he or she has read the evaluation. This acknowledgment refutes any subsequent claim by the employee that he or she was unaware of the contents of the evaluation. The evaluation process is more effective when an employee is permitted to write on the actual evaluation form that he or she is in disagreement with a portion of or all of the evaluation.

Setting goals for the employee to accomplish prior to the next performance review and asking the employee to sign an acceptance of those goals strengthens the commitment between the two parties to the performance review.

LEGAL IMPLICATIONS OF PERFORMANCE APPRAISAL SYSTEMS

Performance appraisals by their nature are based on subjectivity, and as a result are often subject to abuse and criticism. Legal implications of performance appraisals arise when the information in the appraisal is used as the basis for employment-related decisions.

Disparate Impact

The legal implications of performance appraisals arise when information in the appraisals is used as the basis for any employment-related decision. The Uniform Guidelines on Employee Selection procedures apply to the design and use of performance appraisals. A performance appraisal system that has a **disparate impact—**

discrimination based on race, color, religion, sex, national origin, age, or disability that result from a practice that does not seem to be discriminatory, and was not intended to be so, on a protected class—is subject to close scrutiny by the courts.

As discussed at length in Chapter 7, several methods may be employed to determine disparate impact, the most common of which is the "four-fifths rule." In summary, that rule states a presumption of discrimination where the selection rate for any employment decision of the protected group is less than 80% of the selection rate of the nonminority group.

Any employee who disputes a performance appraisal may use the disparate treatment analysis set out in *McDonnell Douglas Corp. v. Green*, 411 U.S. 792 (1973).

The employee most show:

1. that he or she is a member of a protected class;
2. that he or she suffered an adverse employment decision as a result of a performance evaluation;
3. that he or she was qualified to perform the duties of the position; and
4. that he or she was replaced by someone with similar qualifications who is not a member of a protected class.

As is true with other areas of disparate impact, the employer may defend its system of performance appraisal if the performance appraisal was sufficiently job-related.

Disparate Treatment

A performance appraisal may result in **disparate treatment**—intentional discrimination based on a person's race, color, religion, sex, national origin, age, or disability. In the *Hopkins v. Price Waterhouse* case discussed in Chapter 13, a female accounting executive did not receive a promotion to partner based on her performance evaluation. During that evaluation, Ms. Hopkins had been told that she needed to walk, talk, and dress more like a woman, take a charm course, and act less "macho." The Supreme Court ruled in favor of the plaintiff, finding that as long as the sexual stereotype and discriminatory appraisal were "motivating factors" in the denial of the promotion, the motive was illegitimate.

PROMOTIONS

Promotion from within the company is not illegal or unethical. It can be discriminatory, depending on both the process used for the selection of the employee to be promoted and the makeup of the workforce. For example, if the vice president of an insurance company seeks to fill an area manager position by soliciting interest in the position from only a few upper-level management employees, interviews those individuals, extends an offer, and THEN posts a notice of the promotion, discrimination is a possible consequence. That is particularly true if women and minorities are not well-represented in the firm. Such a promotion process might have a disparate impact, even if the purpose of the vice president was to locate and promote the most qualified candidate for the position of area manager.

A less suspect method of selecting employees for a promotion requires that the opening be posted, and all employees are given the opportunity to compete for the position.

TERMS

checklist system
disparate impact
disparate treatment
management by objective
summated scale

REVIEW QUESTIONS

1. An office supply company has a policy that performance appraisals play an important role in employee promotions. Maria Ramirez, a 12-year employee who has consistently received outstanding performance appraisals, has not been promoted, although her name has been submitted for three previous promotions. Ramirez files suit, claiming racial discrimination. Explain the company's potential defenses. Will Ramirez be successful in her lawsuit?

2. Madison Brewing Company relies on its foremen to recommend line employees for promotion. Mel Carter, a white foreman in his 30s, has consistently recommended young white males for promotion. Raul Espinoza, a Hispanic male in his 50s, questions why he has not been promoted during his 15 years with the company. Carter explains that he hasn't really had a chance to get to know him as he has some of the men he recommended for promotion because Espinoza hasn't been bowling with them or going to happy hour on Fridays. Carter admits that he has no guidelines by which he makes promotion decisions; his decisions are purely subjective. Assuming that Espinoza files suit, claiming discrimination, what defenses, if any, may be claimed by Carter and Madison Brewing?

3. Explain the three types of employment evaluations.

4. Discuss the disparate impact of performance evaluations.

5. Explain the disparate treatment potential in performance evaluations.

6. William Durrett is placed on a suspension for excessive absenteeism following one oral warning. Did Mr. Durrett's supervisor follow proper procedures in this case? Why or why not?

7. Assume that Mr. Durrett, in review question 6, had received the proper warnings, and had even signed a written discipline report. Would your answer be the same as in question 6?

8. Does the ADA provide that a disabled employee must be capable of performing essential job duties, marginal job duties, or both?

9. Can you defend an employer's practice of promoting from within the company? Under what situation could you not defend that practice?

10. List the four criteria for proving a disparate impact case involving performance appraisals.

PROJECTS

1. Prepare the outline for an employee handbook that might be used by a law firm.

2. Draft a sexual harassment policy for the employee handbook.

CHAPTER 6

Terminating the Employment Relationship

OVERVIEW

All employment relationships must at some time come to an end, either voluntarily or involuntarily. Under the employment at will doctrine discussed in Chapter 1, an employment relationship for no specific duration may be terminated at any time, for any reason or for no reason at all, at the will of either the employer or the employee. However, an involuntary termination may result in "wrongful discharge," as discussed below.

As discussed extensively in Chapter 1, employment at will is subject to exceptions, including the following:

1. Express written agreement;
2. Oral agreement;
3. Implied contract based on handbooks or policy manuals;
4. Implied contract based on other documents, words, actions, or some combination of the three;
5. Promissory estoppel;
6. Public policy exceptions; and
7. Breach of an implied covenant of good faith and fair dealing.

CONTRACT CLAIMS

Express Contracts of Employment

Whether express or implied, written or oral, an employment agreement for a definite term may supersede the presumption of employment at will. An employee may claim a "wrongful discharge" if he or she allegedly was terminated in breach of either an express or implied employment contract.

Express Written Contracts

The employment at will doctrine does not apply where the parties have entered into a written contract that provides for a definite term of employment. Federal and state courts have held that the mere fact that a contract is in writing does not, however, automatically alter the employment at will doctrine. The issue is generally whether the contract limits the employer's right to terminate an employee at will.

Express Oral Contracts

In numerous states, express contracts (specific promises) to employees may be enforceable even if they are not formal or in writing. Courts have not limited those entitled to bring a lawsuit for breach of contract on the basis of informal promises made orally by a manager or some other individual within the company who was in a position of authority to high-level executives or those covered by union contracts. Courts have permitted individual, lower-level employees to sue for breach of contract on the basis of informal promises.

Implied Contracts of Employment

If the parties have no express oral or written agreement regarding the duration of employment, courts may infer an **implied contract**—a contract that is not expressed, but is created by other words or the conduct of the parties from the circumstances of the relationship.

The courts rely on traditional contract principles in determining whether an implied contract exists. Therefore, the plaintiff must prove some form of offer, acceptance, consideration, and meeting of the minds in order to prove the existence of an implied contract.

In recent years, courts have found implied contracts from references during pre-employment interviews about a "permanent" position, from conversations quoting yearly or other periodic salaries.

Example   If an employee has been told that the job pays $30,000 a year, but he or she is terminated after six months, then the employee would be able to prove a claim for the balance due of $15,000, on the theory that there was an implied contract of one year.

Evidence that courts and juries have considered to determine the existence of an implied contract include:

- Statements made during the preemployment interview about "permanent" employees, or the quoting of periodic salaries (for example, annual salaries) in a case where the employee has been terminated in less than the time quoted in the salary, as discussed above
- Language in employee handbooks that states employees will be discharged only for particular offenses
- Language in progressive disciplinary policies that states employees will be given a chance to improve their performance, but employees were not given such a chance
- An employee's work history that reflects regular good performance evaluations, merit raises, praise, and promotions
- The employer's practice of discharging employees only for good cause.

Employment Policy Manuals or Handbooks

Employment policy manuals or handbooks may be a form of an implied contract. Employers use these tools to communicate company policies to employees. Although a convenient method for a centralized source of policies, policy manuals may present the problem of unwittingly creating implied contracts of employment that negate the employment at will status.

Recent court rulings have held that the regulations and rules contained in the employee handbook may form a contract between the employer and the employee. Many courts have held that statements in policy manuals that employees will be terminated only for "good cause," or that the employee is a "permanent" employee upon successful completion of a probationary period, will create binding agreements between the employer and employee. Such statements have resulted in liability in lawsuits following termination of an employee.

The general rule, however, in some states, such as Texas, appears to be that handbooks or employee manuals are no more than a general statement of policy, and do not limit the employer's rights under the traditional employment at will doctrine.

The specific language of the employee handbooks or manuals, and perhaps the manner in which it is disseminated, may support a court finding that the handbook or manual constitutes an implied contract, limiting the employer's termination rights. *Aiello v. United Air Lines, Inc.*, 818 F.2d 1196 (5th Cir.), *reh'g denied*, 826 F.2d 12 (5th Cir. 1987) is the leading case that holds contractual rights may be implied from a handbook, where the employee proves that company supervisor personnel agreed to or recognized a modification of the employment at will relationship by acknowledging that employees would be discharged for cause only. *Aiello* is different from other employee handbook cases because of its unique facts. The handbook contained an express disclaimer of any contractual rights or obligation, and explicitly stated that all employment was at will. However, the handbook also expressly provided that no employee would be discharged without good cause. Additionally, the employer *stipulated* that the company's policies prohibited discharge without good cause. The Fifth Circuit found that the handbook's limitations on the employer's ability to discharge an employee without good cause constituted an enforceable contract under Texas law.

In a subsequent case, *Zimmerman v. H. E. Butt Grocery Co.*, 932 F.2d 469, 471 (5th Cir.), *cert. denied*, 502 U.S. 984 (1991), the Fifth Circuit listed the following as a basis for finding an enforceable contract in *Aiello*:

a. The handbook provided a detailed disciplinary procedure and obligated the employer to discharge employees only for just cause.
b. The employer in fact followed the procedure and notified the employees that they were entitled to the procedure; and
c. The employer treated the handbook as a contract.

Implied Contracts Based on Other Written Sources

Employees have sought to find an implied contract based on employment applications, evaluation documents, and similar documents. Case law in this area does not tend to give support to those claims of implied contract. Each state's law must be reviewed to determine that state's position in this area.

IMPROPER TERMINATION OF EMPLOYMENT CONTRACT

Overview

Either party to an employment contract may improperly terminate the contract. The type of improper termination could range from terminating the contract before the expiration period to terminating an employee for something other than the listed reasons for termination. As discussed later in this chapter, the employer may also constructively terminate the contract or discharge the employee in violation of public policy. The party that improperly terminates the employment contract may be liable to the other party for damages.

Breach of Employment Contract

Breach of contract cases are decided on a case-by-case basis because the parties' rights are created by the specific contract in question.

Employer Breach

The most common way in which an employer breaches an employment contract is by wrongfully terminating an employee. A **wrongful discharge** is the court's finding that the employer was restricted in its right to terminate employees at will. There are three broad categories of wrongful discharge: discharge in violation of public policy; breach of contract; and breach of implied covenant of good faith and fair dealing.

Constructive discharge (if the employer makes working conditions so intolerable that a reasonable person in the employee's position would have felt compelled to resign) is another common form of employer breach of an employment contract that is discussed subsequently in this chapter.

Employee Breach

The general rule in contract law is that an employee breaches an employment contract if he or she fails to perform the services promised in the contract.

REMEDIES/DAMAGES IN CONTRACT CLAIMS

Overview

In a wrongful discharge action based on a breach of contract, an employee is owed what he or she would have received from the contract, minus what he or she received, or should have received, from employment after the wrongful termination. Compensatory damages are intended to return the employee to the same place that he or she would have been if the breach had not occurred. Lost wages are the most common type of remedy awarded in a breach of employment contract.

Reinstatement

The remedy of reinstatement is not available for breach of employment contract claims. Employment contracts are contracts for personal service. Therefore, an employee or employer cannot be forced to perform the contract. (*See* 11 Williston, *A Treatise on the Law of Contracts* (3d ed.) § 1423)

Past Lost Wages (Back Pay)

Past lost wages or **back pay** is the present value of wages and benefits the employee would have earned for the remainder of the employment term, less any wages and benefits the employee earned or could have earned in the interim, exercising reasonable diligence. In addition, back pay includes any unpaid wages due for services performed prior to the termination of the employment agreement.

Future Lost Wages (Front Pay)

Front pay is the amount of money that the employee would have earned from the date of trial to the conclusion of the employment contract. The calculation of front pay is simple if the contract was for a fixed-term. However, the calculation is more difficult if the contract is not for a specific period of time.

Factors that courts generally consider for determining future damages are the plaintiff's age, probable life expectancy, education, experience, past earning capacity, and probable span of employability.

Loss of Earning Capacity/Mental Anguish

Many states do not permit recovery for loss of earning capacity or mental anguish on a claim of breach of employment contract. Each contract must be reviewed on the basis of the controlling state's laws.

Punitive/Exemplary Damages

Punitive/exemplary damages—damages awarded in addition to actual damages when the defendant acted with recklessness, malice, or deceit and intended to punish and thereby deter blameworthy conduct—generally are not available for breach of an employment contract. In the event the employer acted with malice or fraud, a court may award punitive damages. In that case, the employer's action must be both outrageous and extreme.

If the employer establishes that the employee has failed to mitigate his or her damages, the employer has no additional burden to prove the amount of money that the employee would have earned.

Duty to Mitigate Damages

Employees have a duty to make reasonable efforts to find other employment and reduce their damages in the event of wrongful termination. In *Pennzoil Producing Co. v. Offshore Express, Inc.*, 943 F.2d 1465, 1476 (5th Cir. 1991), the Fifth Circuit wrote that a plaintiff with a valid claim may not recover for post-breach damages that he reasonably could have prevented.

Courts have often ruled that earnings from all other sources, including self-employment, unemployment compensation, and severance pay, will be considered on mitigation issues.

QUASI-CONTRACT-PROMISSORY ESTOPPEL

There are some instances where essential elements of a contract are lacking. In those cases, an employee may be able to argue that a discharge or other adverse employment decision is in violation of a promise, although not necessarily in breach of a contract. In those cases, the doctrine of **promissory estoppel**, defined by *Oran's Dictionary of the Law* as "The principle that when Person A makes a promise and expects Person B to do something in **reliance** upon that promise, then Person B does act in reliance upon that promise, the law will usually help Person B enforce the promise because Person B has *relied* upon the promise to his or her *detriment*. Person A is "stopped" from breaking the promise even when there is no **consideration** to make the promise binding as part of a contract, may prevent the employer from denying an alleged promise."

Elements of Promissory Estoppel Claim

In an employment situation where essential elements of a contract are missing, an employee may be able to argue that a discharge or some other adverse employment decision is in violation of a promise, even if not necessarily in breach of a contract. Under such circumstances, the doctrine of promissory estoppel may prevent the employer from denying an alleged promise.

Elements of a promissory estoppel claim include:

1. the employer made a promise;
2. the employee relied on that promise to his or her detriment; and
3. the employee's reliance was reasonably foreseeable by the employer.

Restatement (Second) of Contracts § 90 (1981).

Promissory estoppel is an exception to the general rule that, in order to be enforceable, a promise must be bargained for with consideration on both sides. Promissory estoppel offers a substitute for such contractual deficiencies as consideration.

Promissory estoppel appears most often in the context of promises to employ and promises not to discharge. An example of a promissory estoppel situation based on a promise to employ is the employee who leaves a job and relocates his or her family to a new job (and possibly a new city) based on a promise of future employment.

Obviously, the employee relied on that promise to his or her detriment, and the employee's reliance was reasonably foreseeable by the employer.

The other major case of promissory estoppel involves the promise not to discharge. An employee may claim that he or she relied upon this promise not to discharge, without just cause, during a particular period of time.

Remedies/Damages Available

The doctrine of promissory estoppel is based on equity. Therefore, the damages available are limited by equity principles. Damages based on promissory estoppel are to be awarded to prevent injustice. Equitable relief is generally a question for the court.

DISCHARGE IN VIOLATION OF COMMON LAW PUBLIC POLICY

Courts have generally held employers liable for employee discharges that violate "public policy." However, there is considerable disagreement over what constitutes public policy, and what constitutes a violation of public policy. Discriminatory discharges on the basis of race, sex, disability, or age are included in this discharge in violation of public policy category. Another major category of public policy discharge is the "retaliatory discharge." Examples of public policy retaliatory discharge include claims by employees that they were terminated for:

a. filing a workers' compensation claim;
b. "whistle blowing"—reporting unlawful activities to law enforcement officials;
c. honoring a legal duty, such as jury service or a subpoena to testify in court;
d. assisting in governmental investigations relating to the employer; and
e. refusing to perform illegal, unethical, or unsafe activities on behalf of the employer.

If there is a state statute permitting an employee to do a certain thing, the employer must exercise care to not terminate employees for engaging in such activity. An example would be "a" above, a statute that permits an employee to file a workers' compensation claim for on-the-job injuries. If an employee files a workers' compensation claim and is terminated for exercising his statutory right, the employee might successfully bring a charge of retaliatory discharge if the employee is in a state that recognizes the public policy exception to employment at will.

A public policy goal that garners little opposition is the goal to prevent employers from using the threat of retaliation to "chill" their employees' use of the laws in question, whether on a state or federal level. The discharge of a whistleblower—an employee who brings organizational wrongdoing to the attention of government authorities—is a common form of public policy violation.

There are a number of federal statutes that contain whistle-blower protections, many of which relate to environmental or workplace health protections. Most of the federal whistleblower statutes apply only to federal employees for reporting violations by government agencies or employees. However, the federal defense contractor statute provides special whistle-blower protection for reporting contract-related violations to the government by the employees of civilian defense contractors that are awarded a contract by:

- The Department of Defense
- The Department of the Army
- The Department of the Navy
- The Department of the Air Force
- The Coast Guard
- The National Aeronautics and Space Administration (NASA)

The various federal statutes providing whistle-blower protection have varying statutes of limitation, some as short as 30 days. Some statutes permit immediate, direct access to the courts for the whistle-blower; others require the exhaustion of administrative remedies first, and some require that a department or agency pursue a claim on behalf of an employee. Figure 6-1 is a chart of federal statutes containing whistle-blower protections.

A number of states have adopted specific whistle-blower statutes Figure 6-2 is a listing of state whistle-blower statutes.

An example of a public policy retaliatory discharge is the employee who is terminated for performing his legal duty to fulfill jury service. Assume that a small-business owner has asked that an employee ignore a jury summons. The employee feels that he

---

- The Whistleblower Protection Act of 1989, 5 U.S.C. § 1221(a)
- Civil Service Reform Act, 5 U.S.C. § 2302(b)(8)
- Whistleblower Protection for Employees of Government Contractors, 10 U.S.C. § 2409
- The False Claims Act, 31 U.S.C. §§ 3729–3733
- National Labor Relations Act, 29 U.S.C. §§ 157 and 158(a)(1)
- Whistleblower Retaliation, 31 U.S.C.A. § 5328 (Relates only to financial institutions)

Figure 6-1
Federal Whistleblower Statutes

State	Language	Source
Arizona	An employee has a claim against an employer if the employee was terminated for refusing to commit an act violating state law; or for disclosing information to the employer that the employer or any employee has violated state law.	Employment Protection Act (ARIZ. REV. STAT. §§ 23-1501 – 13-1502)
California	No employer shall retaliate against an employee for disclosing information to a government or law enforcement agency, where the employee has reasonable cause to believe a violation of state or federal statute, or non-compliance, with a state or federal regulation has occurred.	(CAL. LAB. CODE § 1102.5)
Colorado	No private employer under contract with a state agency shall administer any disciplinary action against an employee for disclosing information that affects the state's interests. An employee must make a good faith effort to provide the information to the employer before disclosing it publicly.	(COLO. REV. STAT. §§ 24-114-101 – 24-114-103)
Connecticut	No employer shall discharge or otherwise penalize an employee for reporting a suspected violation of any state or federal law to a public body, or because an employee is requested by a public body to participate in an investigation. Statute does not apply if employee knows allegations are false.	(CONN. GEN. STAT. § 31-51m)
Florida	No employer may take any retaliatory personnel action against an employee who discloses or threatens to disclose violations of law. However, the employee must first notify the employer in writing of the suspected violations and allow the employer a reasonable opportunity to correct the activity. Also, employer may not take retaliatory action for employee's providing information or testifying before an agency for alleged violations of law.	(FLA. STAT. ANN. §§ 448.101 – 103)
Hawaii	An employer shall not discharge or discriminate against an employee for reporting a violation of law unless the employee knows the report to be false; Employer shall not discharge an employee for participating in an investigation held by a public body.	(Whistleblowers' Protection Act: HAW.REV.STAT. 378-61 to 378-69)
Indiana	An employee of a private employer that is under public contract may report the existence of a violation of state or federal law or the misuse of public resources. Employee must first report the violation to the private employer unless the employer is the source of the violation. If a good faith effort is not made to correct the problem, the employee may submit a written report to any agency or organization.	(IND. CODE § 22-5-3-3)

Figure 6-2
State Whistleblower Statutes

State	Language	Source
Louisiana	No employer shall discharge or discriminate against any employee who testifies or furnishes information in an investigation relative to the labor laws of the state.	(LA. REV. STAT. ANN. § 23:964)
Maine	No employer may discharge an employee who reports a violation of law or a health/safety risk to a public body. Employee must first bring the alleged violation to the attention of employer and allow reasonable opportunity to correct the practice. Employer may not discharge an employee who participates in an investigation or hearing by a public body.	(Whistleblowers' Protection Act: ME.REV.STAT.ANN. tit. 26 §§ 831-840)
Michigan	An employer shall not discharge or otherwise discriminate against an employee who reports a violation of law to a public body unless the employee knows the report to be false.	(Whistleblowers' Protection Act: MICH. COMP. LAW ANN. §§ 15.361 – 15.369)
Minnesota	An employer shall not discharge or otherwise discriminate against an employee for reporting a violation of any federal or state law, or for partici-pating in an investigation. An employee shall not be discharged for refusing to perform an action that violates state or federal law.	(MINN. STAT. §§ 181.931-181.935)
Montana	A discharge is wrongful only if it was in retaliation for the employee's refusal to violate public policy or for reporting a violation of public policy.	(Wrongful Discharge From Employment Act: MONT. CODE ANN. §§ 39-2-901 – 39-2-915)
Nebraska	It shall be unlawful for an employer to discriminate against employees because he or she has opposed any unlawful employment practice; participated in an investigation proceeding; or has opposed any action unlawful under federal or state law.	(Nebraska Fair Employment Practice Act: NEB.REV. STAT. §§ 48-1101 – 48-1125)
New Hampshire	No employer shall discharge or otherwise discriminate against any employee that in good faith reports a violation of any law or participates in an investigation conducted by any governmental entity. Employees must first bring the alleged violations to the attention of employer and allow reasonable opportunity to correct the violation.	(Whistleblowers' Protection Act: N.H.REV.STAT. ANN. §§ 275-E:1 – 275-E:7)
New Jersey	An employer shall not take any retaliatory action against an employee because the employee discloses to a public body a violation of law; provides information to a public body conducting an investigation; or refuses to participate in any activity which the em-ployee reasonably believes violates law or public policy.	(Conscientious Employee Pro-tection Act: NJ STAT. ANN. §§ 34:19 – 34:19-8)

Figure 6-2 (*continued*)

State	Language	Source
New York	An employer shall not take any retaliatory personnel action against an employee for disclosing to a public body an activity that violates a law or presents danger to public health and safety. Also may not retaliate for providing information to a public body or refusing to participate in activities violating law.	(N.Y. LAB. Law § 7400
North Dakota	An employer may not discharge or penalize an employee because an employee in good faith reports a violation of federal or state law; participates in an investigation conducted by a public body, or refuses to perform an action that the employee believes to violate state or federal law.	(N.D. CENT. CODE § 34-01-20)
Ohio	Within 24 hours after employee reports to employer information evidencing criminal violation, employer must notify the employee of any good efforts made to correct the violation. If no remedy has been taken after 24 hour, then the employee may report to a public body without retaliatory conduct by employer.	(OHIO REV. CODE ANN. §§ 4113.51 – 4113.53)
Oregon	An employer shall not take any retaliatory action against an employee because the employee has in good faith reported criminal activity, assisted or cooperated in a criminal or civil investigation, hearing, proceeding, or trial.	(OR.REV.STAT. § 659.550)
Pennsylvania	An employer shall not take any retaliatory action against an employee because the employee reports wrongdoing or waste. Also, an employer may not take such action against an employee for participating in an investigation, hearing or inquiry conducted by a proper authority, or in a court action.	(Whistleblower Law; PA.CONS. STAT. tit.43, §§ 1421-28)
Rhode Island	An employer shall not discharge or otherwise discriminate against an employee for reporting a violation to a public body or discriminate against one who is requested to participate in an investigation conducted by a public body.	(The Rhode Island Whistleblowers Act; R.I.GEN. LAWS §§ 28-50-1 – 28-50-9)
Tennessee	No employee shall be discharged solely for refusing to participate in, or for refusing to remain silent about illegal activities.	(TENN. CODE ANN. § 50-1 304)
Virgin Islands	An employer shall not discharge or otherwise discriminate against an employee because the employee reports a violation of law to a public body. In addition, an employer shall not take such action because an employee participates in an investigation, hearing or inquiry held by a public body, or a court action.	(Whistleblowers Protection Act; V.I. CODE ANN. tit. 10, §§ 121-26)

Figure 6-2 (*continued*)

has an obligation to fulfill his duty by serving on a criminal jury in a case that extends for four weeks. When the employee returns to work, he is terminated because he ignored the employer's orders to ignore the summons for jury service. The employee sues for wrongful discharge. The employer's defense is that the state recognizes employment at will. Many courts would find that the employer violated public policy. If the courts allowed employers to terminate employees who uphold the public policy, such holdings would be inconsistent with the public policy established by the statute.

The fourth type of public policy retaliatory discharge is a discharge that occurs as a result of the employee's cooperation with a governmental investigation of his or her employer. For example, the Justice Department has initiated an investigation of the employer for alleged antitrust activities. If an employee is subpoenaed to testify before a federal grand jury and is subsequently terminated by the employer, the employee has been discharged in violation of public policy.

The final category of public policy retaliatory discharge listed above is discharge for refusing to perform illegal, unethical, or unsafe activities on behalf of the employer. For example, assume that a doctor has demanded that the office manager file fictitious bills with Medicare to obtain money for services not performed. The office manager refuses and is terminated. That employee has a valid claim for wrongful discharge in violation of public policy.

Defenses to Public Policy Claims

Business Reason Defense

An employer may argue in defense of a discharge in violation of public policy claim that the discharge was based on a "legitimate business reason," or that there was no connection between the plaintiff's discharge and his or her alleged refusal to commit an illegal act.

Statute of Limitations

In determining the beginning of the statute of limitations period for a discharge in violation of public policy, courts usually set the clock for the statute at the time that the employee received unequivocal notice of his or her termination or some other allegedly discriminatory conduct by the employer.

This notice period is significant where there is a delay between the time the employee is informed of the allegedly discriminatory employment action and the time the effects of that action are felt. For example, an employee may be given ninety days advance notice of a layoff. Courts are faced with the decision of whether the statute of limitations period should begin at the time of the notice, or the time that the employee was actually laid off. Because of the two options for beginning the statutory period, states vary in the option selected.

Federal Statute Preemption

Federal statutes, including labor laws and ERISA, may preempt state law tort and contract claims relating to employment issues. For example, if a plaintiff's employment is subject to a collective bargaining agreement, state law may be preempted by section 301 of the Labor Management Relations Act. In addition, ERISA "shall supersede any and all State laws insofar as they may now or hereafter relate to an employee benefit plan" (29 U.S.C.A. § 1144(a)(1985). ERISA preempts any claim that the employer wrongfully discharged an employee in violation of public policy to avoid contributing to or paying benefits under an employer pension plan, or that the employee administrator of an ERISA welfare plan was discharged in retaliation for refusing to process allegedly illegal beneficiary loans. (See *Ingersoll-Rand Co. v. McClendon*, 498 U.S. 133 (1990) and *Coker v. Douglas*, No. 04-95-00204-CV, 1996 WL 81911 (Tex. App.—San Antonio Feb 28, 1996, writ denied), *cert. denied*, 117 S.Ct. 1426 (1997) [not designated for publication]. In the latter case, the court held that the plaintiff's claim was preempted by ERISA, because the court could not determine whether the allegedly illegal instruction was illegal without first interpreting the ERISA plan.

After-Acquired Evidence

The **after-acquired evidence doctrine** is a rule that, if an employer discharges an employee for an unlawful reason and later discovers misconduct sufficient to justify a lawful discharge, the employee cannot win on a claim for reinstatement. For example, an employer learns after firing an employee, and before the employee files suit claiming discrimination, that the employee stole company property during his/her employment or that he/she falsified the original employment application.

A leading case on the issue of after-acquired evidence is the *McKennon* case below, in which the Supreme Court held that after-acquired evidence of employee wrongdoing may limit the employee's damages, but does not negate the employee's cause of action if the wrongdoing would have justified the employee's termination even without any discriminatory conduct by the employer. The Supreme Court further clarified that damages under the after-acquired evidence doctrine generally end at the point at which the employer became aware of the misconduct.

McKennon v. Nashville Banner Publ'g Co., 513 U.S. 352, 115 S.Ct. 879 (1995)

Facts:

The plaintiff, a long-time employee, brought an age discrimination suit after she was discharged as part of a reduction-in-force. During the discovery portion of the lawsuit, the employer learned that during her last year of employment she had copied and taken home several confidential documents. Once the employer discovered this conduct, the employer wrote the plaintiff a letter advising her again that she was discharged, and stating that had it known of her conduct, she would have been discharged immediately.

Opinion by Justice Scalia:

In giving effect to the ADEA, we must recognize the duality between the legitimate interests of the employer and the important claims of the employee who invokes the national employment policy mandated by the Act. The employee's wrongdoing must be taken into account, we conclude, lest the employer's legitimate concerns be ignored, the ADEA, like Title VII, is not a general regulation of the workplace but a law which prohibits discrimination. The statute does not constrain employers from exercising significant other prerogatives and discretions in the course of the hiring, promoting, and discharging of their employees. In determining appropriate remedial action, the employee's wrongdoing becomes relevant not to punish the employee, or out of concern "for the relative moral worth of the parties," but to take due account of the lawful prerogatives o the employer in the usual course of its business and the corresponding equities that it has arising from the employee's wrongdoing.

It would be both inequitable and pointless to order the reinstatement of someone the employer would have terminated, and will terminate, in any event and upon lawful grounds. The beginning point in the trial court's formulation of a remedy should be calculation of back-pay from the date of the unlawful discharge to the date the new information was discovered.

Where an employer seeks to rely upon after-acquired evidence of wrongdoing, it must first establish that the wrongdoing was of such severity that the employee in fact would have been terminated on those grounds alone if the employer had known of it at the time of the discharge. The concern that employers might as a routine matter undertake extensive discovery into an employee's background or performance on the job to resist claims under the Act is not an insubstantial one, but we think the authority of the courts to award attorney's fees, mandated under the statute, and to invoke the appropriate provisions of the Federal Rules of Civil Procedure will deter most abuses.

The judgment is reversed, and the case is remanded to the Court of Appeals for the Sixth Circuit for further proceedings consistent with this opinion.

Remedies/Damages Available

Courts have generally found that the following remedies are available for common law public policy claims:

1. Past Lost Wages (Back Pay);
2. Reinstatement or Future Lost Wages (Front Pay);
3. Mental Anguish; and
4. Punitive/Exemplary Damages.

DISCHARGE IN VIOLATION OF IMPLIED COVENANT OF GOOD FAITH AND FAIR DEALING

Good faith and fair dealing cases often involve abusive or highly offensive discharges, such as:

- Retaliation for publicizing or alleging wrongdoing on the part of the employer.
- Termination of an employee to avoid paying a sales commission.
- Retaliation for refusing to become romantically involved with a supervisor.

CONSTRUCTIVE DISCHARGE

Constructive discharge occurs if the employer makes working conditions so intolerable that a reasonable person in the employee's position would have felt compelled to resign. However, this doctrine states that constructive discharge does not occur when all employees are subject to the same working conditions.

An employee's failure to protest allegedly intolerable working conditions, either through internal company procedures or governmental mechanisms, will often refute a complaint of constructive discharge. In determining the issue of constructive discharge, courts consider the working conditions and the reasonableness of the plaintiff's response to these conditions. For example, courts have often not found constructive discharge where an employee immediately resigned after a problem rather than attempting to find alternative ways to resolve the problem; an employee resigned after one instance of name-calling; or the employee resigned while a sexual harassment claim was still under investigation by the employer.

Proving Constructive Discharge

The federal courts disagree on the standard for proving constructive discharge. Most federal courts have adopted an objective test that focuses on whether a "reasonable person" would have felt compelled to resign. However, a minority of federal courts use a "subjective intent" test that focuses on whether the employer *deliberately* made working conditions intolerable.

The reasonable person test requires that the court consider whether working conditions were objectively intolerable, and whether the employee's resignation was an objectively reasonable response to his or her working conditions.

Objectively Intolerable Working Conditions

The plaintiff must prove both an unlawful act (discrimination or retaliation in violation of Title VII) and aggravating circumstances in order to prove objectively intolerable working conditions. If the plaintiff is unable to prove the unlawful act occurred, then constructive discharge claim also fails.

An allegation often relied upon is that the employer either created or allowed to be created an atmosphere of harassment or hostility that rendered working conditions intolerable. To prove such an atmosphere of harassment, the plaintiff must be able to prove that the harassment was more severe or pervasive than the minimum required to prove a hostile working environment. Thus, the burden for proving harassment is quite heavy.

Aggravating Circumstances

The courts consider a number of factors to determine whether aggravating circumstances existed to justify a resignation, including:

(1) Demotion.
See *Stephens v. C.I.T. Group/Equipment Financing, Inc.*, 955 F.2d 1023, 1027 (5th Cir. 1992) (employee was demoted, his salary was cut, and employer badgered him to resign);

(2) Reduction in job responsibilities.
See *Wilson v. Monarch Paper Co.*, 939 F.2d 1138, 1145 (5th Cir. 1991) (company president, a college graduate, was reassigned to janitorial duties);

(3) Reassignment to menial or degrading work.
See *Wilson* above.

(4) Reassignment to work under a younger supervisor.
Example: plaintiff was demoted and required to report to younger supervisor whom he had trained.

(5) Badgering or harassing the employee.
See *Guthrie v. J. C. Penney Co., Inc.*, 803 F.2d 202, 207 (5th Cir. 1986) (constructive discharge shown where employer badgered 60-year-old employee to resign and reprimanded him in the presence of his subordinates)

(6) Offers of early retirement on terms that would leave the employee worse off whether or not the offer was accepted.
See *Downey v. Southern Natural Gas Co.*, 649 F.2d 302, 305 (5th Cir. 1981) (finding fact issues where, after declining early retirement offer, employee was told there was no work for him to do, that he was in danger of being discharged, and that he might lose his benefits), *reh'g denied*, 656 F.2d 704 5th Cir. 1981).

No Finding of Aggravating Circumstances

In the following fact situations, the courts have found that, without aggravating circumstances such as those discussed above, unlawful discrimination is not sufficient to create intolerable working conditions that would justify an employee's resignation:

1. Discrimination on the basis of pay
2. Denial of promotion
3. Discriminatory transfer or demotion
4. Negative performance appraisal

Reasonableness of Resignation

Courts consider the nature of the plaintiff's working conditions and the reasonableness of his or her response to those conditions to determine whether the plaintiff was constructively discharged. For example, in *Landgraf v. USI Film Prods.*, 968 F.2d 427, 430 (5th Cir. 1992), *aff'd*, 511 U.S. 908 (1993), the court rejected the plaintiff's constructive discharge claim in part because she quit her employment while the employer was still investigating her sexual harassment claim.

In *Dornhecker v. Malibu Grand Prix Corp.*, 828 F.2d 307 (5th Cir. 1987), the plaintiff advised her employer that during a short business trip she had been the victim of sexual harassment by a contract consultant retained by the employer. The employer told the plaintiff that she would never have to work with the alleged harasser again. The employer kept its word, but the plaintiff quit her employment without ever having had to work with the harasser after she complained. The Fifth Circuit rejected her claim for constructive discharge on the ground that she did not allow the employer to fully investigate her claims or give the employer a fair opportunity to demonstrate it could stop the harassment before she resigned. The court wrote:

As the Eleventh Circuit recently put it, "part of an employee's obligation to be reasonable is an obligation not to assume the worst and not to jump to conclusions too fast."

Factors that an employer might consider to avoid constructively discharging an employee include asking the employee not to quit and implementing an internal grievance procedure for all harassment and discrimination claims. The internal grievance procedure should be well-publicized and easily accessible, allowing an employee to bypass an immediate supervisor if that supervisor is the source of the discriminatory or harassing conduct.

As discussed above, employees must do what is reasonable *under the circumstances.* If there is an established internal grievance procedure, it would be reasonable, in most instances, for the employee to pursue internal remedies first. However, there may be instances where an immediate resignation is the employee's only recourse. For example, an employee's immediate resignation after a sexual assault by her immediate supervisor (without using the internal grievance procedure) would be constructive discharge.

Remedies for Constructive Discharge

A successful constructive discharge plaintiff is entitled to the same remedies as if she had been formally discharged. Therefore, the plaintiff may be entitled to both equitable remedies, such as injunctive relief and monetary relief (42 U.S.C. § 2000e-5(g)(1)).

Monetary damages available include all actual damages (back pay, front pay, and damages for emotional distress), and may also include punitive damages (42 U.S.C. § 2000e-5(g)(1)). For example, in the *Borg-Warner Protective Servs. Corp. v. Flores*, 955 S.W.2d 861 (Tex. App.—Corpus Christi 1997, no writ), the Title VII plaintiff (who was raped by her supervisor) established constructive discharge and was awarded back pay, front pay, past and future mental anguish damages, and monetary relief for physical pain.

Limits on Recovery of Back Pay

Voluntary Quit versus Constructive Discharge

Whether a termination is deemed a voluntary quit or a constructive discharge has a significant effect on the plaintiff's available relief. In constructive discharge cases, back pay generally begins to accrue on the day the employee resigns. However, if the court finds that the employee voluntarily quit, the employee can recover damages for the unlawful act, but cannot recover back pay for the time following his or her resignation.

An employee who is working in an unsatisfactory, or even discriminatory job, is free to quit the job and file suit. However, that employee cannot hold the employer responsible for his or her economic losses that result from quitting the job, because the employee had the ability to limit the damages prior to resigning. The court in *Hopkins v. Price Waterhouse*, 737 F. Supp. 1202 (D.D.C. 1990) stated that, generally, staying at one's present position until a constructive discharge occurs is part of a Title VII plaintiff's duty to mitigate damages.

Unconditional Offer of Reinstatement

An employee's right to recover back pay may be limited by an **unconditional offer of reinstatement**—an offer by an employer to re-employ the discharged employee under comparable working conditions. The purpose of such an offer is to undo the employer's earlier wrong by restoring the employee to the position that the employee would have occupied before the wrong occurred. Employers often employ the tactic of an unconditional offer of reinstatement because, if it is properly executed, the offer cuts off back pay liability, limits a claimant's damages, and reduces an employer's exposure.

The court in *Ford Motor Co. v. EEOC*, 458 U.S. 219 (1982) set out the following requirements for a valid offer of reinstatement:

(1) Must be for a comparable position;
(2) Must be unconditional (not contingent on the former employee's dismissal of a lawsuit or relinquishing any other rights); and
(3) Must be clearly communicated to the discharged employee.

A reinstatement offer does not have to be identical to the claimant's former position, but it must be for one as sufficiently equivalent as possible. In the *Ford Motor Co.* case, the court explained that "The un- or under-employed claimant need not go into another line of work, accept a demotion or take a demeaning position."

In addition to requiring that the offer be for a comparable position, the offer must be "unconditional." There can be no contingency on the employee's relinquishing or waiving any rights he or she may have.

Refusal of Unconditional Offer

Just as with the voluntary resignation, an employee's refusal of an unconditional offer of reinstatement constitutes a breach of his or her duty to mitigate damages and cuts off the employer's liability for back pay, unless the employee can demonstrate that a reasonable person would have refused the offer (42 U.S.C. § 2000e-5(g)(1)).

A constructive discharge plaintiff who can prove that the conditions of employment had not changed for the better after his or her resignation would have a very strong argument for rejecting an unconditional offer of reinstatement.

Early Retirement Offers

Early retirement offers ("EROs") are designed to enhance the retirement benefits available to employees who fall within the age group protected by the Age Discrimination in Employment Act (ADEA). The question in an ERO is whether acceptance is truly voluntary, or is in effect a constructive discharge as discussed in the *Bodnar* case below.

Bodnar v. Synpol, Inc., 843 F.2D 190, 193 (5th Cir.)
cert. denied, 488 U.S. 908 (1989)

Facts:

Synpol, Inc., formerly a subsidiary of Uniroyal, Inc., produced synthetic polymers in a plant in Port Neches, Texas. In 1983, Synpol's market for a synthetic polymer used in new car tires began to deteriorate drastically, prompting the company to immediately embark on a dramatic cost-reduction program that was announced to all employees in an information bulletin on September 28, 1983. The bulletin informed the employees that one of the cost-reduction programs would be a Special Early Retirement Incentive Program. The SERIP was formulated to include salaried employees who were eligible for early retirement under the company's pension plan, having reached the age of 55 with ten years of company service.

Certain eligible employees deemed essential to the company were not asked to participate in the SERIP. Employees covered by collective bargaining agreements were necessarily excluded from the SERIP.

Twenty-eight employees were offered early retirement under the SERIP on September 27 and 28, 1983 and were given 15 days to accept or reject the offer. The incentive for early retirement was a variable bonus of up to $20,000 cash. The plan was discussed individually with each of the employees to whom it was offered. Twenty-one of those offered the plan accepted the SERIP agreement, which included a release of claims against Synpol. The seven employees who declined early retirement under the SERIP continued their employment with Synpol.

Bodnar and three others filed suit, asserting that the eligible employees were told early retirement option can constitute a constructive discharge " . . . if the employee shows that it sufficiently alters the status quo that each choice facing the employee makes him worse off." (*cert. denied*, 506 U.S. 820 (1992)).

Opinion by Judge Jones:

An employer may implement an early retirement plan that does not extend to all potentially eligible employees if objective factors explain the exclusions.

Appellants' second significant area of objection to SERIP is that they were not really offered a "voluntary" opportunity for an early retirement bonus. Coercion allegedly inhered in (1) the short time afforded appellants for considering their options, (2) the supervisors' "threat" that if not enough employees accepted early retirement and the offeree's job was eliminated he would not receive any severance pay or non-pension benefits and (3) the tone and manner of those who explained the plan. None of these factors, taken singly or cumulatively, constitutes objective evidence that working conditions had become so intolerable as to force appellants' resignation. The fifteen-day time period, although not generous, is a far cry from the twenty-four hour take-it or leave-it proposal considered by the Second Circuit in *Paolillo v. Dresser Industries*, 821 F.2d 81 (2nd Cir. 1987). Appellant Bodnar, for instance, had ample time to and did consult with a lawyer and examine his options. We would be inclined to scrutinize closely any plan that was offered to employees on a shorter schedule, but one must concurrently recognize that a struggling business often has to take rapid and decisive action to stem losses.

That risk inhered in eligible employees' failure to accept the SERIP bonus offer, the risk that their jobs might be eliminated because of economic pressure on the company, is likewise insufficient to suggest age discrimination.

The appellants' vague and subjective impressions of threats conveyed by their supervisors when discussing the ESRIP plan are too insubstantial a reed, in the absence of objective factors or actions suggesting age discrimination, on which to found a jury issue. . . . This conclusion is particularly true in the context of a constructive discharge claim, which relies on an objective test to evaluate what otherwise appears to be voluntary conduct by an employee. Because we do not find evidence in the record sufficient to create a jury issue on whether Appellants were constructively discharged in violation of the ADEA, we AFFIRM the trial court's judgment.

The determination of whether or not offering or accepting an ERO is based on whether the circumstances surrounding the offer support the conclusion that the offer was not discriminatory and the acceptance was voluntary.

INTENTIONAL INFLICTION OF EMOTIONAL DISTRESS CLAIMS IN WRONGFUL DISCHARGE CASES

An **intentional infliction of emotional distress (IIED)** claim includes allegations that the discharge of an employee was carried out in a manner that was intentionally and extremely abusive, degrading, or humiliating. Many states do not recognize IIED claims in the context of employment litigation. Some states provide relief for IIED only through their workers' compensation statutes. In states where IIED claims are recognized, the employer's actions generally must exceed all bounds of decency.

Litigation in the area of IIED often involves claims of sexual or racial harassment that allegedly resulted in severe emotional distress to the employee.

DEFAMATION CLAIMS IN WRONGFUL DISCHARGE CASES

Defamation—transmission to others of false statements that harm the reputation, business, or property rights of a person—is often claimed in cases alleging wrongful termination. The claims in that instance involve allegations by employees that supervisors or coworkers made false statements about them that have injured their reputation.

Examples of defamation include accusing an employee of:

- using or abusing drugs
- theft
- embezzlement
- falsification of records
- arrests or criminal convictions
- having a communicable or venereal disease

Defamatory statements may be in the form of **slander** (oral statements), or **libel** (written statements), and may be communicated to individuals either inside or outside the company. In some states, even a statement made only to the terminated employee may be considered as defamation. For example, if a false reason for termination is placed in the employee's personnel record, and if the employee is compelled to repeat the reason for his discharge (allegedly defamatory) to other persons in searching for a new job, that is known as the doctrine of **self-compelled publication**.

In the employment environment, defamation claims primarily occur in two situations:

1. Discussing an employee's alleged poor performance, misconduct, or reasons for termination beyond the group of people who need to know.
2. Responses to reference checks.

Suggested actions that employers should take to avoid defamation liability include:

1. Investigate and document all incidents of employee misconduct **thoroughly** before imposing discipline.
2. Limit disclosure of the employee's discipline to those who have a legitimate "need to know."
3. Maintain employee medical data (including drug test results) strictly confidential.
4. Obtain a signed release from an employee before releasing any employment data.
5. Limit responses to reference checks to confirmation of the date of employment and the position held.

An employer may utilize a number of defenses in response to a defamation lawsuit, including, truth, consent, statute of limitations, absolute privilege, and qualified privilege.

The truth of an alleged defamatory statement is a complete defense to a defamation suit, because it defeats an essential element (a false statement) of a defamation claim. The Supreme Court has ruled that truth is a complete defense, and true statements, even if damaging to reputation, may not give rise to a legal claim by the employee.

If an employee has consented to the publication or communication of the alleged defamatory statement, this is also a complete defense to a defamation lawsuit. For example, the employee may authorize the employer to provide a reference to a third party.

The statute of limitations also may provide a complete defense to a defamation claim. A statute of limitation fixes the time within which court action for defamatory claims must be initiated.

An employee may not recover damages for defamation if the allegedly defamatory communication is an **absolute privilege**—freedom from all claims of defamation.

Courts have generally recognized absolute privilege for statements made by a legislator during a legislative proceeding, by participants in a judicial or quasi-judicial proceeding, or when there is a legal requirement to make a statement. The employer has complete immunity from a defamation claim, even if the employer made the remark out of malice or sheer ill-will.

A **qualified privilege** exists when otherwise defamatory statements are made under circumstances where the person making the statement has a legitimate and reasonable justification to communicate—for example, in a meeting convened specifically to discuss the employee's conduct, during which negative comments about the employee are made. Under certain, but not all, circumstances, the qualified privilege may serve as a complete defense to an employer's defamatory statement. The employer may lose the qualified privilege by making false statements with a bad or ulterior motive, or by spreading the statements beyond any legitimate business justification.

TERMINATION DECISION

Figure 6-3 lists actions that an employer should consider when faced with discharge decisions relating to its employees.

Any final decision to discharge an employee should be reviewed by management personnel who are responsible for reviewing all terminations, such as the head of the personnel or human resources department. Such a review is necessary to confirm that the discharge will be in accordance with company policy and consistent with the treatment accorded other company employees in similar terminations.

Notifying the employee of the company's decision to terminate is a very important part of the termination process. It is critical for the employee to understand the reason for his or her termination. The actual termination should be brief and candid. Problems and even litigation often arise out of improper handling of the final termination interview with the employee. In the termination atmosphere, employees often become angry and hostile. The human resources personnel sometimes become defensive about the decision to terminate.

Figure 6-4 is a checklist for an employer to follow once the decision to terminate has been made.

UNEMPLOYMENT COMPENSATION FOR TERMINATED EMPLOYEES

Terminated employees may have a right under state laws to file for unemployment compensation, based on the reason for termination. What the employer and

- Was the rule that the employee violated a written rule? When and where was the rule published?
- Did the employee receive a written copy of the rule?
- Did the employee sign for the handbook or manual that contained the rule?
- Was the rule posted?
- Has the employee been warned previously for violation of the rule, and, if so, by whom?
- Was the previous warning for violation of the rule documented and signed by the employee?
- Have any other employees violated this rule?
- Did other employees who violated this rule receive the same disciplinary action as that under consideration for this employee?
- Is the employer's application of rules and standards consistent?
- If the decision to terminate is on the basis of poor performance, has the employee received notice of the poor performance and been given an opportunity to improve his/her performance?
- If the decision to terminate is on the basis of poor attendance, has the employee received notice of the poor performance and been given an opportunity to improve his/her attendance?
- Has the employee been disciplined during the past twelve months?
- Did the employer investigate the incident or accident that resulted in discipline prior to taking the final disciplinary action, including obtaining the employee's version of the events?
- What type of performance appraisals has the employee received over the past year?
- Have other alternatives to termination been considered, such as demotion or opportunity to resign?
- How long has the employee been employed?
- Is the employee working under a written contract?
- Is the employee a member of a protected group (age, race, sex, religion, national origin, or disability)?
- If the employee is a member of a protected group, is the employee receiving the same treatment as employees who are not in a protected group?
- Has the employee ever complained about any company policy or action that he/she considered illegal or immoral, which complaints might lead to a retaliatory discharge claim?
- Does the employee have a protected disability?
- Does the support documentation for the termination include names of witnesses, dates, times, places, and other critical information for the employee's past violations?

Figure 6-3
Checklist for Termination Decisions

employee list as the reason for the termination is often a part of subsequent employment litigation. If the employer disputes the employee's application for unemployment compensation, the matter will proceed to a hearing before the state regulatory agency for unemployment compensation. A favorable decision for the employer by the state's unemployment compensation commission hearing board might result in the employee's decision to not pursue an employment action in the court.

- At the time of the termination, have another member of management present.
- Be organized and prepared for the termination interview. Have all necessary documentation available.
- Don't prolong advising the employee that he/she is being terminated.
- Explain the termination decision clearly and quickly. Make certain that the reason given for termination is truthful. The stated reason for termination is important in the case of subsequent litigation.
- Don't compliment the employee in an attempt to avoid hurting his/her feelings.
- Don't counsel the employee. Counseling should have occurred previously.
- Don't compliment the employee in order to soften the blow of termination.
- Give the employee an opportunity to respond. Listen closely to what the employee has to say. Don't argue with the employee.
- Never refer to age, sex, race, national origin or disability during the termination conference.
- The employer should obtain legal advice prior to terminating a minority employee, older employee, pregnant employee, or employee who has recently experienced an on-the-job injury.
- Remind the employee of any confidentiality or non-compete requirements, if applicable.
- Discuss benefits, including Cobra and unemployment compensation, to which the employee might be entitled. Let the employee know when to expect such benefits. Obtain signatures on all necessary benefit forms.
- Prepare written notes of the termination interview, including what the employee has been told, and what the employee said. The employee and employer personnel should sign the termination interview document.
- Arrange for the return of all company documents, tools, etc. in the employee's personal possession.
- Retrieve IDs and keys. Delete the employee's computer and telephone access. If appropriate, change locks to the building and the employee's locker.
- Permit the employee to leave the premises with as much dignity and as little attention as possible.

Figure 6-4
Checklist for Termination

SEPARATION AGREEMENTS

There are often instances where an employer believes that if it discharges an employee, the employee may file a lawsuit. In such cases, the employer might consider entering into a separation agreement with the employee. The separation agreement must contain two essential elements:

1. The employer must give additional valuable consideration to the employee (such as additional pay or enhanced retirement benefits) to which the employee was not otherwise entitled.

2. After being given time to review the terms of the agreement with a representative of the employee, including an attorney, and in return for the additional valuable consideration, the employee must sign a general release and covenant not to sue.

Properly executed separation agreements tend to dramatically reduce the risk of subsequent employment litigation, and provide an employer with a strong defense against employment claims covered by the release.

Special time requirements and opportunity to review and revoke a separation agreement are set forth in age discrimination law, discussed at length in Chapter 9.

Potential problems with separation agreements are inevitable. In some cases, the company's payment of valuable consideration is limited to only the amount to which the discharged employee is already entitled, even without a separation agreement—for example, vacation pay or severance pay. An employee might reject the agreement and use the proposed agreement as evidence of wrongful termination by claiming that the company must have thought that it was liable for termination, because it offered the terminated employee money to release his or her claims. Failure to specify that the separation agreement is the parties' complete agreement opens the door for claims by either party that there were certain promises not contained in the written agreement.

REPLACING A TERMINATED EMPLOYEE

Employers should exercise caution in replacing a terminated employee. While endeavoring to find the most qualified individual for the position, consideration must be given to avoiding a later charge of discrimination in the termination. One defense in subsequent litigation is often the fact that the terminated employee is replaced by another person of the same race, sex, national origin, or age.

THE MODEL UNIFORM EMPLOYMENT TERMINATION ACT

The Model Uniform Employment Termination Act (UETA) was issued by the National Conference of Commissioners of Uniform State Laws in August 1991. The purpose of this Act was to attempt to bring some uniformity to the myriad of state laws addressing the issue of employment termination. States are not required to adopt a "uniform" act. They also have the option of adopting a similar version, drafting a very similar statute, or adopting no statute at all.

One radical provision of the UETA states that an employer may not discharge an employee without good cause. The UETA also provides that an employee would no longer have the right to bring a court claim against the employer on the basis of wrongful discharge, but would be required to pursue arbitration or another form of state administrative procedure. "Good cause" was interpreted by the UETA drafters to include fighting, theft, insubordination, incompetence, intoxication or drug use, and excessive absenteeism or tardiness.

Under the Act, an employer is permitted to prove a legitimate economic need for the discharge to constitute a good cause requirement. Specifics of the Act do not allow a termination in violation of public policy derived from either constitutional or statutory law, or a retaliatory termination of a **whistle-blower**—an employee who brings organizational wrongdoing to the attention of government authorities.

An employee must have worked for the employer for no less than one year prior to the termination and for an average of 20 hours per week prior to the termination to qualify for UETA protections. As with other employment laws, employers are required to post a copy of the Act or an approved summary in a prominent place in the work area. Violations of this provision may result in a civil fine. UETA carries the same prohibitions against employers' retaliating against employees for pursuing their rights under this Act in any manner, including testifying or filing a claim under UETA.

TERMS

absolute privilege
after-acquired evidence doctrine
back pay
constructive discharge
defamation
front pay
implied contract
intentional infliction of emotional distress
libel
promissory estoppel
punitive/exemplary damages
qualified privilege
self-compelled publication
slander
unconditional offer of reinstatement

whistleblower
wrongful discharge

REVIEW QUESTIONS

1. An employee of a bar refuses to serve alcohol to an intoxicated patron, although it is not a violation of state law. Employee is terminated. Does the employee have a cause of action against the employer? Explain the legal theory for your answer.

2. Assume that there was a state law in question 1 above that prohibited the sale of alcohol to an intoxicated person. Would that change your answer to question 1? Explain the legal reasoning behind your answer.

3. Matthew Carlson received a written offer of employment in the summer of 1999 from Optics Software. The offer outlined his compensation plan, commissions, profit sharing, insurance, benefits, and vacations. Carlson resigned his position and accepted the Optics Software position. Optics failed to honor all of the promises in the offer of employment, and failed to provide Carlson with sufficient training so that he could succeed in the new position. In the fall of 1999, Carlson was terminated. He filed a breach of contract and good faith and fair dealing against Optics. Optics filed a motion to dismiss Carlson's suit, claiming that he was an employee at will and that the offer of employment did not constitute an employment contract. Do you agree or disagree with Carlson's claims? Set out the arguments that Carlson must make to be successful in his lawsuit.

4. Maxine Nelson was hired by Westside Communications to perform a research assistant's duties. Nelson was quoted a $40,000 annual salary. She was terminated after six months, and filed suit against Westside. What would be the legal basis for her suit? Would she be successful? Why or why not?

5. Assume that Matthew Carlson, in review question 3, resigned his current position and accepted the Optics Software position. However, Optics decided not to employ Carlson. What type of claim or claims would Carlson have against Optics Software?

6. After Lou Anderson was injured on her job at Genesis Records, she filed a workers' compensation claim. Anderson was subsequently laid off during a reduction in force. She then filed suit, claiming age discrimination (Anderson was 42) and retaliation for filing a workers' compensation claim. What would Anderson have to prove in order to succeed in her litigation?

7. Lance Cameron is terminated as a result of a reduction in force. After his termination, the employer learns that Cameron had been filing bogus expense reports. Explain whether or not the after-acquired evidence doctrine would apply in this case.

8. Maggie Ramirez was discharged from her employment as a legal assistant with a medical malpractice law firm after she refused to engage in a romantic relationship with the managing partner that he demanded. Is Ramirez's termination a discharge in violation of implied covenant of good faith and fair dealing? Explain the legal reasoning for your answer.

9. An employee was demoted, his pay was cut, and he was badgered by his supervisor to resign constantly. What type of claims would be appropriate for the employee to make in any subsequent litigation?

10. Explain the benefits an employer receives from an unconditional offer of reinstatement to an employee.

PROJECTS

1. Brief *Pennzoil Producing Co. v. Offshore Express, Inc.*, 943 F.2d 1465, 1476 (5th Cir. 1991). Explain the court's ruling relating to a plaintiff's duty to mitigate damages.

2. Search the Internet for news reports of employees who have been disciplined and/or terminated for performing jury duty. List the penalties, if any, imposed on the employers for such terminations.

CHAPTER 7

Overview of Discrimination in Employment Law

OVERVIEW

Discrimination in employment practices had its genesis in early behavior patterns in the home, school, and society in general. An employer who discriminates against an employee on the basis of sex, race, religion, or national origin does not suddenly experience discriminatory thoughts or actions at the office or plant. That employer probably has previously felt and expressed a feeling that another individual is inferior because of skin color or other external characteristics. Employment discrimination consists of more than legal considerations. Social, economic, and ethical considerations generally factor into any act of employment discrimination.

TYPES OF DISCRIMINATORY TREATMENT UNDER TITLE VII

Title VII prohibits discriminatory wage disparities, discrimination in hiring, promotions, discharges, demotions, segregated facilities, and other terms and conditions of employment. The Civil Rights Act also covers both intentional and unintentional discriminatory conduct. However, Title VII only applies to employers with 15 or more employees, based on the number of employees during each working day of twenty or more calendar weeks of the current, or preceding, calendar year (42 U.S.C. § 2000e(b)).

There are two ways to prove a Title VII case: disparate treatment or disparate impact. The disparate treatment cause of action is the easiest and most often utilized.

Disparate Treatment

Disparate treatment is intentional discrimination based on a person's race, color, religion, sex, national origin, age, or disability. Proof of disparate treatment is usually

139

accomplished through a shifting burden of proof standard, as discussed in *McDonnell Douglas v. Green*, 411 U.S. 792 (1973), discussed at length below. The plaintiff must first establish a *prima facie* case of discrimination in the form of an adverse employment event, such as a demotion or termination. If a *prima facie* case is established, the burden then shifts to the defendant to establish a legitimate, nondiscriminatory rationale for the adverse action. If the defendant meets its burden, the burden then shifts back to the plaintiff to prove that the articulated rationale is a pretext. Disparate treatment cases may be classified as individual disparate treatment, mixed motives cases, and systemic disparate treatment.

Individual Disparate Treatment

The theory of **individual disparate treatment** seeks to determine whether the employer deliberately treated the employee bringing a claim of intentional discrimination differently from other employees because of his or her membership in a protected class (age, sex, race, disability, for example). The *McDonnell Douglas* case discussed below set the factors for determining whether a plaintiff has a valid individual disparate treatment case.

McDonnell Douglas Corp. v. Green, 411 U.S. 792 (1973)

Facts:

Green, a black citizen of St. Louis, was employed as a mechanic and laboratory technician from 1956 until August 28, 1964, when he was laid off in the course of a general reduction in McDonnell Douglas's work force. Green was also a long-time activist in the civil rights movement. He protested vigorously that both his discharge and the general hiring practices of McDonnell Douglas were racially motivated. As part of his protest, Green and other members of the Congress on Racial Equality illegally stalled their cars on the main roads leading to the McDonnell Douglas plant for the purpose of blocking access to the plant at the time of the morning shift change.

Subsequent to his arrest and guilty plea for the "stall-in," McDonnell Douglas advertised for qualified mechanics. Green applied for reemployment. McDonnell Douglas rejected his application on the basis of the "stall-in" and "lock-in" activities that resulted in chaining and padlocking the front door of a downtown office building that housed part of McDonnell Douglas' offices.

Shortly after he was denied reemployment, Green filed a formal complaint with the EEOC, claiming that the company had refused to rehire him because of his race and his persistent involvement in the civil rights movement, in violation of Sections 703(a)(1) and 704(a) of the Civil Rights Act of 1964. The district court rejected both of these claims.

The Eighth Circuit affirmed the district court's finding that unlawful protests were not protected activities, but reversed the dismissal of Green's claim relating to racially discriminatory hiring practices and ordered the case remanded for trial of that claim.

The Supreme Court agreed with the Court of Appeals that Green proved a *prima facie* case. McDonnell Douglas had sought mechanics, which was Green's trade, and continued to do so after rejecting his application for reemployment. McDonnell Douglas did not dispute Green's qualifications for the job, and acknowledged that his past work performance was "satisfactory."

The burden then shifted to the employer to articulate a legitimate, nondiscriminatory reason for the employee's rejection. McDonnell Douglas alleged that it failed to rehire Green because of his participation in unlawful conduct against the company.

Green admitted that he had taken part in the carefully planned "stall-in," designed to tie up access to and from the plant at a peak traffic hour.

Opinion by Justice Powell:

Respondent [Green] admittedly had taken part in a carefully planned "stall-in," designed to tie up access to and egress from petitioner's plant at a peak traffic hour. Nothing in Title VII compels an employer to absolve and rehire one who has engaged in such deliberate, unlawful activity against it. In upholding, under the National Labor Relations Act, the discharge of employees who had seized and forcibly retained an employer's factory buildings in an illegal sit-down strike, the Court noted pertinently:

"We are unable to conclude that Congress intended to compel employers to retain persons in their employ regardless of their unlawful conduct-to invest those who go on strike with an immunity from discharge for acts of trespass or violence against the employer's property," *NLRB v. Fansteel Corp.*, 306 U.S. 240 255, 59 S.Ct. 490, 496, 83 L.Ed. 627 (1939).

While Title VII does not, without more, compel rehiring of respondent, neither does it permit petitioner to use respondent's counsel as a pretext for the sort of discrimination prohibited by 703(a)(1). On remand, respondent must, as the Court of Appeals recognized, be afforded a fair opportunity to show that petitioner's stated reason for respondent's rejection was in fact pretext. Especially relevant to such a showing would be evidence that white employees involved in acts against petitioner of comparable seriousness to the "stall-in" were nevertheless retained or rehired. Petitioner may justifiably refuse to rehire one who was engaged in unlawful, disruptive acts against it, but only if this criterion is applied alike to members of all races.

Other evidence that may be relevant to any showing of pretext includes facts as to the petitioner's treatment of respondent during his prior term of employment, petitioner's reaction, if any, to respondent's legitimate civil rights activities; and petitioner's general policy and practice with respect to minority employment. On the latter point, statistics as to petitioner's employment policy and practice may be helpful to a determination of whether petitioner's refusal to rehire respondent in this case conformed to a general pattern of discrimination against blacks. In short, on the retrial respondent must be given a full and fair opportunity to demonstrate by competent evidence that the presumptively valid reasons for his rejection were in fact a coverup for a racially discriminatory decision.

The cause is hereby remanded to the District Court for reconsideration in accordance with this opinion.

Prima Facie *Case—Individual Disparate Treatment*

The discriminatory intent of the employer is the first element that an employee must prove in an individual disparate treatment case. Generally, the courts look to the employer's action to establish discriminatory intent.

The plaintiff in a Title VII case must carry the initial burden under the statute of establishing a *prima facie case* of discrimination by showing:

1. That he or she belongs to a protected group.

   To be liable, the employer must have known that the complainant was a member of a protected group at the time the adverse employment action took place.

2. That he or she applied for and was qualified for a job for which the employer was seeking applicants.

   This second stage of the *McDonnell Douglas* proof standard specifies that the employer must have been "seeking" applicants for the job in question—the job for which the plaintiff was qualified. If the plaintiff cannot show that the employer had an opening for the position applied for, there is no *prima facie* case.

   The necessity of demonstrating that there was a job opening follows the purposes of the original Civil Rights Act of 1964. The Act was not designed to provide a job for every minority member. It was meant to ensure equal opportunity. There is no *prima facie* case if the job opening was filled by the time that the plaintiff applied for the position.

3. That, despite his or her qualifications, he or she was rejected for the job; and if a plaintiff fails to demonstrate that he or she meets the minimum qualifications for the job in question, his or her case will fail. The element of qualification contains two components: the qualifications demanded by the job and the qualifications possessed by the plaintiff. The first component must be established before the second component has any relevance. At this stage the entire burden is on the plaintiff. Therefore, the plaintiff must begin his or her case by demonstrating what the qualifications for the job were. This task is complicated in the area of "subjective qualifications," such as "interpersonal skills," sought by the employer. Courts have held that the plaintiff should not be required, as part of the *prima facie* case, to show that he or she possessed those subjective qualifications, but that the employer should be required to explain the need for, and/or the plaintiff's lack of, such subjective qualifications, in its rebuttal case.

   The courts have generally held that the plaintiff need not prove that he or she is the most qualified candidate for the position, (*Mitchell v. Baldridge*, 759 F.2d 80, 37 FEP 689 (D.C. Cir. 1985)) or is "as qualified as or more qualified than the person actually selected" (*Abrams v. Johnson*, 534 F.2d 1226, 12 FEP 1293 (6th Cir. 1976)). In *Mitchell v. Baldridge*, the District of Columbia Circuit held that it was error for the district court to have required Mitchell to prove that he was as well or better qualified than the person chosen for the position to establish a *prima facie* case. The Court further noted that a plaintiff is only required to show that his qualifications are similar to those of the entire pool from which applications are welcome, rather than to those who are eventually selected. The failure of a plaintiff to prove that he/she was rejected is fatal to a prima facie case.

4. That, after his or her rejection, the position remained open, and the employer continued to accept applications. A common way for a plaintiff to demonstrate this fourth element of a *prima facie* case is to show that the employer subsequently hired someone for the position, and that the person hired had equal or lesser qualifications compared to those of the plaintiff.

Defenses to Individual Disparate Treatment

An employer may rely on two affirmative defenses to an **individual disparate treatment** charge:

1. Bona fide occupational qualification (BFOQ); and
2. Bona fide seniority system.

Under the **bona fide occupational qualification** defense, an employer can adopt an otherwise discriminatory employment practice if it is "reasonably necessary to the normal operations of that particular business . . ." (42 U.S.C. § 2000e-2(e)(1)).

Generally, the BFOQ defense applies to all types of discrimination except race discrimination, because race is not a bona fide occupational qualification. This defense is more often successful in cases where generic sexual characteristics (height or weight) or sexual privacy (hospital nurses or orderlies for same-sex patients) are at issue, as discussed in the case below.

Dothard v. Rawlinson, 433 U.S. 321 (1977)

Facts:

Dianne Rawlinson, a 22-year old college graduate whose major course study had been correctional psychology, was refused employment as a prison guard in Alabama. Ms. Rawlinson failed to meet the minimum 120-pound weight requirement (established by an Alabama statute) for prison guards.

Ms. Rawlinson filed an EEOC charge, received a right to sue letter, and then filed a complaint on behalf of herself and other similarly situated women challenging the statutory height and weight minimum as a violation of Title VII and the Equal Protection Clause of the Fourteenth Amendment.

Opinion by Justice Stewart:

Although women 18 years of age or older compose 52.75% of the Alabama population and 30.80% of its total labor force, they hold only 12.9% of its correctional positions. In considering the effect of the minimum height and weight standards on this disparity in rate of hiring between the sexes, the District Court found that the 5'2" requirement would operate to exclude 33.29% of the women in the United States between the ages of 18–79, while excluding only 1.28% of men between the same ages. The 120-pound weight restriction would exclude 22.29% of the women and 2.35% of the men in this age group. When the height and weight restrictions are combined, Alabama's statutory standards would exclude 41.13% of the female population, while excluding less than 1% of the male population.

. . . [R]eliance on general population demographic data was not misplaced where there was no reason to suppose that physical height and weight characteristics of Alabama men and women differ markedly from those of the national population.

For these reasons, we cannot say that the District Court was wrong in holding that the statutory height and weight standards had a discriminatory impact on women applicants.

We turn, therefore, to the appellants' argument that they have rebutted the prima facie case of discrimination by showing that the height and weight requirements are job related. These requirements, they say, have a relationship to strength, a sufficient, but unspecified amount of which is essential to effective job performance as a correctional counselor. In the District Court, however, the appellants produced no evidence correlating the height and weight requirements with the requisite amount of strength thought essential to good job performance.

For the reasons we have discussed, the District Court was not in error in holding that Title VII of the Civil Rights Act of 1964, as amended prohibits application of the statutory height and weight requirements to Rawlinson and the class she represents.

The judgment is accordingly affirmed in part, and reversed in part, and the case is remanded to the District Court for further proceedings consistent with this opinion.

The court found that the company's seniority system in the *Int'l Bhd. of Teamsters* case discussed at length below was entirely bona fide and applied equally to all races and ethnic groups. In that case, the overwhelming majority who were discouraged from transferring to line-driver jobs were white, not black or Spanish-surnamed employees. The court conceded that the seniority system did not have its genesis in racial discrimination, and that it was negotiated and maintained free from any illegal purpose.

The court further held in this case that "an otherwise neutral, legitimate seniority system does not become unlawful under Title VII simply because it may perpetuate pre-Act discrimination. Congress did not intend to make it illegal for employees with vested seniority rights to continue to exercise those rights, even at the expense of pre-Act discriminatees."

Under the *McDonnell Douglas* model, if a plaintiff succeeds in making a *prima facie* case of discrimination under Title VII, the burden then shifts to the employer to "articulate some legitimate nondiscriminatory reason for the employee's rejection." (*McDonnell Douglas Corporation v. Green*, 411 U.S. 792 (1973)). For years following the *McDonnell Douglas* decision, courts struggled with what kind of "burden" the employer really had. Was it a burden of proving a legitimate, nondiscriminatory reason (lack of a discriminatory motive)? Was the employer required to merely "articulate" or state a valid reason with no further showing? Was the burden somewhere in between?

In 1981, the Supreme Court settled the issue of the employer's "burden" with its decision in *Texas Department of Community Affairs v. Burdine*, 450 U.S. 248, 101 S. Ct. 1089, 67 L. Ed. 2d 207, 25 FEP 113 (1981). The Supreme Court unanimously described the defendant's rebuttal burden as "only the burden of explaining clearly" the nondiscriminatory reasons for its actions. The court continued:

. . . the defendant must clearly set forth, through the introduction of admissible evidence, the reasons for the plaintiff's rejection.

Rebutting the Complainant's Qualifications

One obvious rebuttal of a plaintiff's *prima facie* case claim that he/she was qualified for the position is the introduction of evidence that the plaintiff was in fact not "qualified."

While employment procedures must not be based on discriminatory considerations, the employer is not required to use those procedures that allow it to consider qualifications of the largest number of minority group applicants.

There are numerous other legitimate nondiscriminatory reasons that an employer may assert to rebut a *prima facie* case in addition to qualifications or experience, including poor attitude and an inability to "fit in" and work well with other employees.

Example An employee was terminated because he was not willing to work with others to meet production goals for an assembly line. The employer had transferred him to three different lines before terminating him because of his failure to "get along" with other employees. The employer has a legitimate nondiscriminatory reason to terminate this employee.

An employment action that adversely affects a member of a protected class may be justified for reasons that have nothing to do with the complainant's performance or job qualifications. These reasons may include budget constraints or even cronyism, as discussed in the case below.

Foster v. Dalton, 71 F.3d 52, 69 FEP 1402 (1st Cir. 1995)

Facts:

The female African-American plaintiff applied for a position as a management analyst with the Newport Naval Hospital. When the position became available, the plaintiff was the only applicant who was already working in the hospital. Under the hospital's established hiring procedures, she should have been guaranteed the job. Her name was on the list of potential candidates that was presented to the commander, who had the ultimate authority over hiring.

When the commander questioned why the name of one of his personal acquaintances was not on the list, he was told that the individual could not be offered employment at the grade specified for the position. At that point, the commander ordered that the job description be rewritten to classify the job at a lower grade for which his acquaintance would be eligible. He also ordered that the job description specify certain qualifications that his friend possessed.

The modified job description resulted in a new list with only one name on it—the acquaintance that the commander wanted to hire. Cronyism worked, and the commander's acquaintance was hired. The Court's decision noted that Title VII does not outlaw cronyism, and in this instance it provided a sufficient alternative explanation for the challenged deviation from the standard hiring procedure.

Opinion by Judge Selya:

Where, as here, a disappointed applicant has made no systematic effort to prove *pervasive* cronyism or to show that cronyism, when practiced in a particular workplace, regularly yields a racially discriminatory result, a disparate impact claim goes by the boards.

Because we cannot accept the appellant's invitation to create a presumption that the use of an old boy network in hiring constitutes per se racial discrimination, we are powerless to subvert the district court's election between conflicting inferences.

We need go no further. Title VII "does not presume to obliterate all manner of inequity, or to stanch once and for all, what a Scottish poet two centuries ago termed '[m]an's inhumanity to man,' (quoting Robert Burns, *Man Was Made to Mourn* (1786)). Like the court below, we find the conduct of the naval hierarchy in this case to be deserving of opprobrium, but two wrongs seldom make a right. Discerning no clear error in the district court's finding that favoritism, not racism, tainted Commander Travis' decision making we reject Foster's appeal.

Affirmed.

Person Hired or Promoted Was of Same Minority or Sex as Complainant

Evidence that the person hired or promoted is of the same minority or sex as that of the complainant is extremely helpful to the defendant's rebuttal in supporting a nondiscriminatory justification for its employment action. However, such evidence is not an absolute defense.

It can also be helpful to the defendant's case if the person who made the adverse employment decision was of the same minority or sex as that of the complainant.

Surviving a Pretext Allegation by Plaintiff

Once the plaintiff has established a *prima facie* case, the burden of proof shifts to the employer to prove a legitimate, nondiscriminatory reason for the adverse employment action. If the employer establishes a legitimate reason for its conduct, then the burden of proof shifts again to the plaintiff to prove that the employer's articulated reasons are not the real reasons for its action, but are a mere pretext for discrimination.

Generally, pretext is the critical issue in most individual disparate treatment cases. To prove pretext on the part of the employer, the employee must produce either direct evidence of an intent to discriminate, or circumstantial or inferential evidence of discriminatory intent. The courts have held that an employee's subjective belief alone, even if genuine, will not support a discrimination claim.

Mixed Motives

In many individual disparate treatment cases, the employer offers several reasons for its conduct. A **mixed motives case** is a situation where an employer offers both a legitimate and an illegitimate reason for the adverse action. The issue then becomes whether permissible or impermissible motives "caused" the employment decision at issue.

Prima Facie *Case—Mixed Motives*

The Civil Rights Act of 1991 codified the burdens of proof applicable in mixed motive cases brought under federal law. (*See* Pub. L. No. 102–166, 105 Stat. 107, codified at 42 U.S.C. § 2000e-2(m) (1991)).

The plaintiff states a *prima facie* case of discrimination by proving that race, sex, or some other illegitimate criterion was a motivating factor in the employment decision, even if the employer also considered other, legitimate criteria. Once the plaintiff makes this *prima facie* showing, the employer must prove that it would have taken the same action in the absence of the illegitimate reason, as discussed by the court in the case below.

Hopkins v. Price Waterhouse, 920 F.2d 967 (D.C Cir. 1990)

Facts:

Hopkins, an accountant, alleged that she was denied partnership at Price Waterhouse because of gender-based stereotypes. Although her work had been highly praised, several partners had told her that she was overly aggressive, "macho," and needed a "course at charm school." Another partner advised her to "walk more femininely, talk more femininely, dress more femininely, wear make-up, have her hair styled, and wear jewelry."

In response to the trial court's finding that Price Waterhouse had impermissibly considered the plaintiff's gender, the firm argued that it would have denied her partnership based upon her lack of interpersonal skills even if it had not considered her gender. The Supreme Court affirmed the lower court's finding of unlawful discrimination against the plaintiff and ordered that the firm grant her admission to partnership. The case went back to the district court, and then went up on appeal for a second time.

Opinion by Judge Edwards:

. . . we can upset Judge Gesell's conclusions that Price Waterhouse failed to prove that it would have deferred Ms. Hopkins' candidacy for partnership in 1983 regardless of her sex only if that conclusion "is based on an utterly implausible account of the evidence." Here, we find no such flaw. Therefore, we affirm the District Court's finding of liability.

We find no error in Judge Gesell's finding that Ms. Hopkins was constructively discharged when Price Waterhouse informed her that she would not be renominated for partnership.

. . . [T]he District Court grounded its finding of constructive discharge both in the law of the case doctrine *and* in the fact that this court's earlier constructive discharge ruling has since become the established law of the circuit.

Price Waterhouse also asserts that the District Court had no authority to order admission to partnership to remedy a Title VII violation. Price Waterhouse's argument is apparently that while Title VII extends far enough to protect an employee against discrimination in partnership consideration, it comes to an abrupt halt once a violation has been found, leaving the employee with the promise of fair consideration for partnership but no effective means of enforcing it. This argument seems absurd in the light of the Supreme Court's decision in *Hishon v. King & Spalding*, 467 U.S. 69, 104 S.Ct. 2229, 81 L.Ed. 2d 59 (1984), in which the Court held that "nothing in the change in status that advancement to partnership might entail means that partnership consideration falls outside the terms of [Title VII]." Given the Court's judgment in *Hishon*, and after careful review of Title VII, its legislative history and the case law interpreting it, we find that the District Court clearly acted within the bounds of the remedial authority conferred by the statute.

The Civil Rights Act of 1991 substantially modified the dual motive approach of *Price Waterhouse* in its new § 703(m), which states that "an unlawful employment practice is established when the complaining party demonstrates that race, color, religion, sex or national origin was a *motivating factor* for any employment practice, even though other factors also motivated the practice." (Emphasis added). Accordingly, the plaintiff must state a *prima facie* case of discrimination by proving that his or her protected status of race, sex, or other characteristic was a motivating factor in the employment decision, even if the employer also considered another, legitimate criteria in the employment decision.

The plaintiff's burden is higher in mixed motive cases brought under the Age Discrimination in Employment Act (ADEA). In age cases, the plaintiff must prove "not merely that age was one factor which contributed to the employment decision challenged, but that it was a determining factor," according to the court's findings in *Cunningham v. Cent. Beverage, Inc.*, 486 F. Supp. 59, 60–61 (N.D. Tex. 1980).

Defenses to Mixed Motives

Once the *prima facie* case has been established, the employer must prove that it would have taken the same action in the absence of the illegitimate reason. An employer cannot merely offer a legitimate and sufficient reason for its decision if that reason did not motive the employer at the time of the decision. An employer may not meet its burden of proof by merely showing that at the time of the decision it was motivated only in part by a legitimate reason. The employer must show that its legitimate reason, standing alone, would have induced it to make the same employment decision.

Systemic Disparate Treatment

Systemic disparate treatment is a pattern of discrimination against one general protected group, rather than an isolated case of discrimination against an individual employee.

Prima Facie *Case—Systemic Disparate Treatment*

The employee must show that the employer's policy or policies have a disparate effect on a protected class, and that the disparate effect is a result of the intent to discriminate. A major difference between individual and systemic disparate treatment is the type of evidence that is required to prove the intent.

Evidence of systemic disparate treatment is normally established by direct evidence that establishes the employer has a formal policy of discrimination, or by statistical evidence that reveals an underlying policy of disparate treatment. Few employers today have a formal policy of discrimination. Consequently, most systemic disparate treatment claims are supported by either indirect or circumstantial (statistical) evidence of discrimination. Statistics to show an imbalance of a protected class are valuable because this imbalance is often a sign of discrimination, as noted by the court in the case below.

Int'l Bhd. of Teamsters v. United States, 431 U.S. 324 (1977)

Facts:

This case grew out of alleged unlawful employment practices engaged in by an employer (a common carrier of motor freight with nationwide operations) and a union representing a large group of its employees. Both the district court and the court of appeals held that the employer had violated Title VII by engaging in a pattern and practice of employment discrimination against blacks and Spanish-surnamed Americans, and that the union had violated the Act by agreeing with the employer to create and maintain a seniority system that perpetuated the effects of past racial and ethnic discrimination.

The government carried its burden of proof through both statistical evidence and testimony of individuals who related over 40 specific instances of discrimination. On the statistical side of the case, the government proved that as of March 31, 1971, shortly after the government filed its complaint alleging system-wide discrimination, the company had 6,472 employees. Only 314 (5%) of the employees were blacks and 257 (4%) were Spanish-surnamed Americans. In the higher paying job of line drivers, there were 1,828 in that position, but only 8 (0.4%) were black and 5 (0.3%) were Spanish-surnamed persons, and all of the blacks had been hired after the litigation had commenced. A majority of the blacks (83%) and Spanish-surnamed Americans (78%) who worked for the company held lower-paying city operations and serviceman jobs, whereas only 39% of the nonminority employees held jobs in those categories.

The company claimed that the statistics revealing racial imbalance were misleading because they failed to take into account the company's particular situation as of the effective date of Title VII. While the company conceded that its line drivers were virtually all white in July 1965, it claims that thereafter business conditions caused a drop in its work force. The company argued that low personnel turnover, rather than post-Title VII discrimination, accounted for the more recent statistical disparities. Both the district court and the court of appeals, however, found that the government had proved a *prima facie* case of systemic and purposeful employment discrimination, continuing well beyond the effective date of Title VII.

Opinion by Justice Stewart:

To conclude that a person's failure to submit an application for a job does not inevitably and forever foreclose his entitlement to seniority relief under Title VII is a far cry, however, from holding that nonapplicants are always entitled to such relief. A nonapplicant must show that he was a potential victim of unlawful discrimination. Because he is necessarily claiming that he was deterred from applying for the job by the employer's discriminatory practices, his is the not always easy burden of proving that he would have applied for the job had it not been for those practices.

The known prospect of discriminatory rejection shows only that employees who wanted line-driving jobs may have been deterred from applying for them. It does not show which of the nonapplicants actually wanted such jobs or which possessed the requisite qualification.

For all the reasons that we have discussed, the judgment of the Court of Appeals is vacated, and the cases are remanded to the District Court for further proceedings consistent with this opinion.

In the above case, if the plaintiff proved that an alleged individual discriminatee unsuccessfully applied for a job and therefore was a potential victim of the proven discrimination, the burden of proof then shifted to the employer to demonstrate that the individual applicant was denied an employment opportunity for lawful reasons. The company asserted that a person who had not actually applied for a job (such as line driver) could *never* be awarded seniority relief.

The effects of discriminatory employment practices and the injuries suffered from such practices are not always confined to those who were expressly denied a requested employment opportunity. A consistently enforced discriminatory policy would obviously deter job applications from those employees who were aware of the discriminatory policy and were not willing to subject themselves to the humiliation of certain rejection. The court found that such a person is as much a victim of discrimination as a person who went through the motions of submitting a job application.

However, the court ruled that the known prospect of discriminatory rejection shows only the possibility of deterrence from applying for line-driving jobs, but it does not show which of the nonapplicants actually wanted such jobs, or which of the nonapplicants possessed the requisite job qualifications.

Defenses to Systemic Disparate Treatment

In addition to the defenses listed for an individual disparate treatment claim, an employer may utilize these defenses to a claim of systemic disparate treatment:

- challenge the statistical techniques and analyses used by the employee;
- challenge the facts upon which the plaintiff's statistical case is based; and
- challenge the inference of **discriminatory intent** of the statistics.

Systemic Disparate Impact

Courts have defined **systemic disparate impact** as employment practices that are neutral on their face in the treatment of different groups, but which fall more heavily on one group than another and cannot be justified by business necessity. This theory of employment discrimination is also known as the **adverse impact theory**.

The theory of systemic disparate impact originated in *Griggs v. Duke Power Co.*, 401 U.S. 424 (1971), discussed below, but was drastically changed in *Wards Cove Packing Co., Inc. v. Atonio*, 490 U.S. 642 (1989).

Griggs v. Duke Power Co., 401 U.S. 424 (1971)

Facts:

Black employees brought this action under Title VII of the Civil Rights Act of 1964, challenging the employer's requirement of a high school diploma or the passing of intelligence tests as a condition of employment in or transfer to jobs at the power plant. They alleged that the requirements are not job related and have the effect of disqualifying blacks from employment or transfer at a higher rate than whites.

The court of appeals held that the testing requirement did not violate Title VII because there was no showing of a discriminatory purpose. The Supreme Court reversed, and held that the testing requirement violated Title VII regardless of its intended purpose.

The Supreme Court noted that the black petitioners had long received inferior education in segregated schools, and the Supreme Court had previously expressly recognized those differences in *Gaston County v. United States*, 395 U.S. 285 (1969). In that case, because of the inferior education received by blacks in North Carolina, the Supreme Court barred the institution of a literacy test for voter registration on the grounds that the test would indirectly abridge the right to vote because of race.

Opinion by Justice Burger:

Congress did not intend by Title VII, however, to guarantee a job to every person regardless of qualifications. In short, the Act does not command that any person be hired simply because he was formerly the subject of discrimination or because he is a member of a minority group ... What is required by Congress is the removal of artificial, arbitrary, and unnecessary barriers to employment when the barriers operate invidiously to discriminate on the basis of racial or other impermissible classification ... The touchstone is business necessity. If an employment practice which operates to exclude Negroes cannot be shown to be related to job performance, the practice is prohibited.

The judgment of the Court of Appeals is, as to that portion of the judgment appealed from, reversed.

Prima Facie *Case—Systemic Disparate Impact*

The plaintiff is required to present only enough evidence that, more likely than not, the challenged test, criterion, or practice had a disparate impact. A simple statistical comparison will support a finding that a test had a disparate impact where the pool taking the challenged test is reasonably homogeneous in terms of qualifications and the racial disparity in test results is quite large.

Griggs explains that a *prima facie* case of discrimination can be made by showing that the testing device, neutral on its face, in practice operates to disproportionately bar members of the plaintiff's class from employment. It is not necessary to go through the *McDonnell Douglas* steps to make out a *prima facie* case in the *Griggs* situation, since the issue is the legality of the test itself. Because the objective is to demonstrate the disparate impact of a test or other neutral factor, statistics on the impact of the test or factor on the protected group in question are not only relevant to a *prima facie* showing, but they are often the principal, and sometimes the sole, vehicle for making such a showing.

The *Griggs* type of proof applies also to situations where the crux of the contro-

versy is some intermediate device or practice, such as a seniority system or a classification system, neutral on its face, that can be shown statistically to have a discriminatory impact.

Unlike the disparate treatment case, where the burden of persuasion remains at all times with the plaintiff, in the disparate impact case, once a plaintiff has demonstrated the disparate impact of a test or other neutral device, the burden then transfers to the defendant to persuade the court that the challenged practice is "job related for the position in question and consistent with business necessity" (Civil Rights Act of 1991, PL 102–166, § 105 (1991)). This section of the statute overruled the previous ruling of the Supreme Court in *Wards Cove Packing Co. v. Atonio*, 490 U.S. 642, 109 S. Ct. 2115, 104 L. Ed. 2d 961, 49 FEP 1519 (1989) in which the Court stated that if a *prima facie* case of disparate impact has been made, the burden on the defendant to justify the neutral practice was one of production of evidence, not of proof, and that the burden of proving discrimination remained at all times with the plaintiff.

The line between the disparate impact and disparate treatment case is not always clear. It is not uncommon for both claims to arise in the same litigation, sometimes on the same facts, and for the issue to arise as to what theory or combination of theories is appropriate to the particular fact situation.

The EEOC has issued guidelines interpreting 703(h) of Title VII to permit only the use of *job-related tests*. This interpretation comports with the congressional intent of the Act. While nothing in the Act precludes the use of testing, Congress has forbidden considering testing as a controlling force in an employment decision unless the tests are a demonstrated measure of job performance. Congress has not demanded that the less qualified applicants or employees be preferred over the better qualified simply because of minority origins. Rather, Congress has required that any tests used for employment decisions must measure the person *for the job*.

In *Wards Cove Packing Co. v. Atonio*, 490 U.S. 642 (1989), the Supreme Court modified the *Griggs* disparate impact proof requirement to make it more analogous to the *McDonnell Douglas* discriminatory treatment model discussed above.

The *Wards Cove* case involved the hiring practices of salmon canneries operated in Alaska. Predominantly nonwhite Filipino and Alaska natives staffed the unskilled cannery jobs, while primarily white persons staffed the relatively skilled noncannery positions. The Supreme Court set out the following discriminatory treatment model:

1. The plaintiff must initially establish, through appropriate statistical comparisons, that firm hiring practices have had a disparate impact upon a protected

group, and must identify the specific components of the hiring procedures that have caused the disproportionate impact.

2. Once a *prima facie* disparate impact case has been shown, the defendant employer must offer a nondiscriminatory business justification for the challenged components, but it is not required to prove that the challenged components are job-related.

3. The plaintiff must then rebut the proffered business qualification by demonstrating the existence of a less discriminatory, equally effective alternative selection technique.

The Supreme Court expressly indicated that cost should be considered when a court determines whether a less discriminatory alternative should be considered as effective as the challenged components.

The Civil Rights Act of 1991 codified the basic *Wards Cove* Steps I and III burdens, but reversed the Step II approach and reinstated the traditional *Griggs* burden-shifting concept under which employers must establish that employment criteria that cause a disparate impact on protected groups are job-related.

The employee/plaintiff has the initial burden of proving that the employer's policy or practice has an adverse impact on the members of a protected class. A plaintiff can make its *prima facie* case by proving a statistical imbalance resulting from the policy or practice at issue.

The courts have commonly applied the EEOC's **Four-Fifths or 80% Test** to determine whether an employment action has a discriminatory impact. This test concludes that there is evidence of an adverse impact in the selection process if the excluded group is selected at less than 80% of the selection rate for the preferred group. The courts have also used other statistical tests, such as standard deviation and regression analysis, to determine discriminatory impact of employment actions.

Defenses to Systemic Disparate Impact

Once the plaintiff has established a *prima facie* case, the burden shifts to the employer to prove that either the practice is not discriminatory, or that the discriminatory practice is both job-related and a business necessity.

Even when the employer proves the challenged practice or policy is job-related and there is a business necessity, the plaintiff can establish an unlawful employment practice based on adverse impact if he or she can prove an "alternative employment practice" exists that would achieve the employer's business interests with a less discriminatory effect, and the employer refuses to adopt the alternative practice (*See* 42 U.S.C. § 2000e-2(k)(1)(A)(ii)).

The courts require that the employer's testing procedures accurately "measure the person for the job and not the person in the abstract" (*Griggs*, 433 U.S. at 436). Thus, if the test accurately predicts how well the applicant will perform on the job, it is not discriminatory and is valid under Title VII.

REASONABLE ACCOMMODATION

Reasonable accommodation is a valid theory in employment discrimination cases originating under Title VII, but it primarily applies to cases under the Americans with Disabilities Act or cases involving religious discrimination. For information relating to reasonable accommodation issues in religious discrimination cases, refer to Chapter 12. Chapter 8 discusses what constitutes reasonable accommodation in ADA cases.

RETALIATION

Title VII prohibits retaliation by an employer against an employee or applicant because he or she opposed any employment practice that is unlawful under Title VII, filed a charge, testified, or participated in an investigation or proceeding under the statute.

To establish a *prima facie* case under section 704(a) of Title VII, the plaintiff must establish:

1. statutorily protected expression;
2. adverse employment action; and
3. a causal link between the protected expression and the adverse action.

See *Smalley v. City of Eatonville*, 640 F.2d 765 (5th Cir. 1981), discussed below.

Smalley v. City of Eatonville, 640 F.2d 765 (5th Cir. 1981)

Facts:

The plaintiff filed suit against the town of Eatonville, a small Florida municipality that claims to be the oldest and only all black community in the United States. The mayor, Vereen, was black. Eatonville hired Smalley, a white male, as its Finance Director in May 1975 through the federal Comprehensive Employment and Training Act (CETA) program, and fired him in May 1976.

In terminating Smalley, Eatonville and the other defendants considered several problems.

After he was hired, Smalley was convicted of forgery (a felony) in another state. This fact led the town to believe that it could not obtain the fidelity bond required by federal grants. The mayor also felt that Smalley's work on an important project to reassess property taxes had been inadequate and "grossly insubordinate." The town also considered a letter that Smalley had written to a CETA office complaining of "intolerable conditions caused by racial bias existing at Eatonville" and insinuating that the mayor might manufacture evidence of misconduct to justify terminating him.

The mayor suspended Smalley on May 10, 1976 by a letter that cited the bonding problems, his "gross insubordination" in connection with the reassessment report, and his complaint of "intolerable conditions caused by racial bias." Following his suspension and receipt of a right-to-sue letter from the EEOC, Smalley filed suit claiming racially discriminatory treatment.

Opinion by Judge Godbold:

We assume for purposes of discussion that the letter to Gilmore was protected "opposition" to prove a sufficient causal connection between his "opposition" and his dismissal. A causal connection is suggested by Smalley's direct evidence that the Mayor and Town Council considered his letter to Gilmore. But the City rebutted this showing with evidence of other reasons for discharge.

We cannot say that the letter did not play any part in the decision. But a dismissal based on numerous factors does not violate Title VII merely because an improper consideration played some part in the decision

The other reasons for firing Smalley—the inability to bond a convicted felon as Finance Director and the insubordinate character of Smalley's inadequate progress report—were clearly not a ruse or pretext. We assess the controversy over bonding a felon, the inadequate report, the insinuation that the Mayor might manufacture evidence, and the complaint of racial bias in light of the legal requirement that the plaintiff carry the ultimate burden of proving that he was fired because of his opposition to unlawful employment practices. We conclude that the defendants effectively rebutted Smalley's prima facie case.

AFFIRMED.

The requirement of "statutorily protected expression" requires conduct by the plaintiff that is in opposition to an unlawful employment practice of the defendant. Courts have been divided on whether *proof* of an actual unlawful employment practice is required.

If an employee is successful in establishing a *prima facie* case discriminatory retaliation, the burden shifts to the defendant to articulate a legitimate, nondiscriminatory reason for the employment decision. If the defendant carries its burden, then the plaintiff is entitled to an opportunity to show that the defendant's stated reasons for its employment decision was in fact pretextual. (See *McDonnell Douglas Corp. v. Green*, 411 U.S. 792 (1973), discussed earlier.)

RESPONSIBILITY OF TEMPORARY EMPLOYEES IN DISCRIMINATION CASES

In the *Magnuson* case discussed in Chapter 2, the temporary employee notified her supervisor of the on-site employer's harassing activity, reflecting her perception as to who her "employer" was at the time of the discrimination. While she viewed the temporary agency as her "legal" employer, *Magnuson* obviously viewed the on-site supervisor as an employer also.

To protect his or her rights, a temporary employee who has suffered discrimination should report the situation to the temporary agency immediately. The temporary employee may also want to inform someone in the on-site organization of the discrimination.

Liability of Temporary Agencies in Discrimination Cases

In most instances, the temporary agency is an employer for the purposes of Title VII. Agencies often believe that, because its employees have not committed the harassment, the agency has no liability. In addition, agencies often are afraid that a loss of business will result if it reports that a permanent employee of a client has harassed a temporary employee.

The courts have been clear that a temporary agency's failure to act will lead to a finding of liability on the part of the agency. (See *Magnuson v. Peck Technical Servs. Inc.*, 808 F. Supp. 500 (E.D. Va. 1992), discussed at length in Chapter 2.)

Responsibility of On-Site Employers for Discrimination Involving Temporary Employees

The on-site employer has a choice when a temporary employee accuses a permanent coworker of discrimination. It can assume the position that it is not the employer of the temporary employee and suggest that the temporary employee should contact the temporary agency, or the employer can investigate the allegations.

There are three reasons not to ignore the discrimination claims of a temporary employee:

1. There is a good chance that the on-site employer will be subject to liability as an employer under Title VII.
2. The permanent employee may not have limited his/her discriminatory behavior to the temporary employee. By exposing this behavior, the on-site employer may prevent the occurrence of future incidents.

3. By taking corrective action, the employer notifies all of its employees that the company will not tolerate such behavior.

REMEDIES AND DAMAGES FOR EMPLOYMENT DISCRIMINATION UNDER TITLE VII

Overview

Title VII provides remedies for unlawful employment discrimination that are designed to discourage or prevent the defendant from continuing discriminatory practices, and to return a victim of discriminatory action to the position that he or she would have enjoyed had the discrimination not occurred.

An employer or other defendant might be directed through a court injunction to stop its unlawful conduct and correct discriminatory practices. Another remedy is the return of an individual who is denied a job or fired from a job for discriminatory reasons to that position. This remedy might include awards of back pay, lost benefits, and lost seniority that resulted from the discrimination, or wage increases or promotion that would have most likely occurred had the job not been denied or taken away.

Additional monetary awards also are possible. There are circumstances where the employer is ordered to hire, promote, or reinstate, but individuals may obtain "front pay" in addition to back pay. **Front pay** represents future earnings that are lost because an employee has difficulty securing another job after he or she has suffered discrimination. **Compensatory damages**—damages awarded for the actual loss suffered by a plaintiff—are available under Title VII, the ADA, and other laws for physical or emotional harm suffered from discrimination. Plaintiffs who succeed in litigation also may be entitled to reasonable attorney's fees and court costs.

Punitive damages may be awarded to discourage defendants from acting maliciously or in reckless disregard of the law. Under the federal age discrimination and equal pay laws, the courts award liquidated damages for willful violations, rather than punitive damages. **Liquidated damages** (an amount equal to lost wages and benefits) serve the same purpose as punitive damages.

Plaintiff's Duty to Mitigate Damages

The plaintiff who loses his or her job because of employment discrimination has a duty to **mitigate damages** by using reasonable diligence to seek other employment substantially equivalent to his or her previous position. An employer bears the burden of showing that a plaintiff failed to mitigate his/her damages. If the employer proves failure to mitigate, then the damages are reduced accordingly. (See EEOC Policy Guide on Compensatory and Punitive Damages Under the 1991 Civil Rights Act, § II (A)(1)).

An exception to the mitigation requirement is the case of a plaintiff who has been unable to work because of psychological problems suffered from the sexual harassment. (See *EEOC v. Gurnee Inn Corp.*, 48 FEP Cases 871, 882 (N.D. Ill. 1988) *aff'd* 914 F.2d 815 (7th Cir. 1990)).

Damages Available Prior to 1991

Prior to the 1991 amendment to Title VII, damages available in an employment discrimination lawsuit included solely back pay, front pay, and attorneys' fees, where appropriate. The primary purpose under Title VII relief for a discharge was to award back pay to alleviate the "lingering ill effects" of employment discrimination (See *Ford Motor Company v. EEOC*, 458 U.S. 219, 102 S.Ct. 3057, 73 L.ED.2d 721 (1982)).

Compensatory Damages

The Civil Rights Act of 1991 amended Title VII so that a victim of *intentional* sex discrimination arising after the effective date of the Civil Rights Act of 1991 can recover compensatory damages from private and public employers (42 U.S.C. § 1981a(a)(1). Damages may not be available in certain cases where the employers acted with both legitimate and unlawful motive (mixed motive) (42 U.S.C. § 2000e-2(m). (See also EEOC Revised Enforcement Guide on Recent Developments in Disparate Treatment Theory.)

Compensatory damages may include future pecuniary losses, emotional pain, suffering inconvenience, mental anguish, and loss of enjoyment of life and other nonpecuniary losses. Compensatory damages do not include back pay (discussed below) or interest (42 U.S. C. § 1981a(b) (2) and (3)).

The total amount of compensatory and punitive damages that may be recovered under Title VII is subject to a cap that varies with the size of the employer as follows:

Number of Employees	Cap on Total Amount
15–100	$ 50,000
101–200	$100,000
201–500	$200,000
501 or more	$300,000

Source: 42 U.S.C. § 1981(a)(b)(3).

The number of employees in each category must be maintained in each of 20 or more calendar weeks in the current and preceding year (42 U.S.C. § 1981(a)(b)(3)).

Compensatory damages are awarded to compensate a plaintiff for losses or suffering inflicted due to the discriminatory conduct or act. Compensatory damages include both pecuniary and nonpecuniary losses. A causal connection between the harm and the discriminatory conduct must be established before the plaintiff may be awarded compensatory damages (pecuniary and nonpecuniary).

Nonpecuniary damages (noneconomic losses) are losses for the intangible injuries of emotional harm, such as emotional pain, suffering, inconvenience, mental anguish, loss of enjoyment of life, injury to professional standing, injury to character and reputation, and loss of harm. Emotional harm will not be presumed simply because the plaintiff is a victim of discrimination. In a hostile environment case, if a reasonable person *perceives* the sexual conduct as hostile, no psychological injury is required. Proof that the plaintiff caused some or all the emotional harm, or that the symptoms of emotional harm preceded the discrimination, will undermine or defeat the claim for compensatory damages.

When a plaintiff's emotional harm is due in part to personal difficulties that are not caused or exacerbated by the discriminatory conduct, the employer is liable only for the harm resulting from the discriminatory conduct (See *Vance v. Southern Bell Telephone & Telegraph Co.*, 863 F.2d 1503, 1516 (11th Cir. 1989)), discussed below, in which the plaintiff was awarded over $1 million in damages).

Vance v. Southern Bell Telephone & Telegraph Co., 863 F.2d 1503, 1516 (11th Cir. 1989)

Facts:

Vance, a black woman, found what appeared to be a noose hanging from the light fixture above her work station about a week after her transfer into the department. Two days later, she again found the noose hanging from her light fixture. She removed the noose and threw it into the trash, but did not report the incident to her employer at the time. Vance later reported the incident, but her employer did little about the problem.

Opinion by Judge Fay:

. . . in order to determine whether a hostile environment is severe enough to adversely affect a reasonable employee, the law requires that the finder of fact examine not only the frequency of the incidents, but the gravity of the incidents as well. Viewing all the evidence in context, we believe that Vance satisfied her burden of producing evidence sufficient to create a jury question on her section 1981 claim.

Assuming that Vance is able to show harassment sufficient to sustain a claim under Title

VII or section 1981, there are two theories under which a corporate defendant can be held liable for hostile environment harassment at the workplace. First, where the hostile environment is created by one who is not the plaintiff's employer (i.e., a co-worker) the employer may be held liable through *respondeat superior* if the plaintiff can establish that the employer knew or should have known of the harassment and failed to take remedial action. The plaintiff can prove that the employer knew of the harassment by showing either that she complained to higher management or that the harassment was pervasive enough to charge the employer with constructive knowledge.

Second, where the harasser is himself the plaintiff's employer, or an agent of the employer, the employer is directly, rather than indirectly liable for the harassment. Under this scenario "respondeat superior theory" does not apply and plaintiff need not establish that she gave anyone notice of the harassment." Thus, a jury could properly hold the company liable for damages under section 1981 by finding that the illegal acts were committed by someone deemed to be the plaintiff's employer. In such a case, whether his superiors know or should have known what he did is irrelevant.

Vance produced substantial evidence that Southern Bell failed to investigate the noose incidents even after they were brought to its attention. Vance produced evidence from which a reasonable jury could conclude that in creating a hostile work environment, her supervisor acted as an agent of Southern Bell under the standard outlined above. AFFIRMED in part, REVERSED in part, and REMANDED for a new trial.

Punitive Damages

Since the 1991 amendments to the Civil Rights Act, punitive damages are now available in sexual discrimination lawsuits, but only in disparate treatment cases and only against private employers. An employer must act "with malice or with reckless indifference to the federally protected rights of an aggrieved individual, and egregious intentional discrimination must be found before punitive damages are available (42 U.S.C. § 1981a(b)(1)). **Malice** is defined as ill will, intentionally harming someone, having no moral or legal justification for harming someone.

A liability finding alone does not entitle a plaintiff to an award of punitive damages. The EEOC has set out the following factors that may be considered to determine whether conduct was committed with malice or reckless indifference to the plaintiff's federally protected rights:

1. The degree of egregiousness and nature of the employer's conduct;
2. The nature, extent, and severity of the harm to the complaining party;
3. The duration of the discriminatory conduct;
4. The existence and frequency of similar past discriminatory conduct by the employer;
5. The employer's actions after it was informed of discrimination.

6. Proof of threats or deliberate retaliatory action against complaining parties for complaints to management or filing a charge.

The above list is nonexclusive, and other relevant factors also may be considered. (See EEOC Guide on Compensatory and Punitive Damages under the Civil Rights Act.) Punitive damage awards should "bear some relation to the character of the defendant's act along with the nature and extent of the harm to the plaintiff that the defendant caused." (See *Rowlett v Anheuser-Busch*, 832 F.2d 194, 207 (1st Cir 1987), *quoting Restatement (Second) of Torts*, § 908(2)).

Back Pay

Back pay may be awarded to compensate for economic injury that the plaintiff has suffered as a result of sexual harassment (42 U.S.C. § 2000e-5(g)(1)). The calculation of back pay encompasses not only lost "straight-time" salary, but may include overtime, commissions, bonuses, shift differentials, pay raises, tips, vacation, sick pay, pension, severance pay, profit sharing, and insurance. Back pay is not subject to damages caps. (See EEOC Policy Guide on Compensatory and Punitive Damages under the 1991 Civil Rights Act.)

Interim earnings, or the amount that the plaintiff could have earned with reasonable diligence by the plaintiff, reduces the back pay allowable (42 U.S.C. § 2000e-5(g)(1)). Deductions other than interim earnings are within the discretion of the court.

Back pay liability may not accrue from a date more than two years prior to the filing of the charge or complaint of discrimination (42 U.S.C. § 2000e-5(g)). In actual or constructive discharge cases. back pay accrues from the date of the discharge or resignation. In a case where the plaintiff was denied a promotion, the back pay period begins with the denial of the promotion.

The back pay period typically ends when the court renders judgment. It can end sooner, if, for example, the plaintiff ceases to suffer adverse economic consequences by securing a higher-paying job.

Front Pay

If reinstatement is not ordered because either the plaintiff did not request reinstatement, or the continuing hostility makes reinstatement unwise, a plaintiff may be entitled to front pay. **Front pay** is the difference between what the plaintiff would have earned in the absence of discrimination, and what he or she will earn on a new job. The court has the discretion to determine the point at which front pay will be terminated. Front pay is not subject to the damage caps.

Injunctions

A court-ordered **injunction** requires violators of antidiscrimination laws to cease their discriminatory conduct and to refrain from committing future violations. Injunctive relief also may require employers to alter practices that have a disparate impact. Courts determine the need for injunctive relief based on the likelihood that discriminatory conduct will recur.

Injunctions are generally issued in cases where the acts of discrimination are severe or pervasive, or where an employer has committed other discriminatory violations in the past. However, injunctive relief may be granted on the basis of only one violation.

Injunctions may be either permanent or for a limited duration, depending upon the circumstances. Violations of injunctions are enforced through the courts' contempt power, and contempt may result in an order for further affirmative steps by the employer, supervision of remedial efforts, fines, or even incarceration.

Attorneys' Fees and Costs

Title VII provides for recovery of attorneys' fees by prevailing plaintiffs. Courts have broad discretion to award attorneys' fees in order to provide an incentive to challenge discriminatory practices by employers. Fees may be awarded regardless of an employer's good faith or lack of discriminatory intent.

In order to recover attorneys' fees, a plaintiff must succeed on a significant issue in its lawsuit and must receive at least some of the relief sought in the lawsuit. The success does not have to be on the main issue.

The first step in determining attorney's fees is to multiple the number of hours reasonably expended by a reasonable hourly rate to arrive at a **lodestar** figure. Prevailing market rates in the community determine a reasonable rate. Once a lodestar amount has been determined, a court then adjusts for the following factors:

- extent of success;
- time and labor required;
- difficulty of issues;
- skill required;
- customary fees;
- impact on other legal work;
- amount of money involved;
- experience, reputation and ability of the attorneys; and
- awards in other cases.

(See *Johnson v. Georgia Highway Express, Inc.*, 488 F.2d 714 (5th Cir. 1974)).

Interest

In Title VII cases, courts generally exercise their discretion to order an employer to pay prejudgment and postjudgment interest on the back pay award (See *Loeffler v. Frank*, 486 U.S. 549, 557–558 (1988)).

REMEDIES AND DAMAGES AVAILABLE UNDER THE ADEA

The remedies for a violation of the ADEA include compensatory damages, including back pay, front pay, and reinstatement. Attorneys' fees may also be awarded. A finding that a violation was willful entitles the plaintiff to an award of liquidated damages equal to the amount of back pay.

Compensatory Damages

A showing of a violation under the ADEA entitles the plaintiff to recover compensatory damages, including reinstatement, back pay and front pay. (See Chapter 9.) Whether reinstatement is feasible is a question for the court and may not be submitted to the jury (*Deloach v. Delchamps, Inc.*, 897 F.2d 815, 823 (5th Cir 1990). Factors that the court will consider include:

1. whether the defendant/employer is still in business;
2. whether the particular business for which the plaintiff worked and was qualified is still in operation;
3. whether the same or a comparable position is available;
4. the extent to which the defendant has demonstrated such extreme hostility that a productive and amicable working relationship would be impossible; and
5. the extent to which the litigation itself has created animosity between the plaintiff and defendant. (See *Woodhouse v. Magnolia Hosp.*, 92 F.3d 248, 257 (5th Cir. 1996), discussed in Chapter 9.)

Front pay may only be awarded where reinstatement is not possible or inappropriate, such as in the case of a reduction in force discharge, and, even under those circumstances, several courts have expressed concern over the speculative nature of front pay.

Liquidated Damages

After basic liability is established, a finding that the violation was willful entitles the plaintiff to an award of liquidated damages equal to double the amount owed. The courts have determined that the test for willful violation requires more than a showing of disparate treatment or intentional discrimination, but less than a demonstration of outrageous conduct. An employment decision may be unreasonable without being willful.

Willfulness is a question of fact for a jury to decide. The Supreme Court provided guidance on the willfulness issue in *Hazen Paper Co. v. Biggins,* 507 U.S. 604 (1993). In that case, the Court interpreted the term "willful" in connection with the ADEA to mean that the employer "knew or showed reckless disregard for the matter of whether its conduct was prohibited."

In *Hazen,* the 60-year-old plaintiff was terminated shortly before his pension benefits were to vest, for reasons the employer claimed were unrelated to age. The plaintiff claimed an ADEA violation on the basis that his pension and his age were inextricably intertwined. In that case, the Court found that pensions vest according to years of service, not necessarily age, so an ADEA violation did not exist based on those facts alone.

Hazen set out two separate tiers or degrees of liability—one willful, the other not willful. The Court further held that a plaintiff need not demonstrate outrageous conduct, or that age was the predominant factor, rather than a determinative factor, in order to recover double damages, as some cases previously held.

Punitive Damages Excluded by ADEA

Congress intended ADEA remedies to be compensatory, not punitive. Consistent with this intent, courts have held that ADEA plaintiffs are not entitled to punitive damages or damages for pain and suffering.

Attorneys' Fees and Costs

The ADEA provides for recovery of attorney's fees by prevailing plaintiffs. Courts have broad discretion to award attorneys' fees in order to provide an incentive to challenge discriminatory practices. Fees may be awarded regardless of an employer's good faith or lack of discriminatory intent.

A plaintiff must be successful on a significant issue in the lawsuit and receive at least some of the relief sought in order to recover attorneys' fees. The fact that a plaintiff receives only nominal back pay does not preclude an award of attorney's fees. Additionally, fees will not be denied to a plaintiff who wins back pay but is denied front pay or liquidated damages.

Civil Penalties

The EEOC also may assess civil penalties of up to $1,000 for each willful violation of the ADEA.

DAMAGES AVAILABLE UNDER THE FMLA

Damages available for FMLA violations include:

- wages;
- benefits;
- other compensation denied or lost to the employee;
- actual monetary loss resulting from the violation;
- interest on any amount awarded;
- liquidated damages equal to the amount of actual damages if the court determines that the violation was not in good faith and that the employer lacked reasonable grounds to believe that it was complying with the Act;
- equitable remedies, including employment, reinstatement and promotion;
- attorney and expert witness fees; and
- costs.

(See 29 C.F.R. § 825400(c)).

REMEDIES AND DAMAGES AVAILABLE FOR ADA DISCRIMINATION

Individuals who are successful in ADA lawsuits may be awarded:

1. Money damages, including back pay, compensatory damages (for emotional pain and suffering, mental anguish, loss of enjoyment of life), punitive damages, interest, and, possibly, front pay;
2. Lost benefits;
3. Attorney's fees, expert witness fees, and certain litigation costs; and
4. Injunctive relief (reinstatement or required accommodation).

TERMS

adverse impact
back pay
bona fide occupational qualification
compensatory damages
disparate impact
disparate treatment
front pay
individual disparate treatment

injunction
liquidated damages
lodestar
malice
mitigate damages
mixed motives case
nonpecuniary damages
punitive damages
systemic disparate impact
systemic disparate treatment

REVIEW QUESTIONS

1. Under what circumstances is an employer able to invoke a bona fide occupational qualification defense?

2. Explain the EEOC's Four-Fifths or 80% Test.

3. A female plaintiff who had applied for a job as a welder sued under Title VII, alleging sex discrimination in the defendant's hiring practices. The employer had been reluctant in the past to hire female welders. At the time of the plaintiff's application for employment as a welder, the employer was not hiring any welders, male or female. Would the court find sex discrimination in this case? Why or why not? Would the plaintiff have prevailed in her lawsuit if the employer had been hiring welders at the time of her application? (*East v. Romine, Inc.*, 518 F.2d 331, 11 FEP 300 (5th Cir. 1975)).

4. In question 3 above, would the plaintiff prevail if the employer had an opening, but the position was filled by the time that the plaintiff applied? (*Daves v. Payless Cashways, Inc.*, 661 F.2d 1022, 27 FEP 706 (5th Cir. 1981)).

5. The plaintiff filed a claim with the EEOC the day after a preliminary interview, alleging that she had been discriminated against because of her sex when the employer did not hire her. She claimed that the interviewer had told her that the company was not interested in hiring women for insurance agent positions. Did the employer have an opportunity to actually "reject" her for employment? Would the court find a Title VII discrimination occurred in this case? (*Consor v. Occidental Life Insurance Co.*, 469 F. Supp. 1110 (N.D. Tex. 1979).)

6. A tenured professor in the physical education department at the defendant university, was rejected in her bid for the department chairmanship in favor of a male candidate who had been chosen even before the existence of a vacancy had been publicized. The male candidate lacked previous experience heading other departments of physical education, which was the same qualification that plaintiff had been told was the reason that she had not been selected for the vacancy. Another suspect qualification was the principal reason for the hiring of the male candidate—that "he had gone to a high school in California with two swimming pools, that he could probably teach swimming and that he had a nationwide breadth of experience." Would the court find sex discrimination in this case? On what grounds? (*Greer v. University of Ark. Bd. Of Trustees*, 544 F. Supp. 1085, 33 FEP 77 (E.D. Ark. 1982), *aff'd in pertinent part sub nom.*, *Behlar v. Smith*, 719 F.2d 950, 33 FEP 92 (8th Cir. 1983), *cert. denied*, 466 U.S. 958, 104 S. Ct. 2169, 80 L. Ed. 2 552, 34 FEP 1096 (1984)).

7. The plaintiff alleged that she had been constructively discharged from her employment as a research assistant when she was replaced by a woman who was less qualified in that she did not have a doctorate. Did the fact that she was replaced by a woman negate her claim of discrimination? Why or why not? If the court ruled in the plaintiff's favor, what would be the basis for its ruling? (*Welch v. University of Tex.*, 659 F.2d 531, 26 FEP 1725 (5th Cir. 1981)).

8. Bonaparte, a 54-year-old black female, was employed by the U.S. Postal Service and was in charge of a "dead letter office." Following her demotion, she filed a Title VII claim, charging race, sex, age, and retaliation. The defendant claimed that the reason it demoted the plaintiff was that her supervisors believed that it was her poor management that had caused the problems in the office. Bonaparte failed to show that the defendant's proffered reason was pretextual. Could the court find discrimination in this case? Would the fact that one of the supervisors was a black female older than the plaintiff add to the defendant's rebuttal of pretext? (*Bonaparte v. Frank*, 55 FEP 174 (E.D. Pa. 1990), *aff'd* 925 F.2d 415, 55 FEP 224 (3d Cir. 1991)).

9. In an individual disparate treatment case would it be necessary for a plaintiff to prove that he was as well or better qualified than the person chosen for the position to establish a prima facie case, or is it sufficient to prove that his qualifications are similar to those of the entire pool from which applications are welcome, rather than to those who are eventually selected. (*Mitchell v. Baldridge*, 759 F.2d 80, 37 FEP 689 (D.C. Cir. 1985)).

10. A black female was sent home from an insurance office because she came to work with her hair in what the office manager termed an "African-style." She was told that if she continued to attempt to wear the braids to work, she would be terminated. Does the employee have a claim under Title VII?

PROJECTS

1. Brief *Cunningham v. Cent. Beverage, Inc.*, 486 F. Supp. 59, 60–61 (N.D. Tex. 1980). Explain the court's decision in this case regarding age as the motivating factor in the adverse employment decision reached.

2. Research cases in your state to determine the legality of imposing height and weight restrictions on job candidates by a security company client. Draft a memorandum to your attorney that summarizes your state's position on such restrictions.

CHAPTER 8

The Americans with Disabilities Act

OVERVIEW

The **Americans with Disabilities Act (ADA) of 1990** is one of several landmark civil rights statutes. Congress passed this Act to address discrimination involving an estimated 43 million Americans who suffer from some type of physical or mental disability. (EEOC Technical Assistance Manual). The Act is based in large part on Section 504 of the Rehabilitation Act of 1973, which prohibits discrimination against qualified, disabled individuals by employers who receive federal funds or who are federal contractors.

Title 1 of the ADA, which took effect on July 26, 1992, prohibits private employers, state and local governments, employment agencies, and labor unions from discriminating against qualified individuals with disabilities in all aspects of the employment relationship.

DEFINITIONS UNDER ADA

Employer

The term **employer** means a person engaged in an industry affecting commerce who has 15 or more employees for each working day in each of 20 or more calendar weeks in the current or preceding calendar year, and any agent of such person. **Agent** has been construed to include managers, supervisors, foremen, and agencies used to pre-screen or conduct background investigations on applicants.

Employee

The term **employee** means an individual employed by an employer, and includes U.S. citizens who work for American companies abroad.

Exemptions

Executive agencies of the United States government are exempt from the provisions of the ADA, but are covered under Section 501 of the Rehabilitation Act of 1973. Corporations owned by the United States government, Indian tribes, and private membership clubs that are not labor organizations are exempt from the ADA.

Disability

A **disability** is defined under the ADA to mean:

1. a physical or mental impairment that substantially limits one or more major life activities;
2. a record of such an impairment; or
3. being regarded as having such impairment.

All of the foregoing factors may apply, but an individual need only qualify under one factor in order to be termed disabled.

Qualified Individual with a Disability

A **qualified individual with a disability** is one who, with or without reasonable accommodation, has the requisite education, skill, experience, and other job-related requirements necessary to perform the primary job functions of a position.

The individual with a disability may not be considered unqualified simply because of his or her inability to perform marginal or incidental job functions.

If the individual is qualified to perform essential job functions, except for limitations caused by a disability, the employer must consider whether the individual could perform the functions with a reasonable accommodation.

Physical or Mental Impairment

The ADA definition of **physical impairment** is "any physiological disorder or condition, cosmetic disfigurement, or anatomical loss affecting one or more of the following body systems: neurological; musculoskeletal; special sense organ; respiratory, including speech organs; cardiovascular; reproductive; digestive; genitourinary; hemic and lymphatic; skin and endocrine."

A **mental impairment** is "any mental or psychological disorder, such as mental retardation, organic brain syndrome, emotional or mental illness, and specific learning disabilities."

To further assist in the interpretation of the ADA, the EEOC published an Interpretive Guidance, "[t]he existence of an impairment is to be determined without regard to mitigating measures such as medicines, or assistive or prosthetic devices," 29 C.F.R. § 1630, App. § 1630.2(h) para. 2. As the Tenth Circuit Court of Appeals wrote in *Sutton v. United Air Lines, Inc.*, No. 96-1481 (D. CO. 1996),

The fact that a disorder or condition may be mitigated or correctable does not affect the underlying nature of the disorder or condition. If the underlying disorder or condition makes worse or diminishes in a material respect any of the enumerated body systems of the individual, then it should be considered an "impairment," regardless of whether the individual compensates for this worsening or diminishing by corrective measures. (See *Roth v. Lutheran Gen. Hosp.*, 57 F.3d 1446, 1454 (5th Cir. 1995) (concluding impairment determination made without regard to mitigating measures).

There is no definitive list of physical or mental impairment in the ADA, and each case is evaluated on individual facts regarding the nature and extent of the individual's impairment. However, Figures 8-1 and 8-2 are examples of a number of medical conditions that the EEOC has determined constitute a "physical impairment." or "mental impairment." Examples of learning disabilities covered under the ADA are identified in Figure 8-3. Figure 8-4 lists examples of conditions not covered under the ADA.

Discrimination

Title I of the ADA prohibits limiting, segregating, classifying; participating in a discriminatory contract or other arrangement; using standards, criteria, or methods of administration with discriminatory impact; discrimination because of association with

Figure 8-1
Examples of Physical Impairments under the ADA

- Hearing loss
- Sight loss
- Speech impediments
- AIDS
- Epilepsy
- Cancer
- Osteoporosis
- Arthritis
- Cerebral palsy
- Diabetes
- Heart Disease

Figure 8-2
Examples of Mental Impairments under the ADA

- Mental or psychological disorders as diagnosed by a psychiatrist or psychologist
- Mental retardation
- Organic brain syndrome
- Clinical depression

Figure 8-3
Examples of Learning Disabilities under the ADA

- Dyslexia
- Attention deficit disorder

Figure 8-4
Examples of Conditions Excluded from ADA Coverage

- Current illegal use of drugs, including the unlawful use of prescription drugs
- Temporary conditions such as appendicitis, influenza or broken limbs
- Pregnancy
- Physical characteristics such as height or weight, other than morbid obesity, eye color or hair color that are within normal ranges
- Common personality traits such as a quick temper or poor judgment
- Most sexual behavior disorders
- Compulsive gambling
- Kleptomania
- Pyromania

the disabled; failing to accommodate reasonably; using qualification standards or tests that screen out the disabled; failing to select and administer tests in a way that does not discriminate; or making an inappropriate medical inquiry.

Discrimination is prohibited in all employment practices, including:

- Recruiting and hiring
- Promotion opportunity
- Demotion or transfer

- Rate of pay
- Discipline
- Training
- Evaluation
- Health or insurance benefits
- Discharge

Substantially Limits a Major Life Activity

For protection under the ADA, the impairment must **substantially limit** one or more **major life activities**. However, the ADA does not define either "substantially limits" or "major life activity." The ADA requires that in order for a physical or mental impairment to be "substantially limiting," the individual must be:

(i) Unable to perform a major life activity that the average person in the general population can perform; or

(ii) Significantly restricted as to the condition, manner or duration under which an individual can perform a particular major life activity as compared to the condition, manner, or duration under which the average person in the general populatio.n can perform that same major life activity.

29 C.F.R. § 1630.2(j)(l).

The following factors should be analyzed in determining whether an individual is substantially limited in a major life activity:

1. The type and severity of the impairment;
2. The duration or expected duration of the impairment; and
3. The permanent or long term impact, or the expected permanent or long-term impact resulting from the impairment.

The fact that an employee has a serious health condition does not necessarily mean that individual has a disability that substantially limits the performance of one or more major life activities.

As discussed above, the EEOC's Interpretive Guidance requirement that disability inquiries should be made without regard to mitigating or corrective measures is in conflict with the statutory mandate that the impairment "substantially limit" a major life activity, as the Interpretive Guidance states:

Many impairments do not impact an individual's life to the degree that they constitute disabling impairments. An impairment rises to the level of disability if the impairment substantially limits one or more of the individual's major life activities. . . .

The determination of whether an individual has a disability is not necessarily based on the name or diagnosis of the impairment the person has, but rather on the effect of that impairment on the life of the individual. Some impairments may be disabling for particular individuals but not for others, depending on the stage of the disease or disorder, the presence of other impairments that combine to make the impairment disabling or any number of other factors.

The Tenth Circuit considered the conflict between the EEOC's Interpretive Guidance and the language of the ADA in *Sutton v. United Airlines*, discussed below.

Sutton v. United Airlines, 1307.3d 893 (10th Cir. 1996)

Facts:

Plaintiffs, who are twin sisters, are currently commercial airline pilots for regional commuter airlines. However, they share a "life long goal to fly for a major air carrier." In 1992, the plaintiffs applied for commercial airline pilot positions with United Air Lines, Inc. At their interviews, Plaintiffs were informed that their uncorrected vision disqualified them from pilot positions with United, in that applicants for pilot positions must have uncorrected vision of 20/100 or better in each eye. Plaintiff's uncorrected vision is 20/200 in the right eye and 20/400 in the left eye. Plaintiff's corrected vision is 20/20 in both eyes.

Plaintiffs filed an ADA suit, alleging that United discriminated against them in the hiring process by rejecting their applications because of their "disability," their uncorrected vision, and/or because United regarded them as disabled. Plaintiffs asserted they are disabled under the ADA because their uncorrected vision substantially limits their major life activity of seeing. In addition, Plaintiffs alleged United regarded them as disabled in violation of the ADA because United's policy of requiring uncorrected vision of 20/100 or better blocks Plaintiffs from an entire class of employment, global airline pilots, without any objective evidence of job relatedness or safety.

The district court granted United's motion to dismiss, finding that the Plaintiffs' Amended Complaint failed to state a claim under the ADA. The court ruled that the Plaintiffs were not disabled within the meaning of the ADA because with corrective measures they were "able to function identically to individuals without a similar impairment," and as such they were not substantially limited in the major life activity of seeing. The court reasoned that "[t]o adopt a definition of disabled that would include persons whose vision is correctable by eyeglasses or contact lenses would result in an expansion of disability protection beyond the logical scope of the ADA."

Opinion by Judge Barrett:

The crucial determination becomes whether the EEOC's Interpretive Guidance is correct that disability inquiries should be made without regard to mitigating or corrective measures or is in conflict with the statutory mandate that the impairment "substantially limit" a major life activity. The courts that have considered this issue are split. While some courts have expressly or implicitly followed the EEOC's guidances, others have expressly or implicitly rejected the EEOC's guidance as being in direct conflict with the statutory language requiring a "substantial" limitation.

We join those courts which have rejected this portion of § 1630.2(j) of the EEOC's Interpretive Guidance. We hold that this portion of the EEOC's Interpretive Guidance is in direct conflict with the plain language of the ADA. The determination of whether an individual's impairment substantially limits a major life activity should take into consideration mitigating or corrective measures utilized by the individual. In making disability determinations, we are concerned with whether the impairment affects the individual in fact, not whether it would hypothetically affect the individual without the use of corrective measures.

We hold that Plaintiffs' Amended Complaint alleged sufficient facts to support a conclusion that their uncorrected vision constituted a physical impairment under the ADA. However, for the foregoing reasons, we hold that Plaintiffs cannot present any set of facts showing their vision, when viewed with mitigation and corrective measures, substantially limits the major life activity of seeing. Nor can Plaintiffs show United regarded them as substantially limited in a major life activity of working by finding Plaintiffs unfit for its commercial pilot positions. Therefore, we affirm the district court's dismissal of Plaintiffs' ADA claims for failure to state a claim upon which relief may be granted.
AFFIRMED.

Major life activities are activities that an average person performs with little or no difficulty, including:

walking	sitting	working
speaking	seeing	caring for self
learning	lifting	breathing
hearing	learning	performing manual labor

With respect to the major life activity of "working," the inability to perform a single job does not constitute a substantial limitation. Factors to be considered in determining whether an individual is substantially limited in this major life activity of "working" include:

1. the geographical area to which the individual has reasonable access;
2. the job from which the individual has been disqualified because of an impairment;
3. the number and types of jobs utilizing similar training, skills, or abilities within that geographical area from which the individual is also disqualified because of the impairment; and/or

4. the job from which the individual has been disqualified because of an impairment, and the number and types of other jobs which do not utilize similar training knowledge, skills, or abilities within that geographical area from which the individual is also disqualified because of the impairment.

The restriction on the major life activity must be the result of an impairment. Environmental, cultural and economic disadvantages, advanced age, and physical or personality characteristics are not impairments.

Essential Functions of the Job

ADA regulations define the **essential functions of the job** as the **fundamental** job duties of the position, but not the **marginal** functions of the position.

A written job description is evidence of the essential functions of the job, if the description was prepared in advance of the advertising or interviewing process. By considering the essential functions of the job opening prior to beginning the hiring process, the employer is able to determine whether a person with a disability is qualified for a particular position. If a potential applicant or current employee cannot perform the essential functions of the job, with or without reasonable accommodation, the person is not a qualified individual under the ADA. In the case below, the court found that because a construction inspector could not perform the "essential functions" of that job, his discharge did not violate the Rehabilitation Act.

Chiari v. City of League City, 920 F.2d 311 (5th Cir. 1991)

Facts:

A construction inspector with Parkinson's disease brought action against the city, alleging that his discharge as result of Parkinson's disease violated the Rehabilitation Act. The U.S. district court granted summary judgment for the city, and the employee appealed. The court of appeals affirmed the decision of the U.S. district court. Judge Thornberry's findings, discussed below, concluded that: (1) physician testimony and employer affidavit showed that employee's loss of balance as a result of disease rendered him not "otherwise qualified" to be a construction inspector; (2) city showed that it could not reasonably have accommodated employee's handicap; and (3) because employee could not perform "essential functions" of construction inspector's job, his discharge did not violate Rehabilitation Act.

Opinion by Judge Thornberry:

The City of League City demonstrated that Chiari could not perform the "essential functions" required of a construction inspector and that it could not reasonably accommodate Chiari's handicap. Chiari produced no evidence that would entitle him to a jury determination of either issue. Therefore, he was not "otherwise qualified" to be a construction inspector, and the district court properly granted summary judgment dismissing his section 504 complaint.

The judgment of the district court is AFFIRMED.

Record of Impairment

The ADA protects individuals with a **record of impairment** (history of a disability) from discrimination, whether or not they **currently** are substantially limited in a major life activity. The employer cannot consider, rely upon or refer to prior records relating to a disability when making either employment or benefit decisions. This category is designed to protect people who have a history of disability even though they are not currently suffering from illness, disease, or other conditions.

Regarded as Having Such an Impairment

Individuals who are not disabled, but who are **regarded as having such an impairment** (perceived as disabled) are protected by the ADA from discrimination because of "fears, myths and stereotypes." The case discussed below is best known for deciding that, under the Rehabilitation Act, a *handicapped individual* includes someone whose life activities are limited by other people's fears of contagion of an underlying disease (in this case, tuberculosis).

School Board v. Arline, 480 U.S. 273 (1987).

Facts:

Arline taught elementary school in Nassau County, Florida from 1966 until 1979 when she was discharged after suffering a third relapse of tuberculosis within two years. She brought an action alleging that her dismissal violated the Rehabilitation Act. The U.S. district court entered judgment for the school board and superintendent. Arline appealed. The Eleventh Circuit Court of Appeals reversed and remanded. Certiorari was granted. The Supreme Court, in an opinion by Justice Brennan, held that a school teacher afflicted with a contagious disease, tuberculosis, was a "handicapped individual" within the meaning of the Rehabilitation Act section prohibiting federally funded state programs from discriminating against handicapped individuals solely because of a handicap.

Opinion by Justice Brennan:

We do not agree with petitioners that, in defining a handicapped individual under § 504, the contagious effects of a disease can be meaningfully distinguished from the disease's physical effects on a claimant in a case such as this. Arline's contagiousness and her physical impairment each resulted from the same underlying condition, tuberculosis. It would be unfair to allow an employer to seize upon the distinction between the effects of a disease on others and the effects of a disease on a patient and use that distinction to justify discriminatory treatment.

Few aspects of a handicap give rise to the same level of public fear and misapprehension as contagiousness. Even those who suffer or have recovered from such noninfectious diseases as epilepsy or cancer have faced discrimination based on the irrational fear that they might be contagious. The Act is carefully structured to replace such reflexive reactions to actual or perceived handicaps with actions based on reasoned and medically sound judgments: the definition of "handicapped individual" is broad, but only those individuals who are both handicapped *and* otherwise qualified are eligible for relief. The fact that *some* persons who have contagious diseases may pose a serious health threat to others under certain circumstances does not justify excluding from the coverage of the Act *all* persons with actual or perceived contagious diseases. Such exclusion would mean that those accused of being contagious would never have the opportunity to have their condition evaluated in light of medical evidence and a determination made as to whether they were "otherwise qualified." Rather, they would be vulnerable to discrimination on the basis of mythology-precisely the type of injury Congress sought to prevent. We conclude that the fact that a person with a record of a physical impairment is also contagious does not suffice to remove that person from coverage under § 504.

Because of the paucity of factual findings by the District Court, we, like the Court of Appeals, are unable at this stage of the proceedings to resolve whether Arline is "otherwise qualified" for her job. The District Court made no findings as to the duration and severity of Arline's condition, nor as to the probability that she would transmit the disease. Nor did the court determine whether Arline was contagious at the time she was discharged, or whether the School Board could have reasonably accommodated her. Accordingly, the resolution of whether Arline was otherwise qualified requires further findings of fact.

We hold that a person suffering from the contagious disease of tuberculosis can be a handicapped person within the meaning of § 504 of the Rehabilitation Act of 1973, and that respondent Arline is such a person. We remand the case to the District Court to determine whether Arline is otherwise qualified for her position. The judgment of the Court of Appeals is AFFIRMED

An employer's knowledge of the employee's impairment is insufficient to establish that he "regarded" the employee as disabled. The employee must prove that the employer actually perceived him or her as having such an impairment, or treated the employee as having a substantially limiting impairment that prevents the employee from performing the job.

Association with an Individual with a Disability

The ADA prohibits discrimination because of the known disability of an individual with whom the qualified individual is known to have a relationship or association,

association with an individual with a disability (42 U.S.C. § 12112(b)). The prohibition applies not only to persons with familial relationship, but to any "relationship or association," including same-sex relationships.

The employer has no obligation to provide an employee an accommodation because of the employee's relationship or association with a disabled individual (29 C.F.R. § 1630.8 App.)

Reasonable Accommodation

Reasonable accommodation is any modification or adjustment to the job or work environment to enable a qualified applicant or employee with a disability to participate either in the application process or to perform essential job functions. Reasonable accommodation also includes adjustments to assure that a qualified individual with a disability has the rights and privileges in employment equal to those of employees without disabilities.

Example   An employer constructs a special entrance to an employee lounge to enable Jerry to join his coworkers on breaks.

The accommodation is limited to disability-caused restrictions that prevent the performance of the essential functions of the job, and then (in the majority of jurisdictions) only if the employee requests the accommodation. The person with a disability is responsible for informing the employer that an accommodation is needed.

A request for reasonable accommodation can take the form of a request for an adjustment or change at work for a medical condition. Someone other than the employee, including a family member, friend, health professional, or other representative, may request a reasonable accommodation. The request does not have to be in writing—an oral request is sufficient.

The decision as to the appropriate accommodation must be based on the particular facts of each case. In selecting the particular type of reasonable accommodation to provide, the principal test is that of effectiveness—whether the accommodation will provide an opportunity for a person with a disability to achieve the same level of performance and to enjoy benefits equal to those of a similarly situated person without a disability. If more than one possible accommodation exists, the employer has the ultimate discretion to choose between the accommodations, and may choose the less expensive or easier to provide accommodation.

If a disabled individual refuses an offered accommodation and cannot perform the essential job functions without that accommodation, the individual is no longer protected by the ADA.

The EEOC requires that an employer notify applicants and employees of its obligation to provide reasonable accommodations for otherwise qualified individuals with a disability. This notification can appear on posted notices, job application forms, personnel manuals, job vacancy posting, or may be communicated orally. Posters are available from the EEOC and should be placed in the personnel office and break or lunch rooms.

1. **Types of Reasonable Accommodation**

    The determination of what is a reasonable accommodation is on a case-by-case basis, and may include one or more of the following categories:

    a. **Time**

    Time is a reasonable accommodation, including giving an employee with a disability either time off from work or a modified work schedule. Allowing the employee to take paid or unpaid leave for treatment or recovery is a reasonable accommodation, unless the employee's absence imposes an undue hardship on the operations of the business.

    b. **Physical Changes to Workplace and/or Equipment**

    A simple physical change to the workplace, including placing a room divider, soundproofing, or visual barrier between workspaces, may be an accommodation. The reasonable accommodation extends to other non-work areas used by employees, such as break rooms and restrooms.

    c. **Reassignment**

    Reassignment to another position must be considered as a reasonable accommodation for a current employee when accommodation to the employee's current job would either cause undue hardship or would not be possible. Most courts require the employee to identify a particular position for reassignment. That position must be vacant, or expected to become vacant within a reasonable period of time. The employer need not create a job or bump another employee to facilitate reassignment, and an "equivalent" position is not required if one is not available. Also, the employer does not have to maintain the employee's salary level at the prior rate, unless it does so for other reassigned employees. (See *Hall v. United States Postal Service*, discussed below, relating to the issue of reassignment and accommodation.)

Hall v. United States Postal Service,
857 F.2d 1073 (6th Cir. 1988)

Facts:

A handicapped postal service employee, who was denied the position of distribution clerk, brought suit alleging violation of the Rehabilitation Act. Hall, a 47-year-old woman began working with the United States Postal Service in 1968 as a letter carrier in the Detroit region. At the time she was hired, she passed two tests, one for a clerk's position, and the other for letter carrier. She chose the letter carrier position. In that job, which she held for five years, she sorted and delivered mail on foot.

On June 11, 1973, while delivering mail, an automobile went out of control and struck Hall, injuring her right hip, foot and back. She received workers' compensation benefits as a result of this accident until June 1982, when it was determined that she was no longer disabled.

On October 7, 1984, fifteen months after she stopped receiving workers' compensation benefits under the Federal Employee Compensation Act, she wrote the Detroit postmaster requesting that she be "reinstated as a Distribution Clerk at the General Mail Facility." She did not request reinstatement to her carrier position because she could no longer do all of the walking, lifting, and bending required of that position. She "assumed" that the distribution clerk was the same position that she had previously performed with the postal service during the Christmas rush. She believed that her physical limitations would not prevent her from doing the work that she formerly performed as a clerk at the main post office, stating, "Whatever I was doing then I can do now."

The job description of a distribution clerk states that the position requires, among other things, lifting up to 70 pounds, kneeling, and repeated bending.

During the course of the application process, Hall was found to be unable to perform the physical requirements of the job. The Postal Service's examining physician concurred with Hall's physician that she could not meet the criteria of heavy lifting and bending without serious risk to her health. Therefore, on May 16, 1985, her application was denied.

During the first week of May 1985, prior to her application being formally denied, Hall went to the EEO office at the Detroit post office to file a complaint that she was being discriminated against by the Postal Service due to her physical handicap. Hall alleges that she was told by the EEO officer that she would have to wait until she received the actual denial or termination from the post office before any action could be taken. During the third week of May 1985, when she received the letter denying her application, she went back to the EEO office and renewed her request that an investigation be undertaken regarding her complaint of handicap discrimination.

Opinion by Judge Jones:

In this case, the Postal Service failed to introduce any evidence suggesting that it could not reasonably accommodate Hall. Therefore, the lower court was completely unable to make the kind of individualized inquiry on the accommodation issue that is required by *Arline*. Moreover, while the court was correct in stating that an employer is not required to eliminate an "essential function" in accommodating a handicapped individual, the Postal Service made absolutely no showing that this would occur if they attempted to accommodate Hall. Indeed the court (and the Postal Service in its brief) evidently operated under the assumption that *every* accommodation relating to an essential function of a position necessarily *eliminate* that function, this is simply not the law. Because a particular function is found to be essential does not relieve the federal employer of its burden of showing that the handicapped individual cannot be reasonably accommodated. To hold otherwise, as we think the district court did, is to ignore the reasonable accommodation aspect of the "otherwise qualified" inquiry.

For the foregoing reasons, we REVERSE the grant of summary judgment in the defendant's favor and REMAND to the district court for further proceedings.

d. Providing qualified readers or interpreters

It may be a reasonable accommodation to provide a reader or interpreter for a qualified individual with a disability, if this would not impose an undue hardship on the business. As an alternative, it might be more effective to assign an individual with a visual impairment to a job that does not require reading.

Providing an interpreter on an "as needed" basis may be a reasonable accommodation for a person who is deaf, if this does not impose an undue hardship on the business.

Known Disabilities

An employer is required to make an accommodation for the **known disability** of a qualified applicant or employee if it would not impose an "undue hardship" on the operation of the employer's business.

Hidden Disabilities

If an employer is not aware that an accommodation is necessary, it has no duty to provide an accommodation. Since the ADA prohibits an employer from inquiring whether a person has a disability, or the nature or extent of a disability, an individual with a hidden disability is responsible for informing the employer of the need for an accommodation.

MENTAL AND EMOTIONAL CLAIMS UNDER THE ADA

Overview

The ADA covers mental disabilities as well as physical disabilities. Mental disabilities are difficult to work with in terms of preventing discrimination, because mental disabilities are not as readily obvious as are the majority of physical impairments. In an attempt to facilitate answers to questions of both employers and employees alleging employment discrimination based on a psychiatric disability, the EEOC published its Enforcement Guidance on the Americans with Disabilities Act and Psychiatric Disabilities ("Guidance") on March 26, 1997.

Although the Guidance does not have the force of law, as do the binding regulations under the ADA, it is helpful in interpreting the ADA's application to mental disabilities.

Mental Impairment Exclusion

The Guidance has set out an exclusion for traits or behaviors. Stress that may be shown to be related to a mental or physical impairment could be an impairment. Stress alone is not automatically a mental impairment.

Major Life Activities—Mental Impairment

The determination of major life activities for an individual claiming a mental impairment is more difficult than the determination of a physical impairment. Major life activities are affected differently from person to person in the case of an alleged mental impairment. Irritability or difficulty getting along with others is not an impairment, although interacting with others is listed as a major life activity. Difficulty sleeping is not considered to be an impairment, although sleeping is considered to be a major life activity.

Disclosure of Mental Disability

An employer is charged with accommodating a "known disability" for an applicant or employee, unless doing so would cause an undue hardship on the employer. Disclosure of a mental disability to a potential employer creates concerns for the employee of potential negative consequences because of the disclosure, and the extent to which the employer holds the information confidential.

Prior to making an offer of employment, an employer may not ask questions that would likely elicit information about a mental impairment. The only exception for asking disability-related questions before an offer is made is when the applicant asks for a reasonable accommodation for the hiring process. At that point, the employer may require the applicant to provide documentation concerning his or her disability and functional limitations.

In the case of an applicant with a visible disability, or an applicant with a non-visible disability who informs the employer of the need for reasonable accommodation, the employer may ask the applicant if reasonable accommodation is required, and what type of reasonable accommodation would be needed to perform the functions of the job.

DRUG AND ALCOHOL ABUSE PROVISIONS OF THE ADA

The ADA specifically permits employers the authority to enforce a workplace free from the use of illegal drugs and alcohol. However, the ADA does provide limited protection from discrimination for recovering drug addicts and alcoholics.

An individual who is currently engaged in the illegal use of drugs is not an "individual with a disability." Employers are not prohibited from discharging or refusing to employ persons who currently engage in the illegal use of drugs. However, an employer may not discriminate against a drug addict who is not currently using drugs and who has been rehabilitated, on the basis of a history of drug addiction. Defining "current drug user" is difficult, as each case must be considered individually.

An alcoholic is an "individual with a disability" under the ADA. An employer has the right to discipline, discharge, or refuse to employ an alcoholic whose use of alcohol impairs job performance, or who exhibits conduct such that he or she is not a "qualified individual with a disability."

Employees who use drugs or alcohol are required to meet the same performance and conduct standards as are set for other employees. The employer may give tests for the illegal use of drugs. If an individual tests positive on such a test, the individual will be considered a "current drug user" under the ADA. In that case, it is reasonable for the employer to believe that the individual's drug involvement is an ongoing problem.

Although a current drug user has no protection under the ADA, an employee who currently uses alcohol is not automatically denied protection because of the alcohol use. An alcoholic is entitled to a consideration of accommodation if he or she is qualified to perform the essential functions of a job. However, if an individual's use of alcohol adversely affects job performance or conduct so that he or she is not "qualified" for the job, an employer may discipline, discharge, or refuse to employ that individual.

The ADA protects an addict currently in a drug rehabilitation program who has not used drugs illegally for a long period of time, or an addict who is rehabilitated or who has successfully completed rehabilitation in the past.

DEALING WITH AIDS IN THE WORKPLACE

The issue of AIDS in the workplace involves two critical areas; first, whether the infected person will be able to continue to perform his or her job, and, second, the coworkers' fear of transmission of the disease. According to the Centers for Disease Control (CDC), as of December 1996, there were over 580,000 reported cases of AIDS in the United States, and over 360,000 AIDS-related deaths in that same time period. These statistics confirm the increasing effect of AIDS on the workplace.

However, the number of reported court decisions involving AIDS-infected employees is low compared with the rate of employment complaints involving AIDS. Possible reasons for the small number of court cases in this area include the employee's fear of stigma from publicizing his or her discriminatory treatment; the high settlement rate of AIDS-related complaints; and the lengthy and expensive litigation which might deter the filing of an AIDS discrimination case.

Ability of AIDS-Infected Employee to Continue to Perform a Job

AIDS-infected employees often require repetitive and extensive hospitalization and recuperative time. Employers are faced with the necessity to adhere to ADA requirements while maintaining business operations around possible prolonged absences for the effects of AIDS.

Fear of Transmission of AIDS

The AIDS virus is isolated in various bodily fluids, including blood, semen, saliva, tears, breast milk, urine, cerebrospinal fluid, brain tissue, and cervical secretions, but only blood, semen and possibly breast milk have been implicated in transmission. Consequently, CDC guidelines for preventing transmission of HIV infection in the workplace state that there is no known risk of transmission in workplaces such as offices, schools, factories, and construction sites.

Although none of the transmission methods listed above occur in the normal course of business in most workplaces, fear, not risk, of contamination remains a significant issue for employers. Fear of AIDS, whether justified or not, is very real to some individuals, and often manifests itself in a refusal to work in conjunction with an AIDS-infected employee. However, employment discrimination statutes and work safety laws (discussed at length in Chapter 17) permit an employer to discipline workers who refuse to work around an employee who suffers from AIDS. Employers thus face a balancing test between dealing with certain workers' very real fear of AIDS against a need to accommodate an AIDS-infected employee.

Determining AIDS Impairment under ADA

Frequently, a person who tested positive for antibodies to the AIDS virus has no outward symptoms of AIDS. Is infection alone a disability? In *Bragdon v. Abbott*, 524

U.S. 624, 8 AD Cases 239 (1998), an ADA case, a dentist refused to perform dental services in his office for a HIV patient. The plaintiff claimed that she was an "individual with a disability" because her HIV infection substantially limited her ability to reproduce. The Supreme Court agreed and ruled that her HIV infection, from the moment it occurred, was an "impairment" because it is a physiological condition involving immediate damage to the blood and lymphatic systems. Her ability to reproduce was a "major life activity." Therefore, her HIV status "substantially limited" her ability to reproduce because of the risk of transmitting the virus to her partner or to her unborn child.

Reasonable Accommodation for AIDS

Once a determination has been made that AIDS is a disability under the court's definition and that the person is "otherwise qualified" to do the job, an employee must rebut the employer's argument that reasonable accommodation of the disease was not possible without an "undue hardship," as defined in this chapter.

Discrimination Because of Association with Person with AIDS

ADA forbids an employer from discriminating against an employee because of his or her association with a person with a disability. However, cases involving association with individuals suffering from AIDS are relatively few. (See *Saladin v. Turner*, 936 F. Supp 1571, 6 AD Cases (Okla. 1996)). In the *Saladin* case, the plaintiff was a waiter at the French Hen restaurant. Following his long-time partner's AIDS diagnosis, restaurant patrons asked the plaintiff about his partner's health. The restaurant manager told Saladin not to discuss his partner's condition with customers. Subsequently, the manager met with the restaurant owner who told him to place Saladin on 30 days suspension without pay on the basis of only one identified customer complaint. The court found that Saladin's association with a person with a known disability was the motivating factor in the owner's decision to suspend and discharge Saladin. The court emphasized that "under the ADA, effect may not be given to the public's fears of stereotypes."

Otherwise Qualified Status of Employee with AIDS or HIV Infection

Whether a person with AIDS or HIV infection is "otherwise qualified" under the ADA or Rehabilitation Act is a question of fact, to be decided on individual basis. (See *Holiday v. City of Chattanooga*, 206 F.3d 637, 10AD Cases 501 (6th Cir. 2000)). In this case, the court ruled that summary judgment for the defendant had been improperly granted where there was evidence that the examining physician disqualified the plaintiff from a police officer position solely based on his status as HIV positive, and without determining how the HIV status would affect his ability to fulfill the duties of a police officer.

Even though persons are physically capable of performing their jobs, they may not be considered "otherwise qualified" if they pose a "significant risk" to heath and safety of others due to disability. In *Doe v. University of Md. Medical Sys. Corp.*, 50 F.3d 1261, 4 AD cases 379 (4th Cir. 1995), the court affirmed that an HIV-positive neurosurgery resident was not "otherwise qualified" to continue his training because of the risk to patients involved in "exposure-prone" procedures that are not amenable to reasonable accommodation.

DISCIPLINE OF QUALIFIED INDIVIDUALS WITH A DISABILITY

A qualified individual with a disability is not above company policy. An employer is free to discipline these employees for misconduct or violation of company policy if it would impose the same discipline on an employee with no disability.

Attendance policies are essential in the employment relationship. An employer can terminate an employee for excessive absenteeism, even if the absences are caused by the individual's disability. However, employers should allow employees to use the maximum sick and vacation leaves prior to any consideration of termination. If the circumstances merit, the individual with a disability should be given the option to take leave without pay rather than face termination for excessive absenteeism.

CONFIDENTIALITY

Employers are required under the EEOC regulations to keep all information concerning the medical or mental condition or history of an applicant confidential, including information that the individual voluntarily discloses. This information should be kept in a separate file from the individual's personnel file, and made available only to supervisors and managers who are involved in the work restrictions of the individual or any necessary accommodation, or first aid, nurse, or safety personnel who might be required to assist the individual with a disability.

ADVERSE EMPLOYMENT ACTION RELATED TO DISABILITY— NOT BECAUSE OF DISABILITY

Courts are often asked to determine whether a reason for an adverse employment action was related to or caused by the disability, and the disability itself. For example, discharging an employee who has exhausted all leave benefits does not violate the ADA, even if the employee's disability caused the absences that exhausted the leave benefits.

EEOC FILING PREREQUISITES AND PROCEDURES

A disabled employee who believes that he or she has been discriminated against must first file a claim with the EEOC within 180 days of the alleged violation or within 300 days if the state has a parallel fair employment practices (FEP) agency.

After the charge has been filed, the EEOC initiates an investigation. This investigation may consist of one or more of the following actions:

   a. Interviews with the charging party and the execution of an affidavit by the charging party
   b. Interviews with the employer
   c. Questionnaire to the employer
   d. Employer response to the EEOC charge
   e. Interviews with witnesses for both the charging party and employer
   f. Interviews with the employees
   g. Tour of the job site
   h. Requests for employment records and other relevant data

The EEOC has subpoena power that may be enforced through the federal district courts. Subpoenas may require the production of evidence, attendance and testimony of witnesses, or access to evidence for purposes of examination and the opportunity to copy the evidence.

The investigation process normally begins with the employer's receipt of an EEOC form (Figure 8-5) notifying it that a charge of discrimination has been filed. The employer also will receive a copy of the EEOC charge, and often a Request for Information from the EEOC. The latter seeks an abundance of information and documents. The employer may consider submitting a position statement accompanied by relevant documents to the EEOC as opposed to answering the questionnaire.

The EEOC may then conduct a fact-finding conference with the EEOC representative, the charging party, the employer, the employer's attorney, and possibly witnesses. The questioning is informal, and conducted by the EEOC representative. While the employer's attorney does not have the opportunity to personally question the charging party on behalf of the employer, the attorney may submit questions to the EEOC representative. Testimony is not given under oath, and there is no opportunity for cross-examination.

An on-site investigation may be conducted by the EEOC. The employer has the

CHARGE OF DISCRIMINATION

This form is affected by the Privacy Act of 1974; See Privacy Act Statement before completing this form.

AGENCY	CHARGE NUMBER
☐ FEFA	
☐ EEOC	

_____ and EEOC
State or local Agency, if any

NAME *(Indicate Mr., Ms., Mrs.)*	HOME TELEPHONE *(Include Area Code)*

STREET ADDRESS	CITY, STATE AND ZIP CODE	DATE OF BIRTH / /

NAMED IS THE EMPLOYER, LABOR ORGANIZATION, EMPLOYMENT AGENCY APPRENTICESHIP COMMITTEE, STATE OR LOCAL GOVERNMENT AGENCY WHO DISCRIMINATED AGAINST ME *(If more than one list below)*

NAME	NUMBER OF EMPLOYEES, MEMBERS	TELEPHONE *(Include Area Code)*

STREET ADDRESS	CITY, STATE AND ZIP CODE	COUNTY

NAME	HOME TELEPHONE *(Include Area Code)*

STREET ADDRESS	CITY, STATE AND ZIP CODE	COUNTY

CAUSE OF DISCRIMINATION BASED ON *(Check appropriate box(es))*

☐ RACE ☐ COLOR ☐ SEX ☐ RELIGION ☐ NATIONAL ORIGIN

☐ RETALIATION ☐ AGE ☐ DISABILITY ☐ OTHER

DATE DISCRIMINATION TOOK PLACE
EARLIEST / /   LATEST / /

☐ CONTINUING ACTION

THE PARTICULARS ARE *(If additional space is needed, attach extra sheet(s)):*

☐ I want this charge filed with both the EEOC and the State or Local Agency, if any. I will advise the agencies if I change my address or telephone number and cooperate fully with them in the processing of my charge in accordance with their procedures.

I declare under penalty of perjury that the foregoing is true and correct.

Date _____ Charging Party *(Signature)*

NOTARY– (When necessary for State and Local Requirements)

I swear or affirm that I have read the above charge and that it is true to the best of my knowledge, information and belief.

SIGNATURE OF COMPLAINANT

SUBSCRIBED AND SWORN TO BEFORE ME THIS DATE
(Day, month, and year)

EEOC FORM 5 (Rev. 06/92)

Figure 8-5
Charge of Discrimination EEOC Form

opportunity to exercise some level of control in the investigation by agreeing in advance with the EEOC investigator concerning what records will be inspected and which employees will be interviewed. An individual should be designated by the employer to make copies for or assist with any other needs of the investigator during the on-site visit.

The EEOC will make a "reasonable cause determination" after the investigation is completed. If the EEOC finds no cause, the charging party may appeal the decision to the Determination Review Board of the EEOC within four days. The finding of no cause becomes final if there is no appeal, or if the Determination Review Board upholds the no-cause determination. If reasonable cause is found, the EEOC issues a letter of determination, and the employer is invited to attempt conciliation with the EEOC. That conciliation effort will include meetings of the EEOC representative with the charging party and a conciliation conference with the employer. If conciliation is successful, the EEOC and the employer agree upon a conciliation agreement to be presented to the charging party for his or her signature. Once the charging party, the employer, and the EEOC representative have signed the conciliation agreement, it will be submitted to the EEOC representative's supervisor, and then to the district director of the EEOC for final approval.

If conciliation fails, the EEOC may send the charging party a right to sue notice, or it may file suit on behalf of the charging party in federal district court. The EEOC's final determination is the **notice of right to sue**. At least 180 days must pass after the filing of the charge before the disabled employee may request a right to sue letter from the EEOC. A civil suit must then be brought within 90 days from receipt of a notice of right to sue.

Figure 8-6 is an example of an ADA complaint.

DEFENSES TO AN ADA COMPLAINT

Disabled Individual Poses a Direct Threat

An employer is not required to hire a qualified individual with a disability if that individual poses a direct threat to the health or safety of other individuals in the workplace because of the nature of the job and the specific characteristics of that individual's disability. If the employer uses this exception, the standard must apply to *all* applicants or employees, not just persons with disabilities.

Direct threat means a "significant risk of substantial harm to the health or safety of the individual or others that cannot be eliminated or reduced by reasonable accommodation." The employer should determine whether a person poses a "direct threat"

k. AMERICANS WITH DISABILITIES ACT

§ 1712.20 Complaint for Violation of Americans With Disabilities Act

[F.R.C.P. Rule 8(a); 42 U.S.C.A. § 12111 et seq.]

[Title of Court and Cause]

NATURE OF THE ACTION

This is an action under Title I of the Americans With Disabilities Act of 1990 and Title I of the Civil Rights Act of 1991, to correct unlawful employment practices on the basis of disability and to make whole W. Defendants discharged W, a qualified individual with a disability, cancer, from his position as , because of his disability.

JURISDICTION AND VENUE

1. Jurisdiction of this Court is invoked pursuant to 28 U.S.C. §§ 451, 1331, 1337, 1343, and 1345. This action is authorized and instituted pursuant to Section 107(a) of the Americans With Disabilities Act of 1990 ("ADA"), 42 U.S.C. § 1277(a), which incorporates by reference Sections 706(f)(1) and (3) of Title VII of the Civil Rights Act of 1964 ("Title VII"), 42 U.S.C. § 2000e-5(f)(1) and (3), and pursuant to Section 102 of the Civil Rights Act of 1991, 42 U.S.C. § 1981(A).

2. The employment practices hereafter alleged to be unlawful were and no being committed in the _____ District of , _____ Division.

PARTIES

3. Plaintiff, Equal Employment Opportunity Commission (the "Commission"), is an agency of the United States of America charged with the administration, interpretation and enforcement of Title I of the ADA and is expressly authorized to bring this action by Section 107(a) of the ADA, 42 U.S.C. § 1277(a), which incorporates by reference Sections 706(f)(1) and (3) of Title VII, 42 U.S.C. §§ 2000e-5(f)(1) and (3).

4. At all relevant times, Defendant A has been and is now a *[state]* corporation doing business in *[state]* and *[city]*, and has continuously had and does now have at least twenty-five (25) employees.

5. At all relevant times, Defendant B has been and now is a *[state]* corporation which wholly owns Defendant A.

6. At all relevant times, Defendant C has been the owner of B and A, and is an agent of an Employer within the meaning of Section 101(5)(A) of the ADA, 42 U.S.C. § 12115(A).

7. At all relevant times, Defendant A has continuously been engaged in an industry affecting commerce within the meaning of Section 101(5) of the ADA, 42 U.S.C.

Figure 8-6
Example of ADA Complaint

§ 12111(5), and Section 107(7) of the ADA, 42 U.S.C. § 12117(7), which incorporates by reference Sections 701(g) and (h) of Title VII, 42 U.S.C. § 2000e(g) and (h).

8. At all relevant times, Defendant A has been a covered entity under Section 101(2) of the ADA, 42 U.S.C. § 12111(2).

STATEMENT OF CLAIMS

9. More than thirty (30) days prior to the institution of this lawsuit, W filed a Charge with the Commission alleging violations of Title I of the ADA by Defendants A, B, and C. All conditions precedent to the institution of this lawsuit have been fulfilled.

10. Since the least [*date*], Defendants have engaged in unlawful employment practices in violation of the ADA Sections 102(a), 102(b)(1), and 102(b)(5)(B), 42 U.S.C. §§ 12112(a), 12112(b)(1) and 12112(b)(5)(B), at their Chicago, Illinois facility. These practices include but are not limited to Defendants' discharge of W, a qualified individual with a disability, who was able to perform the essential functions of his position with or without reasonable accommodation, because of his diability, cancer; and Defendants' discharge of W based on the need to make reasonable accommodations to his possible future physical impairments.

11. The effect of the practices complained of above has been to deprive W of equal employment opportunities and otherwise adversely affect his status as an employee because of his disability.

12. The unlawful employment practices complained of above were and are intentional.

PRAYER FOR RELIEF

WHEREFORE, the Commission respectfully prays that this Court:

A. Grant a permanent injunction enjoining Defendant A, its owners, officers, management personnel, employees, agents, successors, assigns; active concert or participation with them, from engaging in any employment practice which discriminates on the basis of disability.

B. Order Defendants A, B, and C to institute and carry out policies, practices, and programs which provide equal employment opportunities to qualified individuals with disabilities, and which eradicate the effects of past and present unlawful employment practices;

C. Order Defendants A, B, and C to make whole W by providing him with appropriate lost earnings and insurance premiums, with pre-judgment interest, in amounts to be proved at trial, and other affirmative relief necessary to eradicate the effects of its unlawful employment practices, including, but not limited to reinstatement of W to the position of;

D. Order Defendants A, B, and C to make whole W by providing compensation for pecuniary losses, including but not limited to costs to be incurred for health and life insurance premiums and costs of seeking new employment, in amounts to be determined at trial;

E. Grant such further relief as the Court deems necessary and proper; and,

F. Grant the Commission its cost in this action.

Figure 8-6 (*Continued*)

based on an individual assessment of the person's current ability to perform the essential functions of that job.

Simply because a person has a history of a psychiatric disability or for being treated for a psychiatric disability does not mean that the individual poses a "direct threat." EEOC regulations permit an employer to refuse to hire someone based on a history of violence or threats of violence if it can show that the individual poses a direct threat. That determination of "direct threat" can only be based on the individual assessment of the individual's present ability to safely perform the functions of the job, considering the most current medical knowledge and/or the best available objective evidence.

Factors to be considered in determining whether there is a direct threat include:

1. duration of the risk;
2. nature and severity of the potential harm;
3. the likelihood that the potential harm will occur; and
4. the imminence of the potential harm.

Part of the reasonable accommodation determination is an analysis of whether the individual can be accommodated to eliminate the direct threat or reduce it to an acceptable level. The EEOC and ADA regulations do not include risk or harm to property in their "direct threat" analysis.

Accommodation Causes an Undue Hardship

An employer is not required to provide a reasonable accommodation if providing the accommodation would cause an undue hardship. **Undue hardship** is defined as any accommodation that would be unduly costly, disruptive or substantial, or that would fundamentally alter the nature or operation of the business. The determination of an "undue hardship" depends on the size and resources of the employer and the nature of the employer's business.

The test for whether an employer can mount a defense of undue hardship includes these factors:

1. The nature and net cost of the accommodation, deducting the available tax credits and/or state or federal funding; and
2. The overall financial resources of the company, the number of employees, and the effect of the accommodation on the company's total resources.

Application for Social Security or Other Disability Benefits

Numerous federal cases have found that an employee who represents on an application for Social Security disability or insurance disability that he is disabled is estopped from alleging that he or she is a "qualified individual" under the ADA. The EEOC has refused to adopt a strict estoppel approach, but has stated that such representations are relevant in its determination of an ADA claim.

After-Acquired Evidence Doctrine

An employer may assert as a defense the "after-acquired evidence doctrine" to bar or limit a former employee's remedies in an ADA case or similar discrimination claims. Chapter 2 contains an extensive discussion of the after-acquired evidence doctrine.

PREVENTIVE ACTION TO AVOID POTENTIAL ADA PROBLEMS

Preemployment Inquiries

As a general rule, questions about specific disabilities or the nature and extent of any disability are not lawful at the job interview stage. This does not mean that an employer can never obtain the health and medical information needed to assess an applicant's qualifications and assure health and safety on the job. Once a job offer has been made and before an individual starts to work, an employer may ask health-related questions and even conduct a medical examination, as long as all candidates who receive a job offer in the same job category are required to respond to the same inquiries or undergo the same examination. There is little leeway for pointed questions at that pre-job offer stage.

The EEOC offers guidance on information that may be requested on an application form or during a job interview without violating the ADA, as well as some additional tips for the pre-offer stage. Figure 8-7 is an example of requests for information during the interview process that violate the ADA, and requests that do not violate the ADA.

Questions about "reasonable accommodation," discussed below, are allowed at the job interview stage in three specific situations:

1. If the employer reasonably believes that the applicant will need reasonable accommodation because of an obvious disability; for example, if the applicant uses a wheelchair or has a severe visual impairment.
2. If the employer reasonably believes that the applicant will need reasonable accommodation because of a hidden disability that the applicant has voluntarily disclosed to the employer. For example, during an interview, the applicant volunteers the fact that he or she has diabetes.
3. An applicant has voluntarily disclosed to the employer a need for accommodation. For example, during an interview, the applicant says that he or she will need periodic breaks to take insulin shots or other medication.

QUESTIONS THAT MAY NOT BE ASKED IN
AN INTERVIEW OR ON JOB APPLICATIONS

- Have you ever had or been treated for any of the following conditions or diseases? (Followed by checklist of various conditions and diseases.)
- Have you ever been hospitalized? If so, for what condition?
- Have you ever been treated for any mental condition?
- Have you ever been treated by a psychiatrist or psychologist? If so, for what condition?
- How many days were you absent from work because of illness last year? Do you have any physical defects that preclude you from performing certain kinds of work? If yes, describe such defects and specific work limitations?
- Do you have any disabilities or impairments that may affect your performance in the position for which you are applying? Is there any health-related reason you may not be able to perform the job for which you are applying?
- Are you taking any prescribed medications?
- Have you ever been treated for drug addiction or alcholism?
- Have you ever filed a workers' compensation claim?

Figure 8-7
Example of Request of ADA Information

Physical Examinations

The ADA allows an employer to require a physical exam only after an offer of employment has been made, and only if the exam is given to all potential employees in the same job category. Current employees may be required to submit to medical exams if they serve a legitimate business purpose.

Coordination with FMLA

An employee who is covered by the ADA may also be covered by the federal Family and Medical Leave Act (FMLA), discussed at length in Chapter 14. However, a "disability" under the ADA and a "serious health condition" under the FMLA, even though neither would qualify as a disability, are different concepts and should be analyzed separately.

Under the FMLA, short term or nonchronic impairments, such as a broken leg or a hernia, generally do not qualify as disabilities for purposes of the ADA. However, the FMLA includes any serious health condition that prevents the employee from being able to work for three consecutive days and requires continuing medical treatment. Thus, a broken leg or hernia may be a serious health condition under the FMLA, even though neither would qualify as a disability.

REMEDIES FOR ADA VIOLATIONS

Individuals who are successful in ADA lawsuits may be awarded:

1. Money damages, including back pay, compensatory damages (for emotional pain and suffering, mental anguish, loss of enjoyment of life), punitive damages, interest, and, possibly front pay
2. Lost benefits
3. Attorneys' fees, expert witness fees, and certain litigation costs
4. Injunctive relief (reinstatement or required accommodation)

TERMS

agent
Americans with Disabilities Act of 1990
association with an individual with a disability
direct threat
disability
employee
employer
essential functions of the job
known disability
major life activity
mental impairment
notice of right to sue
physical impairment
qualified individual with a disability
reasonable accommodation
record of impairment
regarded as having such an impairment
substantially limit
undue hardship

REVIEW QUESTIONS

1. Under the ADA, is diabetes considered an impairment if the symptoms of the disease are totally controlled by medicine or insulin?

2. A female welder suffered a serious injury to her right arm in a gun accident. While she testified that she could take care of her normal activities of daily living, such as feeding herself, driving her car, washing dishes, vacuuming, and taking out trash with her injured right arm, she could not do heavy lifting, repetitive movement, and climbing (a requirement of her job). Would the court find that her injury/impairment limited a major life activity? Would the fact that there were other jobs that she could perform play a role in the court's decision?

3. If an individual who uses alcohol is often either late to work or unable to perform his or her job responsibilities, is the employer permitted to discipline the individual on the basis of the poor performance and conduct? Can the employer discipline the alcoholic employee more severely than it does other employees for the same offenses?

4. A former deputy marshal, who had been committed to a hospital for psychiatric evaluation and diagnosed with a mental disorder, was terminated after the employer was unable to find a position for him that did not require him to carry a gun. Would the court rule that the termination was proper? Why or why not? Would the employer be required to accommodate the employee by transferring him to an administrative position? Why or why not?

5. A former employee, who suffered from manic depression, had indicated on her employment application ten years previously that she did not suffer from any physical or mental condition that would limit her capacity to perform the job for which she applied. Several years later, she began to suffer from what was termed "situational stress reaction." She failed to return to work, and the employer was informed by her family members that she was "falling apart," and the family was attempting to get her admitted into a hospital. The employer then wrote the employee and requested that she return to work within a short period of time, or provide a medical excuse. She failed to respond, and was terminated. Explain whether the employer had a duty to accommodate the employee.

6. A postal worker unable to continue carrying mail because of acute asthma problems made several trips to the emergency room and was hospitalized as a result of working outdoors. Would a court find that the employee was substantially limited in the major life activity of working? Why or why not?

7. Describe potential accommodations in the case of an employee lounge that is inaccessible to an employee using a wheelchair. Would the provision of a location that did not enable the individual to take a break with coworkers be an acceptable accommodation?

8. Could an employer refuse to hire an applicant whose spouse has a disability because of the employer's "assumption" that the spouse's disability would require the applicant to lose an excessive amount of time from work? Do employment statutes protect a disabled employee's spouse?

9. Mary Stewart is unable to read because of dyslexia. Is her dyslexia considered to be an impairment under the ADA? If Mary Stewart's inability to read was because she had never been taught to read, would the inability to read be an impairment under the ADA?

10. If the employer reasonably believes that the applicant will need reasonable accommodation because of an obvious disability—for example, if the applicant uses a wheelchair or has a severe visual impairment—is it permissible for the employer to ask about the need for reasonable accommodation during the interview process? Why or why not?

PROJECTS

1. Contact your regional EEOC office and determine the number and type of ADA claims filed last year. Determine how many of those claims resulted in findings against an employer. Prepare a chart to summarize those findings.

2. Brief the *Bragdon v. Abbott*, 524 U.S. 624, 8 AD Cases 239 (1998) case. Discuss the court's basis for finding the existence of an impairment for the plaintiff.

CHAPTER 9

Age Discrimination

OVERVIEW

Age Discrimination in Employment Act of 1967

Although Title VII was intended to regulate discrimination when it was enacted in 1964, Title VII did not prohibit age discrimination. Congress passed separate, comprehensive legislation, the **Age Discrimination in Employment Act of 1967** (ADEA)(29 U.S.C.A. § 621 et seq.) to specifically address age discrimination in employment.

The ADEA, as does Title VII, covers all aspects of workplace discrimination: hiring, assignments, promotions, compensation, work environment, and discharge. Specifically the ADEA states that it is unlawful for an employer to:

- Fail or refuse to hire or to discharge any individual or otherwise discriminate against any individual with respect to his/her compensation, terms, conditions, or privileges of employment because of such individual's age (29 U.S.C.A. § 623(a)(1));
- Limit, segregate, or classify employees in any way which would deprive or tend to deprive any individual of employment opportunities, or otherwise adversely affect his or her status as an employee, because of such individual's age (29 U.S.C.A. § 623(a)(2));
- Reduce the wage rate of any employee in order to otherwise comply with the ADEA (29 U.S.C.A. § 623(a)(3)); or
- Discriminate or retaliate against an employee for opposing any practice made illegal under the ADEA, or for participating in an investigation, proceeding, or litigation involving a charge of discrimination under the ADEA (29 U.S.C.A. § 623(d)).

It is age discrimination to impose on workers of one age group requirements or conditions not imposed on other age groups. Standards of performance and discipline must be applied equally to all age groups, as discussed by the court in the case below.

Shager v. Upjohn Co., 913 F.2d 398 (7th Cir. 1990)

Facts:

Shager was employed by a seed manufacturer that was bought by Asgrow in 1983, when he was fifty years old. His job was sales representative for the state of Wisconsin, and required him to supervise the company's sales force in the state. Shager reported to John Lehnst, Asgrow's youngest district manager, who was thirty-five years old at the time. There were nine sales representatives, six older than Lehnst, of whom five were in their fifties.

Shortly after the acquisition, Asgrow hired a second sales representative for Wisconsin, Eugene Stouffer, who was 48 years old. Troubled by the disparity in ages between himself and most of his subordinates, Lehnst asked Stouffer several times during the pre-hire interview whether he would mind being supervised by a younger man. Stouffer stated he would not mind.

Two years later, Lehnst actively recruited and hired Lane Schradle, who was twenty-nine years old and had no previous experience in the seed business, to be a third Wisconsin sales representative. In April 1986, Lehnst rated the sales performance of both Shager and Schradle marginal, but made excuses for Schradle's poor performance, while placing Shager on probation for alleged deficiencies in collecting accounts receivable and in the management of salesmen. When the deficiencies persisted, Lehnst recommended to Asgrow's Career Path Committee that Shager be fired, and in July 1986, Shager was terminated. The district court dismissed Shager's case on the defendants' motion for summary judgment, and Shager appealed to the Seventh Circuit Court of Appeals.

Opinion by Judge Posner:

There is evidence that Shager's deficiencies were exaggerated and in any event that they pale beside his outstanding sales performance, inexplicably rated marginal by his hostile supervisor. There is also some although not much evidence of Lehnst's animosity toward older workers. He was heard to say to one of Shager's younger salesmen, "These older people don't much like or much care for us baby boomers, but there isn't much they can do about it." He also was heard to make frequent comments to the effect that "the old guys know how to get around things." And in Schradle's first performance evaluation, Lehnst wrote: "It is refreshing to work with a young man with such a wonderful outlook on life and on his job," though in fact Schradle's performance had not been distinguished.

Of course, it is not a violation of the age discrimination law to fire an employee for insufficient cause, merely because the employee is more than forty years of age and is replaced by a younger person. The statute is not a guarantee of tenure for the older worker, although not all juries understand this. But the question before us in reviewing the grant of summary judgment is only whether Shager produced evidence from which a rational factfinder could infer that the company lied in saying that it fired Shager because he was an unsatisfactory worker. If the only reason an employer offers for firing an employee is a lie, the inference that the real reason was a forbidden one, such as age, may rationally be drawn.

. . . the issue before us is not whether Shager was in fact fired because of his age, which remains to be determined at trial, but whether the question whether he was fired because of his age is genuinely contestable; it is.

It is genuinely contestable for the further reason that Stouffer and Shager were not identically situated. Stouffer was old by Lehnst's standards but had assured Lehnst that he had no problem with being supervised by a much younger man. He was docile old. Shager was, perhaps, "uppitty" old. An employer can fire a worker for being uppity or for any other reason good or bad, without violating the age discrimination law, provided that the reason is not the worker's age. But if the employer would not fire an uppitty worker unless he was also an old worker—if it admired high spirits and an independent attitude only in the young— then age would be a causal factor in the worker's termination. This may have been the case with Asgrow's firing Shager while retaining Stouffer.

The statute does not protect merely the older worker who is perfect from the standpoint of his employer; such a worker needs no protection except from irrational employers, an they are rare. It protects, as a practical matter, the imperfect older worker from being treated worse than the imperfect younger one.

So, we must reverse. We are not entirely happy in doing so, being perplexed that the middle-aged should be thought an oppressed minority requiring the protection of federal law. But that is none of our business as judges. We also are sympathetic to the argument that if Asgrow allowed Lehnst to push out a good worker because of Lehnst's own insecurity as a supervisor, Asgrow will pay a price in the competitive marketplace, and that the threat of such market sanctions deters age discrimination at lower cost than the law can do with its cumbersome and expensive machinery, its gross delays, its frequent errors, and its potential for rigidifying the labor market. But this sanguine view of the power of the marketplace was not shared by the framers and supporters of the Age Discrimination in Employment Act, and we shall not subvert the Act by upholding precipitate grants of summary judgment to defendants.

REVERSED.

During the 1990s, as companies merged, restructured, and scaled back their workforces, millions of job displacements occurred. Statistics confirm that the older a displaced worker is, the more difficult it is for the worker to find a new job. Consequently, the EEOC reported that over 15,000 charges of age discrimination were filed in fiscal year 1997.

The ADEA prohibits employers, employment agencies, and labor unions from taking adverse action against workers because they are 40 years of age or older. Employees who are under age 40 cannot file age discrimination claims on their own behalf, even though they were denied work or were otherwise treated adversely because of their age. Most workers remain in the workforce as long as they want to and are able to work. Accordingly, the ADEA has no maximum age limit for protection. Exceptions generally exist only for certain executives and policymakers, or for a "bona fide occupational qualification" based on safety or other considerations.

Age Discrimination Act of 1975

The **Age Discrimination Act of 1975** applies to employers that receive federal grants or financial assistance and contains no minimum age limit for protected status. Therefore, some younger workers may be able to obtain remedies under this statute. There is no requirement in this Act that administrative remedies must be exhausted before a lawsuit is filed. Consequently, administrative remedies are considered exhausted 180 days following a complaint. Individuals also must give at least 30 days' notice to the defendant, the attorney general, and the secretary of Health and Human Services before commencing litigation.

Older Workers' Benefits Protection Act of 1990

In 1990, the **Older Workers' Benefit Protection Act** (OWBPA) amended requirements for employee benefit plans. The act also spelled out standards for waivers of age discrimination claims, including those used in company severance programs. Waiver standards are discussed at length later in this chapter.

COVERED PERSONS AND ENTITIES UNDER THE ADEA

Employers

The ADEA applies to employers, employment agencies, and labor organizations (29 U.S.C.A. § 623(a)–(c)). An **employer** is defined as a "person engaged in an industry affecting commerce who has twenty or more employees for each working day in each of twenty or more calendar weeks in the current or preceding calendar year" (29 U.S.C.A. § 623(a)). The term "employment agency" is defined at 29 U.S.C.A. § 623(c) and the term "labor organization" is defined at 29 U.S.C.A. § 623(d).

Individual Supervisor as Employer

The United States Supreme Court has not yet addressed the issue of whether an individual supervisor might be an "employer" under the ADEA. A majority of federal courts have held that the ADEA provides no basis for relief against supervisory personnel in their individual capacities, unless the individual otherwise qualifies as an "employer" under the statute, as reflected in *Stults v. Conoco, Inc.*, 76 F.3d 651, 655 (5th Cir. 1996), "[t]he ADEA provides no basis for individual liability for supervisory employees."

The Single Employer Test

Sometimes it is difficult to identify the employee's actual employer. In civil rights actions, distinct entities may be exposed to liability upon a finding that they represent a single, integrated enterprise, a **single employer**.

To determine whether a parent corporation and its subsidiary may be regarded as a "single employer" under the ADEA, the courts apply a four-part test, as set out in *Schweitzer v. Advanced Telemarketing Corp.*, 104 F.3d 761 (5th Cir. 1997), discussed below.

Schweitzer v. Advanced Telemarketing Corp., 104 F.3d 761 (5th Cir. 1997)

Facts:

Schweitzer, who was employed by a subsidiary, brought an ADEA action against the subsidiary and its parent corporation. The United States District Court for the Northern District of Texas entered judgment in her favor, and the employer appealed. Eunice Schweitzer began working at ATC, a subsidiary of NRP, in 1985 as a sales representative, and eventually reached the rank of senior supervisor. In the summer of 1992, the department she worked in was reduced and she was transferred to the GTE Customer Service Department as a supervisor.

The GTE Department was an inbound department responsible for taking orders for GTE services and responding to GTE customers who called in with problems. In August and September of 1992, the GTE Customer Service Department chose to reduce its work force because of a significant reduction in call volume. To effectuate the layoff, the department retained those employees with greater seniority, and laid off employees with less. Schweitzer was laid off in September 1992. She sued NRP and ATC, alleging age discrimination. At trial, the jury found that ATC and NRP were a single employer of Ms. Schweiter.

Opinion by Judge Duhe:

Evidence revealed that: the three members of the ATC Board of Directors all sat on the NRP board, NRP had a 99.5% share of ATC stock, NRP guaranteed ATC's line of credit and ATC had a negative net worth until it achieved a positive cash balance in 1994. Testimony also showed, however, that NRP provided no human resource functions or policy direction to ATC and had no operational involvement with ATC. ATC employees were solely responsible for decisions regarding the hiring, firing or reduction in force of personnel at ATC and had no operational involvement with ATC. Indeed, the vice president of ATC testified NRP was unlikely to know when ATC was forced to reduce staff and was never involved in making such decisions involving personnel.

In civil rights actions, "superficially distinct entities may be exposed to liability upon a finding they represent a single, integrated enterprise: a single employer." *Trevino v. Celanese Corp.*, 701 F.2d 397, 404 (5th Cir. 1983). *Trevino* set out a four-part formula to determine when a parent corporation should be considered the employer of a subsidiary's employee. The formula focuses on *actual control* of employees by the parent company.

Trevino's four part test considers (1) interrelation of operations; (2) centralized control of labor relations; (3) common management; and (4) common ownership or financial control. The second of these factors has traditionally been most important, with courts refining their analysis to the single question, "What entity made the final decisions regarding employment matters related to the person claiming discrimination."

Trevino and the hybrid test are similar, since, under the hybrid test, the right to control an employee's conduct is the most important component. However, we hold that while the *Trevino* and hybrid tests are similar, and will frequently yield the same results, the tests should not be used interchangeably. Rather, the hybrid test should be used as an initial inquiry to resolve, if need be, whether a plaintiff is an employee of the defendant (or one of the defendants, in a multi-defense case) for the purposes of Title VII. If the plaintiff is found to be an employee of one of the defendants under the hybrid test, but questions remain whether a second (or additional) defendant is sufficiently connected to the employer-defendant so as to be considered a single employer, a *Trevino* analysis should be conducted. The *Trevino* analysis will establish if the second or additional defendant is also an employer of the plaintiff.

Since neither ATC nor NRP disputed that Ms. Schweiter was an employee of ATC for the purposes of the ADEA, there was no need for the district court to instruct on the hybrid test. In this case, the *Trevino* test was the proper analysis to determine if ATC and NRP were a single employer.

The district court erred in not following the *Trevino* test to determine single employer status. The district court's instruction did not focus on control of labor relations but instead on a multitude of other factors.

Judgment is REVERSED, and the case is REMANDED for a new trial.

As evidenced by the above case, the controlling factor among the four parts of the *Trevino* test is whether the parent corporation was the final decision maker in the employment matters underlying the litigation, and whether the parent corporation was involved in the daily employment decisions of the subsidiary.

The Fifth Circuit decided whether a parent corporation may be held liable for the allegedly discriminatory conduct of its subsidiary in the case discussed below.

Lusk v. Foxmeyer Health Corporation, 129 F.3d 773 (5th Cir. 1997)

Facts:

The plaintiffs were employed by a subsidiary and terminated as a result of a reduction-in-force. The subsidiary was wholly-owned by a holding company with no employees.

However, the two corporations shared the same board of directors and executive officers. The holding company was a wholly-owned subsidiary of another holding company that had approximately fifteen employees and was affiliated with nearly forty other corporations. The three corporations shared one corporate headquarters.

The plaintiffs alleged that the three corporations engaged in unlawful discrimination under the ADEA by directing lower-level managers to consider age as a factor in determining which employees to discharge. Under the ADEA, the second holding company could not be held liable unless it qualified as an "employer" under the statute. Although the plaintiffs produced evidence establishing common management and ownership between the subsidiary and the holding companies, the court held that those factors alone were insufficient to establish single employer status. There was no evidence to show that the second holding company was involved directly in the subsidiary's daily decisions, shared employees, services, records, and equipment with the subsidiary, commingled bank accounts, receivables, inventories, and credit lines, maintained the subsidiary's books, issued the subsidiary's paychecks or prepared and filed the subsidiary's tax returns. Thus, the court stated that the plaintiffs needed to point to evidence that when the officers and directors of the subsidiary approved the reduction-in-force plan, they were acting in their capacity as officers of the second holding company.

The United States District Court for the Northern District of Texas granted the corporation's motion for summary judgment, and the former employees appealed.

Opinion by Judge Jolly:

The evidence of common management and ownership between NII and its FoxMeyer subsidiaries, taken together with their shared use of a common headquarters building and main telephone number, does not permit an inference that NII is responsible for the decision to terminate employees of FoxMeyer Drug. This conclusion is supported by uncontradicted evidence that NII was nothing more than a holding company with no involvement in or control over the daily operation or employment decisions of its FoxMeyer subsidiaries. Accordingly, the judgment of the district court is
AFFIRMED.

Individual Employees Protected

The ADEA protects individuals 40 years of age and older from age discrimination. However, the ADEA does not prohibit compulsory retirement of any employee who is 65 years of age and older and for the two-year period immediately before retirement, was employed in a bona fide executive or a high policy-making position, if the employee was entitled to an immediate, nonforfeitable annual retirement benefit that equals at least $44,000 (29 U.S.C. § 631(c)).

THE EFFECT OF THE ADEA ON HIRING PRACTICES

Age as a Selection Criterion

The ADEA expressly provides that employment notices for job applicants shall not include any "preference, limitation, specification or discrimination based on age." It is unlawful for employers to state or imply age preferences in newspaper advertisements, Internet postings, orders placed with employment agencies, or other job listings. The use of age-reference language by employment agencies is also unlawful. Applicants may rely on the contents of employment ads or job descriptions as evidence that they were rejected because of their age.

Education and Experience Requirements of Applicants

An employer can lawfully request that applicants furnish their education, experience, and salary histories, even though that information could indicate that an applicant is over the age of 40.

Requesting Age or Date of Birth from Applicants

Requesting an applicant to furnish his or her age or date of birth is not, alone, unlawful. However, the actual use of that information for a discriminatory purpose is prohibited. The EEOC advises that any inquiry about age or date of birth should be accompanied by a notice that the ADEA prohibits discrimination against persons age 40 or older (29 CFR §§ 1625.4(b) and 1625.5).

Requiring Salary History from Applicants

In professional and management personnel searches, employers often require that an applicant state his or her salary position. Exclusion of candidates with high salaries on the basis of that question obviously has a disparate impact on older workers.

Use of the salary history question to purposely exclude older applicants would be unlawful. The requirement, by itself, probably does not provide direct evidence of that purpose.

Impact of Use of Term Overqualified with Applicants

In *EEOC v. District of Columbia Dept. of Human Services*, 729 F. Supp. 907 (D.D.C. 1990), *vacated without opinion*, 925 F.2d 488 (DC Cir. 1991), the court decreed:

Denying employment to an older job applicant because he or she has too much experience, training or education is simply to employ a euphemism to mask the real reason for refusal, namely, in the eyes of the employer the applicant is too old.

The court continued that it "defies common sense" to find that a younger person with less experience and training is more qualified.

An employer normally has no obligation to hire a more experienced person at a higher salary than a younger applicant. There is no obligation for the employer to consider experience other than what is relevant to the skills and responsibilities of the available position. Legitimate concerns about "overqualified" applicants include the possibility that the individual will be bored in the job or that the applicant will not be a team player.

THE EFFECT OF THE ADEA ON PROMOTION REQUIREMENTS

A company is not required to promote on the basis of seniority or the individual who is "next in line" for a promotion, unless the company has previously agreed to do so. The ADEA prohibits promotion on the basis of age, not on the basis of desirable skills, performance traits, philosophies, or other factors.

Objective job descriptions and performance evaluations make for persuasive evidence in promotion cases. Although it is not unlawful to use subjective criteria in promotions, it is more difficult for management to provide factual support for its decisions.

THE EFFECT OF THE ADEA ON RETIREMENT ISSUES

Mandatory Retirement Age and Exempt Employees

With few exceptions, a mandatory retirement age is prohibited. The protections of the ADEA in this area have been substantially expanded over the years. The original law protected workers only between the ages of 40 and 65. The maximum mandatory retirement age was later increased to age 70, and then was eliminated totally in 1986.

There are two statutory exceptions to the mandatory retirement age for specific types of employees:

- Individuals who for the two years preceding retirement were employed as a qualifying executive or high policymaker, and who were entitled to an imme-

diate, nonforfeitable annual retirement benefit from this employer of at least $44,000 per year (29 U.S.C.A. § 631c; 29 CFR § 1627.17); and
- Firefighters and law-enforcement personnel.

Qualifying Executive

For an exception under the "bona fide executive" category, the individual must meet the following requirements:

- spend at least half of his or her working time managing an enterprise, department or subdivision;
- customarily and regularly direct the work of at least two other employees;
- possess the authority to hire and fire or suggest changes in job status of other employees;
- customarily and regularly exercise discretionary powers; and
- spend less than 20% of weekly work hours on nonexempt work (40% for a retail or service establishment).

The foregoing requirements are the same standards that exempt an executive from overtime compensation under the Fair Labor Standards Act. (See Chapter 3).

Even if the standards are met, mandatory retirement may still be prohibited. The executive must receive a retirement benefit in excess of $44,000. The exception does not extend to middle management employees, regardless of their income.

The phrase "bona fide executive" was clarified in *Wendt v. New York Life Ins. Co.*, 76 Fair Empl. Prac. Cas. (BNA) 1500 (S.D.N.Y. 1998). In this case, the plaintiff had worked for the defendant for forty-four years and retired pursuant to his employer's mandatory retirement policy in 1993. Wendt challenged the policy one year later, claiming that, although he had "executive authority up until 1989, he was only a "middle-level manager" upon his retirement four years later. He based this assertion on the fact that from 1989 on, he was forced to report to the executive vice president of the company. However, the plaintiff retained the title "Senior Vice President" until he retired.

The court's findings included:

- Only eight officers in the company ranked higher than the plaintiff;
- Plaintiff received incentive awards for the last two years before retirement, and those awards were normally reserved for employees at the highest management level;
- Plaintiff attended monthly executive officers meetings and departmental status meetings;
- Plaintiff was one of only two individuals in the company authorized to approve claim payments exceeding $250,000;

- Plaintiff supervised a division with forty-five employees and an operating budget of approximately $8.7 million per year; and
- Plaintiff sat on the board of directors of at least seven of the defendant's subsidiaries during the two years preceding his retirement.

The court's opinion stated that "an employee's title and salary cannot automatically place that person within the bona fide executive or high policy-making exemption." However, the court utilized the factors set out in the Code of Federal Regulations regarding the bona fide executive exemption to conclude that the plaintiff was exempt from ADEA overage.

High-Level Policymakers

An individual who plays a significant role in the development and implementation of corporate policy, although not an executive, is exempt from a mandatory retirement age. Consequently, mandatory retirement of high government officials, such as state judges, at a fixed age does not violate the ADEA.

Firefighter and Law-Enforcement Personnel

Setting a mandatory retirement age and a maximum hiring age for firefighters and law-enforcement officers is lawful. The age limitation must have been either in effect under state or local law on March 3, 1983, or enacted after September 20, 1996. Mandatory retirement ages enacted after September 20, 1996 must be set at age 55 or older.

The 1996 law contemplated that the secretary of Health and Human Services would issue regulations on fitness testing by the year 2000. After the issuance of these regulations, employers who want to waive an age restriction must provide their employees with annual opportunities to demonstrate their continued fitness for the job. These two statutory exceptions do not apply to federal agencies. Additionally, elected public officials and their personal staff members are not "employees," and therefore can be forced to retire. Employers must establish the existence of a bona fide occupational qualification for any other workers to avoid mandatory retirement issues.

Most age BFOQ cases have focused on public safety concerns relating to the continued employment in such positions as police officer, firefighter, airline pilot, and bus driver.

Early Retirement Incentives

Early retirement incentives naturally affect older workers in disproportionate numbers. However, the ADEA authorizes voluntary early retirement incentives motivated by economic considerations that would otherwise be prohibited. The election to participate or not participate must be voluntary. However, the courts have determined that a choice between retirement with benefits or a discharge without benefits, for example, is not really a voluntary selection. Additionally, a choice between early retirement and transfer to an undesirable location may actually be a constructive discharge.

REDUCTION-IN-FORCE AND THE ISSUE OF AGE DISCRIMINATION

With the increase in economic competition during the latter part of the twentieth century, a large number of American companies have been forced to utilize a combination of corporate layoffs, plant closings, and reductions-in-force to compete both nationally and internationally. Many employers, in an effort to operate more efficiently, have been forced to undertake significant downsizing to achieve those goals.

Under the ADEA, it is unlawful for an employer effectuating a reduction-in-force to consciously refuse to consider retaining or relocating an individual because of the individual's age, or to regard age as a negative factor in such a consideration, as discussed below.

Thornbrough v. Columbus and Greenville R. Co.,
760 F. 2d 633 (1985)

Facts:

At the time of his discharge from C&G Railroad, Thornbrough was fifty-six years old and held the position of Vice President of Federal Projects. He had worked in the railroad business for approximately thirty-one years, the last five with the C&G Railroad.

In 1982, the railroad determined that, in order to cut its losses, it had to reduce its work force. Including retirements, the railroad's work force was reduced by 46 employees, from 106 to 60.

On June 30, 1982, the railroad "furloughed" Thornbrough. Apparently, no one replaced him; his duties were divided between three individuals who were approximately 47, 30, and 54 years old. The railroad also retained several other younger employees in positions similar to Thornbrough's and hired two new employees with little railroad experience.

Thornbrough brought suit against the railroad, alleging both a violation of the ADEA and breach of contract. He alleged that he was better qualified than the younger employees whom the railroad retained and hired, including the three persons who assumed his former duties. According to Thornbrough, the fact that younger, less well-qualified employees were retained and hired in preference to him was evidence that the railroad had discriminated based on age.

The district court granted the railroad's motion for summary judgment on the ADEA claim on the ground that Thornbrough had failed to establish a *prima facie* case, and dismissed without prejudice his claim for breach of contract. Thornbrough appealed.

Opinion by Judge Goldberg:

If a plaintiff is able to offer sufficient direct evidence of intentional discrimination he obviously should prevail. Usually, however, this is not the case. Unless the employer is a latter-day George Washington, employment discrimination is as difficult to prove as who chopped down the cherry tree. Employers are rarely so cooperative as to include a notation in the personnel file, "fired due to age," or to inform a dismissed employee candidly that he is too old for the job.

The only evidence offered by Thornbrough in support of his claim of age discrimination was that several younger, allegedly less qualified employees were retained during the Railroad's reduction-in-force, and that, at the time of his discharge, two younger, allegedly less well-qualified employees were hired. In our view, these allegations, limited though they are, are sufficient to support a prima facie case. They exude that faint aroma of impropriety that is sufficient to justify requiring the Railroad to give reasons for its decision.

In a reduction-in-force case, what creates the presumption of discrimination is not the discharge itself, but rather the discharge coupled with the retention of a younger employee.

The issue in this case is not whether Thornbrough or the retained employees were better qualified. The railroad is entitled to make that decision for itself. The ADEA was not intended to be a vehicle for judicial second-guessing of business decisions, nor was it intended to transform the courts into personnel managers. However, if the factfinder determines that Thornbrough was clearly better qualified than the employees who were retained, it is entitled to conclude that the railroad's articulated reasons are pretext. Everyone can make a mistake— but if the mistake is large enough, we may begin to wonder whether it was a mistake at all.

In *Simmons v. McGuffey Nursing Home*, 619 F.2d 369 (5th Cir. 1980), we upheld a grant of summary judgment, noting, "the possibility of a jury drawing a contrary inference sufficient to create a dispute as to a material fact does not reify to the point even of a thin vapor capable of being seen or realized by a reasonable jury. *Id.* at 371. Here, through the dim mists, we perceive a thin vapor. Whether it will precipitate into a victorious shower is a question for the jury. It should not have been dispersed by means of summary judgment.

REVERSED AND REMANDED.

A reduction-in-force (RIF) violates the ADEA if it was prompted by a desire to eliminate older workers. However, a RIF prompted by economic conditions which results in older workers being laid off, standing alone, does not create a *prima facie* case of age discrimination.

In a reduction-in-force situation, terminated employees are not replaced. Their jobs are eliminated, although portions of their work may be transferred to other employees or to a newly reorganized position. The issue in downsizing is whether the employer utilized age as a determinative factor in deciding whom to keep and whom to let go. The ADEA specifically permits employer to utilize seniority, laying off the most junior employees. Alternatively, the employer must devise an objective, non-age based system for determining which positions will be abolished, or the employer may adopt an objective system for evaluating performance of individual employees and base layoffs upon such evaluations.

In some instances, terminations are merely disguised as reductions-in-force, and the employer's real goal may be to replace older or highly-paid workers with younger, lower-paid personnel.

Targeting Higher-Paid Workers in Downsizing

It may be difficult to prove discriminatory motivation if an employer targets higher-paid middle manager positions for elimination while retaining lower-paid, primarily younger workers in other classifications. However, such a policy may have a disparate impact on older workers that would have to be justified.

A company that is in financial difficulty has more leeway to use relative salaries in downsizing issues. An employer may use relative pay to force the retirement of older workers if the employer can establish:

1. that cost reductions are *necessary* to avoid the company's liquidation; and
2. that forced retirement of the higher paid workers is the *least detrimental alternative* for the reduction of costs.

In the case discussed below, the Supreme Court reviewed a claim that an employer used pension eligibility as a basis for termination. The court concluded that when a decision is based solely on a factor other than age, even though that factor is correlated with age, the problem of inaccurate and stigmatizing stereotypes disappears. Therefore, the court found no disparate treatment in the *Hazen* case. That reasoning applies also to the issue of pay considerations.

Hazen Paper Co. v. Biggins, 507 U.S. 604, 113 S.Ct. 1701 (1993)

Facts:

Biggins was hired as technical director of Hazen Paper Co. in 1977. He was fired when he was 62 years old and apparently a few weeks short of the years of service he needed for his pension to vest. Biggins brought an action under ADEA and ERISA. Hazen asserted that he had been fired for doing business with Hazen's competitors.

The U.S. district court entered judgment finding ADEA and ERISA violations, but finding that the violation was not willful, and the case was appealed. The First Court of Appeals affirmed in part and reversed in part. The case was appealed to the U.S. Supreme Court.

Opinion by Justice O'Connor:

An employer does not violate the ADEA by interfering with an older employee's pension benefits that would have vested by virtue of the employee's years of service. In a disparate treatment case, liability depends on whether the protected trait—under the ADEA, age—actually motivated the employer's decision. When that decision is wholly motivated by factors other than age, the problem that prompted the ADEA's passage—inaccurate and stigmatizing stereotypes about older workers' productivity and competence—disappears. Thus, it would be incorrect to say that a decision based on years of service—which is analytically distinct from age—is necessarily age based. None of this Court's prior decisions should be read to mean that an employer violates the ADEA whenever its reason for firing an employee is improper in any respect. The foregoing holding does not preclude the possibility of liability where an employer uses pension status as a proxy for age, of dual liability under ERISA and the ADEA, or of liability where vesting is based on age rather than years of service. Because the Court of Appeals cited additional evidentiary support for ADEA liability, this case is remanded for that court to reconsider whether the jury had sufficient evidence to find such liability.

We now clarify that there is no disparate treatment under the ADEA when the factor motivating the employer is some feature other than the employee's age.

Because age and years of service are analytically distinct, an employer can take account of one while ignoring the other, and thus it is incorrect to say that a decision based on years of service is necessarily "age based."

Perhaps it is true to say that older employees of Hazen Paper are more likely to be "close to vesting" than younger employees. Yet a decision by the company to fire an older employee solely because he has nine-plus years of service and therefore is "close to vesting' would not constitute discriminatory treatment on the basis of age. The prohibited stereotype ("Older employees are likely to be_____") would not have figured in this decision, and the attendant stigma would not ensue.

We do not mean to suggest that an employer *lawfully* could fire an employee in order to prevent his pension benefits from vesting. Such conduct is actionable under Section 510 of ERISA, as the Court of Appeals rightly found in affirming judgment for respondent under that statute. But it would not, without more, violate the ADEA. That law requires the employer to ignore an employee's age (absent a statutory exemption or defense); it does not specify *further* characteristics that an employer must also ignore.

We do not preclude the possibility that an employer who targets employees with a particular pension status on the assumption that these employees are likely to be older thereby engages in age discrimination. Pension status may be a proxy for age, not in the sense that the ADEA makes the two factors equivalent, but in the sense that the employer may suppose a correlation between the two factors and act accordingly. Nor do we rule out the possibility of dual liability under ERISA and the ADEA where the decision to fire the employee was motivated both by the employee's age and by his pension status. Our holding is simply that an employer does not violate the ADEA just by interfering with an older employee's pension benefits that would have vested by virtue of the employee's years of service.

Although there was no direct evidence of petitioners' motivation, except for two isolated comments by the Hazens, the Court of Appeals did note the following indirect evidence; Respondent was asked to sign a confidentiality agreement, even though no other employee had been required to do so, and his replacement was a younger man, who was given a less onerous agreement. In the ordinary ADEA case, indirect evidence of this kind may well suffice to support liability if the plaintiff also shows that the employer's explanation for its decision—here that respondent had been disloyal to Hazen Paper by doing business with its competitors—is "unworthy of credence." But inferring age-motivation from the implausibility of the employer's explanation may be problematic in cases where other unsavory motives, such as pension interference, were present. We therefore remand the case for the Court of Appeals to consider whether the jury had sufficient evidence to find an ADEA violation.

WAIVER OF AGE DISCRIMINATION CLAIMS

Voluntary waivers are a means by which employers can protect themselves from liability under the ADEA when faced with a reduction-in-force. An employer may encourage employees to waive their rights under the ADEA by offering added incentives in addition to what the employees are already entitled to upon discharge. The waiver of age discrimination claims in return for receipt of severance benefits or participation in an early retirement programs is valid, assuming the waiver meets specific statutory standards. These standards apply to both voluntary and involuntary terminations.

Congress amended the ADEA by enacting the **Older Workers Benefit Protect Act** (OWBPA) to provide specific requirements for waivers of rights and claims under the ADEA. To bar a claim under the ADEA, a release must conform to the requirement of the OWBPA.

Knowing and Voluntary Requirement for Waivers

Under the OWBPA, a waiver is not effective unless it is made knowingly and voluntarily. Minimum standards for "knowingly and voluntarily" are set forth in the statute as follows:

1. The waiver must be part of a written agreement between the employer and the employee that is calculated to be understood by the individual, or by the average individual eligible to participate.
2. The waiver must not have the effect of misleading, misinforming, or failing to inform participant and affected individuals.

3. The waiver should not exaggerate the benefits or minimize the limitations of any advantages or disadvantages.
4. The waiver must refer specifically to rights or claims arising under the ADEA.
5. The waiver cannot cover claims that might arise after the waiver is signed.
6. The waiver must provide for consideration in addition to that to which the individual is already entitled in the absence of the waiver.
7. The employee must be advised in writing to consult with an attorney before signing the waiver.
8. The employee must have at least 21 days to consider the agreement (45 days for a group or class of employees). The time period runs from the date of the employer's final offer. Material changes to the final offer will restart the running of the period.
9. There must be a "cooling-off" period of at least seven days following execution of the waiver, during which the employee may revoke the agreement before it becomes effective.

The parties may not agree to shorten the revocation period for the waiver. However, an employee may sign a release prior to the end of the 21- or 45-day period. An employee's decision to shorten the 21- or 45-day period must be knowing and voluntary, and not induced by fraud, misrepresentation, a threat to withdraw or alter the offer prior the expiration of the 21- or 45-day period, or by providing incentives to employees who sign the release prior to the expiration of the period.

PROVING AN AGE DISCRIMINATION CLAIM

The ultimate issue in an age discrimination case is whether the employer intentionally discriminated against the plaintiff. In employment discrimination cases, the plaintiff is rarely able to produce *direct evidence* of discrimination. To ease the evidentiary burdens on employment discrimination plaintiffs, the courts have established a shifting standard of proof to prove age discrimination.

Elements of a *Prima Facie* Case—Disparate Treatment

Initially, a plaintiff must establish a *prima facie* case of discriminatory motivation by demonstrating by a *preponderance of the evidence* that:

1. The plaintiff was discharged (or suffered other adverse employment action).
2. The plaintiff was within the protected group (age 40 or older) at the time of discharge or other adverse employment action.

3. The plaintiff was qualified to do the job from which he or she was discharged or in which he or she was adversely affected.
4. The plaintiff was either replaced by someone outside the protected class, replaced by someone younger, or otherwise show that he or she was discharged or suffered adverse effects because of his or her age.

The court in *Scott v. University of Mississippi*, 148 F.3d 493 (5th Cir. 1998), discussed below, considered those four factors in reaching its decision.

Scott v. University of Mississippi, 148 F.3d 493 (5th Cir. 1998)

Facts:

Scott was hired as a reference librarian in the Law School Library in 1991. In 1993, when she was 54 years old, Scott applied for the position of legal writing specialist, a ten-month contractual, non-tenure track position. The hiring decision was made by a four-member committee. From 26 total applicants, the committee selected six finalists. Scott was ranked third in the finalists. The committee initially offered the position to the first finalist, who rejected the offer, and then to the second finalist, a 33-year-old applicant, who accepted the position. Scott filed a charge of age discrimination with the EEOC, and then filed this lawsuit.

In early 1995, when a legal writing specialist position again became available, she applied for the position. Of 33 applicants, Scott was again a finalist, but was not offered the job.

Scott brought action against the university, alleging that the university's failure to hire her as a legal writing specialist on two separate occasions constituted discrimination and retaliation, in violation of the ADEA. The jury rendered a verdict for the employee on her discrimination claim and for the university on the retaliation claim. The Fifth Circuit wrote that Scott and her expert did nothing more than present a difference of opinion as to whether Scott or the candidate selected was better qualified for the job, and therefore, did not establish either directly or through inference that the university intentionally refused to hire Scott because of her age. The court added that the evidence was insufficient to conclude that Scott was *clearly* better qualified and, therefore, did not suffice to present a jury question as to pretext. The court agreed with the district court that the finalist who accepted the job had clerked for a federal judge and had more extensive writing experience than Scott. The court also found that Scott's assertions that the jury was entitled to infer discrimination from evidence that she was treated differently from the other applicants in that the committee did not call her references, did not tell her to bring a writing sample to her interview, and did not take her to lunch when she was interviewed. The court explained that the committee made a decision to call the references of only the top two candidates, did not take all finalists to lunch, and that the committee's failure to tell her to provide writing samples until the date of her interview may support a reasonable inference that the committee was less than conscientious about her application, but "it does not represent even a mere scintilla of evidence of age discrimination."

Opinion by Judge Garza:

The ADEA cannot protect older workers from erroneous or even arbitrary personnel decisions, but only from decisions which are unlawfully motivated. Such disputes do not support a finding of discrimination and have no place in front of a jury.

In denying the University's first partial summary judgment motion, the district court noted that "it may be significant that the law school has hired only one person in the over-forty age bracket since 1986 as a regular full-time professor" and that [t]hose in the protected age group who have been employed were hired as 'visiting professor' or 'adjunct professor' or 'professor emeritus' or 'acting professor.'" We have previously stated that while statistical evidence "may be probative of pretext in limited circumstances" it "usually cannot rebut the employer's articulated nondiscriminatory reasons."

For the foregoing reasons, the decision of the district court denying the University's motion for judgment as a matter of law is REVERSED and judgment is hereby RENDERED in the University's favor.

Preferential Treatment within the Protected Age Group

An individual may be able to establish unlawful preference or treatment in favor of other workers within the protected age group. The age difference must be substantial in order to prove discriminatory motivation, as discussed in *O'Connor v. Consolidated Coin Caterers Corp.*, 517 U.S. 308, 116 S.Ct. 1307 (1996). In that case, the Supreme Court found that a 56-year-old employee who was replaced by a 40-year-old employee met the "substantially younger" requirement.

Elements of a *Prima Facie* Case—Reduction in Force

In age discrimination cases involving a reduction in force, the courts use slightly different standards for the prima facie case. The plaintiff must show that a discharge or layoff had a specific impact on workers within the protected age group, as compared to younger workers, by proving the following:

1. the plaintiff was discharged or laid off;
2. the plaintiff was within the ADEA's protected class when discharged or laid off;
3. the plaintiff was qualified to assume another position at the time of his/her discharge or layoff; and
4. circumstantial or direct evidence exists from which a fact-finder reasonably might conclude that the employer intended to discriminate on the basis of age in discharging or laying off the plaintiff.

The case below discusses such evidence of intent to discriminate.

Woodhouse v. Magnolia Hosp., 92 F.3d 248 (5th Cir. 1996)

Facts:

Woodhouse, who was 53 years old at the time of her discharge, had been employed by Magnolia Hospital for two separate periods totaling 23 years. Woodhouse, a registered nurse, served as Magnolia's director of admission for 14 years preceding her termination.

During 1993, Magnolia eliminated 61 full-time positions due to a loss of approximately $1.2 million in operating revenues. The administrative staff selected the positions to be eliminated, and the head of the department inserted the names of the employees who held that position. Woodhouse's position as director of admissions was chosen for elimination. Woodhouse was discharged on January 24, 1994. In November 1994, she applied for a clinical nursing position at Magnolia. Magnolia did not rehire her, ostensibly because she had not been involved in clinical nursing services for 14 years.

Woodhouse sued Magnolia under the ADEA, alleging that she was discharged and denied a clinical nursing position because of her age. The jury awarded her $50,700 in back pay and $50,700 in liquidated damages.

Opinion by Judge Benavides:

The crucial inquiry involves Magnolia's proffered reasons why Woodhouse was chosen for termination and why it refused to rehire her as a clinical nurse.

In the instant cause, Woodhouse presented evidence that Tommy Alexander, chairman of Magnolia's board of trustees and a practicing gynecologist, and Vicky Franks, an employee in the business office who was also terminated, discussed the impending terminations two weeks before the RIF. According to Franks, Alexander advised her that Magnolia was planning to lay off the "older employees." Eight months later, Franks called Alexander and surreptitiously taped a subsequent conversation. The tape contained the following admission:

FRANKS: You know back in January when I came in for my pap smear. [A]nd I told you I thought I was having stress headaches from being worried about being laid off, and you said, don't worry about being laid off, you're not gonna get laid off. They're gonna lay off those old people and the people that needed done been—

ALEXANDER: That's what they told me.

At trial, Alexander testified that he did not remember making the statement and that no one ever told him Magnolia was planning to discharge older employees.

The jury apparently chose to believe that Alexander made the statement and that Magnolia intended to use age as one criteria in its discharge decision. We conclude that the jury could properly consider the statement as evidence that Magnolia intentionally discriminated against Woodhouse because of her age.

Interestingly, Magnolia was unable to clearly identify either the person who made the decision to eliminate Woodhouse's position or the process by which Woodhouse's position was chosen for elimination.

Based on the foregoing, we affirm the judgment of the district court.

The court additionally found that conflicting evidence was introduced on whether the refusal to rehire Woodhouse was based on her qualifications. At trial, the hospital personnel testified that Woodhouse had no clinical nursing experience in the past 14 years and had taken no refresher courses in the interim. No one at Magnolia ever told her that she needed to take a refresher course. The director of nursing services testified that this requirement for a refresher course was found in a "nursing newsletter." Woodhouse rebutted that testimony by saying that the refresher course requirement only pertained to nurses who did not have a current license, which she had. Woodhouse also presented evidence that none of the 76 nurses hired by the time of trial were her age or older. Therefore, the court concluded that the jury was thus entitled to find that the refresher requirement was a pretext for discrimination.

In RIF cases, plaintiffs do not have to establish that they were qualified for the job or that they met the legitimate expectations of their employer. The question is often what their level of performance was relative to younger coworkers who were retained, or whether they were qualified for any jobs that remained open after the cutback, not their former position.

Elements of a *Prima Facie* Case—Hostile Work Environment Claims

Standards for a hostile work environment relating to older workers are the same as those for sexual harassment:

- The plaintiff must be 40 years of age or older.
- The harassment must be age-related.
- The harassment must be unwelcome.
- The harassment must affect a term or condition of employment; and
- The employer knows, or should have known, about the harassment, and fails to take prompt effective action.

Employers are liable for their supervisors' acts of harassment. Incidents where a supervisor creates intolerable working conditions for an older employee and forces a retirement or resignation are unlawful, as discussed in the case below.

EEOC v. Massey Yardley Chrysler Plymouth, Inc.,
117 F.3d 1244 (11th Cir. 1997)

Facts:

EEOC brought this action in the district court alleging Massey Yardley Chrysler Plymouth, Inc. willfully violated the ADEA by unlawfully discriminating against Paigo in her place of employment by subjecting her to a hostile work environment and harassing and constructively discharging her because of her age.

Paigo was hired as a title clerk at Massey Yardley in 1987, at the age of 54. In the early 1990s she began going through menopause. Although her work performance remained good, she gained weight, had hot flashes, cried easily, and became nervous and sensitive about her age. She claimed that James Cox, her immediate supervisor, and Bonnie Griffin, the comptroller and general manager, in particularly began making demeaning, age-related comments on a daily basis. Griffin's comments included demeaning statement about Paigo's mental capacity. Paigo testified that she told Griffin that she would understand how it felt when she went through menopause, whereupon Griffin responded that "she would never go through it and become an old lady like [Paigo] was."

On several occasions, Paigo told Cox and Griffin that she was going to complain directly to the president of the dealership. They warned her, in an "authoritative" tone of voice, against taking such action. When she twice attempted to talk with him, Yardley told her to work it out with Griffin directly because he would not interfere between her and her supervisor.

The situation came to a head when Paigo returned from a week's vacation to find her office in a mess, with new files and mail strewn around, instead of neatly stacked. A short while later, she drafted a letter demanding a large raise and an end to the age-related comments, and left copies in the offices of Cox, Griffin, and Yardley.

The next day, the switchboard operator showed her a newspaper ad for a "title clerk" and asked if she were quitting. When Paigo confronted Cox and Griffin about the ad and her letter, Griffin told her that a new "helper" would be starting, and that the company had forgotten to tell her. Griffin denied her raise request, told her that she had no authority to stop the age-related comments, and told her that Paigo was "too sensitive" and would "just have to get used to it" since she was "an old lady." Paigo quit at that point.

Her replacement started immediately. Company records confirm that she was hired as a title clerk, not as a helper, the day that Paigo quit.

Paigo searched for employment for two years, and took a job in a position that paid less than she was earning at Massey Yardley.

After the filing of the EEOC claim, Massey Yardley offered an "unconditional offer of reinstatement," with a return to her old job, with no back pay or a raise, and a policy statement reaffirming its policy not to discriminate. Paigo rejected the offer because she believed the harassment would continue and she did not want to work under Cox and Griffin. Just before trial, Massey Yardley offered to institute an antidiscrimination policy and place her in a dealership operated by Yardley's sons, where she would seldom encounter Cox or Griffin. Paigo refused the offer.

Opinion by Judge Campbell:

The case was submitted to the jury by means of four questions set out in a so-called "Special Verdict Form." Responding to these, the jury found (1) that Paigo was subjected to a hostile work environment because of her age; (2) that a reasonable person would have found the hostile working conditions she was subjected to so difficult or unpleasant as to have felt forced to resign; (3) that Paigo lost $10,513.86 in back pay and fringe benefits because of her constructive discharge, but (4) that defendant's conduct with regard to Paigo was not done with knowledge or reckless disregard as to whether it was a violation of the ADEA.

After the verdict, the EEOC moved to renew its motion for judgment as a a matter of law on willfulness and further moved to conform the damages to the evidence (i.e. by increasing the $10,513.86 award), and for equitable relief that, among other things would enjoin defendant from further employment discrimination. Massey Yardley renewed its motion for judgment as a matter of law. All motions were denied by the court without comment.

The EEOC now appeals, and Massey Yardley cross-appeals, from the court's denial of the parties' post-judgment motions. We affirm in part, vacate in part, and remand.

The court held that: (1) whether supervisor's and manager's age-related comments were unwelcome was for jury; (2) whether employer's violation was willful was for jury, but (3) district court abused its discretion in turning down all equitable relief sought by EEOC.

A small number of poorly chosen comments about age do not necessarily create a hostile work environment. Comments by a supervisor that "old people should be seen and not heard," and that "women over 55 should not be working," were not sufficient to create a hostile work environment in *Crawford v. Medina General Hospital*, 96 F.3d 830 (6th Cir. 1996).

The harassment by a non-management employee's peers of older workers may subject the employer to liability. Such harassment might include jokes and cartoons, age-related insults, verbal abuse, or even physically threatening behavior. In an egregious case, a coworker insulted an older worker, slapped her, and called her a "senile old thing" when she complained about the coworker's taking work from her. The employer fired the older worker without talking to her and did not punish the abuser. (*See Blake v. J.C. Penney Co., Inc.*, 894 F.2d 274 (8th Cir. 1990)).

EMPLOYER'S BURDEN OF PROOF

Legitimate Nondiscriminatory Reason for Employer's Decision

Once a plaintiff establishes a *prima facie* case, the burden of proof shifts to the employer. To overcome the presumption of intentional discrimination created by plaintiff's establishment of a *prima facie* case, the employer must articulate a legitimate, nondiscriminatory reason for the employment decision at issue. If the employer fails to articulate a legitimate reason, the presumption requires the fact finder to rule for the plaintiff.

The ADEA does not protect older employees from erroneous or even arbitrary personnel decisions that are unrelated to the plaintiff's age. In *EEOC v. Texas Instruments, Inc.,*100 F.3d 1173, 1182 (5th Cir. 1996), as discussed below, the court refused to accept the plaintiff's argument that the employer's ignorance of its own termination procedures was evidence of pretext.

---

*EEOC v. Texas Instruments, Inc.,*100 F.3d 1173, 1182 (5th Cir. 1996)

Facts:

Sweeping cutbacks in national defense spending and dramatically reduced procurements by the United States Department of Defense forced TI to reorganize its Defense Systems and Electronics Group ("DSEG") to lay off approximately 850 out of 1700 DSEG manufacturing employees between 1988 and 1994. The EEOC studied many of the layoffs but attempted to make a case for illegal discrimination only in regard to six manufacturing supervisors in the DSEG (the "Six Supervisors"), victims of TI's reduction-in-force, who were protected by the Age Discrimination in Employment Act of 1967.

TI's traditional policy favoring senior employees was not followed in the RIF. Douthit, the head of DSEG's manufacturing division, suggested to management that TI's policy favoring senior employees would impose significant costs on the company, as supervisor staff was concentrated in high pay grades. Furthermore, unwavering commitment to seniority promised a reorganized workplace that would not have the contemporary skills necessary to assimilate new technologies.

Not only did TI eschew reliance on seniority in its RIF of the manufacturing supervisors, it also did not consider either performance evaluations or the company's Key Personal Assessments (KPAs).

Opinion by Judge Jones:

As we have stated, the ADEA was not created to redress wrongful discharge simply because the terminated worker was over the age of forty . . . To make out an ADEA claim, the plaintiff must establish some nexus between the employment actions taken by the employer and the employee's age.

TI carefully outlined why it disregarded the seniority protection typically afforded to its employees in a RIF and why it did not consider performance evaluations or KPAs when determining which supervisors to retain. The ECOC failed to undermine this decision.

TI's decision to replace a seniority system that would impede its ability to reduce its workforce while maximizing the efficiency and expertise of the remaining employees does not, without a clear nexus to discrimination, create an inference of age discrimination.

The agency's case, in sum, confused a quarrel with the merits of the company's business decision—a quarrel in which the ADEA plays no role—with a case of illegal age discrimination.

For the following reasons, the district court's award of summary judgment to TI on the merits of the claims brought by the EEOC is AFFIRMED.

An example of a reasonable business decision in an age discrimination case can be found in *Dilla v. West*, 4 F. Supp. 2d 113 (M.D. Ala. 1998), 76 Fair Empl. Prac. Cas. (BNA) 1414 (M.D. Ala. May 7, 1998). In that case, the Fort Rucker Army base had an opening for an air traffic control specialist. Sixteen applicants were considered to be highly qualified for the position. A panel of supervisors, headed by the chief of the division with the vacancy, considered each applicant's qualifications and arrived at a joint consensus on who should be selected. The applicant pool consisted of, among others, three air traffic controllers over the age of 40, and Kevin Nolan, who was 29 years old. Nolan was eventually offered the job.

The panel justified its decision on the following facts:

- Fourteen employees in the division that had the opening were close to retirement age. Thus, the panel wanted an applicant who would remain in the division for some time.
- The division was under pressure to save money, and an applicant with less experience would receive a lower salary than an applicant with a higher level of expertise.
- The panel was able to distinguish who was close to retirement without knowledge of the applicants' age, since there was a fixed retirement plan in the division based on years of experience only.

The court in this case was forced to answer the question of whether a refusal to hire based on the likelihood of an applicant's retirement in the near future violated the ADEA. The court wrote that in cases where a link exists between the proffered reason for termination or denial of employment and the plaintiff's age, the employer must have made hiring or firing decisions based on "inaccurate and stigmatizing stereotypes" in order for age discrimination to have occurred.

The court also found that "the mere fact that there exists a perfect correlation, or even a direct link between age and the factor purportedly relied upon by the employer does not perforce mean that the employer has impermissibly relied on age." *Id.* at 1142–1143. The defendant's explanation for how its decision was made to hire an applicant with less experience was sufficient to support the conclusion that they focused on the candidates' retirement-eligibility status without reliance upon their ages or age-biased assumptions regarding older employees' propensity to retire earlier.

Age as a Bona Fide Occupational Qualification

Reliance on a person's age is permitted if that age is a bona fide occupational qualification, or BFOQ. For example, employers have claimed that age is a BFOQ for airline captains and flight officers, bus drivers, law-enforcement officers and campus security officers.

Any claimed BFOQ must relate to the ability to perform the specific job, and safety generally is the justification for an age-related BFOQ, with physical or mental illness usually the issue. The alleged inability of older workers to perform their jobs safely must be supported by objective evidence.

Reasonable Factors Other Than Age Defense

The ADEA states that there is no unlawful discrimination when an employer relies on a **reasonable factor other than age** (known as the RFOA defense) (29 U.S.C.A. § 623(f)(1)). RFOA includes uniformly required credentials such as education, prior experience, and systems that measure merit or the quality or quantity of performance. So long as performance standards are uniformly applied, persons who do not measure up to those standards may be discharged "for good cause" regardless of their age (29 U.S.C.A. § 623(f)(3)).

Cost savings and budget constraints are most often listed as RFOA defenses, but these have only been successful when the dispute has involved a term or condition of employment other than an employee benefit plan. Costs are not considered to be a legitimate factor if they are too closely linked to age.

Market forces can also be a RFOA. Salaries higher than those paid to incumbent workers doing similar work can be paid to attract younger professionals. However, it will be age discrimination for any employer who pays higher salaries to attract new, and presumably younger, workers to not match bona fide offers made to older employees or applicants.

The RFOA exception has been successful when selecting employees for a reduction in force (RIF) on the basis of relative job performance and qualification for remaining positions. Additionally, the RFOA exception appears to be more relevant in a disparate impact case. Even though a policy may have a disparate impact on older workers, it is lawful if it is based on RFOA.

PLAINTIFF'S ULTIMATE BURDEN-PROVING PRETEXT

By articulating legitimate reasons for the employment decision in controversy, the employer rebuts the presumption of discrimination, and the burden of persuasion shifts back to the plaintiff to prove that the reasons articulated by the employer are not true reasons, but a *pretext* for discrimination.

Standard of Proof

The Fifth Circuit in *Rhodes v. Guiberson Oil*, 75 F.3d 989 (5th Cir. 1996), as discussed below, clarified the standard of proof to establish pretext, including:

1. The plaintiff must show that a material fact issue exists as to whether each of the employer's stated reasons for the termination actually motivated the employer, and;
2. The plaintiff must present substantial evidence to create a reasonable inference that age was a determining factor in the employer's decision.

Proof of pretext is not required when the plaintiff presents direct evidence of discrimination.

Rhodes v. Guiberson Oil, 75 F.3d 989 (5th Cir. 1996)

Facts:

The employer told the 54-year-old Rhodes, both in termination papers, and at the time of his discharge, that he was being terminated because of a reduction in force. At trial, the employer had to explain why a 42-year-old employee had filled his position within six weeks of the "lay-off." A company supervisor testified that Rhodes actually was fired because of poor work performance, not because of a reduction in force. The employer testified that it did not tell Rhodes the real reason for his termination in an effort to spare his feelings. On the basis of this evidence, the Fifth Circuit Court of Appeals, *en banc*, overturned a lower court decision and affirmed a $200,000 jury verdict for the plaintiff. The court held that the company's inconsistent reasons for the plaintiff's termination could support the jury's inference of pretext and discrimination.

Opinion by Judges Davis and Duhe:

The evidence necessary to support an inference of discrimination will vary from case to case. A jury may be able to infer discriminatory intent in an appropriate case from substantial evidence that the employer's proffered reasons are false. The evidence may, for example, strongly indicate that the employer has introduced fabricated justifications for an employee's discharge, and not otherwise suggest a credible nondiscriminatory explanation.

The Fifth Circuit failed to find pretext in *Scott v. University of Mississippi*, 148 F.3d 493 (5th Cir. 1998), discussed on next page.

Scott v. University of Mississippi, 148 F.3d 493 (5th Cir. 1998)

Facts:

A state university law library employee claimed age discrimination and denial of promotion. While Scott was highly qualified for the legal writing specialist position that she sought, she was not considered the most qualified because she lacked the legal writing experience and federal clerkship qualification that the successful candidate possessed. Statistical evidence that the five legal writing teachers hired by the university during the relevant period were under 40 was found to be flawed, since there was no comparison of the persons hired to the pool of qualified applicants.

Opinion by Justice Scalia:

" . . . while statistical evidence may be probative of pretext in limited circumstances, it usually cannot rebut the employer's articulated nondiscriminatory reasons."

Arbitrary, Capricious, or Nonsensical Employment Decisions

Proof that the employer's decision was arbitrary, capricious, or nonsensical may support a finding that the employer's "articulated reason" for the employment action is a pretext for discrimination (See *Dodd v. Runyon*, 114 F.3 726, 730 (8th Cir. 1997)). In that case, the court found that the employer's irregular and arbitrary administration of its seniority system was a pretext for discrimination.

Age-Related Comments

Individuals claiming age discrimination often search for something that a manager or supervisor said to show that age was a factor in their adverse employment decision. Such remarks are particularly damaging if made by a management person who actually participated in the adverse employment decision, close in time to the event. Similar remarks by an individual who was not a decision maker may have little effect on the amount of damage caused by an age-related comment. However, juries often attach more weight to the remarks of a decision maker for other reasons.

Examples of language that has supported age bias claims in the past include:

1. "younger blood" desired (*EEOC v. G-K-G, Inc.*, 39 F.3d 1247 (8th Cir. 1997));
2. "too old to learn anything new" (*Greanias v. Sears, Roebuck & Co.*, 774 F. Supp. 462 (N.D. Ill. 1991));

3. "We've got to get rid of these old gals and get some young gals in here." (*Tibbits v. Van Den Bergh Foods Co., div. of Conoco, Inc.*, 859 F. Supp. 1168 (N.D. Ill. 1994));
4. "These older people don't much like or much care for us baby boomers, but there isn't much they can do about it." (*Shager v. Upjohn Co.*, 913 F.2d 398 (7th Cir. 1990)).

In some situations, excessive age-related comments, jokes, or insults can help the plaintiff prove pretext. Such remarks will be considered evidence of discrimination if they are:

1. age-related;
2. proximate in time to the adverse employment action;
3. made by a person with authority over the employment decision at issue; and
4. related to the employment decision at issue.

Biased or age-related comments such as those listed above are not always treated as direct evidence. There must be a sufficient link between the statement and the decision-making process. Someone who had the ability to affect the decision must make the age-related statement, and the remark must indicate that it had some bearing on the decision.

"Stray remarks" by persons who were not involved in the employment decision, or which were too remote in time or too isolated to be strong evidence of discrimination, are not direct evidence.

PERSONNEL RECORDS TO BE MAINTAINED UNDER THE ADEA

Appendix E lists the types of records that must be maintained under the ADEA. Record retention periods for these documents are discussed in Appendix C.

ADMINISTRATIVE PROCEDURES UNDER THE ADEA

The ADEA, like Title VII, is administered by the Equal Employment Opportunity Commission (EEOC). Generally, the same EEOC administrative procedures govern Title VII and ADEA cases.

There are three key differences, however, between the two statutes. Unlike Title VII, the ADEA provides that the charging party has a right to a jury trial, regardless of whether he or she seeks equitable relief in addition to legal remedies.

Second, the ADEA provides that if a state law prohibits age discrimination in employment and establishes or authorizes a state authority to grant or seek relief from such discrimination, the plaintiff may not file suit under the ADEA until 60 days after proceedings have been commenced under state law. The United States Supreme Court has interpreted this provision as requiring a complainant to resort to appropriate state administrative proceedings prior to bringing suit in federal court (See *Oscar Mayer & Co. v. Evans*, 441 U.S. 750, 753 (1979)).

Third, a complainant alleging age discrimination under the ADEA need not wait for the EEOC or FEP to make a determination on the charge and issue a notice of right to sue letter before filing a civil action. Once the ADEA charge has been filed with the EEOC and the FEP, a civil action may be commenced after a 60-day waiting period.

REMEDIES AVAILABLE UNDER THE ADEA

Successful ADEA plaintiffs may recover:

1. Back pay, including the value of the lost benefits, less mitigation amount;
2. Reinstatement or front pay;
3. Liquidated (double) damages (if a willful violation is proved); and
4. Attorneys' fees and costs.

Review the case below for that court's analysis of remedies available under the ADEA:

McKennon v. Nashville Banner Pub. Co., 513 U.S. 356, 115 S.Ct. 879 (1995)

Facts:

A discharged employee sued the employer under ADEA. The U.S. district court found that the employee's subsequently discovered misconduct in removing confidential documents from the office precluded recovery, and granted summary judgment for the employer. The employee appealed. The court of appeals affirmed. The case was appealed to the U.S. Supreme Court, which reversed and remanded.

Opinion by Justice Scalia:

In giving effect to the ADEA, we must recognize the duality between the legitimate interests of the employer and the important claims of the employee who invokes the national employment policy mandated by the Act. The employee's wrongdoing must be taken into account, we conclude, lest the employer's legitimate concerns be ignored, the ADEA, like

Title VII, is not a general regulation of the workplace but a law which prohibits discrimination. The statute does not constrain employers from exercising significant other prerogatives and discretions in the course of the hiring, promoting, and discharging of their employees. In determining appropriate remedial action, the employee's wrongdoing becomes relevant not to punish the employee, or out of concern "for the relative moral worth of the parties," but to take due account of the lawful prerogatives of the employer in the usual course of its business and the corresponding equities that it has arising from the employee's wrongdoing.

It would be both inequitable and pointless to order the reinstatement of someone the employer would have terminated, and will terminate, in any event and upon lawful grounds. The beginning point in the trial court's formulation of a remedy should be calculation of backpay from the date of the unlawful discharge to the date the new information was discovered.

Where an employer seeks to rely upon after-acquired evidence of wrongdoing, it must first establish that the wrongdoing was of such severity that the employee in fact would have been terminated on those grounds alone if the employer had known of it at the time of the discharge. The concern that employers might as a routine matter undertake extensive discovery into an employee's background or performance on the job to resist claims under the Act is not an insubstantial one, but we think the authority of the courts to award attorney's fees, mandated under the statute, and to invoke the appropriate provisions of the Federal Rules of Civil Procedure will deter most abuses.

The judgment is reversed, and the case is remanded to the Court of Appeals for the Sixth Circuit for further proceedings consistent with this opinion.

TERMS

Age Discrimination Act of 1975
employee
employer
Older Workers' Benefit Protection Act
reasonable factor other than age
single employer

REVIEW QUESTIONS

1. A 42-year-old applicant filed a claim against an employer with whom she interviewed, claiming that the ad to which she responded did not list communication skills as a requisite for the open position. However, the employer cited the outstanding communication skills of the 28-year-old who was selected from the applicant pool.

2. A supervisor recommended whom to discharge, but did not make the final decision to terminate. Would a jury consider his age-related comments as direct evidence of discrimination? Explain the legal reasoning behind your answer.

3. During a reduction in force in an automobile manufacturing plant, two departments were combined, requiring the elimination of one supervisory position. Greg Woodward was 57 years old at the time, with 24 years' seniority at the plant, 15 of which were spent in supervisory positions. Jerry Hatchell was 43 years old, with 10 years of supervisory experience. The plant laid off Woodward because it did not believe that he could handle the management of two departments. What does Woodward need to prove to convince a court that the plant was guilt of age discrimination?

4. Does the ADEA prohibit discrimination by an employer who establishes a minimum age requirement for prospective employees because of the cost of insurance premiums?

5. A telecommunications company offers 20 employees over the age of 60 additional benefits if they voluntarily retire within the next six months. No pressure is placed on these employees and the employer takes no retaliatory action against those who decline its offer of early retirement. Is the employer's action permissible under the ADEA?

6. David Jacobson applies for a job as a bankruptcy paralegal with a small Milwaukee law firm. The administrator advises him that he was not selected for the vacancy because he has "too much experience and education." Is that a valid reason for denying Jacobson a position? Is that a pretext for discrimination on the basis of age?

7. Is it possible that a policy that results in a disparate impact is not prohibited under the ADEA if it is based on a reasonable factor other than age?

8. Courts often are required to determine whether a statement relating to age is direct evidence or merely a stray remark. Explain the factors that courts might find to be direct evidence of age discrimination.

9. Discuss the differences between the ADEA and Title VII.

10. Can a state require the retirement of an elected judge at a particular age? Explain the legal basis for your answer.

PROJECTS

1. Review your city's newspaper advertisements for employment opportunities. Compile a list of any advertisements that might give rise to age discrimination claims.

2. Using the facts outlined in the *Thornbrough v. Columbus and Greenville R. Co.* case discussed in this chapter, draft an age discrimination complaint.

CHAPTER 10

Race and Color Discrimination

OVERVIEW

Title VII lists race and color as separate prohibitions against discrimination. However, the two categories often overlap, and for that reason, will be discussed together in this chapter.

Race has been defined by the courts as any identifiable class of persons, and Title VII protects not only individuals who are members of minority racial groups, but individuals of *all races*. Race discrimination in employment is often incorrectly linked to the beginning of slavery. At that period of time, the Constitution offered no legal protection to blacks, and even contained language sanctioning the slave trade. During the days of slavery, both free and enslaved blacks were limited almost entirely to agricultural work and domestic service. The enactment of the Thirteenth Amendment in 1865 abolished the institution of slavery, but did not otherwise address the civil rights of blacks. Following the legal end to slavery, deep suspicion, prejudice, and hatred persisted, and blacks continued to be employed in less desirable occupations.

The Civil Rights Act of 1866 declared persons of every race and color to be United States citizens, and to have the same right to make and enforce contracts, to inherit, purchase and convey property, to sue and be sued, and to have the same benefit of the laws as white citizens. In 1868 the Fourteenth Amendment was ratified, with its familiar due process and equal protection provisions.

Although new legal protections now existed for all races, many years passed without there being useful tools to avoid employment discrimination. The courts simply did not address private discrimination. One reason for the failure to address the issue of racial discrimination was the courts' pervasive acceptance of the doctrine of employment at will, under which a worker has no constitutionally recognized property right in his or her job, and can be discharged at any time for any reason.

Four years after the enactment of the Civil Rights Act of 1964, the Supreme Court ruled that the Act prohibited private as well as governmental discriminatory activity. (See *Jones v. Alfred H. Mayer Co.*, 392 U.S. 409, 88 S. Ct. 2186, 20 L. Ed. 2d 1889 (1968)). In 1975, the Supreme Court articulated the fact that the 1866 Act's assertion of equal rights in the making and enforcement of contracts applied to employment contracts, thereby barring private acts of employment discrimination.

Discrimination against blacks was not the only discrimination that existed in the United States prior to the enactment of Title VII. Asians and Native Americans also suffered intense discrimination during that time period.

RACE DISCRIMINATION UNDER TITLE VII

When the Civil Rights Acts of 1866 and 1871 were enacted, the focus was on equal rights for African Americans. Subsequently, Title VII established that other racial categories also were entitled to equal job opportunities. For purposes of Title VII enforcement, the EEOC currently identifies the following five racial categories:

1. *White*—All persons with origins in the original peoples of Europe, North Africa, or the Middle East;
2. *Black*—All persons with origin in black racial groups of Africa;
3. *Hispanic*—All persons of Mexican, Puerto Rican, Cuban, Central or South American, or other Spanish culture or origin regardless of race;
4. *Asian or Pacific Islander*—All persons with origin in the original people of the Far East, Southeast Asia, the Indian subcontinent or Pacific islands; and
5. *American Indian or Alaskan Native*—All persons with origin in the original peoples of North America, and who maintain cultural identification through tribal affiliation or, community recognition.

White employees, as well as minority employees, may claim race discrimination in violation of Title VII.

Because of the issue of multiracial identity, the federal Office of Management and Budget has directed changes in racial classifications used by the EEOC and other agencies (62 FR 58782, October 30, 1997). Hispanic, or Latino, will become an ethnic, rather than racial category. Individuals in the future will be able to designate themselves as belonging to more than one category.

Issues of racial status, national origin, and religion may be difficult to distinguish. For example, an issue may be whether an adverse action was taken because the individual was African American or Muslim. As a result, claims of ethnic discrimination have been recognized under the Civil Rights Act of 1866 when national origin appears inextricable from issues of race.

Employment policies often appear race neutral on their face, but in reality they may have a disparate impact on racial minorities. Such policies are unlawful, unless they can be justified by business necessity. For example, refer to *Griggs v. Duke Power Co.*, discussed later in this chapter.

RACIAL HARASSMENT

In addition to liability for race discrimination under Title VII, the employer may also be liable for racial harassment in the workplace. The employer's responsibility includes any racial harassment by the employer and the employer's supervisor if it is permitted in the workplace. Abuse, threats, slurs, jokes, and epithets that are based on race may constitute unlawful harassment if they are sufficiently severe and pervasive to affect terms or conditions of employment. Employers have a duty to take prompt action to remedy a work environment that is hostile to a racial minority.

REVERSE DISCRIMINATION

Under Title VII, an individual is either discriminated against or not, and all races are equally protected from illegal discrimination. The term **reverse discrimination** applies to situations in which the employee feels discriminated against, specifically because of a remedy applied by a court to redress wrongs found to have existed, or by an employer under an affirmative action plan. For example, if a court found that an employer had discriminated against blacks in promotions in a municipal police department, the remedy imposed by the court could be to promote one black police officer until the desired ratio between races is reached. White police officers could feel that they had been adversely affected by the affirmative action plan, all because of the color of the skin, in violation of Title VII. However, an employer who has been ordered by a court to remedy racial discrimination may not avoid the remedy because of the possibility of a "reverse discrimination" lawsuit. In the event an employer maintains a judicially imposed or voluntary affirmative action plan, the employer will not be liable to employees for "reverse discrimination."

COLOR DISCRIMINATION

Skin color cannot provide the basis for an employment decision, regardless of race. Because color often relates to race or ethnicity, darker skinned individuals of Arab and Hebrew ancestry have been permitted to file discrimination claims, even though they may be considered to be of the Caucasian race.

TYPES OF RACE AND COLOR DISCRIMINATION

Disparate Treatment

Disparate treatment racial discrimination is intentional discrimination against an individual because of his or her race. An employer commits an unlawful employment practice if, on the basis of race or color, the employer:

- fails or refuses to hire an individual, discharges an individual, or discriminates in any other manner against an individual in connection with compensation or the terms, conditions, or privileges of employment; or
- limits, segregates or classifies an employee or applicant for employment in a manner that would deprive or tend to deprive an individual of any employment opportunity or adversely affect in any other manner the status of an employee.

Individual Disparate Treatment Case

The theory of **individual disparate treatment** seeks to determine whether the employer deliberately treated the employee bringing a claim of intentional discrimination differently from other employees because of his or her membership in a protected class (age, sex, race, disability, for example). (See *McDonnell Douglas Corp. v. Green*, 411 U.S. 792 (1973), discussed below). The *McDonnell Douglas* case has served as the model for determination of the existence of individual disparate treatment case.

Mixed Motives Case

In a **mixed motives case**, the employer has both lawful and unlawful reasons for taking the adverse employment action.

The plaintiff's burden of proof in a mixed motive case consists only of demonstrating that race was a motivating factor, even though other factors also motivated the challenged practice. Direct evidence of a discriminatory motive is necessary to meet the plaintiff's burden of proof.

Once the plaintiff proves race was a factor in the employment decision, the employer cannot win. The employer is entitled to a partial reduction of damages, however, if it can demonstrate that it would have taken the same action even if it had not considered race as a factor. Upon such a showing by the defendant, the court may grant the plaintiff declaratory and injunctive relief, and attorneys' fees and costs, but may not award damages or order reinstatement, hiring, promotion, or back pay, as discussed below.

Systemic Disparate Treatment

Systemic disparate treatment is a pattern of discrimination against one general protected group, rather than an isolated case of discrimination against an individual employee.

Disparate Impact

Courts have defined **disparate impact** as employment practices that are neutral on their face in the treatment of different groups, but that fall more heavily on one group than another and cannot be justified by business necessity. This theory of employment discrimination is also known as the **adverse impact theory**.

The theory of disparate impact originated in *Griggs v. Duke Power Co.*, 401 U.S. 424 (1971), discussed extensively in Chapter 6, but was drastically changed in *Wards Cove Packing Co., Inc. v. Atonio*, 490 U.S. 642 (1989).

ESTABLISHING A *PRIMA FACIE* CASE OF RACE DISCRIMINATION

In order to establish a prima facie case of race discrimination, a plaintiff must show (1) that he or she is a member of a protected class; (2) he or she applied for and was qualified for the position sought; (3) he or she was rejected despite being qualified (or an adverse employment action occurred); and (4) the posted job remained vacant after the plaintiff was rejected (or the plaintiff was replaced by a person not in the protected class). Once the plaintiff has established a *prima facie* case of race discrimination, the burden of proof shifts to the employer to articulate a legitimate, nondiscriminatory reason for the allegedly unequal treatment.

After the employer has stated a legitimate, nondiscriminatory reason for the allegedly unequal treatment, the burden shifts back to the plaintiff to prove that the employer's articulated reasons are a mere pretext for unlawful discrimination, as discussed in the following case.

McDonnell Douglas Corp. v. Green, **411 U.S. 792 (1973)**

Facts:

Green, a black citizen of St. Louis, was employed as a mechanic and laboratory technician from 1956 until August 28, 1964, when he was laid off in the course of a general reduction in McDonnell Douglas's work force. Green was also a long-time activist in the civil rights movement. He protested vigorously that both his discharge and the general hiring practices of McDonnell Douglas were racially motivated. As part of his protest, Green and other members of the Congress on Racial Equality illegally stalled their cars on the main roads leading to the McDonnell Douglas plant for the purpose of blocking access to the plant at the time of the morning shift change.

Subsequent to his arrest and guilty plea for the "stall-in," McDonnell Douglas advertised for qualified mechanics. Green applied for reemployment. McDonnell Douglas rejected his application on the basis of the "stall-in" and "lock-in" activities that resulted in chaining and padlocking the front door of a downtown office building that housed part of McDonnell Douglas' offices.

Shortly after he was denied reemployment, Green filed a formal complaint with the EEOC, claiming that the company had refused to rehire him because of his race and persistent involvement in the civil rights movement, in violation of Sections 703(a)(1) and 704(a) of the Civil Rights Act of 1964. The district court rejected both of these claims.

The Eighth Circuit affirmed the district court's finding that unlawful protests were not protected activities, but reversed the dismissal of Green's claim relating to racially discriminatory hiring practices and ordered the case remanded for trial of that claim.

The Supreme Court agreed with the court of appeals that Green proved a *prima facie* case. McDonnell Douglas had sought mechanics, which was Green's trade, and continued to do so after rejecting his application for reemployment. McDonnell Douglas did not dispute Green's qualifications for the job, and acknowledged that his past work performance was "satisfactory."

The burden then shifted to the employer to articulate a legitimate, nondiscriminatory reason for the employee's rejection. McDonnell Douglas asserted that it failed to rehire Green because of his participation in unlawful conduct against the company. The court found that this sufficed to discharge the burden of proof and to meet the *prima facie* case of discrimination.

Green admitted that he had taken part in the carefully planned "stall-in," designed to tie up access to and from the plant at a peak traffic hour.

Opinion by Justice Powell:

On remand, respondent must, as the Court of Appeals recognized, be afforded a fair opportunity to show that petitioner's stated reason for respondent's rejection was in fact pretext. Especially relevant to such a showing would be evidence that white employees involved in acts against petitioner of comparable seriousness to the "stall-in" were nevertheless retained or rehired. Petitioner may justifiably refuse to rehire one who was engaged in unlawful, disruptive acts against it, but only if this criterion is applied alike to members of all races.

Other evidence that may be relevant to any showing of pretext includes facts as to the petitioner's treatment of respondent during his prior term of employment, petitioner's reaction, if any, to respondent's legitimate civil rights activities; and petitioner's general policy and practice with respect to minority employment. On the latter point, statistics as to petitioner's employment policy and practice may be helpful to a determination of whether petitioner's refusal to rehire respondent in this case conformed to a general pattern of discrimination against blacks. In short, on the retrial respondent must be given a full and fair opportunity to demonstrate by competent evidence that the presumptively valid reasons for his rejection were in fact a coverup for a racially discriminatory decision.

The cause is hereby remanded to the District Court for reconsideration in accordance with this opinion.

PROVING PRETEXT

The Supreme Court addressed the issue of pretext in *St. Mary's Honor Center v. Hicks*, 509 U.S. 502 (1993), discussed below.

St. Mary's Honor Center v. Hicks, 509 U.S. 502 (1993)

Facts:

A halfway house in Maryland hired Hicks, a black man, as a correctional officer in 1978. Hicks' employment record was satisfactory until changes were made at the management level of the establishment. Soon after those changes, he was subjected to repeated and increasingly severe disciplinary actions and finally demoted to his former position for repeated rules violations by his subordinates. In mid-1984, Hicks was fired for threatening his supervisor during a verbal confrontation.

Hicks filed a racial discrimination claim under Title VII. In a bench trial, the district court found that although he had proved the employer's stated reasons for his termination were pretextual, he had not proved that the "crusade to terminate" him was "racially rather than personally motivated." *Id.* at 508.

The Eighth Circuit Court of Appeals reversed, holding that because Hicks had proved the defendant's proffered reasons for its actions were pretextual, he was entitled to judgment as a matter of law. The Supreme Court reversed and remanded, holding that the court of appeals had erred in concluding that Hicks was entitled to judgment as a matter of law. The Court stated that even though Hicks had proved that the employer's proffered reasons were a pretext for his discharged he had failed to prove that race was the employer's true motivation.

Opinion by Justice Scalia:

[A] reason cannot be proved to be a pretext for *discrimination* unless it is shown *both* that the reason was false, *and* that discrimination was the reason.

It is not enough, in other words, to *dis*believe the employer; the factfinder must believe the plaintiff's explanations of intentional discrimination.

The Court's decision in *St. Mary's Honor Center* sets a **pretext plus** standard. A limited number of jurisdictions, including the Fifth Circuit as expressed in *Rhodes v. Guiberson Oil Tools*, 75 F.3d 989 (5th Cir. 1996), have applied this standard. However, the majority of courts require the plaintiff to prove only pretext.

DEFENSES AGAINST RACE DISCRIMINATION CLAIMS

Available defenses against race discrimination claims include:

1. nondiscriminatory motive;
2. affirmative action program; and
3. bona fide seniority or merit system.

Nondiscriminatory Motive Defense

As discussed in *McDonnell Douglas Corp. v. Green*, 411 U.S. 792 (1973) above, the employer can argue that it did not *intentionally* discriminate against the plaintiff

Affirmative Action Program

A contractor or subcontractor with 50 or more employees and a nonconstruction contract of $50,000 or more must develop a written **affirmative action plan** that is designed to remedy racially discriminatory practices suffered in the past by members of certain minority groups within 120 days of the beginning of the contract.

Large contractors are also required to perform a **workplace assessment** measuring the workplace for the representation of women and minorities in each of seven employment categories, ranging from unskilled workers to management employees. The employer is also required to compare the percentage of women and minority employees in those positions with the percentage of such employees available in the workforce from which the employer's workforce is drawn.

Although the Civil Rights Act was enacted in 1964 to facilitate equal employment rights for all workers, no significant employment affirmative action case was decided by the U.S. Supreme Court until the case of *United Steelworkers of America, AFL-CIO v. Weber*, 443 U.S. 193 (1979), discussed below.

United Steelworkers of America, AFL-CIO v. Weber, 443 U.S. 193 (1979)

Facts:

In 1974, United Steelworkers of America and Kaiser Aluminum entered into a master collective-bargaining agreement. This agreement included an affirmative action plan designed to eliminate conspicuous racial imbalances in Kaiser's then almost exclusively white craft-work forces. The plan reserved 50% of the openings in the in-plant craft-training programs for blacks until the percentage of black craftworkers in a plant was commensurate with the percentage of blacks in the local labor force. In 1974, only 1.83% of the skilled craftworkers at one of Kaiser's plants were black, even though the local work force at the time was approximately 39% black. During the plan's first year, seven black and six white craft trainees were selected from the plant's production work force. The most senior black trainee had less seniority than several white production workers whose bids for admission were rejected. Thereafter, Weber, one of the white production workers, filed this class action in Federal District Court, alleging that the affirmative action program had resulted in junior black employees' receiving training in preference to senior white employees, causing discrimination in violation of Title VII. The district court agreed that the affirmative action plan violated Title VII, entered judgment in favor of the plaintiff class, and granted injunctive relief. The court of appeals affirmed, holding that all employment preferences based upon race, including those preferences incidental to bona fide affirmative action plans, violated Title VII's prohibition against racial discrimination in employment.

Opinion by Justice Brennan:

Challenged here is the legality of an affirmative action plan—collectively bargained by an employer and a union—that reserves for black employees 50% of the openings in an in-plant craft-training program until the percentage of black craftworkers in the plant is commensurate with the percentage of blacks in the local labor force. The question for decision is whether Congress, in Title VII of the Civil Rights Act of 1964, left employers and unions in the private sector free to take such race-conscious steps to eliminate manifest racial imbalances in traditionally segregated job categories. We hold that Title VII does not prohibit such race-conscious affirmative action plans.

We need not today define in detail the line of demarcation between permissible and impermissible affirmative action plans. It suffices to hold that the challenged Kaiser-USWA affirmative action plan falls on the permissible side of the line. The purposes of the plan mirror those of the statute. Both were designed to break down old patterns of racial segregation and hierarchy. Both were structured to "open employment opportunities for Negroes in occupations which have been traditionally closed to them." 110 Cong. Rec. 6548 (1964) (remarks of Sen. Humphrey).

At the same time, the plan does not unnecessarily trammel the interests of the white employees. The plan does not require the discharge of white workers and their replacement with new black hires. Nor does the plan create an absolute bar to the advancement of white employees; half of those trained in the program will be white. Moreover, the plan is a temporary measure. It is not intended to maintain racial balance, but simply to eliminate a manifest racial imbalance. Preferential selection of craft trainees at the Gramercy plant will end as soon as the percentage of black skilled craftworkers in the Gramercy plant approximates the percentage of blacks in the local labor force.

We conclude, therefore, that the adoption of the Kaiser-USWA plan for the Gramercy plant falls within the area of discretion left by Title VII to the private sector voluntarily to adopt affirmative action plans designed to eliminate conspicuous racial imbalance in traditionally segregated job categories. Accordingly, the judgment of the Court of Appeals is
REVERSED.

Bona Fide Seniority or Merit System

An employer can challenge a claim of race discrimination on the grounds that the challenged employment decision was made pursuant to a bona fide seniority or merit system. The employer must show that the employee, in fact, was not treated differently than others would have been treated under the same circumstances. Evidence in this type of case might include: bona fide personnel policies listing job qualifications, conditions of employment, grounds for termination or prerequisites for pay increases or advancement, such as a ranking by seniority, production quotas, or merit-based systems. Personnel policies are bona fide only if they are not intentionally devised for discriminatory purposes, and are justified by a business necessity.

BFOQ Defense Not Generally Available in Race Discrimination Claims

An employer generally may not rely on the bona fide occupational qualification ("BFOQ") defense in a race discrimination case. The BFOQ defense allows an employer to adopt an otherwise racially discriminatory employment practice if "reasonably necessary to the normal operation of that particular business" (42 U.SC. § 2000e-2(3)(1)). Race or color, however, generally is *not* a bona fide occupational qualification in employment decisions.

ADVERSE IMPACT RACE DISCRIMINATION

If a racially neutral employment policy unintentionally discriminates against a disproportionate number of persons on the basis of race, the policy can be challenged on the grounds that it has a **systemic disparate impact** (adverse impact) on a protected class. Disparate impact discrimination is unintentional discrimination. Thus, the issue in adverse impact cases is the policy's effect on the protected group, not the employer's motive, as discussed in *Griggs v. Duke Power Co.*, 401 U.S. 424 (1971).

Plaintiff's *Prima Facie* Case

To prove a *prima facie* case of adverse impact racial discrimination, the plaintiff must demonstrate that the employment practice adversely affects a protected group on the basis of race. The plaintiff must identify a particular employment practice that causes the disparity, and provide sufficient evidence to raise an inference of causation. Statistical evidence is not *required*. In some cases, a showing that all or substantially all members of a protected class are adversely affected will be sufficient to establish a *prima facie* case.

Business Necessity Defense to Adverse Impact Claim

In defense of an adverse impact claim, the employer might argue:

1. the practice does not cause an adverse impact, or
2. the unintentionally discriminatory practice is job-related for the position in question and consistent with business necessity.

The *Griggs* case discussed below was the first ruling by the Supreme Court on the disparate impact of employment tests on a racial minority.

Griggs v. Duke Power Co., 401 U.S. 424 (1971)

Facts:

Thirteen African-Americans challenged the employer's requirement of either a high school diploma or a passing score on two separate intelligence tests as a condition of employment or job transfer. Neither test was intended to measure the ability to learn to perform a particular job or category of jobs at the plant. The testing requirement applied equally to blacks and whites, but the employer failed to show that the tests had a demonstrable relationship to successful performance of the jobs for which the tests were used. The testing requirement was not retroactive. Employees hired before the testing was required were performing satisfactorily and were being promoted. According to a company vice president, the company imposed testing requirement to "improve the overall quality of the workforce."

The court of appeals relied on a subjective test of the employer's intent and found no showing of a discriminatory purpose in the diploma or test requirements and found no violation of Title VII. The Supreme Court disagreed, as reflected in the court's opinion below.

Opinion by Justice Burger:

The Act [Title VII] proscribes not only overt discrimination but also practices that are fair in form but discriminatory in operation. The touchstone is *business necessity*.

Good intent or absence of discriminatory intent does not redeem employment procedures or testing mechanisms that operate as 'built-in headwinds' for minority groups and are unrelated to measuring job capability. [The employer has the] burden of showing that any given requirement [has] a manifest relationship to the employment in question.

Defeating the Business Necessity Defense

The plaintiff must demonstrate that an alternative policy exists and would be as effective in serving the employer's legitimate business needs, with less discrimination, in order to overcome a proffered business necessity defense. In *Fitzpatrick v. City of Atlanta*, 2 F.3d 1112 (11th Cir. 1993), the plaintiffs challenged a requirement that all city firefighters be clean-shaven. They alleged that the policy has an adverse impact on African-American men who suffer disproportionately from pseudo-folliculitis barbae (PFB), an infection to the face caused by shaving. The city's defense was based on the necessity of the policy for safety reasons. An affidavit from a safety expert cited OSHA regulations requiring that firefighters' respirator masks be sealed securely to the face.

The plaintiffs offered alternative policies, but no support of expert testimony or documentation to support their suggested policies. The trial court granted summary judgment for the City of Atlanta. On appeal, the Eleventh Circuit affirmed the judgment on the grounds that, without expert testimony, the plaintiffs had failed to overcome the business necessity defense in support of the city's "no beard" policy.

REMEDIES

Title VII provides comprehensive remedies for employment discrimination. The primary remedy, however, is back pay. Back pay includes regular wages, overtime, shift differentials, premium pay, and fringe benefits. A defendant has several possible deductions from the back pay award. Such deductions include severance pay, retirement benefits, and unemployment compensation. In addition, a defendant is entitled to a back pay reduction for a failure to mitigate (42 U.S.C. § 2000e-5(g)).

A successful plaintiff is also entitled to reinstatement. If reinstatement is not feasible, then front pay is awarded to make the plaintiff whole. Front pay is awarded from the date of judgment until the plaintiff obtains the position that he or she would have had but for the discrimination. The award and amount of front pay is an equitable remedy, and is within the court's discretion.

The Civil Rights Act of 1991 expressly added compensatory and punitive damages available for three successful Title VII plaintiff. (42 U.S.C. § 1981a (1986 and 1994)). The Civil Rights Act of 1991 caps the recovery of compensatory damages by the number of employees:

Less than 101	$ 50,000
Less than 201	$100,000
Less than 501	$200,000
More than 500	$300,000

However, these caps do not limit recovery of backpay or other remedies and do not apply to compensatory damages for racial discrimination under section 1981. Mental anguish damages are available for a successful plaintiff in a racial discrimination lawsuit.

Title VII grants the court, upon proof of intentional discrimination, the discretion to enjoin a defendant from continuing the discriminatory behavior (42 U.S.C. § 2000e-5(g)).

Finally, the prevailing plaintiff in a racial discrimination lawsuit can recover his or her attorneys' fees. However, the award of the fees is in the discretion of the court.

TERMS

adverse impact theory
affirmative action plan
disparate impact
disparate treatment racial discrimination
individual disparate treatment
mixed motives case
race
reverse discrimination
systemic disparate impact
systemic disparate treatment
workplace assessment

REVIEW QUESTIONS

1. An employer favors lighter skinned African Americans over employment candidates who are more qualified, but who have dark skin. Could a darker-skinned African American claim color discrimination?

2. A successful financial officer is denied a promotion to vice president of a major bank. She files an EEOC claim of discrimination because she believes that the denied promotion was a result of her marriage to a minority. When she confronted the CEO about her belief, he confirmed her suspicions by stating, "Well, Carole, I just can't see your husband fitting in with us fishing trips and golf excursions. Some of the country clubs where we play golf don't welcome blacks or other minorities. I just wouldn't want you to be embarrassed." Do you accept the CEO's reason? Will Carole be successful in her EEOC claim? How could she succeed if she isn't a minority herself?

3. A black female is terminated during a reduction-in-force. Decisions on employees to be terminated were made on the basis of performance ratings. The terminated

employee had never received a negative performance review because the employer was afraid that she would file a claim of discrimination. However, her performance had been substandard for several years. The employee files a discrimination charge after termination, claiming that the termination itself was discriminatory, and that the employer's failure to give her the appropriate negative feedback during previous reviews had not permitted her to correct the problems that indirectly resulted in her termination. Does the employee win one or both charges of discrimination? Why? Why not?

4. In the *Griggs* case discussed earlier in the chapter, do you think that Duke Power could have argued that the diploma requirement and intelligence test were a business necessity? Outline any argument that you believe could be made for a business necessity.

5. In the *McDonnell Douglas Corp. v. Green* case discussed earlier, do you think that the Court should require actual evidence of discrimination in disparate treatment cases, rather than permitting an inference? Why or why not?

6. Did the court order the employer in the *McDonnell Douglas Corp. v. Green* case to keep Green on as an employee in spite of his illegal activities? Explain why or why not.

7. A prominent national discount store hires a large number of black employees. However, these employees typically work in lower-pay positions. Management positions are filled predominantly by white employees. Will the store be successful in its defense that because of the number of black employees, it does not discriminate on the basis of race? Explain.

8. An African American engineer was replaced by another African American. Does he have a claim for discrimination? Explain the basis for your answer.

9. A coworker repeatedly utters racial epithets to an Iranian, referring to him as "the Ayatollah." Are these epithets sufficient to establish a *prima facie* case of racial discrimination?

10. Assume that the individual who utters the racial epithets in question 9 is a supervisor rather than a coworker. Does this make a sufficient enough difference to establish a *prima facie* case of racial discrimination?

PROJECTS

1. Brief the *Wards Cove Packing Co., Inc. v. Atonio*, 490 U.S. 642 (1989).

2. Draft a memorandum outlining the differences in the *Wards Cove* case and the *Griggs* case discussed in this chapter.

CHAPTER 11

National Origin Discrimination

OVERVIEW

Discrimination based on national origin existed long before World War II. This discrimination was rampant after World War II for persons of Japanese ancestry who were living in many regions of the West Coast, as curfews were imposed on those individuals and they were excluded from large areas of the West Coast.

For years, discrimination based on national origin affected millions in the United States in all walks of life, including employment. The types of jobs occupied during the period after World War II reflect the same disparities evident in unemployment and income, as 30.4% of employed Caucasians occupied managerial and professional jobs, while only 14.2% of employed Hispanic Americans held such positions. (Bureau of Labor Statistics, U.S. Department of Labor, *Geographic Profile of Employment and Unemployment*, 1991 at 16 (1992)).

STATUTORY REQUIREMENTS AFFECTING NATIONAL ORIGIN DISCRIMINATION

Title VII of the Civil Rights Act of 1964 makes it unlawful for employers of 15 or more employees to discriminate against any employee or applicant because of the individual's national origin. The EEOC guidelines on national origin discrimination prohibit discrimination on the basis of:

- The employee's particular place of origin or an ancestor's place of origin
- Physical, cultural, or linguistic characteristics of a national origin group
- Marriage to or association with persons, membership in organizations, or attendance at schools or churches associated with a national origin group

- A name or spouse's name associated with a national origin group
- Height or weight specifications that are not related to successful job performance
- Aptitude or other employment tests, unless such requirements are applied equally to all applicants, and relate to successful job performance
- An accent or manner of speaking, unless there is a legitimate, nondiscriminatory reason for the action.

It is unlawful to prefer someone for employment or promotion because the individual was born in the United States over someone from another country. There is no national origin discrimination when the choice is between two individuals from the same national origin group.

National origin is closely associated with race. For example, someone with origins in Asia, Africa, or Latin America may allege both race and national origin discrimination, and may pursue claims under both the Civil Rights Act of 1866 and Title VII. A claim for national origin discrimination may be made without regard to race.

Ethnic slurs and other harassment based on national origin or ancestry are also unlawful.

Workplace Rules Relating to Language

English-proficiency or English-only rules relate to the language used at work. **English-proficiency rules** require that employees or job applicants have the ability to write, speak, and understand English at a given level of proficiency. **English-only** rules normally require that employees not communicate in the workplace in any language other than English. Two types of English-only rules may be utilized in the workplace:

- Absolute rules—rules that apply at all times and at all places while the employee is at work.
- Limited rules—rules that require employees to speak only in English at certain times (such as working hours), or in certain places (such as while in the presence of customers).

Language Discrimination as National Origin Discrimination

Challenges to English-only rules question whether employees who are affected by such rules are within the scope of Title VII. These challenges seek to determine whether employees who suffered an adverse employment decision or effect because of an English-only rule have been discriminated against under Title VII. Answering these challenges has been complicated by the fact that to date the Supreme Court has decided only one case dealing with "national origin" discrimination.

In *Espinoza v. Farah Manufacturing Co.*, 414 U.S. 86 (1973) (discussed below), the employer refused to hire a citizen of Mexico who was a legally admitted resident alien because she was not a citizen of the United States.

Espinoza v. Farah Manufacturing Co., 414 U.S. 86 (1973)

Facts:

The plaintiff claimed in her Title VII complaint that by imposing the citizenship requirement the employer had discriminated against her on the basis of national origin. The United States District Court for the Western District of Texas found against the employer, and the employer appealed. The court of appeals reversed. The Supreme Court, speaking through Justice Marshall, wrote that nothing in the equal employment opportunities provisions makes it illegal to discriminate on the basis of citizenship or alienage.

Opinion by Justice Marshall:

There are other compelling reasons to believe that Congress did not intend the term "national origin" to embrace citizenship requirements. Since 1914, the Federal government itself, through Civil Service Commission regulations, has engaged in what amounts to discrimination against aliens by denying them the right to enter competitive examination for federal employment. But it has never been suggested that the citizenship requirement for federal employment constitutes discrimination because of national origin, even though since 1943, various Executive Orders have expressly prohibited discrimination on the basis of national origin in federal government employment. Moreover, 701(b) of Tit. VII, in language closely paralleling 703, makes it "the policy of the United States to insure equal employment opportunities for Federal employees without discrimination because of . . . national origin."

Congress itself has on several occasions since 1964 enacted statutes barring aliens from federal employment.

[T]he issue presented in this case is not whether Congress has the power to discriminate against aliens in federal employment, but rather, whether Congress intended to prohibit such discrimination in private employment. Suffice it to say that we cannot conclude Congress would at once continue the practice of requiring citizenship as a condition of federal employment and, at the same time, prevent private employers from doing otherwise. Interpreting 703 as petitioners suggest would achieve the rather bizarre result of preventing Farah from insisting on United States citizenship as a condition of employment while the very agency charged with enforcement of Tit. VII would itself be required by Congress to place such a condition on its own personnel.

There is no indication in the record that Farah's policy against employment of aliens had the purpose or effect of discrimination against persons of Mexican national origin. It is conceded that Farah accepts employees of Mexican origin, provided the individual concerned has become an American citizen. Indeed, the district court found that persons of Mexican ancestry 'make up more than 96% of the employees at the company's San Antonio division, and 97% of those doing the work for which Mrs. Espinoza applied.' While statistics such as these do not automatically shield an employer from a charge of unlawful discrimination, the plain fact of the matter is that Farah does not discriminate against persons of Mexican national origin with respect to employment in the job Mrs. Espinoza sought. She was denied employment, not because of the country of her origin, but because she had not yet achieved United states citizenship. In fact, the record shows that the worker hired in place of Mrs. Espinoza was a citizen with a Spanish surname.

Aliens are protected from illegal discrimination under the Act but nothing in the Act makes it illegal to discriminate on the basis of citizenship.

AFFIRMED.

In the *Espinoza* case, the Supreme Court defined national origin discrimination as discrimination based on ancestry, and found that both disparate treatment and disparate impact analyses were applicable in determining national origin discrimination. However, the Court decided that the prohibition against "national origin" discrimination was not intended to protect against discrimination because of citizenship status. Citizenship is not one of the ethnic traits that comprise national origin according to *Espinoza*.

Whether one's language is an ethnic trait defining national origin has been the subject of some debate within the EEOC and court system. In early decisions, the EEOC recognized that a rule prohibiting languages other than English from being spoken in the workplace "at all times" discriminated on the basis of national origin. Numerous courts of appeals have disagreed on the definition of national origin.

In 1980, the EEOC issued a set of guidelines concerning national origin discrimination and the issue of English-only rules. The EEOC broadly construed the term **national origin discrimination** to include adverse employment actions based on a person's or his or her ancestors' place of origin or the "physical, cultural or linguistic characteristics of a national origin group." The guidelines also note that the "primary language of an individual is often an essential national origin characteristic" and in various cases the EEOC has held that English-only rules could constitute national origin discrimination (EEOC Compl. Man. (BNA) § 623.1 (1989)).

Under the EEOC guidelines, language is one of the ethnic traits included in the definition of national origin. Workplace rules that discriminate with respect to language may be challenged under the national origin provision of Title VII.

Discrimination Issues in English-Only Rules

English-only rules have been challenged under disparate treatment, disparate impact, and hostile environment theories of discrimination, discussed in Chapter 7. The Supreme Court in *Espinoza* found that both disparate treatment and disparate impact theories were available in raising a Title VII complaint based on national origin discrimination. The EEOC has also issued a manual that analyzes English-only rules under both the disparate treatment and the disparate impact theories of discrimination.

Disparate Treatment

An English-only rule is a term and condition of employment, and the unequal application of the rule may constitute disparate treatment under Title VII. For example, if an employer's rule does not apply equally to all national origin groups because it requires a particular ethnic group to speak English at work, but allows other languages to be spoken by other national origin groups, a disparate treatment analysis would be appropriate. If the rule is neutral on its face but is applied differently against employee members of a particular national origin group, disparate treatment analysis would also be applicable.

Direct evidence of discriminatory motive could be in the form of statements by the employer, such as that it has prohibited the speaking of Spanish at work but not other languages "because persons speaking Spanish are generally loud and disruptive" that indicate a bias against members of a particular group (EEOC Compl. Man. (BNA) § 623.3(a)(2)).

Statistical evidence may also be used to establish that an English-only rule has been applied differently to similarly situated employees of a different national origin than that of the charging party. For example, statistical evidence might show that the frequency and severity of disciplinary actions for noncompliance with the employer's English-only rule varies substantially for different national origin groups, could be evidence of disparate treatment.

The defendant must produce evidence of the stated reason for the adverse employment action sufficient to raise a "genuine issue of fact" as to whether discrimination occurred (*Texas Dep't of Community Affairs v. Burdine*, 450 U.S 248, 254 (1981)).

Courts have generally been reluctant to accept challenges to English-only rules under the disparate treatment model. An example of that reluctance is illustrated in the case below.

Dimaranan v. Pomona Valley Hospital Medical Center, 775 F. Supp. 338 (C.D.Cal. 1991)

Facts:

In this case, the employer introduced a rule that Tagalog (a language spoken frequently by Filipino nurses in the unit) was not to be spoken in a particular hospital unit. Non-Tagalog-speaking nurses complained that the other nurses' use of Tagalog was "rude and disruptive" and that they felt "left out when Tagalog was spoken." Some of the nurses additionally thought that the plaintiff, who was assistant head nurse in the unit and who frequently spoke Tagalog, showed a preference for her Tagalog-speaking friends "and had essentially divided the unit into two groups as a result." Prior to this time, the plaintiff had enjoyed above-standard performance evaluations. Suddenly she received a negative performance review at the time that the coworkers' unhappiness with the language problem surfaced.

Opinion by Judge Rafeedie:

It is clear that the restriction on the use of Tagalog was not the result of racial animus. Tagalog was spoken for many years, without complaint from management. However misguided and ineffective the Hospital's language restriction may have been, there is simply no basis for concluding that it was motivated by ethnic animosity. This action should never have been a Title VII case. Language was clearly never the central focus of management, and Tagalog was, so to speak, merely caught in the cross-fire. The Court, therefore, cannot conclude that the Hospital's language rules violated Title VII by intentionally discriminating against plaintiff on the basis of her national origin.

The Court finds that plaintiff's disparate impact argument must fall, because she has not identified a facially-neutral employment practice. Rather, the employment practice of which plaintiff complains was expressly non-neutral, in both word and fact. As announced at the various staff meetings, only Tagalog was prohibited. The policy was not what could be deemed a facially-neutral "English-Only" policy. Both sides agree that Spanish was spoken on the Unit without complaint.

The plaintif's demotion and transfer resulted from a mixture of legitimate motives and impermissible retaliation. The Court is not convinced that plaintiff would have been demoted had she not opposed the defendant's language directives and filed the EEOC charge and this lawsuit. Because plaintiff's resistance to the Hospital's language directive was an essential ingredient in the demotion decision, it is the conclusion of the Court that plaintiff suffered unlawful retaliation and should be afforded an appropriate remedies.

The Court orders expungement of all plaintiff's employment records, dated after December 1987, that reflect poor performance evaluations during her tenure as AHN on the night-shift. Plaintiff is entitled to the differential between what she received in terms of pay and benefits after her demotion, and what the other nurses holding the same rank as plaintiff who were not demoted received from the time of plaintiff's demotion up until the time that the position was abolished, and through the date of entry of judgment.

Plaintiff should be offered a position in Pediatrics in a nursing position for which she is qualified, and is ordered restored to the same position in terms of salary, benefits, and assignments as other assistant head nurses whose positions in the M/B Unit were abolished.

IT IS SO ORDERED.

Legitimate Business Reasons for English-Only Rule

Courts have been largely in agreement with employers' arguments that the adoption of the English-only rule is based on legitimate business reasons. Employers have argued that, as in *Dimaranan*, a rule limiting the use of languages other than English was necessary to maintain cohesion in the appropriate unit. Employers have also argued that English-only rules are necessary to ensure that management understands what is being said in order to effectively evaluate employees in all work-related communications.

Disparate Impact of English-Only Rule

In the context of English-only rules in the workplace, it is appropriate to use the disparate impact analysis in a situation where the defendant has a policy prohibiting the speaking of any language other than English at work, the rule is applicable to all employees, and it is alleged that the rule disproportionately affects a protected group. The EEOC Compliance Manual concludes that most English-only cases would be analyzed under the disparate impact model of discrimination.

The traditional disparate impact case raises three issues in the context of English-only rules:

- Can the plaintiff establish that the rule has a disparate impact with respect to specific employment opportunities?
- Was appropriate notice given prior to the implementation of the rule?
- Is there justification for the "business necessity" defense?

The EEOC presumes that rules requiring employees to speak only English in the workplace adversely affect an employee's employment opportunities on the basis of national origin. Whether the rule is applied at all times or only at certain times, and whether the employees affected by the rule received adequate notice of the rule, will determine the level of scrutiny to be used in judging the imposition of those rules.

According to the EEOC guidelines, an English-only rule that is applied at all times in the workplace constitutes a burdensome term and condition of employment. Prohibiting employees from speaking their primary language at all times in the workplace might cause the employee to feel inferior, isolated, or intimidated based on national origin. Therefore, the EEOC will presume that such a rule violates Title VII and will closely scrutinize the rule.

Successful pursuit of a business necessity defense for an absolute English-only rule is difficult because the EEOC has stated that there will rarely, if ever, be a need for an absolute prohibition against speaking any language other than English at all times and in all places in the workplace. However, an employer may have a rule requiring that employees speak only in English at certain times if the employer can show that the rule is justified by necessity—situations in which employees are required to speak English while dealing with customers or while in areas of the employer's premises that are open to the public.

Courts' Disagreement with EEOC on English-Only Rule

Disparate impact challenges to English-only rules have explicitly rejected the EEOC approach in all courts. The courts require the plaintiff to establish a rule's discriminatory effect before shifting the burden to the employer to justify the English-only requirement.

Garcia v. Spun Steak Co, 998 F.2d 1480 (9th Cir. 1993), *later proceeding*, 114 S.Ct. 1292, and *cert denied*, 114 S.Ct. 2726 (1994)

Facts:

Spun Steak, a poultry and meat producer, employed 33 workers, 24 of whom were Spanish-speaking. Two of the 24 employees spoke no English, and the others had varying degrees of English proficiency. Spun Steak instituted an English-only rule to promote racial harmony in the workplace and enhance worker safety and productivity following complaints that some workers were harassing and insulting other workers in a language they could not understand. The plaintiffs challenged the English-only rule under the disparate impact theory.

The plaintiffs argued that since an individual's primary language is an important link to his/her cultural and ethnic identity, the English-only rule denied them the ability to express their cultural heritage on the job. The plaintiffs also argued that the rule denied them a privilege of employment that the monolingual employees enjoyed—the ability to converse in the language with which they felt most comfortable. Additionally, the plaintiffs also argued that the rule created an atmosphere of inferiority, isolation, and intimidation that was prohibited by the EEOC guidelines.

Opinion by Judge O'Scannlain:

It is clear that Congress intended a balance to be struck in preventing discrimination and preserving the independence of the employer. In striking that balance, the Supreme Court has held that a plaintiff in a disparate impact case must prove the alleged discriminatory effect before the burden shifts to the employer. The EEOC Guideline at issue here contravenes that policy by presuming that an English-only policy has a disparate impact in the presence of proof. We are not aware of, nor has counsel shown us, anything in the legislative history to Title VII that indicates that English-only policies are to be presumed discriminatory. Indeed, nowhere in the legislative history is there a discussion of English-only policies at all.

[In reversing the grant of summary judgment in favor of the plaintiff and remanding with instructions to grant summary judgment in favor of Spun Steak, the Court found, as follows:]

(1) disparate impact claim may be based upon challenge to practice or policy that has significant adverse impact on "terms, conditions, or privileges" of employment of protected group under title VII; (2) employees who spoke both Spanish and English failed to show that employer's requirement that bilingual workers speak only English while on job had significant adverse effect on terms, conditions, or privileges of their employment; and (3) genuine issue of material fact existed as to whether employee who spoke no English was adversely affected by English-only rule.

The Ninth Circuit in *Garcia v. Spun Steak Co.* noted that Title VII does not protect the ability of individuals to express their cultural heritage at the workplace, and an employer is not required to allow employees to express their cultural identity. The court further found that the privilege enjoyed by the monolingual employee was the privilege to converse on the job, not the privilege to converse in a particular language. Finally the court rejected the argument that the English-only rule created an atmosphere of inferiority, intimidation, and isolation that resulted in ethnic tension in the workplace.

Notice of the English-Only Rule

The EEOC had stated that proper notice must be given to all employees of the implementation of the rule. A company's failure to provide an effective notice, in conjunction with an adverse employment decision against an individual based on a violation of the rule, will be considered as evidence of discrimination on the basis of national origin.

Employees should be made aware of the provisions of the rule, such as the scope of its applicability, working hours, conversations, and the consequences of violating the rule. Notification might include written communication, posting the notice, conducting a meeting to inform employees of the rule, or a combination of those methods.

Business Necessity Defense of English-Only Rules

In the context of English-only rules, employers have utilized three basic arguments.

Lessening of Racial Tension

In *Garcia v. Gloor, 618 F.2d 264* (5th Cir. 1980), *cert denied* 101 S. Ct. 903 (1981), the employer claimed that customers who understood no Spanish became irritated when employees spoke Spanish to each other. Courts have been willing to accept the argument that English-only rules are necessary to reduce racial tensions in cases where failure to speak in English would not have affected job performance. The EEOC has warned that the fears of coworkers and customers that employees speaking in a language other than English are talking about them are unfounded, and the product of individual conversation in a language other than English increases productivity, since employees are able to express their concerns about such issues as production problems more accurately in their primary language.

Enable More Effective Supervision

Another justification for English-only rules is that they enable more effective supervision. The English-only rule must significantly enhance a supervisor's ability to monitor job performance. However, in situations where job performance can be measured by means other than the content of employees' conversation (a typical production-line job, for example), the content of employee conversations does not relate to important tasks of the job, and the effective supervision justification is likely to fail.

Safety and Efficiency

In a workplace environment involving hazards and possible emergencies, a limited English-only rule can be justified on the grounds that it improves communication and reduces confusion. In a petroleum company, the EEOC found that adoption of an English-only rule was not a violation of Title VII. The employer justified the rule on the basis that constant and open communication among employees working with potentially dangerous equipment was necessary to avoid fires and explosions, and to be able to respond quickly at the time of an accident.

A challenge can be mounted to an English-only rule in a case where the rule may decrease the effectiveness of communication and therefore interferes with the ability of a person whose primary language is not English to learn safety procedures and to properly respond to emergencies.

Hostile Environment

Conduct related to an individual's national origin that has the purpose or effect of creating an intimidating, hostile, or offensive working environment, or unreasonably interfering with an individual's work performance, or that otherwise adversely affects an individual's employment opportunities, creates a hostile environment and thus is prohibited under Title VII (29 C.F.R. 1608.8(b)(1997)). There is a basis on which to challenge English-only rules and other language rules under the hostile environment discrimination to the extent that language is one of the traits protected under the national origin aspect of Title VII.

In *Prado v. L. Luria & Son*, 975 F. Supp. 1349 (S.D. Fla. 1997), discussed below, the English-only rule was challenged under the hostile environment discrimination theory.

Prado v. L. Luria & Son, 975 F. Supp. 1349 (S.D. Fla. 1997)

Facts:

Prado was born in Cuba, immigrated to the United States in 1979, and was initially employed by the defendant in 1987. During the next ten years, she voluntarily left her employment and was rehired a year later. Prado received promotions and was assigned to a number of different positions with various degrees of responsibility. The plaintiff claimed that her supervisor began to make fun of her accent at least once a day for a period of two months in 1994. She argued that after she started working at a different location, the new supervisor made comments about his dislike of having to work with "Spanish-speaking people," and asked the plaintiff, who had hiring responsibilities at the time, "not to employ any blacks or persons with heavy Spanish accents." The new supervisor then began to make fun of the plaintiff's accent and began to strictly enforce the store's English-only policy. Soon after that series of events, the plaintiff resigned.

The *Prado* court considered whether the defendant's English-only rule imposed a discriminatory employment environment on an employee whose preferred language was Spanish. The district court utilized the hostile environment test developed by *Harris v. Forklift Systems*, 510 U.S. 17 (1993):

1. The frequency of the discriminatory conduct
2. The severity of the discriminatory conduct
3. Whether the conduct was physically threatening or humiliating, or a mere offensive utterance
4. Whether it unreasonably interfered with an employee's work performance

In this case, the district court considered not only the English-only rule, but also the other alleged conduct, including the comments about employees with heavy Spanish accents, and the instances in which the supervisors made fun of the plaintiff's accent.

The court failed to find the existence of a hostile work environment. Only two facts were determined to be of key significance. Most of the alleged hostile behavior had occurred over a three-month period. However, the plaintiff had worked for the defendant for a number of years, and over that time her experiences had been favorable. The court also found that over

90% of the workforce at one of the defendant's stores and approximately 70% of management were Hispanic. The court used this majority status in its determination that there was no discriminatory intimidation.

Opinion by Judge Ferguson:

Generally, an employer may adopt or maintain any worksite policy governing employees which has as its principal purpose a furthering of the employer's legitimate business interests so long as the policy does not infringe on individual rights, is not detrimental to the health or safety of the employees and, on balance, does not create an unfair advantage or disadvantage to any discrete group. More particularly, an English-only workplace rule adopted with a principal purpose of providing for effective supervision and evaluation of employees furthers a legitimate business interest without violating protected rights.

On the record presented there is no showing that the policy, separate from aberrant behavior of one or two individuals entrusted with its enforcement, created a hostile employment environment. Where an employer acts promptly to discipline or remove an offending supervisor, offers re-employment to the employee who has resigned before reporting the offensive conduct, and further offers the employee a choice of working locations to ensure an environment which accommodates personal sensitivities, it cannot be said that the employer has created a workplace environment hostile to the employee.

Foreign Accent Discrimination

Courts have accepted the argument that, although it is not as permanent as race or color, an accent is not easily changed for a person who was born in and has lived in a foreign country for a long time. Unlike the English-only cases, there has been almost total agreement by the courts that accent discrimination is actionable under the national origin protection of Title VII.

The EEOC has identified four situations in which the issue of accent discrimination could arise:

1. The case in which the employer denies using the employee's accent when making the employment decision at issue.
2. The case in which an employer may admit that the individual's accent was the reason for the adverse employment decision, but argues that the individual's accent interfered with his or her job performance. (The analysis then will focus on whether the accent would "materially interfere" with the individual's job performance.)
3. The case in which an employer admits that the individual's accent was a factor, but argues that other facts were utilized as well. (The analysis would then

be based on whether the use of accent was a "substantial" or "motivating" factor in the employment decision.)

4. The case in which an employer may admit that the individual's accent was the only factor in the adverse employment decision, without any regard to the intelligibility of speech and how it would affect job performance. (The employer admits to national origin discrimination.)

A key determination in accent discrimination cases is whether accent interferes with job performance. A foreign accent that interferes with an employee's ability to perform a task may also constitute a legitimate nondiscriminatory reason for an adverse employment decision.

To determine whether an accent "materially interferes" with job performance, the EEOC considers three factors:

- The level and type of communication demands in the job, including the frequency and complexity of oral communication, and the severity of a single incident of miscommunication.
- Whether the employee's speech was fairly evaluated as to its intelligibility.
- The level to which the employee's accent would present difficulties in the job at issue.

ENGLISH PROFICIENCY RULES

Rules requiring employee fluency in English or any other language may constitute unlawful discrimination under Title VII. In many cases, such English proficiency rules are used as employee selection devices by employers and are justified on the basis that fluency in a particular language is a necessary job qualification.

In the context of a discrimination charge involving a language fluency requirement, it may be appropriate to consider the applicability of the bona fide occupational qualification (BFOQ) exception where the respondent alleges that a language fluency requirement justifies restricting an employment opportunity to members of a particular national origin (EEOC Compl. Man. (BNA) § 623.9).

TERMS

english-only rules
english-proficiency rules
national origin discrimination

REVIEW QUESTIONS

1. Would a school be able to legitimately discharge a teacher who, though fluent in English, speaks with an accent so heavy that it makes him or her incomprehensible to the students? Explain why or why not.

2. Can an employer legally justify the termination of an office employee whose foreign accent did not interfere with her ability to perform the duties of her position? If so, on what basis?

3. Could a company require job applicants to take employment-related test in English? Why or why not?

4. If a job requires English proficiency, is an employer guilty of national origin discrimination if it declines the application of an applicant who has only been in the United States for two years and speaks very limited English?

5. A county in California used two written examinations (both in English) for applicants, and instituted a height requirement for its law enforcement personnel. Several Mexican American applicants filed suit, claiming that these requirements had a disparate impact on Mexican American applicants. The suit claimed that these applicants' national origin tended to produce shorter applicants. A further claim was made that many Mexican American applicants were not comfortable with English examinations. Would the county prevail in this lawsuit? What type of evidence could the county produce to support its employment requirements relating to testing and height?

6. A Chinese restaurant advertised for a "Chinese wait person," in an effort to add to the authenticity of its business. An applicant from a South American country applies for the position, believing that his ten years of experience in the restaurant industry should qualify him for the position. Can the restaurant legally reject his application? If not, on what basis can it deny him employment?

7. If a Guatemalan applied for a position as front desk clerk for a major resort hotel in San Francisco, would the hotel management commit national origin discrimination if it denied her the position because of her limited ability to communicate in English with hotel guests? Should the hotel offer her employment as an auditor, a position that does not require communication with guests?

8. A security company refuses to hire a female applicant when it learns that her husband is from a country that the U.S. deems to be a security risk. The company is concerned that her employment might be an attempt to infiltrate the company for an attack by radicals from her husband's country. Can the security

company legally refuse to hire this applicant because of her husband's national origin?

9. A furniture design company considered two applicants for a sales manager position. One was a U.S. citizen and the other was from Japan. The human resources manager decided to hire the U.S. citizen because of his personal preference for working with U.S. citizens. Does this constitute national origin discrimination?

10. Does Title VII categorize employment discrimination on the basis of citizenship as a violation of the Act?

PROJECTS

1. Brief the *Texas Dep't of Community Affairs v. Burdine*, 450 U.S 248 (1981) case.

2. Search the Internet for recent cases in your state involving the issue of English-only use in the workplace. Prepare a summary of the courts' position on that issue.

CHAPTER 12

Religious Discrimination

OVERVIEW

As originally enacted, Title VII contained no definition of the word "religion." However, the 1972 amendments to Title VII included the language, "The term **religion** includes all aspects of religious observance and practice, as well as belief, unless an employer demonstrates that he is unable to reasonably accommodate an employee's or prospective employee's religious observance or practice without undue hardship on the conduct of the employer's business." A key word in the definition above is "belief." To survive a court challenge, the belief must be loosely held and must take the place of religion in the employee's life. For Title VII purposes "belief" encompasses atheism as a religion. An employer is not permitted to question the sincerity of the belief simply because the belief may appear unorthodox to the employer.

The right to follow one's religious beliefs was a large part of what made the early settlers in America break away from Great Britain and its state-imposed religious beliefs. Religious belief was such an important part of the early colonial process that the right to pursue religious freedom was included in the U.S. Constitution. Since the Founding Fathers addressed religion in the Constitution, religious freedom has been protected in American law. Title VII advanced this protection into the arena of employment.

Litigation for Title VII violations relating to religion does not occur as often as some other categories of discrimination, but religious violations remain a justifiable concern for both employers and employees. Unlike the other protected categories of Title VII, there is no absolute prohibition against discrimination on the basis of religion. Title VII provides within the category of religious protection a duty to reasonably accommodate the employee's religious beliefs, unless to do so would cause an undue hardship on the employer. The only other reasonable accommodation requirement under Title VII is found in the Americans with Disabilities Act, as discussed in Chapter 8.

UNLAWFUL EMPLOYMENT PRACTICES RELATING TO RELIGION

Title VII provides in part:
> It shall be an unlawful employment practice for an employer—

> (1) to fail or refuse to hire or to discharge any individual, or otherwise to discriminate against any individual with respect to his compensation, terms, conditions, or privileges of employment, because of such individual's . . . religion . . . or
> (2) to limit, segregate, or classify his employees or applicants for employment in any way which would deprive or tend to deprive any individual of employment opportunities or otherwise adversely affect his status as an employee, because of such individual's religion . . . (42 U.S.C. § 20002–2(a)).

PROTECTED ACTIVITY

As discussed above, religion is expansively defined to include "all aspects of religious observance and practice, as well as belief."

Religious Observance and Practice

An individual's religious observance and practice do not need to be responsive to the commands of a particular religious organization to be protected under Title VII. The individual's practice must simply stem from a sincerely held religious belief. The prohibition against religious discrimination includes personal religious beliefs that are not in the mainstream of religious thought, or that are not common to all members of a particular religious group (See 29 C.F.R. § 1605.1 (1996)).

Religious Beliefs

A **religious belief** is a sincere and meaningful belief that is not confined in either source or content to traditional or parochial concepts of religion. Title VII extends protection to the employee's freedom not to hold a belief in a supreme being or other religious tenets, often referred to as **atheism**. In *Young v. Southwestern Sav. & Loan Ass'n*, 509 F.2d 140 (5th Cir. 1975), the employer compelled the plaintiff, an atheist, to attend monthly staff meetings that began with a prayer and religious presentation. Young resigned to avoid attending further staff meetings. The Fifth Circuit decided that the employer's conduct constituted discrimination based on religion, and that the plaintiff had suffered a constructive discharge based on his religious belief.

Ministerial Duties

Title VII's protection of religious practices in the workplace extends to ministerial duties such as teaching a weekly Bible study class or attending a church's monthly business meetings.

REASONABLE ACCOMMODATION

Overview

While Title VII contains no absolute prohibition against discrimination on the basis of religion, for the first time in the Act the category of religion contains a **duty to reasonably accommodate** (a legal obligation to try to find a way to avoid a conflict between workplace policies and an employee's religious practices or beliefs), unless to do so would cause **undue hardship** (a burden imposed on an employer by accommodating an employee's religious conflict that would be too onerous for the employer to bear, discussed later), on the employer. Title VII contains no duty to accommodate for race, gender, color, or national origin. Only religion and ADA are afforded accommodation rights under Title VII.

The duty to accommodate originated in the 1966 EEOC Guidelines on Discrimination Because of Religion. These guidelines required an employer not only to refrain from discrimination, but to affirmatively accommodate the reasonable needs of its employees where such accommodation could be made without serious inconvenience to the conduct of business (29 C.F.R. § 1605.1(b)(c)). This duty to accommodate is necessary to negate the impact of racially neutral employer policies upon its employees who hold sincere convictions about working on the Sabbath or other religious observances that affect their ability to either obtain employment or continue that employment. In summary, the concept of accommodation is consistent with the premise that apparently neutral policies violate Title VII if they have an adverse impact upon protected groups.

Selection of Accommodation

It is generally the employer's responsibility to examine the accommodation options, and offer an accommodation to an employee once the employer is notified that a conflict exists between a particular employment practice and the employee's religious observance or practice. If the employer is unable to devise any reasonable accommodation, it must accept any reasonable accommodation offered by the employee. The employee is not required to suggest any accommodations to the employer.

Employee's Duty to Cooperate with Employer on Accommodation

The courts have held that all that is required for religious accommodation under Title VII is for the employer to make any reasonable accommodation—not necessarily the *most* reasonable accommodation. Additionally, the employee must also be reasonable in considering possible accommodation alternatives.

Factors used by courts and the EEOC to determine whether an employer has met its burden of reasonably accommodating the employee's religious conflict include:

1. Whether the employer made an attempt to accommodate;
2. The size of the employer's workforce;
3. The type of job involved in the conflict;
4. The cost of accommodation, and
5. The administrative efforts involved in accommodation

Types of Accommodations

Work Schedules

Work scheduling is one of the most common issues in religious discrimination case, because religious practices and beliefs often require time off from work for Sabbath days and religious holidays. Thus, EEOC guidelines address potential work scheduling accommodations, including:

*   Creation of a flexible work schedule for individuals requiring accommodation
*   Assignment of a voluntary substitute with similar qualifications
*   Consideration of a lateral transfer or a change in job assignment to resolve the conflict

While an employer must attempt to accommodate an employee's need for a schedule change to attend Sabbath services or participate in religious holidays, the employer is not required to grant the time off with pay.

Religious Dress and Grooming Practices

Safety concerns or other business necessities may justify limitations on religious attire, beards worn for religious reasons, religious jewelry, or other types of religious dress or appearance. Employers have an obligation to seek reasonable accommodations for a particular religious attire or appearance before prohibiting it completely. With the exception of safety concerns, employers will have difficulty establishing a business necessity for limitations on religious attire or appearance.

Testing and Screening

Employers who utilize employment tests must accommodate individuals who cannot attend a scheduled test because of their religious practices, unless the accommodation is an undue hardship.

Preemployment inquires about an applicant's availability during normal work hours may exclude individuals who have certain religious practices from employment opportunities. Such inquiries could be used as evidence of discrimination. No public or private employer should inquire about an applicant's need for religious accommodation until after the hiring decision has been made.

Undue Hardship

What constitutes undue hardship varies from situation to situation. Employers differ in critical factors such as size, financial strength, and corporate structure. An undue hardship for a sole proprietorship grocery store is obviously not automatically an undue hardship for a major supermarket chain. Many of the EEOC guidelines on undue hardship factors in accommodation are duplicative of those listed above for a finding of accommodation. These factors for determining undue hardship include:

1. The nature and type of the employer's workplace.
2. The type of position for which accommodation is requested.
3. The cost of the accommodation.
4. The possibility of a transfer of the employee and its effect on the employer's business.
5. The number of employees available for accommodation.

The courts and the EEOC have often differed on their interpretation of what constitutes undue hardship, as discussed in the following case.

Trans World Airlines, Inc. v. Hardison, 432 U.S. 63 (1977)

Facts:

Hardison was employed by Trans World Airlines in a maintenance and overhaul department that operated 24 hours a day. Hardison was subject to a seniority system in a collective-bargaining agreement between TWA and the International Association of Machinists &

Aerospace Workers that gave senior employees first choice for job and shift assignments. Junior employees were required to work when enough employees were not available at a particular time or in a particular job to meet TWA's needs.

Because Hardison's religious beliefs prohibited him from working on Saturday, TWA attempted to accommodate his scheduling. These attempts were successful for a time, mainly because of his seniority. Hardison later requested and received a transfer to another job where he was asked to work Saturdays. Because of his low seniority, problems ensued. TWA agreed to ask the union to seek a change of work assignments, but the union refused to violate its seniority system. TWA next rejected a proposal that Hardison work only four days a week because this would impair critical functions in the airline operations. No accommodation could be reached, and Hardison was discharged for refusing to work on Saturdays. The Court of Appeals held that TWA had not made reasonable efforts to accommodate Hardison's religious needs.

Opinion by Justice White:

Hardison and the EEOC insist that the statutory obligation to accommodate religious needs takes precedence over both the collective-bargaining contract and the seniority rights of TWA's other employees. We agree that neither a collective-bargaining contract nor a seniority system may be employed to violate the statute, but we do not believe that the duty to accommodate requires TWA to take steps inconsistent with the otherwise valid agreement. Collective bargaining, aimed at effecting workable and enforceable agreements between management and labor, lies at the core of our national labor policy, and seniority provisions are universally included in these contracts. Without a clear and express indication from Congress, we cannot agree with Hardison and the EEOC that an agreed-upon seniority system must give way when necessary to accommodate religious observances.

It was essential to TWA's business to require Saturday and Sunday work from at least a few employees even though most employees preferred those days off. Allocating the burdens of weekend work was a matter for collective bargaining. In considering criteria to govern this allocation, TWA and the union had two alternatives: adopt a neutral system, such as seniority, a lottery or rotating shifts; or allocate days off in accordance with the religious needs of its employees. TWA would have had to adopt the latter in order to assure Hardison and others like him of getting the days off necessary for strict observance of their religion, but it could have done so only at the expense of those who had strong, but perhaps nonreligious, reasons for not working on weekends. There were no volunteers to relieve Hardison on Saturdays, and to give Hardison Saturdays off, TWA would have had to deprive another employee of his shift preference at least in part because he did not adhere to a religion that observed the Saturday Sabbath.

Title VII does not contemplate such unequal treatment. It would be anomalous to conclude that by "reasonable accommodation" Congress meant that an employer must deny the shift and job preference of some employees as well as deprive them of their contractual rights, in order to accommodate or prefer the religious needs of others, and we conclude that Title VII does not require an employer to go that far.

To require TWA to bear more than a de minimis cost in order to give Hardison Saturdays off is an undue hardship.

In the absence of clear statutory language or legislative history to the contrary, we will not readily construe the statute to require an employer to discriminate against some employees in order to enable others to observe their Sabbath. **REVERSED.**

Cost Considerations

Employers are not required to make accommodations if the costs that would be incurred are more than *de minimis*, as reflected by the Supreme Court in the *Hardison* case discussed above. Such considerations are not limited to the direct expenditure of money. Costs might be in the form of efficiency or public health, safety, and welfare considerations. The court in *Favero v. Hunstville Indep. Sch. Dist.*, 939 F. Supp. 1281, 1286 (S.D. Tex. 1996), *aff'd*, 110 F.3d 793 (5th Cir. 1997) found that permitting school bus drivers unpaid leave for religious observances would be an undue burden, because the school district would have to provide replacement drivers, involving increased cost and inconvenience.

Impact on Other Employees

A significant consideration in determining undue hardship is the effect of a requested or needed accommodation on other employees. The Supreme Court held in the *Hardison* case that it would be unreasonable to require either TWA or the union to act inconsistently with a valid collective bargaining agreement, accept replacement workers with increased costs incurred, and impose an unwanted shift on other employees.

It is also an undue hardship to require an employer to force employees to permanently switch shifts over their objections to accommodate another employee's different observance of the Sabbath.

Collective Bargaining Agreements

Scheduling accommodations constitute an undue hardship when they adversely affect seniority rights or impair neutral work scheduling requirements under an employer's collective bargaining agreement with a labor organization.

An employer is not required to deviate from its seniority system in order to give an employee a shift preference for religious reasons, according to the Court's decision in *Hardison*.

Religious Activities in the Workplace

An accommodation that would allow an employee to engage in religious activities during working hours constitutes an undue hardship. For example, a manufacturing plant's production would suffer if an employee passed out religious pamphlets or read the Bible during the time that the employee was scheduled to be working on a production line.

PROVING DISCRIMINATION

The plaintiff in a religious accommodation must demonstrate the following in order to establish a *prima facie* case:

1. He or she has a sincere belief, observance or practice that conflicts with an employment requirement;
2. Such belief, observance, or practice is religious in nature;
3. The plaintiff informed the employer of this belief, observance, or practice; and
4. The religious observance or practice was a motivating factor for plaintiff's discharge or other adverse employment decision.

Once the plaintiff has established a *prima facie* case, the burden then shifts to the employer to prove that it made a reasonable accommodation or that an accommodation would have resulted in undue hardship.

Sincerity of Beliefs

The employer may concede the sincerity of an employee's religious beliefs. In some cases, however, the employer has contested the sincerity of an employee's beliefs. Such a contest might be won or lost by an employee based on his or her consistency in observing the religious practice. For example, an employee might argue that he had held a lifelong belief against working on Sundays, but frequently worked on Sunday until shortly before his termination. In that case, a court could determine that the employee's religious belief was more about "convenience" than sincerity.

Nature of Beliefs

Political beliefs are not afforded statutory protection against religious discrimination. The court in *Slater v. King Soopers, Inc.*, 809 F. Supp. 809 (D. Colo. 1992), dismissed a claim of religious discrimination brought by a member of the Ku Klux Klan when his employer discharged him for organizing a pro-Nazi rally. The court found that this discharge was based on the Klansman's political and social views, rather than on genuine religious beliefs. A number of courts have also ruled that an employee's cultural beliefs are not religious beliefs in cases involving employee's African-style head wraps and berets.

Notice to Employer

A primary element of the plaintiff's *prima facie* case is notice to the employer. The plaintiff must prove that he or she informed the employer of the conflict between the plaintiff's religious observances or practices and an employment requirement. The notice may be oral rather than written.

Courts have held that the employer's knowledge that the plaintiff has strong religious beliefs is not sufficient to put the employer on notice that the employee's religious observances or practices may conflict with an employment requirement (*Chalmers v. Tulon Co. of Richmond*, 101 F.3d 1012 (4th Cir. 1996)).

Causation

The plaintiff must prove by a preponderance of the evidence that a motivating factor for an adverse employment decision was the plaintiff's failure to comply with an employment requirement that conflicted with the employee's religious beliefs.

Disparate Treatment

A small number of religious discrimination cases involve only disparate treatment claims. In those cases, as discussed at length in Chapter 7, the courts normally apply the *McDonnell Douglas* burden-shifting model. To establish a *prima facie* disparate treatment case, the plaintiff must establish:

1. The plaintiff has sincere religious beliefs;
2. The plaintiff is qualified for the position at issue;
3. The plaintiff suffered an adverse employment decision; and
4. The employer selected another person for the position who did not hold the plaintiff's particular religious beliefs.

Once the plaintiff establishes a *prima facie* case, the burden shifts to the defendant to establish a legitimate, nondiscriminatory reason for its employment action. Next, the plaintiff must prove by a preponderance of evidence that the legitimate reasons articulated by the employer were a pretext for intentional discrimination on the basis of religion.

Consider the elements of a *prima facie* case as discussed by the court in the following case.

Hall v. Baptist Memorial Health Care Corp.,
27 F. Supp. 2d, 1029, 78 FEP 1756 (W.D. Tenn. 1998)

Facts:

Although the defendant was found to be exempt from Title VII, the court found that Hall was not terminated because of religious beliefs or practices, but because she was ordained into a leadership position in an organization (church) that "espoused beliefs" on homosexuality that were "diametrically opposed to those held by the College." That conclusion was supported by the fact that when the plaintiff's supervisor found out that she was a member of this church, nearly a year after she was hired, he went to his supervisor to express his concerns about the "reputation" of that church and was told that her choice of church was not a concern of the college. When she became an ordained minister in church, she told her supervisor that she was a lesbian. Concern about her role at the defendant college arose after this disclosure.

Opinion by Judge Donald:

This court concludes that Defendant is a religious educational institution under 2000e-1(a) and is exempt from any Title VII liability arising from Plaintiff's claim of religious discrimination. Even if Defendant were not exempt from Title VII liability for religious discrimination, Plaintiff's claim would not survive Defendant's motion for summary judgment. Plaintiff has not offered any credible evidence that Defendant's asserted reason for terminating her was pretextual. Absent such evidence, Plaintiff does not raise an issue of fact for a jury.

Plaintiff has failed to offer any credible evidence that Defendant terminated her for any reason other than the conflict of interest existing between Plaintiff's leadership role at Holy Trinity and her employment as a student services specialist at the College. Where the Defendant has asserted a legitimate, nondiscriminatory reason for Plaintiff's discharge, and Plaintiff has failed to prove pretext, this court must grant Defendant's motion for summary judgment.

Defendant's MSJ on Plaintiff's claim of religious discrimination under Title VII is granted.

Judge Donald explained that the plaintiff satisfied the first three elements of a *prima facie* case for religious discrimination: member of protected group, subject to adverse employment decision, and qualified for position. However, Judge Donald wrote that the plaintiff did not prove that she was replaced by a person outside the protected class. He also found that the plaintiff did not demonstrate that the college had ever treated an employee who assumed leadership role in an organization expressing public support for homosexuals and homosexual lifestyle any differently than it treated her, and without this proof, the plaintiff could not establish a *prima facie* case of religious discrimination.

Religious Harassment

Religious harassment is prohibited by Title VII. Such harassment may be either *quid pro quo* harassment or hostile environment harassment.

Quid Pro Quo Harassment

***Quid pro quo* religious harassment** is defined as the conditioning of an economic or other job benefit upon an employee's submission to the employer's religious observances or practices in the workplace, or punishing the employee for failure to comply with those religious observances or practices.

To establish *quid pro quo* harassment, an employee must show:

1. the employer's religious observances or practices are unwelcome;
2. the harassment was motivated by a supervisor's religious beliefs;
3. the employee's reaction to the supervisor's religious observances or practices affected a tangible part of his employment; and
4. employer liability is established.

An employer may be strictly liable for *quid pro quo* harassment by a supervisor (29 C.F.R. § 1606 (1996)).

Hostile Environment Harassment

A plaintiff must establish the following to prove hostile environment harassment:

- The plaintiff belongs to a protected class—all employees covered by Title VII are protected from religious discrimination;
- The plaintiff was subjected to unwelcome harassment;
- The harassment was based on the plaintiff's religious practices or beliefs;
- The harassment affected a term, condition, or privilege of employment; and
- The employer knew or should have known of the harassment and failed to take prompt remedial action.

As in the case of harassment based on age, religious harassment normally consists of repeated, outrageous, and derogatory comments by a supervisor or coworker regarding the affected worker's religion or religious practices. Isolated or stray remarks do not constitute religious harassment.

To prevail in a hostile environment case based on religious practices or belief, a plaintiff must establish that the employer had actual or constructive notice of the offensive conduct and failed to take prompt actions to remedy the wrong.

DEFENSES TO RELIGIOUS DISCRIMINATION CLAIMS

An employer may utilize any of the following defenses to religious discrimination claims.

Undue Hardship

As discussed above, an employer can defend against a religious discrimination claim based on the duty of accommodation by proving that it is unable to reasonably accommodate the religious observance or practice of the plaintiff without undue hardship.

Business Necessity

An employer does not commit an unlawful employment practice if a practice has a discriminatory effect and would otherwise be prohibited by Title VII if the employer establishes that the practice is not intentionally designed or utilized to circumvent the prohibitions of the statute, and the practice is justified by business necessity. An employer can impose practices or conditions of employment that discriminate against certain religious groups if the practices or conditions are necessary to the normal operation of the business. As discussed earlier in this chapter, an employer may prohibit facial hair even if it conflicts with the employee's religious belief, because the prohibition was based on business necessity—the employee was required to wear a respirator that needed to be tightly sealed against his face.

Bona Fide Occupational Qualification

Religious organizations are generally exempt from Title VII prohibitions relating to religion. Religion *may* provide a **bona fide occupational qualification** (BFOQ), an employer's legitimate need to discriminate in hiring. For example, Title VII would not require that a Baptist church in Virginia hire a Catholic priest as its minister. However, if the Baptist church has sectarian activities, such as a day care center, religious bookstore, or health club or gym that does not involve religion, those activities do not offer the same exemptions from Title VII.

In addition, Section 703(e)(2) of Title VII states that it is not unlawful for a university, college, school, or other educational institution to hire employees of a particular religion if the institution is in whole or in substantial part owned, supported, controlled, or managed by a particular religion or religious association, or if its curriculum is directed toward propagating a particular religion.

RELIGIOUS ADVOCACY IN THE WORKPLACE

Constitutional guarantees of free speech and religion do not apply to private employers. Employers act unlawfully if they tolerate conduct that amounts to harassment of employees based on their religious beliefs or practices. The only time that management can reasonably intercede in religious advocacy is when the activity is aggressive and intimidates other employees, as discussed in the following case:

Wilson v. U.S. West Communications dba Northwestern Bell Telephone Co., 58 F.3d 1337 (8th Cir. 1995)

Facts:

In late July 1990, Wilson, a Roman Catholic, made a religious vow that she would wear an antiabortion button "until there was an end to abortion or until [she] could no longer fight the fight." The button was two inches in diameter and showed a color photograph of an eighteen to twenty-week old fetus. The button also contained the phrases "Stop abortion," and "They're Forgetting Someone." Wilson wore the button at all times, unless she was sleeping, or bathing, because she believed that if she took off the button she would compromise her vow and lose her soul.

Wilson began wearing the button to work in August 1990. The button caused disruptions at work. Employees gathered to talk about the button. Wilson acknowledged that the button caused a great deal of disruption. Some employees threatened to walk off their jobs because they found the button offensive and disturbing for "very personal reasons," such as infertility problems, miscarriage, and death of a premature infant, unrelated to any stance on abortion or religion.

Shortly after she began wearing the button, Wilson met with her supervisors, Jensen and Gail Klein, five times. Jensen and Klein are also Roman Catholics who oppose abortion. Klein noted a 40% decline in the productivity of the information specialists after Wilson began wearing the button.

Wilson told her supervisors that she should not be singled out for wearing the button because the company had no dress code. She also suggested that coworkers offended by the button should be asked not to look at it. Klein and Jensen offered Wilson three options: (1) wear the button only in her work cubicle, leaving the button in the cubicle when she moved around the office; (2) cover the button while at work; or (3) wear a different button with the same message but without the photograph. Wilson said she could neither cover nor remove the button because it would break her promise to God to wear the button and be a "living witness." She suggested that management tell the other information specialists to "sit at their desk[s] and do the job U.S. West was paying them to do."

Information specialists accused Jensen of harassment for not resolving the button issue to their satisfaction. Two employees filed grievances based on Wilson's button. Eventually,

U.S. West told Wilson not to report to work wearing anything depicting a fetus, including the button and T-shirt. U.S. West sent Wilson home when she returned to work wearing the button and fired her for three consecutive unexcused absences.

The parties stipulated that Wilson's religious beliefs were sincerely held, and the district court ruled that she made a *prima facie* case of religious discrimination. The court then considered whether U.S. West could defeat Wilson's claim by demonstrating that it offered Wilson a reasonable accommodation. The district court found that requiring Wilson to cover the button while at work was a reasonable accommodation.

Wilson appealed the district court's decision.

Opinion by Judge Gibson:

U.S. West's proposal allowed Wilson to comply with her vow to wear the button and respected the desire of coworkers not to look at the button. Hence the district court did not err in holding that U.S. West reasonably accommodated Wilson's religious beliefs.

We recognize that this case typifies workplace conflicts which result when employees hold strong views about emotionally charged issues. We reiterate that Title VII does not require an employer to allow an employee to impose his religious views on others. The employer is only required to reasonably accommodate an employee's religious views.

We affirm the district court's judgment.

TERMS

atheism
bona fide occupational qualification
duty to reasonably accommodate
quid pro quo religious harassment
religion
religious belief
undue hardship

REVIEW QUESTIONS

1. A welding shop refuses to permit men to wear beards because of OSHA requirements for the use of closely fitting breathing apparatus. An applicant whose religious beliefs necessitate a beard is denied employment because of the prohibition against beards. Does this prohibition constitute religious discrimination?

2. An employee is required to work on Saturday, which the employer knows is the

employee's Sabbath. Will the employee be successful in his religious discrimination lawsuit? What accommodation could the employer have offered?

3. A bus company requires that its female drivers wear pants. Claiming a religious prohibition against wearing pants, a female employee refuses to wear pants on the job. Will the court require the employer to accommodate the employee's religious beliefs in this case?

4. After a store clerk was hired by a small grocery store, she joined a religious group who celebrated Saturday as its Sabbath. When she refused to work on Saturday, she was terminated. The store owner claimed that because his wife and the clerk were the only employees, he could not handle the store's business on Saturday without the clerk. Is there a reasonable accommodation option in this case? Would allowing the clerk to take Saturday off create an undue hardship for the store owner? Would a court likely find for the plaintiff or defendant? Why?

5. A paralegal voluntarily resigns from her employment with a large law firm. After her resignation, she becomes a Seventh Day Adventist. She reapplies for employment with the law firm two years later. In the interview and on her application, she requires a "guarantee" that she would not be required to work during her Sabbath (from sundown on Friday to sundown on Saturday). The firm administrator advises that the firm could not give such a "guarantee," but she promises to attempt to at least limit overtime requirements during that period. Would a court find that the paralegal's requirement of a "guarantee" against working on her Sabbath created an undue hardship on the law firm? Would the court find that the employee was unwilling to assist in the accommodation?

6. Could a Jesuit university establish a hiring policy to recruit only Jesuit professors? Is this requirement a BFOQ for the position?

7. Buddhist employees who do not celebrate Christmas resent the fact that they are required to take off on the Christmas holiday, but must use personal days or annual leave when they are off for their own religious holidays. Is the employer required to give the Buddhist employees paid time off for their own religious holidays, in addition to paid time for the Christmas holiday? Why or why not?

8. An elementary teacher uses Christian terms as spelling words, decorates the classroom with religious items on Christian holidays, and reads Biblical stories to the students. Muslim parents complain to the principal, who advises the teacher that she must immediately refrain from any religious activity in her classroom. The teacher refuses, claiming that her religion requires that she be a "wit-

ness" to her faith in all areas of her life. What action, if any, should the principal take to resolve the conflict between the Muslim parents and the teacher?

9. The FBI terminates an agent for his refusal to investigate pacifist antiwar protestors. Was this termination a violation of Title VII's reasonable accommodation requirement?

10. The United States Postal Service terminates an employee who refuses to distribute draft registration materials. Should the employer have attempted to accommodate the postal clerk's religious beliefs that prohibit military service? Is this failure to accommodate a violation of Title VII?

PROJECTS

1. Use the facts in *Trans World Airlines, Inc. v. Hardison* to draft a complaint.

2. Search legal Internet cites for cases involving a religious group that practices the use of peyote. Locate any case that involves religious discrimination in the workplace on the basis of peyote use.

CHAPTER 13

Sex Discrimination

OVERVIEW

As a result of a number of federal laws, most notably Title VII of the Civil Rights Act of 1964, employment practices that discriminate on the basis of sex are prohibited. These anti-discrimination statutes cover all but the smallest employers (those with fewer than 15 employees), and prohibit sex discrimination in hiring, advancement, or any other condition of employment.

It can be difficult to determine exactly what constitutes a distinction made "on the basis of sex." Title VII and the other relevant federal statutes, unfortunately, do not provide a definition. Courts interpreting the statutes have held that sex discrimination involves a comparison of one gender to the other that results in differing treatment, and that claims may be brought by a member of either gender.

Sex discrimination in employment has been an issue for less than two hundred years. Prior to the mid-1800s, few women were a part of the workplace. However, the growth of industrialization in the United States triggered a marked increase in the number of women working outside the home. By 1890, over 40% of single women under the age of 25 were engaged in industry jobs, and more than one million women were working in factories. (Smuts, *Women and Work in America*, pgs. 23–24 (1971)).

The ratio of female workers to the total work force in 1991 had grown from 20% in 1920 to 45%. (*Geographic Profile of Employment and Unemployment*, p. 5 (1991)). During the period 1975–1985, women held more than three-fifths of the almost 22,000,000 new jobs created. (Women's Bureau, U.S. Department of Labor, *20 Facts on Women Workers*, par. 1 (1986)).

Although sex discrimination has occurred at all salary and skill levels, the most significant disparities appear to have been those occurring in professional and management levels. (*Background Facts on Women Workers in the United States*, pp. 11–12, Tables 7 and 8 (1970)). The thirty-year period since these studies has seen active enforcement of the numerous anti-sex-discrimination laws, and has seen large strides in correcting disparities between the sexes. By 1985, the number of women in executive, administrative, and managerial positions had increased to 36%. However, the patterns of employment in lower-paying, traditionally female positions, saw little change. In 1985, four out of five administrative support workers were female.

According to a 1993 study, 99% of secretaries and 93% of bookkeepers and nurses in 1992 were women. (National Association for Female Executives, *Women in the American Workforce and Power Structure, A Contemporary Snapshot* (1993)). Statistics released by the National Committee on Pay Equity indicate that in 1992 women earned 69.8% of the salary earned by white men, while black males earned 72.1%, and black women earned 63%. (*Women and People of Color in the Workforce: 1991 Percentages of Year-Round, Full-Time Workers in the Workforce by Race/Ethnicity, Sex, and Wage Gap*, National Committee on Pay Equity).

DEFINITION OF SEXUAL HARASSMENT—TITLE VII

Sexual harassment is a form of sex discrimination. Since 1964, Title VII of the Civil Rights Act has made it unlawful for an employer to "fail or refuse to hire or to discharge any individual, or otherwise to discriminate against any individual" because of that individual's sex (42 U.S.C. § 2000e-2(a)(1)(1994)). As a practical matter, sexual harassment was not defined for many years. A court first interpreted this prohibition against discrimination as extending to sexual harassment in 1976. Shortly after that decision, the Equal Employment Opportunities Commission published guidelines to define sexual harassment.

DEFINITION OF SEXUAL HARASSMENT—EEOC

The EEOC "Guidelines on Discrimination Because of Sex" define **sexual harassment** as unwelcome sexual advances, requests for sexual favors and other verbal or physical conduct of a sexual nature in the following situations:

1. Submission to the sexual conduct is made, explicitly or implicitly, a term or condition of an individual's employment;
2. Submission to or rejection of the conduct by an individual is made the basis for employment decisions affecting such individual; or
3. Such conduct is for the purpose or effect of unreasonably interfering with an

individual's work performance, or creating an intimidating hostile or offensive working environment (29 C.F.R. § 1604.11).

CATEGORIES OF SEXUAL HARASSMENT

Title VII recognizes three categories of sexual harassment:

1. *Quid pro quo*;
2. Hostile work environment; and
3. Retaliation.

Quid Pro Quo Sexual Harassment

Definition

Quid pro quo harassment occurs when a manager or supervisor engages in unwelcome sexual conduct in a manner that, expressly or implicitly, makes submission to that conduct a term or condition of employment, or uses the employee's response as a basis for employment decisions affecting that person (29 C.F.R. § 1604.11(1) and (2)).

The Behavior Must Be Sexual in Nature or Sexually Motivated

An express demand for sexual relations is not required. The conduct of the alleged harasser must be reasonably interpreted to demand sexual favors in exchange for tangible job benefits. The behavior might consist of a demand for sexual favors; proposal for a date; advances limited to kissing or touching; or encouraging the harassed employee to wear provocative attire in the office.

The unlawful act is the manager or supervisor's use of power to affect an employee's job for sexually motivated purposes. In return for the employee's submission to sexual advances, the harasser either expressly or implicitly offers a favorable job assignment, a pay raise, a promotion, or saving a job that was scheduled to be deleted. The *quid pro quo* might be termination, failure to promote, elimination of a job, or other adverse employment action if the employee spurns the manager or supervisor. A constructive discharge might be sufficient to establish sexual harassment. However, the effect on the employee's terms and conditions of employment must be tangible, not merely psychological.

The Behavior Must Be Unwelcome

In *Meritor Savings Bank v. Vinson*, 477 U.S. 57, 106 S.Ct. 2399, 91 L.Ed.2d 49 (1986), the United States Supreme Court wrote that the question is not whether the victim acted "voluntarily," but whether the sexual advances were "unwelcome." For example, a secretary engages in a sexual relationship with a supervisor. On the surface, the relationship appears to be voluntary. However, when examined by a court, the secretary testifies that she doesn't consider the relationship voluntary at all. Rather, she feels that she has no choice but to comply with the supervisor's advances. Thus, the supervisor's behavior is actually unwelcome.

Extenuating circumstances that courts examine to determine whether the behavior is welcome or unwelcome might include an employee's participation in sexual jokes, sexual teasing, or sexual banter with other employees. Additionally, the courts examine the facts of a sexual harassment case to determine whether the employee complained to anyone about the alleged unwelcome behavior, or tried to evade the unwelcome behavior.

Example   A supervisor told a female worker that he could make her life hell and then assigned her onerous work, would not allow her to attend a conference that would have helped her do her job, and engaged in other cumulative actions. (*Reinhold v. Commonwealth of Virginia*, LEXIS 19532 (4th Cir. 1998)).

Hostile Work Environment

Definition

Conduct that "has the purpose or effect of unreasonably interfering with an individual's work performance, creating an intimidating, hostile or offensive work environment," may form the basis for a claim of sexual harassment in a **hostile work environment** (29 C.F.R. 1604.11(a)(3)). In this situation, the plaintiff is not required to show a loss of a tangible job benefit to establish the existence of a hostile work environment, as decided by the Supreme Court in the case discussed below.

Harris v. Forklift Systems, Inc., 510 U.S.17, 114 S.Ct. 367, 126 L.Ed.2d 295, *on remand* 14 F.3d 601 (1994)

Facts:

Harris worked as a manager at Forklift Systems, Inc., an equipment rental company, from April 1985 until October 1987. The Court found that throughout Harris' time at Forklift Charles Hardy, the president of Forklift, often insulted her because of her gender and often made her the target of unwanted sexual innuendo. Hardy told Harris on several occasions, in the presence of other employees, "You're a woman, what do you know?" He also told her at least once that she was a "dumb ass woman." In front of other workers he suggested that he and Harris "go to the Holiday Inn to negotiate [Harris'] raise." Hardy occasionally asked Harris and other female employees to get coins from his front pants pockets.

In mid-August 1987, Harris complained to Hardy about his conduct. Hardy expressed surprise that she had been offended, claimed that he was only joking, and apologized to her. He also promised he would stop his previous actions, and based on this assurance, Harris remained on the job. However, in early September, Hardy asked Harris in front of other employees about a deal that she was arranging with one of Forklift's customer and whether she had promised the guy sex on Saturday night. On October 1, 1987, Harris collected her paycheck and quit.

Harris then sued Forklift, claiming that Hardy's conduct had created an abusive work environment for her because of her gender.

Opinion of Justice O'Connor:

When the workplace is permeated with "discriminatory intimidation, ridicule, and insult," 477 U.S. at 65, 106 S. Ct., at 2405, that is "sufficiently severe or pervasive to alter the conditions of the victim's employment and create an abusive working environment," *id*, at 67, 106 S.Ct., at 2405 (internal brackets and quotation marks omitted), Title VII is violated.

. . . we can say that whether an environment is "hostile" or "abusive" can be determined only by looking at all the circumstances. These may include the frequency of the discriminatory conduct; its severity; whether it is physically threatening or humiliating, or a mere offensive utterance; and whether it unreasonably interferes with an employee's work performance. The effect on the employee's psychological well-being is, of course, relevant to determining whether the plaintiff actually found the environment abusive. But while psychological harm, like any other relevant factor, may be taken into account, no single factor is required.

We therefore reverse the judgment of the Court of Appeals, and remand the case for further proceedings consistent with this opinion.

So ordered.

A hostile work environment can be created through the conduct of persons with supervisory authority, coworkers, or even a nonemployee such as an independent contractor, customer, client, or vendor.

To meet the test of Title VII in hostile environment cases, the sexual harassment must be sufficiently severe or pervasive to alter the conditions of the complainant's employment and create an abusive work environment. Serious flirtation or even vulgar language probably will not establish a hostile work environment. The harassment must be viewed in its totality. The more severe the conduct, the less pervasive it must be. Potential factors regarding hostile work environment include:

- Whether the conduct was verbal, physical, or both;
- Whether the conduct was a one-time occurrence or was repeated;
- Whether the conduct was hostile and patently offensive;

- Whether the alleged harasser was a co-worker or a supervisor;
- Whether others joined in perpetrating the harassment; and
- Whether the harassment was directed at more than one individual.

Pervasiveness

What constitutes *pervasiveness* in the context of a hostile work environment? A single incident or a few isolated instances of offensive sexual conduct or remarks generally will not be enough to create an abusive environment. Title VII does not create a claim of sexual harassment for every crude joke or sexually explicit remark on the job.

Severity

A single sexual advance *may* constitute harassment, if it is linked to either granting or denying an employment benefit. Additionally, a single, unusually severe incident of harassment may establish a Title VII violation, particularly when the harassment is physical.

Example   The rape of an employee by the harasser would constitute actionable sexual harassment.

Example   Extremely vulgar and offensive sexual slurs pervaded a complainant's work place, even though the conduct did not directly affect her paycheck.

Example   The complainant was subjected to sexual propositions by supervisors and sexual intimidation was "standard operating procedure" in the work place.

Reasonable Person Standard

The reasonable person standard is utilized to determine if the sexual harassment is severe or pervasive. Conduct that does not substantially affect the work environment of a reasonable person is not actionable harassment (See EEOC Policy Guidance on Sexual Harassment § C (1); *Harris v. Forklift Systems, Inc.* 114 S.Ct. at 370 (1993)). In *Harris*, the Supreme Court wrote "conduct that is not severe or pervasive enough to create . . . an environment that a **reasonable person** would find hostile or abusive . . . is beyond Title VII purview." In the hostile work environment harassment case, the conduct must be severe or pervasive enough to create an objectively hostile or abusive work environment that a "reasonable person" would find hostile or abusive. In addition, the environment must be such that the plaintiff herself subjectively finds it offensive.

Hostile work environment sexual harassment is actionable only if the conduct in question adversely affects the work performance and well-being of not only the complainant, but also would have affected a reasonable person.

Reasonable Woman Standard

Some courts have adopted a **reasonable woman** standard, recognizing that what women find offensive may be acceptable to men. This standard is subjective in nature, as it allows the complainant to decide what is unacceptable conduct.

Retaliation

Retaliation for sex discrimination occurs where the claimant alleges he or she suffered an adverse employment action because he or she filed a charge of discrimination, made a complaint of discrimination, participated in a discrimination investigation, or otherwise opposed sex discrimination by the employer (42 U.SC. § 2000e-3(a)).

If an employer retaliates after a complainant files a charge of sexual harassment, a second charge for retaliation may be filed, regardless of the merit of the original complaint. However, some developing case law has not been favorable to the filing of a second charge.

This prohibition against retaliation also protects employees who have communicated an intent to file a charge, who have testified on behalf of a coworker who filed a sexual harassment charge, who have refused to testify on behalf of the employer, or who have filed charges against other employers. Employees who are not the direct victims of sexual harassment, but who oppose it or report it on behalf of another employee, also are protected from retaliation by Title VII. Conduct that disrupts the workplace or that seriously affects the job performance of the person who opposed the sexual harassment is not protected.

Necessary elements of a claim of retaliation include proof of the following:

1. That the plaintiff engaged in an activity protected by Title VII;
2. That an adverse employment action occurred; and
3. That a causal connection exists between the plaintiff's participation in the protected activity and the adverse employment action.

To prove retaliation, the plaintiff must first establish a *prima facie* case. The burden then shifts to the employer to articulate some legitimate nondiscriminatory reason for the alleged acts or reprisal. Finally, the burden returns to the plaintiff, who is given an opportunity to demonstrate that the employer's reasons are a mere *pretext* for discrimination in retaliation for the plaintiff's participation in protected activity. (See *McDonnell Douglas Corp. v. Green*, 411 U.S. 792, 93 S.Ct. 1817, 36 L.Ed.2d 668 (1973)), discussed at length in Chapter 4.

The plaintiff is not required to prove that the protected activity was the *sole* factor motivating the employer's action to prove a causal link. The Fifth Circuit held in *Long v. Grossfield College*, 88 F.3d 300 (5th Cir. 1996) that evidence of a supervisor's knowledge of the protected activity, and subsequent recommendation of termination, was sufficient to prove a *prima facie* causal link between the activity and the termination. *Long*, 88 F.3d at 306.

SAME-SEX HARASSMENT

The phrase **affinity orientation**, defined generally as a person attracted to those of her or his own gender, has replaced the previous designation of homosexuality or sexual orientation and has gained attention in the area of employment law in the last twenty years. Issues such as AIDS funding, the ban on gays in the military, and the 1992 presidential election, in which President Clinton voiced support for gays and later appointed the first gay to a high-level government position, are responsible for much of the emphasis placed on this segment of the workforce. Not surprisingly, courts were asked for the first time during the 1990s to decide the question of whether the fact that a harasser and a victim belong to the same sex precludes a finding of unlawful sexual harassment.

The Supreme Court ruled unequivocally that Title VII protects both men and women from discrimination based on sex in the landmark case discussed below. The Court noted that the critical question is whether members of one sex are treated differently than the other. This opinion held that there must also be discrimination, not merely offensive behavior.

Oncale v. Sundowner Offshore Serv., Inc., 118 S.Ct. 998 (1998)

Facts:

Oncale worked for Sundowner Offshore Services on a Chevron U.S.A., Inc. oil platform in the Gulf of Mexico. He was a roustabout on an eight-man crew. On several occasions, he was forcibly subjected to sex-related, humiliating actions against him by three of the crew, two of whom had supervisory authority, in the presence of the rest of the crew. Two of the crew also physically assaulted him in a sexual manner and one of the two threatened him with rape.

Oncale's complaints to supervisory personnel produced no remedial action. In fact, the company's safety compliance clerk told Oncale that the two men picked on him all the time too and called him a name suggesting homosexuality. Oncale eventually quit, and asked that his record reflect that he "voluntarily left due to sexual harassment and verbal abuse."

Oncale filed a complaint against his employer in the United States district court for the Eastern District of Louisiana, alleging that he was discriminated against in his employment because of his sex. The district court found that, as a male, he had no cause of action under

Title VII for harassment by male coworkers. On appeal, a panel of the Fifth Circuit followed binding precedent and affirmed. The Supreme Court granted certiorari.

Opinion by Justice Scalia (reflecting unanimous decision of the Court):

If our precedents leave any doubt on the question, we hold today that nothing in Title VII necessarily bars a claim of discrimination "because of . . . sex" merely because the plaintiff and the defendant are of the same sex.

We have never held that workplace harassment, even harassment between men and women, is automatically discrimination because of sex merely because the words used have sexual content or connotations. The prohibition of harassment on the basis of sex . . . forbids only behavior so objectively offensive as to alter the "conditions" of the victim's employment. "Conduct that is not severe or pervasive enough to create an objectively hostile or abusive work environment—an environment that a reasonable person would find hostile or abusive— is beyond Title VII's purview." *Harris v. Forklift Systems, Inc.*, 510 U.S. 17, 21. We have always regarded that requirement as crucial, and as sufficient to ensure that courts and juries do not mistake ordinary socializing in the workplace—such as male-on-male horseplay or intersexual flirtation for discriminatory "conditions of employment." A professional football player's working environment is not severely or pervasively abusive, for example, if the coach smacks him on the buttocks as he heads onto the field—even if the same behavior would reasonably be experienced as abusive by the coach's secretary (male or female) back at the office. Common sense, and an appropriate sensitivity to social context, will enable courts and juries to distinguish between simple teasing or roughhousing among members of the same sex, and conduct which a reasonable person in the plaintiff's position would find severely hostile or abusive

Because we conclude that sex discrimination consisting of same-sex sexual harassment is actionable under Title VII, the judgment of the Court of Appeals for the Fifth Circuit is reversed, and the case is remanded for further proceedings consistent with this opinion.

Consistent with the Supreme Court guidelines on same sex harassment, the EEOC states that same-sex harassment is unlawful when it is based on sex, not sexual preference, and employees of the opposite sex are not treated the same way.

CONSTRUCTIVE DISCHARGE

Constructive discharge occurs when an employer imposes working conditions so intolerable that they foreseeably would compel a reasonable person to resign rather than stay on the job. Some courts have ruled that the employer's conduct must be deliberate, while other courts have set no requirement of specific intent. The lack of an effective complaint procedure may be a key factor in determining whether a constructive discharge situation exists.

Monetary liability for harassment often increases substantially in a constructive discharge situation. In addition to back pay and front pay, compensatory and punitive damages may be awarded.

Example   A hotel worker who claimed sexual harassment was awarded approximately $150,000 in back pay and $234,000 in front pay alone. (*See Virgo v. Riviera Beach Associates, Ltd. dba Sheraton Ocean Inn*, 30 F.3d 1350 (11th Cir. 1994)).

PREPARING TO LITIGATE FROM THE PLAINTIFF'S PERSPECTIVE

Administrative Proceedings

Filing a Complaint with the Employer

The first action to be taken by an employee who has suffered sexual harassment is the filing of a complaint with the employer, using the employer's sexual harassment complaint form. The form should include relevant personnel data, description(s) of incidents of sexual harassment, including dates, times, places, and witnesses, and a section for administrative use. The administrative section should detail the investigation, including the results of the interview of the accuser and the accused, witness interviews, the final determination of the investigation, and a description of consequences for the harasser. Figure 13-1 is an example of a sexual harassment complaint form.

Filing a Complaint with the EEOC

In the event that the employee is not satisfied with the employer's handling of the sexual harassment complaint, the next available remedy is filing a complaint with the EEOC. A complaint made to the EEOC within 180 days of the adverse employment action is a prerequisite for filing a suit alleging discrimination (42 U.S.C. § 2000e-5(e)). If a state has an agency with the power to grant relief for the type of adverse action, the plaintiff must first file a complaint with the state agency (FEP). After proceedings have commenced under state law, a complaint cannot be filed with the EEOC until the state agency terminates proceedings, or until the expiration of sixty days (42 U.S.C. § 2000e-5 (c)).

Once a charge has been filed with the EEOC, the commission will evaluate the merits of the claim. If the EEOC believes that the allegations are true, it will first try informal conciliation, and ultimately has the right to bring a civil action on behalf of the plaintiff (42 U.S.C. § 2000e-5(b)). In cases where the EEOC determines there is a lack of reasonable cause on the merits of the claim, the EEOC will dismiss the

[This type form may be used to file a complaint with your employer of sexual harassment within your workplace]

SECTION I.
Personal Information

Current Date: _____

Name: _____

Employee ID#: _____

Company Name: _____

Company Location: _____

Complainant's Department: _____

SECTION II.
Personal Information

[Identifies the violator]

Name of violator: _____

Indicate violator's position to complainant:

- ☐ Executive Manager
- ☐ Supervisor
- ☐ Department Manager
- ☐ Co-Worker
- ☐ Agent or Affiliate of Employer
- ☐ Non-employee
- ☐ Client
- ☐ Other (Describe) _____

Date(s) of incident(s): _____

SECTION III.
Description of act

1. Indicate the type of complaint by checking all that apply:

- ☐ unprovoked touching
- ☐ personal space invasion
- ☐ found yourself cornered
- ☐ unwarranted sexual banter
- ☐ continuous sexual comments
- ☐ inquiries of personal sexual orientation of self or friends/family
- ☐ exposure to offensive photos or other types of lewd pictures
- ☐ evocative looks
- ☐ condescending references about personal appearance
- ☐ continued pressure to engage in sexual activity
- ☐ job status or employment threatened

Figure 13-1
Sexual Harrassment Complaint Form

2. Explain the actual incident in full extent.

_____

_____

_____

_____

3. Were you pressured into the act? If so, explain.

_____

_____

_____

_____

4. What did you do to end the act? (check all that apply)
   ☐ Did not take action
   ☐ Submitted a written or verbal complaint with your supervisor or manager
   ☐ Ended the problem through department intervention
   ☐ Other actions (please specify) _____

5. What was your management's response to your actions taken? (List only if action taken)

_____

_____

_____

_____

6. If you did not take action to prevent harassment, explain why.

_____

_____

_____

_____

7. Have you felt physical or psychological suffering as a result of the harassment? If so, describe your emotions.

_____

_____

_____

_____

Figure 13-1 (*continued*)

8. With whom have you shared your experience(s), including professional, personal and in-house.

_____

_____

_____

_____

9. If you complained, did you have work-related penalties or objections? Explain.

_____

_____

_____

_____

10. If your harassment has suffered or other fears have developed as a result, explain in what capacities your performance has been hindered.

_____

_____

_____

_____

11. Does your place of employment provide for employee assistance? If so, and you had a session regarding the act, explain your feelings and emotions, then explain if you felt the assistance helped you overcome your fears. If you did not attend a session, explain why.

_____

_____

_____

_____

12. Enter any additional comments you wish to make regarding the act.

_____

_____

_____

_____

Figure 13–1 (*continued*)

charges and issue a determination to both the employer and employee that it found no discrimination in violation of Title VII has taken place.

Right to Sue Letter

A claimant can take a charge away from the EEOC after the expiration of 180 days by requesting in writing a **right to sue letter**. The claimant must file suit within 90 days of receiving the right to sue letter from the EEOC, or forever lose the right to bring suit (42 U.S.C. § 2000e-5(f)).

Determining Parties to Sue

Categories of Persons Committing Sexual Harassment

Supervisors

Under the *quid pro quo* theory, the doctrine of *respondeat superior* applies. The employer is strictly liable for the conduct of its agents and supervisors, regardless of whether the specific acts complained of were authorized or even forbidden by the employer, and regardless of whether the employer knew or should have known of the specific acts (29 C.F.R. § 1604.11(c)).

Coworkers

An employer is liable for acts of sexual harassment in the workplace by coworkers where the employer or its agents or supervisory employees know or should have known of the conduct, unless the employer can show that it took prompt remedial action (29 C.F.R. § 1604.11(d)).

The employer's actual knowledge of harassment may come from its observance of the conduct or by disclosure of the conduct by the victim or other employees. A complaint to management can establish knowledge on the part of the employer. However, what level of management must be notified often depends on the particular circumstances.

Example   Employees of a local restaurant franchise complained to their store manager of harassment, but it was not until they placed a call to the vice president that action was taken. The court stated that notice to the lower-level supervisor was not constructive notice to the employer—the notice must go to higher management. (*Kilgore v. Thompson & Brock Management, Inc.,* 93 F.3d 752 (11th Cir. 1996)).

Nonemployees

An employer may also be responsible for the acts of nonemployees such as vendors in the workplace, where the employer or its agents or supervisory employees know or should have known of the conduct and fail to take prompt remedial action (29 C.F.R. § 1604.11(e)).

Prompt, effective action may be reporting the problem to a superior, in the case of the outside vendor who has been accused of harassment, and working with the superior to investigate and reach a solution. Prompt action might also include replacement of the offending representative or, possibly the most severe action of all, cancellation of the business relationship with the outside vendor

Witnesses Affected by Offensive Conduct

An employer may be liable for acts of sexual harassment even if the employee is not the person being harassed, but witnessed the offensive conduct and was affected by it. (See *Childress v. City of Richmond*, 134 F.3d 1205 (4th Cir. 1998)).

DETERMINATION OF EMPLOYER'S LIABILITY FOR SEXUAL HARASSMENT/HOSTILE WORK ENVIRONMENT

New Standard for Employer Liability—Post–*Faragher* and *Ellerth* Supreme Court Decisions

During its 1998 term, the U.S. Supreme Court issued two landmark decisions, *Burlington Industries, Inc. v. Ellerth*, 118 S.Ct. 2275 (1999) and *Faragher v. Boca Raton, Fla.*, 118 S.Ct. 2275 (1998), that establish a new standard for employer liability in cases where a supervisor creates a sexually hostile work environment without imposing any tangible job detriment. Prior to these landmark decisions, most courts analyzed sexual harassment claims by categorizing the alleged conduct as either *quid pro quo* or hostile environment sexual harassment, with different liability standards for the two categories. Although the Supreme Court acknowledged that it was responsible, in part, for creating these two categories, the Court dismissed their usefulness in assessing employer liability.

Identical language was used by the court in *Faragher* and *Ellerth* to explain the new standard of employer liability under Title VII of the 1964 Civil Rights Act for supervisor harassment of an employee when no tangible job detriment has occurred:

An employer is subject to vicarious liability to a victimized employee for an actionable hostile environment created by a supervisor with immediate (or successively higher) authority over the employee. When no tangible employment action is taken, a defending employer may raise a affirmative defense to liability or damages . . . The defense comprises two necessary elements: (a) that the employer exercised reasonable care to prevent and correct promptly any sexually harassing behavior, and (b) that the plaintiff employee unreasonably failed to take advantage of any preventive or corrective opportunities provided by the employer or to avoid harm otherwise.

The traditional Title VII defense that an employer lacked actual and constructive knowledge of the harassment now applies only in those cases where the harassment was committed by a nonsupervisor. Employers can be held liable for a supervisor's harassing conduct regardless of whether the employer was negligent or at fault for the employee's conduct. **Vicarious liability**—indirect legal responsibility for the acts of an employee—has supplanted negligence as the standard for employer liability in a case of harassment by a supervisor.

Additional points raised by the court in these two cases include:

- An employer without disseminated sexual harassment policies and complaint procedures will be automatically ("vicariously") liable for harassing conduct by supervisors, regardless of whether the harassment is *quid pro quo* or hostile environment harassment.
- An employer will also be vicariously liable for sexual harassment by supervisors, regardless of the existence of a sexual harassment policy if the harassment results in a tangible employment action, which the court defined to include a significant change in employment status, such as hiring, firing, failing to promote, reassignment with significantly different responsibilities, or a decision that causes a significant change in benefits.

The traditional sexual harassment categories of "quid pro quo" and "hostile environment" no longer control for purposes of imposing employer liability. The critical factor is whether the harassment by a supervisor culminates in a tangible employment action. If so, the employer is vicariously liable. If not, then the employer's new affirmative defense quoted above is available.

Neither of the plaintiffs in the *Ellerth* or *Faragher* case suffered any tangible job detriment in their alleged sexually hostile work environments.

Facts of the Ellerth Case

After 15 months as a salesperson for Burlington Industries, Kimberly Ellerth quit as a result of alleged sexual harassment by a supervisor, Ted Slowik. Slowik was not Ellerth's immediate supervisor, but was a mid-level manager with the authority to make hiring and promotional decisions (although subject to higher approval).

Ellerth cited three incidents where she felt that Slowik's comments threatened to deny her job benefits unless she acquiesced to his advances. Ellerth never informed anyone in authority at Burlington of Slowik's conduct during her employment with the company, despite her admitted knowledge of the company's sexual harassment policy.

In her complaint, Ellerth alleged that the sexual harassment forced her constructive discharge in violation of Title VII. A federal district court dismissed her sexual harassment claim on summary judgment. The district court described her claim as hostile environment but with a *quid pro quo* component, and applied a negligence standard to determine employer liability. The federal district court held that while Ellerth could prove the existence of a hostile work environment, there was no evidence that Burlington "knew or should have known" of the harassment. The U.S. Court of Appeals for the Seventh Circuit, *en banc*, produced eight separate and confusing opinions in this case.

Justice Kennedy authored the opinion in the 7–2 decision of the Supreme Court. The Court remanded the case to give Burlington the opportunity to establish its affirmative defense.

Facts of the Faragher Case

Beth Ann Faragher worked as a lifeguard for the city of Boca Raton, Florida between 1985 and 1990 while attending college. She alleged that two supervisors, Bill Terry and David Silverman, created a hostile work environment by subjecting her to offensive touching and lewd remarks. Terry was chief of the Marine Safety Division in which Faragher worked, and had the authority to hire, supervise, and reprimand lifeguards.

In 1986, the city adopted a sexual harassment policy that was promulgated to all employees by a memorandum. In May 1990, the city revised the policy and issued a statement describing it. The city, however, failed to circulate the policy among employees of the Marine Safety Division, so that Terry, Silverman, and many lifeguards were not aware of the policy.

Faragher (like Ellerth) did not complain to upper management about Terry or Silverman. She did disclose their behavior to Robert Gordon, her other immediate supervisor, although she did not regard those discussions as formal complaints. Other female lifeguards also spoke to Gordon about the conduct of Terry and Silverman, but Gordon never reported those complaints to Terry, who was his supervisor, or to any other city official.

In 1992, Faragher sued the city, Terry, and Silverman. At the conclusion of a bench trial, a federal district court held that the conduct of Terry and Silverman created a hostile environment under Title VII. The court also held the city liable for the harassment, because the conduct was severe enough that the city had at least "constructive knowledge" of it, because Terry and Silverman were acting as agents of the city, and Gordon's failure to act on Faragher's reports to him added a further basis on which to impute liability to the city.

A divided Eleventh Circuit, sitting *en banc*, reversed the judgment against the city and held that Terry and Silverman were acting outside the scope of their employment in committing the harassment, and that because neither threatened to fire or demote Faragher, their agency relationship with the city did not assist them in committing the harassment. The Eleventh Circuit also disagreed with the district court's ruling that the city had "constructive knowledge" of the harassment.

Justice Souter authored the 7–2 opinion of the Supreme Court, reversing the Eleventh Circuit's holding and reinstating the district court's judgment for Faragher. The Supreme Court found that the city had no "serious prospect" of successfully invoking the affirmative defense because it failed to disseminate its policy against sexual harassment, and because its officials made no attempt to track the conduct of supervisors like Terry and Silverman. Justice Souter also noted that the city's sexual harassment policy contained no assurance that the harassing supervisors could be bypassed in registering complaints to the city.

Liability for Sexual Harassment by Non-Supervisory Individuals

Following the *Faragher* and *Ellerth* decisions, an employer continues to be liable for sexual harassment by non-supervisors (coworkers, customers, vendors, and independent contractors) based on a negligence standard that applies if the employer "knew or should have known" of the harassment and failed to take corrective action.

DEFENDING SEXUAL HARASSMENT CLAIMS—EEOC AND COURT

Investigating the Claim—Investigation by the Employer

The investigation process of an external sexual harassment complaint generally begins with the employer's receipt of a notice from the EEOC (or FEP) that a charge has been filed. In most instances, the employer will also receive a copy of the charge and a Request for Information from the EEOC.

Counsel for the employer should be furnished a copy of the documents received from the EEOC to advise the employer of not only the issue of whether the charge is timely filed, but whether jurisdiction is at issue. Title VII applies to employers who are engaged in interstate commerce and who have 15 or more employees, including part-time on each working day in each of 20 or more calendar weeks in the current year in which the alleged discrimination occurred or preceding year (42 U.S. § 21.002 (6)(A)). If the requisite number of employees is not met, the EEOC (or FEP) lacks jurisdiction of the charge or complaint of discrimination, and a court would also lack subject matter jurisdiction of the alleged discrimination.

Once the employer's counsel has determined that the charge is both timely filed and that jurisdiction is not an issue, either the employer or counsel should immediately undertake a comprehensive investigation, including interviews with all personnel who might possibly have knowledge of the allegations contained in the charge, and a review of all pertinent documents in the employer's possession. The investigation should be prompt, thorough, and documented.

A human resources employee or a member of management typically handles in-house investigations. The investigator should be knowledgeable on company policies and issues, able to communicate effectively, and able to act with impartiality.

The following are important steps to be taken by the person conducting the interview of an accused harasser:

- Provide the accused harasser a fair opportunity to confirm, deny, or explain the situation;
- If the accused harasser perceived the conduct as welcome, determine the reason for that belief;
- Remind the accused harasser that retaliation is *unlawful* and *prohibited*.

Improper handling of the investigation can lead to a finding of liability against the employer, just as the harassment itself.

Once an investigation has been completed, both the harassed and the harasser are entitled to a decision from the employer and a letter communicating that decision, if the employer was unable to determine what happened in a "he said/she said" situation.

If the investigation finds harassment, the harasser should be disciplined on the basis of the circumstances, and that discipline should then be recorded in the employee's personnel file. Discipline might include a warning, reprimand, probation, suspension, transfer, or a denial of a pay increase. The perpetrator should also be warned not to retaliate against the victim because of the discipline he or she received.

Notes of the investigation, including interview notes, witness statements, and communications in the investigation, should be retained, but not in personnel files.

Responding to EEOC Charge

The EEOC normally provides a questionnaire that seeks an abundance of information and documents that may or may not be relevant to the charge. Since any information provided may be used against the employer in the future, the employer and its counsel should determine whether the questionnaire will be answered at this stage of the investigation.

Once the employer's investigation is complete, it should consider submitting a

Position Statement to the EEOC as opposed to answering the questionnaire. This Position Statement permits the employer to set out facts that are directly related to the charge and to articulate the reasons for the action taken against the charging party. The Position Statement may be accompanied by any documents that the employer believes are relevant to its defense against the charge.

Answering the Complaint/Petition/Removal to Federal Court

Counsel for the employer should determine if the case is a candidate for removal to federal court, and determine any applicable defenses, such as failure to mitigate, lack of jurisdiction, or failure to exhaust administrative remedies. Figure 13-2 is an example of a Notice of Removal.

If counsel determines that the case should remain in state court, a general denial is often filed, with an amended answer filed subsequent to further investigation of the facts in the case.

Notice to Insurance Carrier

The employer should give all of its insurance carriers notice of a sexual harassment claim immediately upon receipt of the EEOC charge. The carriers then will advise the employer of the applicability of coverage for the incidents contained in the charge.

Individual Defendants

If an individual within the company is sued, the employer and counsel are faced with the decision of whether joint representation is appropriate. In the case of an individual defendant who admits or totally denies the sexual conduct, a joint defense is probably not in the best interest of the employer, and separate counsel should be obtained to avoid a conflict of interest. Separate representation also preserves the employer's argument that the individual defendant acted outside the course and scope of employment. If an attorney is representing both the employer and the alleged harasser, the attorney cannot ethically recommend that the employer discipline the other client (Model Code of Professional Responsibility DR 5–105(B)).

Initiation of Corrective Action—Prompt and Effective Remedial Action

Prompt and effective remedial action starts before harassment even occurs when the employer has in effect a strong, well-communicated policy that prohibits sexual

IN THE UNITED STATES DISTRICT COURT
FOR THE SOUTHERN DISTRICT OF TEXAS
HOUSTON DIVISION

(Style of Case)

NOTICE OF REMOVAL PURSUANT TO 28 U.S.C. § 1446

TO: Plaintiff, by and through his attorney of record (name and address of attorney)

NOTICE IS HEREBY GIVEN that Defendant (Name) seeks removal of Cause No. 776934 from County Court at Law No. 3 of Harris County, Texas to the United States District Court for the Southern District of Texas, Houston Division.

1. Removal of this civil action is proper because:

_____

_____

2. The Citation and Plaintiff's Original Petition were received by Defendant on _____, 2001, thus, this Notice of Removal is being filed within thirty days after receipt of the Citation and Petition as required by 28 U.S.C. § 1446(b).

3. A copy of this Notice of Removal will be filed with the Clerk of the County Court, Harris County, State of Texas, as required by 28 U.S.C. § 1446(d).

WHEREFORE, Defendant respectfully requests that this case be removed from the County Court at Law No. 3 of Harris County, Texas, to this Court and proceed in this Court as an action properly removed thereto.

Dated: _____, 2001.

Respectfully submitted,

_____

[Signature Block and Certificate of Service]

Figure 13-2
Notice of Removal

harassment and establishes effective procedures for receiving and resolving employee complaints concerning sexual harassment. Workers must know that the employer takes sexual harassment seriously.

Every employer should have a written sexual harassment policy, with reporting procedures designed to encourage victims of sexual harassment to come forward. Such a policy reduces the likelihood that inappropriate conduct will occur. It also may provide a defense against liability when such inappropriate conduct does occur. The policy should ensure confidentiality and offer a complainant protection from retaliation. All employees should be given a form to sign as acknowledgment that they have read and understand the company's sexual harassment policy.

Sexual harassment policies must be more than just written down. They must be well-communicated and enforced, as suggested below:

- Distribute, read and explain the policy to all employees;
- Post the policy on bulletin boards and in recreation or lunch rooms;
- Educate employees to recognize and report harassment;
- Train supervisors about inappropriate behavior and sensitive handling of complaints;
- Notify all personnel of available employee assistance programs;
- Conduct follow-up training sessions to make certain that all employees are aware of what constitutes sexual harassment; and
- Document attendance at training sessions.

Elements of an effective sexual harassment policy are listed in Figure 13-3.

Case law has established that appropriate and effective remedial action might include the following:

---

1. "No tolerance" language
2. Definition of sexual harassment
3. Dissemination of sexual harassment policy
4. Responsibility of employees to report incidents of harassment
5. Individuals to whom reports of incidents must be made
6. Methods for investigating complaints of harassment
7. Posting of policy and reporting procedures
8. Confidentiality of reporting process
9. Prohibition against retaliation for reporting harassment
10. Acceptance of policy-signed by employee

Figure 13-3
Components of Effective Sexual Harassment Policy

- An immediate meeting with the complaining employee;
- Agreement to investigate and inform the complaining employee of the employer's decision;
- Sensitivity toward the worker (granting the worker time off after the worker has come forward to complain of sexual harassment);
- Prompt investigation, including interviews with the parties and other witnesses;
- Offering a transfer, schedule adjustment, or other action to separate the parties;
- Training and educating employees and supervisors on harassment issues; and
- Following up to make certain that the harassment has not continued.

In a discharge or constructive discharge case, the employer may be able to limit economic damages by offering the complainant an unconditional offer of reinstatement to a position at least substantially equivalent to the complainant's former position. This unconditional offer of reinstatement ends the accrual of back pay liability, which is discussed later in this chapter.

Offer of Judgment

If the case has been filed in federal court or removed to federal court, the employer may make an offer of judgment pursuant to Rule 68 of the Federal Rules of Civil Procedure. An **offer of judgment** is the offer of a specified amount that the plaintiff could obtain if the case went to trial. If, after the offer of judgment, the plaintiff is granted a judgment at trial either less than or equal to the offer of judgment, the employee is not entitled to any costs or attorneys fees incurred after the offer, and must pay the employer's post-offer costs and attorneys fee. If the plaintiff prevails at trial in an amount greater than the offer, the offer has no effect. (*See Marek v. Chesney*, 473 U.S. 1, 9 (1985)).

Discovery Conducted by the Defendant Employer

The defendant's discovery in a sexual harassment lawsuit should focus on either disproving or limiting liability and damages. Written and oral discovery must address the causes of action pled by the plaintiff and the elements of proof of injury and actual and compensatory damages.

Once a plaintiff has claimed **nonpecuniary damages** (damages that cannot be estimated and monetarily compensated), the range of discovery available to the defendant substantially increases. Discovery should address the following areas:

1. previous reports of sexual harassment at the plaintiff's former workplace;
2. history of emotional or mental illness;

3. family history of emotional or mental illness;
4. military records;
5. medical records;
6. tax returns;
7. previous litigation;
8. police reports;
9. use of drugs or alcohol;
10. workers' compensation claims;
11. psychological tests or records;
12. divorce records; or
13. records of financial difficulties, such as bankruptcy filings or liens against the plaintiff and his or her property.

A plaintiff's claim for compensatory damages places his or her mental condition at issue. When the medical condition is at issue and there is good cause shown, the employer may be entitled to compel the plaintiff to undergo a mental, psychiatric, and/or psychological evaluation (Fed.R.Civ.P. 35).

SEX-PLUS DISCRIMINATION

Sex-plus discrimination is discrimination of a subclass of a protected group. Relatively early in the history of Title VII, the courts established that sex-plus discrimination, such as discrimination against a class of women—for example, married women or women with children, and not the entire gender—violated Title VII. For example, prior to the passage of the PDA, the U.S. Supreme Court struck down the hiring practice of an employer who hired 75–80% women for the position in question, but refused to hire women with pre-school age children. (See *Phillips v. Martin Marietta Corp.*, 411 F.2d 1 (5th Cir. 1969), *cert. granted*, 397 U.S. 960 (1970), *vacated*, 400 U.S. 542 (1971) (per curium). In the *Phillips* case, the Supreme Court found this sex-plus discrimination was just as much a violation of Title VII as discrimination based solely on sex. *Id.* at 544.

Sex Plus Marriage

The EEOC Guidelines state that employer policies that forbid or restrict the employment of married women and do not apply to married men constitute discrimination based on sex in violation of Title VII, 29 C.F.R. § 1604.4(a) (West 1997). The EEOC's position is clear—the fact that the policy applies only to married women and not to all women is irrelevant—as long as sex is a factor in the application of the rule, the application involved discrimination based on sex.

Sex Plus Parenthood

The U.S. Constitution restrains public employers from discrimination on the basis of parenthood. However, this protection from discrimination does not normally extend to employees of private entities. For example, in *Boyd v. Harding Academy of Memphis, Inc.*, 88 F.3d 410 (6th Cir. 1996), the plaintiff, an unmarried preschool teacher for a religious-affiliated school, became pregnant during her employment. The school fired her because of a school policy prohibiting teachers from engaging in extramarital sexual intercourse. The plaintiff sued for gender discrimination, claiming that she was terminated because she was pregnant. The Sixth Circuit affirmed the judgment in favor of the school based on uncontroverted trial testimony that the school had terminated at least four individuals, both male, and female, who had engaged in extramarital sexual relationships that did not result in pregnancy.

Sex Plus Grooming and Appearance Policies

Courts have generally held that private employers may require certain grooming standards, and may require male employees to adhere to different modes of dress and grooming than female employees. In *Tavora v. New York Mercantile Exch.*, 117 S. Ct. 1821 (1997), the court found that a policy that requires male employees to have short hair, but imposes no such restrictions on female employees, does not constitute sex discrimination in violation of Title VII.

Based on the same rationale followed by the *Tavora* court, other courts have held that sex-based makeup requirements do not violate the law. In a highly-publicized case, *Craft v. Metromedia, Inc.*, 766 F.2d 1205, 215 (8th Cir. 1985), cert. denied, 475 U.S. 1058 (1986), the court held that a television station's appearance standards did not constitute sex discrimination against a female anchor, since such standards were applied equally to males.

Sex Plus Race or Other Protected Classification

If an employer improperly considers sex plus another protected classification, such as race, the employer's conduct violates Title VII and gives rise to a claim of discrimination on *both* grounds.

Discrimination on the Basis of Physical Characteristics

Hiring criteria based on physical characteristics can be held to be discriminatory if they adversely impact one gender. Minimum height and weight requirements, for example, tend to exclude more women than men, and have been held discriminatory if the employer cannot demonstrate a clear business necessity for the requirement.

GLASS CEILING ISSUES IN DISCRIMINATION

The term "glass ceiling" was originally coined by *The Wall Street Journal* to describe the so-called "invisible" barriers thought to prevent the advancement of women and minorities in the workplace. As an increasing number of women have recently advanced into the higher echelons of law, accounting, academia, and other professions, special legal issues have arisen. With regard to the issue of sex discrimination in particular, the Department of Labor (DOL) has embraced the metaphor of the "glass ceiling." The DOL, through the Office of Federal Contract Compliance ("OFCCP") designed and launched the Glass Ceiling Initiative during the Bush Administration.

In its pilot program, the OFCCP probed nine Fortune 500 companies in search of obstacles that impeded the progress of women and minorities in reaching upper-management positions. That pilot study revealed that almost all women and minorities at higher levels of management were in staff functions, as opposed to operational functions. The study also showed that the glass ceiling for minorities existed at a lower level than the glass ceiling for women.

The case of *Emmel v. Coca-Cola Bottling Co. of Chicago*, 95 F.3d 627 (7th Cir. 1996), is indicative of the way in which gender stereotypes contribute to the glass ceiling imposed for upper-management positions.

Emmel v. Coca-Cola Bottling Co. of Chicago, 95 F.3d 627 (7th Cir. 1996)

Facts:

Coca-Cola hired Emmel in 1976 as an account manager. She was then promoted to route manager in 1981, a supervisory position that she held for seven years. In 1986 she was recognized as "route manager of the year." In 1988, she moved to district sales manager in the syrup division. In 1989, because of her expertise in both syrup and cans, the vice president of sales for the north zone offered her the position of cold drink specialist.

In July 1992 Coca-Cola created five new upper-management positions called area development managers. All five employees promoted to those positions had considerably shorter careers with Coca-Cola and much less time in supervisory positions than Emmel. Additionally, all five were men. Upon learning that she had been passed over, Emmel confronted Vice President Walsh, who said, "Let's close the door and speak honestly." He then advised, "Karen, you know, as we all know, they wanted men in these positions in the past to run—

to have D licenses [a truck driver's license, and to run strike duty. Emmel asked "[W]as I qualified for any of these positions, to which Walsh replied, "You are the only other one qualified."

After trying unsuccessfully to speak with Coca-Cola's president and vice president for companywide sales, Emmel filed a complaint with EEOC that evolved into a lawsuit. In September 1993, after Emmel's lawsuit was filed, Coca-Cola announced the creation of three new upper-management "key account executive positions," filled by the promotion of three male employees with less time and less supervisor experience.

Because she was again passed over for positions for which she felt that she was more qualified, Emmel filed another complaint with the EEOC, which was eventually consolidated into this lawsuit.

Opinion by Judge Manion:

Emmel introduced evidence of a number of statements by the top officers at Coca-Cola indicating a corporate bias against women holding upper-management positions. Duane Hallstrom, vice president of the south zone, in the presence of Thomas Noxon, vice president of company-wide sales, told Joan Fitzimons as she was being transferred out of her route manager position that "Marvin Herb, the owner of [Coca-Cola] no longer wanted women in route management." Coca-Cola president William O'Rourke was quoted at a gathering of company management at the Brookwood Country Club as saying "that he didn't think the beverage industry was where women were meant to be," and "that he wouldn't have his own daughters be managers of Coca-Cola Company, and that "it was a man's business." At another management meeting at McDonald's Lodge, vice president of sales, Tom Noxon was quoted as stating, "Let's have the women stand. We're filling our quotas nicely."

These statements not only corroborate Walsh's statement that "they" wanted men in these positions, they prevent Coca-Cola from effectively arguing that Walsh's statement was merely an isolated instance of a loose tongue misstating company policy.

The failure to promote Emmel was not an isolated instance of discrimination by a single supervisor, but the predictable outcome of not-so-secret company practice. The evidence indicated that Emmel was not promoted as a direct result of that practice. In light of the significant evidence that Coca-Cola maintained a policy of intentional disregard for the statutory rights of its female employees, we cannot say the maximum punitive damage award was inappropriate in this case.

For the foregoing reasons, the decision is AFFIRMED.

NONSEXUAL GENDER HARASSMENT

"Nonsexual" gender harassment has become actionable subsequent to the enactment of Title VII. Recent court decisions hold that **nonsexual gender hostility**—where female employees are treated qualitatively different from their male counterparts in a hostile or abusive manner—may state a claim for which relief may be granted. In *Cline v. General Electric Credit Auto Lease, Inc. ("Cline I")*, 748 F. Supp. 650 (N.D. Ill. 1990) and in *"Cline II,"* 757 F. Supp. 923 (N.D. Ill. 1991), the court ruled that the harsh treatment a female employee received from her supervisor, although unrelated to sexual activity, was qualitatively different from the treatment received by men in her department. The evidence in this case reflected that the supervisor yelled mostly at older women, and never yelled at men. Additionally, the plaintiff offered evidence from several other females who were allegedly mistreated by the same supervisor.

Other courts have concurred with the court in *Cline* that hostile environment sexual harassment is actionable under Title VII when there is a pattern of pervasiveness, although the harassment is not necessarily sexual in nature.

OVERVIEW OF PREGNANCY DISCRIMINATION

Title VII was amended to establish the **Pregnancy Discrimination Act of 1978**, thereby erasing any confusion that the original language in Title VII's prohibition on sex discrimination did not include discrimination based on pregnancy, childbirth, or related medical conditions. Employers cannot deny job opportunities to women based on a concern that their current or future pregnancy may lead to time lost from work or additional insurance payments. Employers also should not assume that pregnant women might be unable to perform work in a satisfactory and safe manner.

Pregnancies should be treated in the same manner as other temporary disabilities. In that regard, the law does not prohibit management from disciplining pregnant employees for performance or absentee problems. Discipline may include termination. Pregnant employees may also be selected for inclusion in a reduction-in-force on a nondiscriminatory basis.

Example   A registered nurse was lawfully terminated because she lacked essential job skills and had been involved in several incidents of incompetent or unsafe patient care, not because of her pregnancy. (See *O'Hare v. Saint Francis Hospital, Inc.*, 917 F. Supp. 1523 (N.D. Okla. 1995)).

Example   An employer discharged an employee who was on maternity leave. The employer's stated reason for the termination was the reduction of managerial positions. (See *Smith v. F.W. Morse & Co., Inc.* 76 F.3d 413 (1st Cir. 1996)).

HIRING ISSUES RELATING TO PREGNANCY DISCRIMINATION

Employers should not ask female applicant whether they are pregnant, whether they have family responsibilities, or about their future childbearing plans. Adverse employment decisions based on the answers to such questions are unlawful. However, employers generally are not required to hire pregnant applicants who are physically unable to perform the job (See *International Union v. Johnson Controls*, 499 U.S. 187).

ACCOMMODATIONS FOR PREGNANT EMPLOYEES

Pregnant employees are entitled to the same job reassignments and light-duty accommodations that are provided to other workers who temporarily cannot perform their regular work.

Example   A pregnant employee was given medical restrictions that limited her to four hours standing and four hours sitting while on the job. The employee produced evidence that other employees were allowed to sit on stools while working, and that a union contract specifically permitted temporary light-duty assignments. The court agreed with the pregnant employee that she should receive the same treatment (See *Ensley-Gaines v. Runyon*, 100 F.3d 1220 (6th Cir. 1996)).

PREGNANCY LEAVE AND BENEFITS

Title VII does not explicitly require employers to grant pregnancy leave, although it does prohibit pregnancy discrimination, nor does it permit employers to force a pregnant employee to go on pregnancy leave. The leave option is available if the pregnant employee wants to exercise it. However, Title VII does require employers to grant medical leaves that are applicable to pregnant women. The Family and Medical Leave Act and similar state laws also confer certain leave rights relating to pregnancy and childbirth.

An employer may require a pregnant worker to take a leave of absence, but only if the employee is unable to perform her job duties. However, it is unlawful for the employer to require a pregnant worker to take a leave at a specific point—for example, in the seventh or eighth month of the pregnancy.

A pregnant employee may be required to return to work within a specific period of time after delivery, or after her physician has certified that she can return to work.

Requests for pregnancy leave should be handled in the same manner as requests for leave for other temporary disabilities. The employer has no obligation to provide any greater leave rights for pregnancy than for other temporary disabilities. For example, if an employer requires a doctor's statement prior to granting a leave or other accommodation, it also can require a doctor's statement prior to granting a pregnancy leave.

Where a leave policy is unrelated to actual job duties, a disparate impact claim may be valid (See *Garcia v. Woman's Hosp. of Tex.*, 97 F.3d 810 (5th Cir. 1996)). In the *Garcia* case, when the plaintiff was two months pregnant and returning to work from medical leave, her doctor restricted her from pushing, pulling, and lifting over 150 pounds during her pregnancy. The hospital leave policy prohibited her return to work until she had no medical restriction. Another hospital policy provided that any employee on medical leave for more than six months was to be discharged. After six months, the plaintiff would be in her eighth month of pregnancy, and still would be under the medical restriction. The hospital's policies effectively resulted in the plaintiff's termination.

In the *Garcia* case, the plaintiff claimed disparate impact under the PDA. The Fifth Circuit was asked to review the decision of the district court to not allow the plaintiff to reopen her case after a Rule 50 motion to dismiss had been granted. The Fifth Circuit concluded that *Garcia* had failed to prove a disparate impact claim of showing that pregnant women as a group would be adversely affected by the hospital's policies. If she was the only perosn adversely affected, her disparate impact claim could not survive. The case was remanded to the district court to allow the plaintiff to present evidence of an adverse impact on pregnant workers as a group. The court added that if the plaintiff's expert could testify that doctors would restrict ALL pregnant women from lifting over 150 pounds, a *prima facie* case could be made.

State statutes sometimes require that employers provide a specific period of time for pregnancy or maternity leave. In those cases governed by state statutes regarding pregnancy or maternity leave, an employer provides a benefit not accorded for other temporary disabilities, without violation of federal law.

POSITIONS HELD OPEN FOR PREGNANCY OR MATERNITY LEAVE

Positions must be held open on the same basis that they are held open for other employees on sick or disability leave, unless the pregnant employee has informed management that she does not intend to return to her job. If a company policy stipulates that employees have a right to a job only if one is available, then that is the limit of the pregnant employee's right.

Even in a case where the employer's policy contemplates automatic reinstatement following a leave of absence, the particular circumstances under which a new mother is not reinstated may result in a finding of no discrimination. For example, in *Piantanida v. Wyman Ctr., Inc.*, 927 F. Supp. 1226 (E.D. Mo. 1996), *aff'd*, 116 F.3d 340 (8th Cir. 1997), the plaintiff was informed that she would have to take another, lower-paid position when she attempted to return to work after the birth of her child.

Plaintiff sued under the PDA and lost. The court found that the plaintiff had been demoted for performance-related reasons based on trial testimony by the plaintiff's replacement, who reported that a large number of the plaintiff's tasks had not been completed in a timely manner prior to her maternity leave. The court also determined that the plaintiff did not establish a claim of constructive discharge, because she could not proffer evidence that the low salary was offered with the intent to make her quit.

Seniority benefits that are provided in other sick or disability leave situations must be accorded to employees returning from pregnancy or maternity leave.

HEALTH BENEFITS FOR PREGNANCY

An employer who provides health insurance or other income maintenance benefits during temporary periods of disability must provide that same level of benefits for pregnancy, childbirth, and related medical conditions. Additionally, the FMLA requires that health insurance benefits remain in effect during leave granted under that law.

PROVING PREGNANCY DISCRIMINATION

Proving pregnancy discrimination under the PDA is essentially the same as proving gender discrimination under Title VII. Once the plaintiff proves a *prima facie* case, the burden of proof shifts to the employer to show a lawful reason for its action. The plaintiff, however, must carry the ultimate burden of proving discrimination, including showing that the employer's conduct was motivated by her pregnancy. The burden of proving discrimination is more than proving mere unfairness or lack of compassion. For example, in *Elie v. K-Mart Corp.*, 1994 WL 50250, 64 Fair Empl. Prac. Cas. (BNA) 957 (E.D. La. 1994), the plaintiff, who was 19 weeks pregnant, asked for a reassignment to a job that did not require heavy lifting. She was given a job at the service desk that required she work evenings and weekends. The plaintiff refused to work the scheduled hours because of difficulty obtaining child care. The company fired her, and she sued for pregnancy discrimination. The court dismissed her claim because she failed to provide disparate treatment (that other employees who were reassigned for medical reasons and who objected to the reassignment were not terminated.) The court's decision explained:

The statutes [Title II and the PDA] do not protect against arbitrary, unfair, or erroneous employment decisions. They protect against employment decisions which are unlawfully motivated by an intent to discriminate. The law does not guarantee that pregnant employees will not suffer any adverse employment decisions. It protects only against employment decisions which, for discriminatory reasons, are different from decisions relating to persons who are not pregnant.

The courts have set standards of evidence that a pregnant employee needs to produce to win a pregnancy discrimination case. Any one of the following three types of evidence will demonstrate discrimination by the employer:

1. Evidence of suspicious timing, behavior, comments, and other situations from which an inference of discriminatory intent might be drawn (even when the timing of the discharge is suspect), the plaintiff still must prove causation to support a claim of pregnancy discrimination. (See *Smith v. F. W. Morse & CO.*, 76 F.3d 413 (1st Cir. 1996), in which the court upheld the employee's termination during maternity leave based on evidence that the plaintiff would have been terminated even in the absence of the pregnancy);
2. Evidence of employees with a similar situation, other than pregnancy, who received better treatment; or
3. Proof that the pregnant employee was qualified for the job in question, but was passed over in favor of, or replaced by, a nonpregnant employee.

Numerous cases, including *Troupe v. May Dep't Stores Co.*, 20 F.3d 734 (7th Cir. 1994), have helped to clarify what constitutes discrimination against pregnant employees. In the *Troupe* case, Kimberly Troupe requested and received part-time employment status when she began to experience morning sickness. However, she continued to be tardy for work due to her morning sickness. She received a written warning and was placed on a 60-day probation. During the probationary period, she was tardy 11 more times and consequently was terminated the day before taking maternity leave. Troupe was unable to prove that she was treated differently than other employees in similar circumstances, as the court stated, "Troupe would be halfway home if she could find one non-pregnant employee of Lord & Taylor who had not been fired when about to begin a leave similar in length to hers . . . Given the absence of other evidence, her failure to present any comparison evidence doomed her case." *Id.* at 738.

The *Troupe* court concluded "[if] an employee who . . . does not have an employment contract cannot work because of illness, nothing in Title VII requires the employer to keep the employee on the payroll." *Id.* at 737. In addition to the *Troupe* case, the case law in this area clearly establishes that an employer can terminate a pregnant employee who is unable to perform her job satisfactorily.

Discriminatory motive can be established in pregnancy employment situations through a supervisor's negative comments about pregnancy, or a newly hostile attitude toward the pregnant employee.

Example   A manager's comment that she did not like pregnant women working for her was direct evidence of discrimination. (See *EEOC v. Freedom Adult Foster Care Corp.*, 929 F. Supp. 256 (E.D. Mich. 1996)).

Denying employment or terminating employees because of pregnancy is obviously unlawful. Employment decisions, such as hiring, job assignments, promotions, and terminations, should be based on a pregnant employee's ability to perform the work, *not her condition, or how it believes customers or clients might respond to that condition*.

FETAL PROTECTION POLICIES

Fetal protection policies are policies adopted by an employer that limit or prohibit employees from performing certain jobs or working in certain areas of the workplace because of the potential harm presented to pregnant employees, their fetuses, or the reproductive system or capacity of employee. The Supreme Court held in *United Auto Workers v. Johnson Controls, Inc.*, 499 U.S. 187 (1991), discussed below, that employers may not bar women from jobs on the basis that the job may be hazardous to yet unborn (or unconceived) children.

United Auto Workers v. Johnson Controls, Inc., 499 U.S. 187 (1991)

Facts:

Johnson Controls' fetal protection policies exclude women with childbearing capacity from lead-exposed jobs. Employees involved in the suit include: Elsie Nelson, a 50-year-old divorcee, who suffered a loss in compensation when she was transferred out of a job where she was exposed to lead. Mary Craig, who chose to be sterilized in order to avoid losing her job, and Donald Penny, who was denied a request for leave of absence for the purpose of lowering his lead level because he intended to become a father.

Opinion by Justice Blackmun:

In this case we are concerned with an employer's gender-based fetal protection policy. May an employer exclude a fertile female employee for certain jobs because of its concern for the health of the fetus the woman might conceive? Our answer is no.

The policy classifies on the basis of gender and childbearing capacity, rather than fertility alone. The employer does not seek to protect the unconceived children of all it employees. Despite evidence in the record about the debilitating effect of lead exposure on the male reproductive system, Johnson Controls is concerned only with the harms that may befall the unborn offspring of its female employees. Johnson Control's policy is facially discriminatory because it requires only a female employee to produce proof that she is not capable of reproducing.

It is word play to say that the job at Johnson Controls is to make batteries without risk to fetuses in the same way the job at an airline is to fly planes without crashing. Decisions about the welfare of future children must be left to the parents who conceive, bear, support and raise them rather than to the employers who hire those parents.

Concern for a woman's existing or potential offspring historically has been the excuse for denying women equal employment opportunities. Congress and the PDA prohibited discrimination on the basis of a woman's ability to become pregnant. We do no more than hold that the PDA means what it says.

It is no more appropriate for the courts than it is for individual employers to decide whether a woman's reproductive role is more important to herself and her family than her economic role. Congress has left this choice to the woman as hers to make. REVERSED and REMANDED.

REPRODUCTION DISCRIMINATION

The protection of the PDA may extend to women who are trying to become pregnant, as well as to those who are already pregnant (See *Cleese v. Hewlett-Packard Co.*, 911 F. Supp. 1312 (D. Or. 1995). The plaintiff, Cleese, claimed that she was treated differently, and ultimately discharged, because she was trying to become pregnant. She also claimed disparate impact discrimination, alleging that her use of fertility drugs caused the dependability problems cited as a defense by the employer. The court held that the PDA did extend protection in such circumstances, based on the legislative history of the PDA. This history included a finding that the capacity of women to become pregnant had contributed to them being viewed as marginal workers who did not deserve the full benefits of compensation and consideration for advancement. *Id.* at 1318.

In *Pacourek v. Inland Steel Co.*, 858 F. Supp. 1393, 65 Fair Empl. Prac. Cas. (BNA) 758 (N.D. Ill. 1994), a district court within the Seventh Circuit Court of Appeals held that the PDA covers infertility treatment as a "pregnancy-related condition."

The Sixth Circuit has held that the PDA also protects, as a pregnancy-related condition, an employee's decision to have an abortion. (See *Turic v. Holland Hospitality, Inc.*, 85 F.3d 1211 (6th Cir. 1996)). In that case, the plaintiff was discharged because she had become the subject of controversy among the hotel staff as a result of her announced consideration of an abortion. The district court found that her discharge violated the PDA and awarded compensatory and punitive damages, and back pay. The Sixth Circuit affirmed this decision, and pointed out in its opinion that the fact that the plaintiff did not actually have an abortion had no effect on its decision. *Id.* at 1214.

PRIMA FACIE VIOLATIONS OF THE PDA

Under the PDA, it is a *prima facie* violation of Title VII for an employer to:

- Refuse to hire, fail to promote, or discharge a female employee because of a pregnancy or pregnancy-related condition;
- Deny fringe benefits, such as disability insurance, sick leave, or health insurance, for pregnancy or pregnancy-related conditions, while other employees who are unable to work for different medical reasons receive such benefits;
- Force a pregnant employee to go on leave of absence before she is unable to perform her job (at least at the same level as other employees with medical conditions);
- Deny an extension of leave to a pregnant employee or an employee with a pregnancy-related disability, while employees with other medical conditions are granted such extensions;
- Cease the accrual of seniority (or vacation or sick leave credits), while employees on leave with other medical conditions continue to accrue seniority for the purpose of employee benefits;
- Deny child care leave after pregnancy, while similar leaves have been granted to employees for non-medical, personal reasons;
- Deny reinstatement rights to employees on pregnancy leave, while employees on leave due to other temporary disabilities have been granted reinstatement rights; or
- Establish an arbitrary rule requiring pregnant employees on leave to remain on leave for a predetermined period of time.

(EEOC Guidelines on Discrimination Because of Sex, 29 C.F.R. § 1604.10(a) (West 1997)).

STATISTICS ON EEOC AND FEP PREGNANCY DISCRIMINATION CHARGES FILED

Figure 13-4 is a chart that represents the total number of charges filed and resolved under Title VII between 1992 and 1999 that alleged pregnancy discrimination as an issue. The data in that table were compiled by the Office of Research, Information, and Planning from the EEOC's Charge Data System—National Database.

	1992	1993	1994	1995	1996	1997	1998	1999
No. of charges received	3,385	3,577	4,170	4,191	3,743	3,977	4,219	4,166
No. of Resolutions to charges	3,045	3,145	3,181	3,908	4,186	4,595	4,467	4,343
Resolutions by type: Settlements	457 15.0%	420 13.4%	373 11.7%	440 11.3%	388 9.3%	395 8.6%	424 9.5%	505 11.6%
Withdrawals w/Benefits	237 7.8%	311 9.9%	341 10.7%	362 9.3%	323 7.7%	379 8.2%	328 7.3%	359 8.3%
Administrative Closures	762 25.0%	756 24.0%	920 28.9%	1,155 29.6%	1,098 26.2%	1,103 24.0%	1,026 23.0%	897 20.7%
No Reasonable Cause	1,497 49.2%	1,552 49.3%	1,435 45.1%	1,851 47.4%	2,276 54.4%	2,432 52.9%	2,534 56.7%	2,389 55.0%
Reasonable Cause	87 2.9%	104 3.3%	104 3.3%	96 2.5%	97 2.3%	279 6.1%	154 3.5%	188 4.3%
Successful Conciliations	56 1.8%	62 2.0%	60 1.9%	51 1.3%	55 1.3%	71 1.5%	66 1.5%	81 1.9%
Unsuccessful Conciliations	31 1.0%	42 1.3%	44 1.4%	45 1.25	42 1.0%	208 4.5%	88 2.0%	107 2.5%
Merit Resolutions	781 25.6%	835 26.6%	818 25.7%	898 23.0%	808 19.3%	1,053 22.9%	906 20.3%	1,052 24.2%
Monetary Benefits (Millions)*	$3.7	$3.9	$4.0	$4.7	$4.1	$5.6	$5.3	$6.7

*Does not include monetary benefits obtained through litigation.

Figure 13-4
Pregnancy Discrimination Charges Filed With EEOC and FEP for Years 1992–1999

TERMS

affinity orientation
constructive discharge
fetal protection policies
hostile work environment
non-pecuniary damages
offer of judgment
quid pro quo harassment
reasonable person standard

reasonable woman standard
retaliation
sexual harassment
vicarious liability

REVIEW QUESTIONS

1. Mary Webster is terminated by a female supervisor, and her position is filled two months later by a female. The employer defends its decision against Mary's charge of discrimination by claiming that there can be no finding of discrimination, since the supervisor making the termination decision is female and the position was filled by a female. Will this defense be successful? Explain.

2. Is it possible for a clerical employee to sexually harass a supervisor? Why or why not?

3. John Lincoln greets Abby Crandall, "Good morning! You look great today! That dress is very attractive." He then pauses and says, "I'm sorry. I shouldn't have said that. That's sexual harassment." Is John correct? Explain your answer.

4. Tammy sued her employer for sexual harassment, because her supervisor once rubbed her shoulders and made an "embarrassing" comment to her. Discuss whether Tammy will win her suit.

5. A provision in a collective bargaining agreement allows female, but not male, employees to take one year of childbearing leave. Does this provision violate Title VII?

6. An employee tells the store manager in confidence that he has a hunch that one of the other employees is gay. As a manager, what is your response to the employee?

7. James is the manager of a restaurant. Homer, one of the restaurant employees reports to work wearing an earring. James becomes enraged and, in front of other employees and customers, orders Homer to get rid of the earring or face immediate termination. Homer refuses. If James follows through with his threat and terminates Homer, does Homer have a cause of action against James? Does he have a cause of action against the owner of the restaurant?

8. A female construction worker sued her employer for gender discrimination, alleging the failure to furnish adequate sanitary toilet facilities at her construction site. Does she have grounds for a Title VII claim?

9. Marcella resisted repeated propositions by her supervisor and was terminated. Do mere propositions constitute sexual harassment?

10. A female employee sued her former employer on the basis of gender discrimination and sexual harassment because of the constant vulgarity of her supervisor and because of the tasteless posters he placed on the community billboard. Does the supervisor's behavior constitute sexual harassment?

PROJECTS

1. Brief the *Boyd v. Harding Academy of Memphis, Inc.*, 88 F.3 410 (6th Cir. 1996) case.

2. Prepare a form sexual harassment complaint based on the facts of *Harris v. Forklift Systems, Inc.*, 510 U.S.17, 114 S.Ct. 367, 126 L.Ed.2d 295, *on remand* 14 F.3d 601 (1994).

CHAPTER 14

The Family and Medical Leave Act

OVERVIEW

The **Family and Medical Leave Act** (FMLA) was enacted to enable employees to take time off from work to tend to personal or family medical problems without fear of reprisal from their employers. The FMLA took effect on August 6, 1993 for employers not subject to a collective bargaining agreement, and on February 5, 1994 for employers operating under an employer/union agreement.

EMPLOYERS COVERED BY FMLA

All public employers are subject to the FMLA. Private employers that employed 50 or more people for at least 20 weeks in the current or previous calendar year are also covered. Full-time, part-time, and temporary employees, employees on layoff status who are subject to recall, and employees on leave who are expected to return to work are all counted toward the 50 employees necessary to trigger application of the Act. A corporation is considered to be a single employer, even if it has multiple divisions or facilities. Owners of a company are counted if they are also employees.

Independent contractors do not count as "employees" under the FMLA, because they perform work based on an independent contractual relationship, rather than an employment relationship. A temporary staffing agency and an employer are considered joint employers for purposes of determining employer coverage and employee eligibility under the FMLA. Workers who are stationed outside the United States, its territories, or possessions also are not counted for FMLA purposes.

EMPLOYEES ENTITLED TO LEAVE

Under the FMLA, covered employers are required to permit eligible employees to take up to 12 weeks of job-protected leave per year. To be eligible for FMLA leave, an employee must meet the following criteria:

1. The individual must be employed by a covered employer in the United States or in one of its territories or possessions;
2. The employee must work at a site where the employer employs 50 or more employees at or within 75 miles of that worksite;
3. The employee must have worked for the employer for at least 12 months, which need not be consecutive; and
4. The employee must have worked at least 1,250 hours for the employer during the 12-month period immediately preceding the date leave will begin.

LEAVE REQUIREMENTS

Purpose of Leave

The FMLA permits eligible employees to take up to 12 workweeks of job-protected leave during a 12-month period for the following reasons:

- The birth of a child and in order to care for the newborn;
- The placement of a child with the employee for adoption or foster care;
- To care for a spouse or an immediate family member (spouse, parent, or child) who has a serious health condition; or
- The employee's own serious health condition that prevents the employee from performing the functions of his or her position.

Length of Leave

An eligible employee is entitled to 12 workweeks of job-protected unpaid leave per year for a qualifying reason. If a couple work for the same employer, they are limited to a total of 12 workweeks, not 12 for each party. For purposes of what constitutes 12 workweeks of leave under the FMLA, it is necessary to consider the employee's usual workweek and workday schedule.

For FMLA-eligible employees working part-time or on variable schedules, calculating FMLA leave requires comparing the employee's typical schedule with the hours or days of FMLA leave. FMLA leave entitlement for part-time or variable-schedule employees should be based on an average of the hours worked during the 12 weeks immediately preceding the employee's commencement of leave.

Calculation of the 12-Month Period

The FMLA gives each employer the right to select a uniformly applied 12-month period during which employees may take up to 12 workweeks of FMLA leave. The 12-month period utilized by the employer will affect how eligible employees may use leave. An employer may chose one of the following methods for determining the 12-month period in which leave may be used:

1. The calendar year;
2. Any fixed 12-month leave year, such as a fiscal year, a year based on the employee's "anniversary date," or a year required by state law;
3. The 12-month period following the start date of the employee's first FMLA leave; or
4. A "rolling" 12-month period measured backward from the date the employee uses any FMLA leave.

An employer may change its method of calculating the 12-month period, but only after giving employees at least 60 days notice of the change. An employer must use the same methodology for all eligible employees.

Unpaid Leave Versus Paid Leave

Although the FMLA is, by definition, unpaid leave, the FMLA contemplates that some FMLA leave may actually be paid leave. An eligible employee may elect to substitute available paid company leave for unpaid FMLA leave (See 2 C.F.R. § 825.027). In the event that the employee fails to make such an election, the employer may require the employee to substitute any accrued paid leave (such as paid sick leave, family or personal leave, or accrued vacation time) for unpaid FMLA leave to prevent employees from taking paid company leave before or after taking unpaid FMLA leave. All leave taken for an FMLA-qualifying reason, paid or unpaid, will count against the employee's 12-week FMLA entitlement.

Either the employee or the employer may choose to have the employee's 12-week leave entitlement run concurrently with a workers' compensation absence when a serious health condition results from an on-the-job injury. If the leave is taken concurrently as both FMLA leave and workers' compensation leave, the employee need not return to work even if cleared for a "light duty job" for purposes of workers' compensation.

Designation and substitution of paid leave for unpaid leave *must be made in writing* to the employee. Good faith efforts should be made to render a preliminary designation within two business days after the employer learns of the possible FMLA-qualifying reason for the absence.

An employer can retroactively designate an absence as FMLA under two circumstances:

1. When the employer does not know the reason for an absence at the time that it occurs, and the employer makes the designation within two business days after the employee returns from the absence; or
2. When the employer preliminarily designates the absence as FMLA leave and is awaiting a medical certification.

The employee must claim that the absence was for an FMLA-qualifying reason within two business days after returning from an absence.

Intermittent Leave or Reduced Leave Schedule

The FMLA requires that employees have the option to take intermittent leave or leave on a reduced leave schedule when medically necessary due to the employee's serious health condition or that of an immediate family member (29 C.F.R. § 825.203). Intermittent leave is FMLA leave taken in blocks of time due to a single qualifying reason, instead of all 12 weeks in one continuous period. A reduced leave schedule is one that reduces an employee's usual number of working hours per workweek or per workday.

Leave taken after the birth of a child, or for the placement of a child for adoption or foster care, may only be taken intermittently or on a reduced leave schedule if the employer agrees. The employer is not required to provide intermittent or reduced leave in this situation, but if the employer does allow the leave, it should do so on a consistent, nondiscriminatory basis. An intermittent or reduced leave schedule may be taken when it is medically necessary for planned or unanticipated medical treatment for a serious health condition.

An absence from work to handle the funeral arrangements of a deceased family member does not qualify for FMLA leave, even if the employee was on FMLA leave to care for that family member's serious health condition when the family member died, as discussed in the case below.

Brown v. J. C. Penney Corp., **924 F. Supp. 1158 (S.D. Fla. 1996)**

Facts:

Ross Brown worked as a customer service supervisor at the J. C. Penney store at the Dadeland Mall. In late July 1994, he requested an FMLA leave to care for his terminally ill father in New Jersey. He requested a twelve-week leave, but indicated on his leave application that his absence might end sooner than that. The last day Brown worked was July 24, 1994. On September 1, 1994, while Brown was still on leave, J. C. Penney placed Sonia Cannon in Brown's position of customer service supervisor.

Brown's father died on September 23, 1994; however, Brown did not contact J. C. Penney management about this occurrence. Instead, he reported in person to the Dadeland Mall store on October 22, 1994. At that time, he was told that he would not be given his old job, but had been assigned as a sales associate in the Men's Sportswear Department at his former rate of pay. Brown refused to accept this position, and the company terminated him.

Brown claimed in his lawsuit that the employer had an obligation to restore him to his former position, or provide him with a comparable job. According to the employer, Brown relinquished his rights under the FMLA by failing to return to work after his father's death on September 23, 1994, or in the alternative, that the statutory maximum of twelve weeks FMLA leave expired on October 17, 1994, five days before Brown reported to work.

Opinion by Judge Marcus:

According to the Defendant, "Plaintiff's approximate one month absence from work subsequent to September 23rd was no longer covered as FMLA leave because he no longer satisfied the criteria for covered leave" under the statute. As a result, the Defendant maintains its alleged refusal to restore Brown to his former position (or a comparable position) upon his return on October 22, 1994 did not violate the FMLA. We agree.

J. C. Penney insists that the "serious health condition" justifying the Plaintiff's FMLA leave ended when Brown's father died. In essence, the Plaintiff is arguing that his father's "serious health condition" did not end with his death. This argument has no support in the language of the statute or the relevant regulations. The language seems to contemplate that the term "serious health condition" is limited to health problems that afflict an individual who is alive."

Put simply, if Congress wanted to ensure that employees on FMLA leave could take additional time off after a family member died from a serious health condition, it easily could have said so in the statute.

The Plaintiff places a great deal of emphasis on the fact that while he was on leave, the Defendant gave his job as Customer Service Supervisor to Sonia Cannon. Brown states that J.C. Penney violated the statute as of September 11, 1994 (two weeks before his father died). As the Defendant explains, however, the FMLA does not require that an employee be returned to the exact position that he held prior to embarking on his leave. This language makes clear that J.C. Penney did not violate the statute through the mere act of substituting Cannon for Brown as Customer Service Supervisor on September 11, 1994, even if it intended this change to be permanent. If a violation did occur, it took place when Brown returned from his FMLA leave and J.C. Penney offered him position of Sales Associate. However, even assuming arguendo that the Sales Associate post was not the "equivalent" of Brown's former position, this job assignment was not made until *after* the Plaintiff had relinquished his protected status under the FMLA.

For all of the foregoing reasons, it is hereby
ORDERED AND ADJUDGED that the Defendant's Motion for Summary Judgment is GRANTED.

QUALIFYING REASONS FOR FMLA LEAVE

Serious Health Condition

The FMLA requires covered employers to grant leave to eligible employees to care for the employee's spouse, child, or parent with a serious health condition, and for the employee's own serious health condition that prevents the employee from performing the functions of his or her job (29 C.F.R. § 825.112(a)).

In most instances, care for grandparents, siblings, or in-laws is not included in FMLA coverage, even if those individuals are dependent upon the employee. The definition of "spouse" is narrowly construed to include only legally-married or common-law spouses. Therefore, employers are not required to grant FMLA leave to an eligible employee for the care of his or her unmarried domestic partner.

One of the most difficult areas of FMLA interpretation relates to the definition of "serious health condition." The legislative history of this Act reveals that **serious health condition** covers those conditions that require absences beyond those usually provided for by an employer's sick leave policy. Legislation comments for the Act included the following as serious health conditions:

- Heart attacks
- Heart conditions requiring heart bypass or valve operations
- Most types of cancer
- Back conditions requiring extensive therapy or surgical procedures
- Strokes
- Spinal injuries
- Severe respiratory conditions
- Appendicitis
- Pneumonia
- Emphysema
- Severe arthritis
- Severe nervous disorders
- Pregnancy-related conditions including morning sickness and miscarriages. (See H.R. Rep. No. 8, 103rd Cong., 1st Sess., pt. 1 at 29 (1993).

The above list is not all-inclusive. The Department of Labor's regulations set out the definitive test that courts must apply to determine whether a serious health condition exists. The regulations state that a serious health condition is an illness, injury, impairment, or physical or mental condition that meets one or more of the following criteria:

1. Inpatient care;
2. Continuing treatment by a health care provider for more than three days;
3. Any period of incapacity due to pregnancy, or for prenatal care;
4. Any period of incapacity for treatment of a chronic serious health condition;
5. Permanent or long-term incapacity due to a condition for which treatment may not be effective (for example, Alzheimer's disease, severe stroke, or the terminal stages of a disease);
6. Any period of absence for multiple treatments of non-chronic conditions that would result in incapacity for three or more days without such treatment (for example, chemotherapy, radiation, physical therapy for severe arthritis, or dialysis for kidney disease); or
7. Alcohol and substance abuse

This protection also applies to employees who provide care for eligible family members whose alcohol or substance treatment program meets the requirements of a serious health condition. The FMLA does not prevent employers from taking employment action against those employees. For example, an employer may have a policy by which an employee can be terminated for alcohol or substance abuse whether or not the employee is presently taking FMLA leave, so long as the policy is applied in a nondiscriminatory manner and is clearly communicated to all employees (29 C.F.R. § 825.112(g)). That exception only applies to employees who themselves suffer from alcohol or substance abuse. An employer may not take employment action against an employee who is merely providing care for an eligible family member with an alcohol or substance abuse problem.

Health Care Provider Defined

A **health care provider** for purposes of the FMLA includes doctors of medicine or osteopathy who are licensed to practice medicine or surgery by the state in which the doctor practices, or any other person determined by the Secretary of Labor to be capable of providing health care services. Subject to the nature of the health condition, health care providers might include dentists, nurse practitioners, nurse-midwives, clinical psychologists and social workers, and optometrists.

Proof that Condition Prevents Performance of Job Functions

In addition to satisfying the requirements for a serious health condition, employees taking FMLA leave due to their own serious health condition must also show that their condition prevents them from performing the functions of the job. An employee is unable to perform the functions of his or her job if a health care provider finds that he or she is either unable to work at all, or unable to perform an essential function of his or her job (as defined by the ADA and 29 C.FR. § 1630.2(n)). This requirement does not mean that the employee's physical condition itself actually renders the person incapable of working.

Employee Needed to Care for a Family Member

An employer may require that an employee who requests FMLA leave to care for a seriously-ill spouse, child, or parent provide a medical certification by a qualified health care provider to show that the employee is needed to care for that family member.

Birth of Child or Placement of Child for Adoption or Foster Care

In addition to leave for prenatal care and incapacity due to pregnancy, the FMLA provides leave for the birth and the care of the newborn child, and the placement with the employee of a child for adoption or foster care. Employers must grant FMLA equally to both male and female employees in those instances. Employers are not required, however, to grant intermittent or reduced schedule leave.

Parents may take FMLA leave for adoption or foster care before the actual placement of the child. This could include counseling sessions, court appearances, or consultations with attorneys or doctors.

EMPLOYEE PROTECTIONS UNDER THE FMLA

The FMLA provides covered employees with substantial job and benefit protections, including the following, when they take leave time protected by the Act.

Right of Reinstatement to the Same or Equivalent Position

An employee returning from FMLA is entitled to be returned to the same position he or she held prior to taking leave, or to an equivalent position with equivalent benefits, pay, and other terms and conditions of employment. The employer must reinstate the returning employee even if the employee has been replaced, or his or her position has been restructured to accommodate the employee's absence.

However, if the returning employee is no longer able to perform an essential function of the position because of a physical or mental condition, the employer has no obligation to return the employee to his or her prior position. This is true even if the inability results from the serious health condition that originally entitled the employee to FMLA leave.

Equivalent Pay

The employee who is returning from FMLA leave must be given any pay raises, such as cost of living increases, which the employer has given while the employee was out on leave. "Equivalent pay" also includes pay an employee would have received from overtime hours worked prior to taking FMLA leave.

Bonuses

Whether an employee returning from FMLA leave is entitled to a bonus for job-related criteria such as perfect attendance, safety, or exceeding production goals depends upon the purpose of the bonus. To the extent that the employee met the requirements for such a bonus prior to taking FMLA leave (for example, had perfect attendance prior to taking leave), he or she continues to be qualified for such bonuses upon returning to work.

Benefits

"Equivalent position" also requires that the employer give an employee returning from FMLA leave equivalent benefits to those he or she enjoyed prior to taking leave.

Employee Requests

An employee returning to work following a serious health condition may not always want to be reinstated to the same job duties he or she held prior to an illness. An employer is not prohibited under FMLA from accommodating an employee's request to be restored to a different shift, schedule, or position that better suits the employee's personal needs. However, the employer cannot attempt to induce the employee to accept a different position against his or her will.

LIMITATIONS AND EXCEPTIONS TO THE EMPLOYER'S FMLA OBLIGATION

General

An employee has no greater right to reinstatement or to other benefits and conditions of employment than if the employee had been continuously employed during the FMLA leave. If the employer would have terminated the employee—even if he or she had not taken FMLA—the employer can refuse to reinstate the employee to the same or equivalent position.

For example, if a shift has been eliminated or overtime hours have been reduced while the employee was on FMLA leave, the employee is *not* entitled to return to the shift or overtime hours he or she had prior to taking leave. In addition, the employer has *no obligation* under the FMLA to create a new position for a returning employee who cannot perform all the essential functions of a job, although the ADA may impose an obligation for the employer to make reasonable accommodations.

Key Employees Exception

One of the most important exceptions to the employer's general duty to reinstate an employee under the FMLA involves "key employees." Generally, an employer may deny restoration of employment to a key employee when the employer determines that the restoration will cause "substantial and grievous economic injury" to its operations.

A **key employee** is defined as a salaried, FMLA-eligible employee who is among the highest paid 10% of all of the employees within 75 miles of the employee's work site at the time the employee gives notice of the need for leave. Generally, this definition includes executive, administrative, and professional employees. However, in determining the highest 10% of all employees, the employer must consider both salaried and nonsalaried employees within 75 miles of the work site, whether or not all of these employees are eligible under the FMLA. Earnings must include wages, incentive pay, and nondiscretionary and discretionary bonuses. It does not include uncertain incentives such as stock options.

Rights of Key Employees

The FMLA requires an employer to give one, and under certain circumstances two, written notices to a key employee of his or her rights. As soon as the employer has made a good faith determination that it will suffer a grievous and substantial economic injury if the key employee is reinstated, it must provide written notice, either in person or by certified mail, containing the following information:

- The employer cannot deny FMLA leave to the employee;
- The employer intends to deny employment to the employee on completion of the FMLA leave; and
- An explanation of the employer's reasons for finding that substantial and grievous economic injury will result if the employee is restored.

If the employee is already on FMLA leave when this notice is given, the employer must also give the employee a reasonable period of time in which to return to work.

"Reasonable" is defined by the circumstances of each case, with the employer required to consider such factors as the length of the employee's leave and the business urgency for the employee to return.

There are occasional situations where an employer is not able to immediately determine if it will suffer harm from the absence of a key employee. In those cases, the employer must provide written notice to the employee when the employee notifies the employer of his or her intention to take FMLA leave. The written notice must contain the following information:

- A statement that the employer believes that it may be entitled to deny reinstatement to the employee; and
- An explanation of the potential consequences with respect to reinstatement and the maintenance of health benefits if the employer determines that it will suffer substantial and grievous economic consequences.

Written notice is necessary in order to preserve the employer's rights under the "key employee" exception. Failure to provide such notice automatically results in the loss of the employer's right to deny reinstatement, even if it will suffer a grievous and substantial economic injury.

Continuation of FMLA Leave to Key Employees

The employer must be very careful *not* to take any action denying benefits to a key employee who does not return to work in response to the written notifications above while the employee remains on FMLA leave. A key employee's rights to protection under the FMLA continue up to the point that he or she either notifies the employer that he or she does not wish to return to work, or the employer actually denies reinstatement at the conclusion of the FMLA leave.

Request for Reinstatement

Even if the employee has received written notice from the employer that he or she will not be reinstated upon returning to work, the employee is still entitled to request reinstatement at the end of the FMLA leave period, even if the employee refused to return to work in response to the employer's notice. When the employer receives such a request, it is required to determine once again whether it will suffer a grievous and substantial economic injury based on the facts as they exist at that time. If the employer finds that it will suffer such an injury, it must again notify the employee in writing either in person or by certified mail.

Grievous and Substantial Economic Injury

There is no precise test for this standard. In many cases, an employer meets the standard if it would suffer a substantial, long-term economic injury. In deciding the issue, an employer may take into account its ability to temporarily replace a key employee on FMLA leave. If permanent replacement is unavoidable, then the cost of reinstating the employee can be considered. The employer must base its decision on the effect on the absent employee's reinstatement, not on the effect of his or her absence while on FMLA.

Light Duty Assignment

The FMLA's requirements are separate and distinct from any rights under the ADA or any other statute. If an employee qualifies for FMLA leave, he or she must receive it. The Department of Labor has stated that nothing prohibits an employer from accommodating an employee *if* the employee requests reassignment. However, the employee cannot be induced to accept a different position against his/her wishes. An employer must avoid the temptation to assign an employee who is entitled to FMLA leave to a mandatory light duty assignment in lieu of FMLA leave, or to assign the employee to a job that the employer believes will reasonably accommodate the employee's serious health condition.

Benefit Protection

Generally, the FMLA requires an employer to maintain the employee's coverage under any group health plan on the same condition as coverage would have been provided if the employee had been continuously employed during the entire leave period.

If an employer provides a new plan, benefits, or if it changes health plan benefits while an employee is on FMLA, it must provide that employee with the new or changed plan/benefits to the same extent as if the employee were not on leave.

The employee on leave is required to pay the same amount of group health plan premiums as he or she paid prior to the leave. If the premium is raised or lowered while the employee is on leave, he or she must pay the new premium rate.

The same rules that apply to reinstating an employee to an equivalent position with equivalent benefits also apply to an employer's retirement plans. An employee who returns from FMLA leave is entitled to resume retirement plans in the same manner as the employer provided when the leave started. Any changes that the employer instituted that affected its entire workforce while an employee was on FMLA leave also apply to the returning employee.

FMLA leave must *not* be treated as a break in service for purposes of vesting and eligibility to participate. If an employer's retirement plan or pension plan requires an employee to be employed on a specific date in order to be credited with a year of service for vesting, contribution, or participation purposes, an employee on unpaid FMLA leave on that date will be deemed to have been employed on that date.

THE EMPLOYEE'S OBLIGATIONS UNDER THE FMLA

Prior Notice

Generally, an employee must give his or her employer at least 30 days advance notice before the FMLA leave is scheduled to begin if the leave is foreseeable for an expected birth, placement for adoption or foster care, or planned medical treatment for a serious health condition of the employee or of a family member. If the employee is not able to give 30 days notice because he or she has no advance knowledge of when the leave will need to begin, the employee must give notice "as soon as practicable." An example of an inability to give 30 days notice is the placement or adoption of a child.

Notice must be given only once, even if the FMLA leave is to be intermittent leave. However, the employee is required to notify the employer as soon as practicable if the dates of scheduled leave change or are extended.

Verbal notice of the need for an FMLA leave is sufficient to make the employer aware of the need for the leave, the anticipated starting time of the leave, and the expected duration of the leave. An employee is not required to use the phrase "FMLA" specifically. If the employer is uncertain whether the employee's reason for leave raises an FMLA issue, it should inquire further about the reason the employee is requesting a leave.

An employer may waive the employee's FMLA notice requirement.

Notice should be given to the employer either in person or by telephone, telegraph, or facsimile. If the employee is unable to give notice personally, it may be given by the employee's spokesperson (spouse, adult family member, or other responsible party).

If an employee fails to give the 30 days notice for foreseeable leave and fails to give a reasonable excuse for his or her failure to give notice, the employer is allowed to *delay* the commencement of FMLA leave until at least 30 days after the employee actually gives proper notice.

Medical Certification

An employer may require a medical certification from an employee's health care provider when an employee requests FMLA leave for a serious health condition or to care for the employee's seriously-ill spouse, child, or parent. If the FMLA leave is for a family member's condition, the employer may require a certification from that family member's health care provider. When an employee fails to provide certification, the employer may delay the taking of FMLA leave until the certification is provided.

The employer should given written notice to an employee at least 15 days before it requires a medical certification. This notice should be given no later than two days after the employee gives notice of the need for FMLA leave. In the case of unforeseeable FMLA leave requests, the employer's notice should be given within two days after the leave begins. An employer that does not make an initial request for certification can still require it at a later date if it has reason to question the appropriateness of the leave or its duration.

At the time an employer notifies an employee that it will require certification, it must also explain the consequences if the employee fails to respond. Additionally, the employer is required to immediately notify an employee whenever it believes that a certification is incomplete, and provide the employee with a reasonable time to cure any deficiency.

An employer may use Department of Labor form WH-380 (Figure14-1), or request certification concerning only the following five areas:

1. Facts surrounding "serious medical condition";
2. Date the serious health condition began, its probable duration, and whether it will be necessary for the employee to take an intermittent or reduced leave schedule;
3. Additional treatments that may be required for the medical condition;
4. Employee's ability to work; and
5. Absence to care for family members.

THE EMPLOYER'S OBLIGATIONS

Notice to Employee Regarding FMLA Rights

An employer must notify employees of their rights under the FMLA. This duty may be satisfied by:

- Posting approved FMLA notices; and
- Either incorporating the FMLA policy into an existing employee handbook, or providing written guidance outlining FMLA rights and employee obligations.

All employers covered by the FMLA must post an approved DOL notice (WH Publication 1420) that explains the provisions of the FMLA and provides information on the filing of a complaint. The DOL notice must be placed in a conspicuous place on the premises of the employer, where notices to employees and employment applicants are customarily posted. If a significant portion of an employer's workforce is not literate in English, the employer must provide the notice in a language in which the employees are literate.

Certification of Health Care Provider
(Family and Medical Leave Act of 1993)

U.S. Department of Labor
Employment Standards Administration
Wage and Hour Division

*(When completed, this form goes to the employee, **not to the Department of Labor**.)*	OMB No.: 1215-0181 Expires: 06/30/02

1. Employee's Name	2. Patient's Name *(If different from employee)*

3. Page 4 describes what is meant by a **"serious health condition"** under the Family and Medical Leave Act. Does the patient's condition[1] qualify under any of the categories described? If so, please check the applicable category.

   (1) _____   (2) _____   (3) _____   (4) _____   (5) _____   (6) _____ , or None of the above _____

4. Describe the **medical facts** which support your certification, including a brief statement as to how the medical facts meet the criteria of one of these categories:

5. a. State the approximate **date** the condition commenced, and the probable duration of the condition (and also the probable duration of the patient's present **incapacity**[2] if different):

   b. Will it be necessary for the employee to take work only **intermittently or to work on a less than full schedule** as a result of the condition (including for treatment described in Item 6 **below**)?

      If yes, give the probable duration:

   c. **If** the condition is a **chronic condition** (condition #4) or **pregnancy,** state whether the patient is and the likely duration and frequency of **episodes of incapacity**[2]:

---

[1] Here **and** elsewhere on this form, the information sought relates **only** to the condition for which the employee is taking FMLA

[2] "Incapacity," for purposes of FMLA, is defined to mean inability to work, attend school or perform other regular daily activities condition, treatment therefor, or recovery therefrom.

Form WH-380
Revised December 1999

Figure 14-1
United States Department of Labor form WH380 (Source: United States Department of Labor)

6. a. If additional **treatments** will be required for the condition, provide an estimate of the probable number of such treatments.

   If the patient will be absent from work or other daily activities because of **treatment** on an **intermittent** or **part-time** basis, also provide an estimate of the probable number of and interval between such treatments, actual or estimated dates of treatment if known, and period required for recovery if any:

   b. If any of these treatments will be provided by **another provider of health services** (e.g., physical therapist), please state the nature of the treatments:

   c. **If a regimen of continuing treatment** by the patient is required under your supervision, provide a general description of such regimen (*e.g.*, prescription drugs, physical therapy requiring special equipment):

7. a. If medical leave is required for the employee's **absence from work** because of the **employee's own condition** (including absences due to pregnancy or a chronic condition), is the employee **unable to perform work** of any kind?

   b. If able to perform some work, is the employee **unable to perform any one or more of the essential functions of the employee's job** (the employee or the employer should supply you with information about the essential job functions)? If yes, please list the essential functions the employee is unable to perform:

   c. If neither a. nor b. applies, is it necessary for the employee to be **absent from work for treatment**?

Figure 14-1 (*continued*)

8. a. If leave is required to **care for a family member** of the employee with a serious health condition, **does the patient require assistance** for basic medical or personal needs or safety, or for transportation?

   b. If no, would the employee's presence to provide **psychological comfort** be beneficial to the patient or assist in the patient's recovery?

   c. If the patient will need care cnly **intermittently** or on a part-time basis, please indicate the probable **duration** of this need:

Signature of Health Care Provider

Type of Practice

Address

Telephone Number

Date

To be completed by the employee needing family leave to care for a family member:

State the care you will provide and an estimate of the period during which care will be provided, including a schedule if leave is to be taken intermittently **or** if it will be necessary for you to work less than a full schedule:

Employee Signature

Date

Figure 14-1 (*continued*)

A civil penalty of up to $100 can be required for each willful failure to comply with the posting requirements. If an employer fails to post the notice and an employee fails to give proper advance notice of an FMLA leave, the employer cannot take adverse action against the employee.

Workplace Policies and Employee Handbooks

If a covered employer with eligible employees has an employee handbook or other written guidance on employee benefits or rights, the handbook must include an FMLA policy outlining FMLA rights and employee obligations.

Even though an employer may violate the FMLA by not explaining benefits and leave rights in its employee handbook, there is not necessarily a violation if the employee receives all of the FMLA benefits to which he or she is entitled.

If an employer does not have a handbook or other written policies, the employer must still provide written guidance concerning the employer's rights and obligations under the FMLA. The DOL's FMLA Fact Sheet (Figure 14-2) satisfies this written guidance requirement.

Required Notices to Employees Requesting FMLA Leave

To protect the employer, required notices should either be hand-delivered to the employee at work, with acknowledgement of their receipt obtained, or mailed via certified mail.

The employer is responsible for designating time off as FMLA leave, paid or unpaid, when the employer knows the leave is for an FMLA-qualifying reason. The employee should be told that the leave of absence will count against his or her 12-week FMLA entitlement.

According to the DOL regulations, designation of time off as FMLA leave must be given promptly after the employee requests leave. In the absence of extenuating circumstances, the employer should notify the employee of this designation within one or two business days. The notice may be given orally, but written confirmation designating the time off as FMLA leave must be given no later than the next pay day, or if the next pay day is less than one week after the oral designation, by the subsequent pay day.

Notice of Employee's Rights and Obligations under the FMLA

If the employee requests FMLA leave and/or the employer designates time off as FMLA leave, the employer must provide the employee with written notice including details of the specific obligations of the employee and any consequences for failing to

A "**Serious Health Condition**" means an illness, injury impairment, or physical or mental condition that involves one of the following:

1. Hospital Care

   Inpatient care (*i.e.*, an overnight stay) in a hospital, hospice, or residential medical care facility, including any period of incapacity[2] or subsequent treatment in connection with or consequent to such inpatient care.

2. Absence Plus Treatment

   (a) A period of incapacity[2] of **more than three consecutive calendar days** (including any subsequent treatment or period of incapacity[2] relating to the same condition), that also involves:

      (1) **Treatment**[3] **two or more times** by a health care provider, by a nurse or physician's assistant under direct supervision of a health care provider, or by a provider of health care services (*e.g.*, physical therapist) under orders of, or on referral by, a health care provider; or

      (2) **Treatment** by a health care provider on **at least one occasion** which results in a **regimen of continuing treatment**[4] under the supervision of the health care provider.

3. Pregnancy

   Any period of incapacity due to **pregnancy**, or for **prenatal care**.

4. Chronic Conditions Requiring Treatments

   A **chronic condition** which:

      (1) Requires **periodic visits** for treatment by a health care provider, or by a nurse or physician's assistant under direct supervision of a health care provider;

      (2) Continues over an **extended period of time** (including recurring episodes of a single underlying condition); and

      (3) May cause **episodic** rather than a continuing period of incapacity[2] (*e.g.*, asthma, diabetes, epilepsy, etc.).

5. Permanent/Long-term Conditions Requiring Supervision

   A period of **Incapacity**[2] which is **permanent or long-term** due to a condition for which treatment may not be effective. The employee or family member must be **under the continuing supervision of, but need not be receiving active treatment by, a health care provider**. Examples include Alzheimer's, a severe stroke, or the terminal stages of a disease.

6. Multiple Treatments (Non-Chronic Conditions)

   Any period of absence to receive **multiple treatments** (including any period of recovery therefrom) by a health care provider or by a provider of health care services under orders of, or on referral by, a health care provider, either for **restorative surgery** after an accident or other injury, **or** for a condition that **would likely result in a period of Incapacity**[2] **of more than three consecutive calendar days in the absence of medical intervention or treatment**, such as cancer (chemotherapy, radiation, etc.), severe arthritis (physical therapy), and kidney disease (dialysis).

This optional form may be used by employees to satisfy a mandatory requirement to furnish a medical certification (when requested) from a health care provider, including second or third opinions and recertification (29 CFR 825.306).

Note: Persons are not required to respond to this collection of information unless it displays a currently valid OMB control number.

---

[3] Treatment includes examinations to determine if a serious health condition exists and evaluations of the condition. Treatment does not include routine physical examinations, eye examinations, or dental examinations.

[4] A regimen of continuing treatment includes, for example, a course of prescription medication (*e.g.*, an antibiotic) or therapy requiring special equipment to resolve or alleviate the health condition. A regimen of treatment does not include the taking of over-the-counter medications such as aspirin, antihistamines, or salves; or bed-rest, drinking fluids, exercise, and other similar activities that can be initiated without a visit to a health care provider.

Figure 14-2
United States Department of Labor FMLA Fact Sheet (Source: United States Department of Labor)

meet these obligations. If a significant number of workers are not literate in English, the employer is required to provide the Employer Response Form in a language in which the employees are literate.

Figure 14-3, the DOL's "Employer Response to Employee's Request for Leave" form, satisfies the written notice requirement.

(Date)

TO: _____
                    (Employee's Name)

FROM:_____
                    (Employer Representative)

SUBJECT: Request for Family/Medical Leave

On _____, you identified us of your need to take family/medial leave due to:
        (Date)

- The birth of your child, or the placement of a child with your for adoption or foster care, or;
- A serious health condition that makes you unable to perform the essential functions of your job; or
- A serious health condition affecting your spouse, child, parent, for which you need to provide care.

You notified us that you need this leave beginning on _____, and that you expect the
                                                                                    (date)

leave to continue until or about _____.
                                                      (date)

Except as explained below, you have a right under the FMLA for up to 12 weeks of unpaid leave in a 12 month period for the reasons listed above. Also, your health benefits must be maintained During any period of unpaid leave under the same conditions a if you continued to work, and you must be reinstated to the same or an equivalent job with the same pay, benefits, an terms and conditions of employment on your return from leave. If you do not return to work following FMLA leave for a reason other than: (1) the continuation, recurrence, or onset of a serious health condition which would entitle you to FMLA leave; or (2) other circumstances beyond your control, you may be required to reimburse us for our share of health insurance premiums paid on your behalf during your FMLA leave.

This is to inform you that: (*check the appropriate boxes*, explain where indicated)

1. You are _____ eligible _____ not eligible for leave under the FMLA.

2. The requested leave _____ will _____ will not be counted against your annual FMLA leave entitlement.

3(b). You _____ will, _____ will not be required to furnish medical certification of a serious health condition. If required, you must furnish certification by _____ (*insert date*) (must be at least 15 days after you are notified of this requirement) or we may delay the commencement of your leave until the certification is submitted).

Figure 14-3
Family and Medical Leave Act of 1993 Employer Response to Employee Form

4. You may elect to substitute accrued paid leave for unpaid FMLA leave. We _____ will _____ will not require that you substitute accrued paid leave for unpaid FMLA leave. IF paid leave will be used the following conditions will apply: (*Explain*)

5(a). If you normally pay a portion of the premiums for your health insurance, these payments will continue during the period of FMLA leave. Arrangements for payment have been discussed with you and it is agreed that you will make premium payments as follows: (*Set forth dates or pay periods that specifically cover the agreement with the employee.*)

5(b). You have a minimum 30 day (or, indicate longer period, if applicable) grace period in which to make premium payments. If payment is not made timely, your group health insurance may be canceled, *provided* we notify you in writing at least 15 days before the date that your health insurance will lapse or, at our option, we may pay your share of the premiums during FMLA leave, and recover these payments from you upon your return to work. We _____ will _____ not pay your share of health insurance premiums while you are on leave.

5(c). We _____ will _____ will not do the same with any other benefits (e.g., life insurance, disability, insurance, etc.) while you are on FMLA leave. If we do pay your premiums for the benefits, when you return from leave you _____ will _____ will not be expected to reimburse us for the payments made on your behalf.

6. You _____ will _____ will not be required to present a fitness-for-duty certificate prior to being restored to employment. If such certification is required but not received, your return to work may be delayed until the certification is provided.

7(a). You _____ are _____ are not a "key employee" as described in 825.218 of the FMLA regulations. If you are a "key employee," restoration to employment may be denied following FMLA leave on the grounds that such restoration will cause substantial and grievous economic injury to us.

7(b). We _____ have _____ have not determined that restoring you to employment at the conclusion of FMLA leave will cause substantial and grievous economic harm to us. (*Explain (a) and/or(b) below See 825.219 of the FMLA regulations*).

8. While on leave, you _____ will _____ will not be required to furnish us with periodic reports every _____ (*indicate interval of periodic reports, as appropriate for the particular leave situation*) of your status and intent to return to work (*see* 825.309 of the FMLA regulations). If the circumstances of your leave change and you are able to return to work earlier than the date indicated on the reverse side of this form, you _____ will _____ will not be required to notify us at least two work days prior to the date you intend to report to work.

9. You _____ will _____ will not be required to furnish recertification relating to a serious health condition. (*Explain below, if necessary, including the interval between certificates as prescribed in 825.308 of the FMLA regulations*).

Figure 14-3 (*continued*)

If an employer fails to provide the notice outlined above, the employer may not take any action against the employee for failure to comply with any provision contained in the notice.

Nondiscrimination or Interference

It is unlawful for an employer to interfere with an employee's rights under the FMLA. An employer may not discriminate or retaliate against any employee for opposing unlawful practices under the FMLA, or for participating in any proceedings related to enforcement of the FMLA.

The FMLA specifically states that FMLA leave may not be counted under attendance policies, including "no fault" policies, and employers cannot use an employee's FMLA leave as a negative factor in employment actions such as hiring, promotions and disciplinary actions.

BURDEN OF PROOF IN FMLA DISCRIMINATION CASES

A plaintiff must establish a *prima facie* case for discrimination or retaliation under the FMLA by demonstrating that:

- He is protected under the FMLA;
- He suffered an adverse employment decision, and either he was treated less favorably than an employee who had not requested leave under the FMLA, or the adverse decision was made because of the plaintiff's request for leave.

If the plaintiff makes its *prima facie* case, the burden shifts to the employer to articulate a legitimate nondiscriminatory or nonretaliatory reason for the termination. Once the employer has established its case, the plaintiff must show by a preponderance of the evidence that the employer's reason is a pretext for discrimination or retaliation.

EXAMPLE OF INTERFERENCE/DISCRIMINATION FOUND BY THE COURT

In the case of an employee handbook that offered 16 weeks of leave but failed to notify employees that any leave in excess of the 12 weeks mandated by the FMLA would result in a loss of the right to reinstatement to the same or comparable position, the court determined that this policy interfered with the employee's FMLA rights (See *Fry v. First Fidelity Bancorporation*, No. CIV.A95–6019, 1996 WL 36901, 1996 U.S. Dist. LEXIS 875, 3 WH Cases 2d 115 (BNA)(E.D. Pa. 1996)).

EXAMPLE OF NO INTERFERENCE/DISCRIMINATION FOUND BY THE COURT

Where supervisors had discovered and reported the plaintiff's expense irregularities, conducted an investigation and recommended her termination *before* the employee requested medical leave, the court found no discrimination. See *Beno v. United Tele. Co. of Florida*, 969 F. Supp. 723 (M.D. Fla. 1997), as discussed below:

Beno v. United Tele. Co. of Florida, 969 F. Supp. 723 (M.D. Fla. 1997)

Facts:

Beno was employed by United Telephone Company of Florida from August 1977 until May 1, 1996. At the time of her termination, Beno held the position of "System Designer I—Marketing." On April 2 and 3, 1996, Beno attended a training session out of town. After the trip, Beno submitted an expense statement to her immediate supervisor, Monica Pfister, for reimbursement of meal expenses.

Pfister found the accounts submitted by Beno to be suspiciously high and conducted an investigation. After contacting the accounting department at the restaurant where Beno had eaten dinner, Pfister determined that Beno was not entitled to $18.00 of the reimbursement that she requested. Beno admitted that she took her mother with her on the trip, and that they went to the restaurant together, but claimed that she ordered the two dinners for herself.

Seeking reimbursement for expenses other than those incurred for "a valid business purpose" violated United's policies and procedures and constitutes a terminable offense. United had terminated people in the past for similar violations involving as little as $3.00.

On April 19, United's Security Manager interviewed Beno, and on April 22, reported results of his investigation to the legal department. On April 24, after consulting with the attorney about the security manager's findings, Pfister decided to recommend Beno's termination. Before Beno, Pfister had never recommended that a United employee be terminated.

On April 26, Pfister received a facsimile from Beno's doctor stating that she needed to be off work for three weeks. Her request was granted. During a conference call on April 30 between Pfister, Pfister's supervisor, the security manager, the attorney, two managers of employee relations, and the director of human resources, the group agreed that Beno should be terminated for falsifying the expense reported. On May 1, while still on medical leave, Beno was notified, by telephone and by letter, that her employment at United had been terminated.

Beno claimed that United terminated her employment in violation of the FMLA, and sought reinstatement to her job, back pay, front pay, liquidated damages, attorneys' fees and costs.

Opinion by Judge Kovachevich:

Before Beno requested medical leave, her supervisors had already discovered and reported Beno's expense irregularity, conducted an investigation, and recommended her termination. Thus, Beno's allegation of pretext—that she was terminated because of her request for medical leave—is undermined by the undisputed fact that United's steps toward termination were already underway before Beno requested leave. Based on these undisputed facts, summary judgment must be granted on the FMLA claim as a matter of law because Beno does not prove all of the elements of a *prima facie* case.

RECORDKEEPING REQUIREMENTS UNDER THE FMLA

Information to be Maintained

Covered employers with eligible employees must maintain records as outlined in Appendix C.

Maintaining the Confidentiality of Medical-Related Records

The FMLA requires that all records and documents created for purposes of the FMLA relating to medical certifications, recertifications, or medical histories of employees or employee's family members be maintained separately and treated as confidential medical records, except as follows:

- Supervisors and managers may be informed about necessary restrictions on the work or duties of an employee and necessary accommodations;
- First-aid and safety personnel may be informed, when appropriate, if the employee's physical or mental condition might require emergency treatment; and
- Disclosure is permitted to government officials investigating compliance with laws.

Retention Period

An employer must keep FMLA records for at least three years. However, covered employers with no eligible employees are only required to maintain basic payroll information and identifying employee data. Refer to Appendix E for information regarding retention requirements under the FMLA.

EMPLOYEE PROTECTIONS UNDER THE FMLA

Interference

The FMLA protects employees who assert FMLA rights or request leave by prohibiting interference with an employee's rights provided by the Act, with legal proceedings, or with inquiring relating to an employee's rights. An example of interfering with an employee's rights include refusing to authorize FMLA leave and discouraging an employee from requesting or taking FMLA leave.

Retaliation

Employers are prohibited from retaliating against any person for complaining about or opposing any practice unlawful under the FMLA (*See* 29 C.F.R. § 825.220(a)).

Discrimination

Employers are prohibited from discharging or otherwise discriminating against an individual who has:

- Filed a charge or complaint with the Secretary of Labor;
- Instituted a lawsuit to enforce the Act;
- Given (or is about to give) information pursuant to an inquiry relating to a right protected by the Act; or
- Testified (or is about to testify) at an inquiry relating to a right protected by the Act.

Additionally, employers may not discriminate against employees or prospective employees who have taken FMLA leave by using the taking of leave as a negative factor in employment actions such as hiring, promotions, disciplinary proceedings, or in performance evaluations.

Protected Class

All individuals, not just employees, are protected against an employer's retaliatory actions (*See* 29 C.F.R. § 825.220(e)).

ENFORCEMENT PROCEEDINGS

Complaints Filed with the Secretary of Labor

An employee (or the employee's representative) may file a complaint with the Secretary of Labor. The complaint may be filed in person, by telephone, or by mail with any local office of the Wage and Hour Division, Employment Standards Administration, U.S. Department of Labor. The regulations provide that the complaint must be in writing and include a full statement of the acts and/or omissions believed to violate the Act.

Complaints must be filed within a "reasonable" time of the employee's discovery that his or her FMLA rights have been violated. The regulations provide that any complaint must be filed within two years of the violation, or within three years of a willful violation. The DOL investigates allegations of every complaint and may file suit against the employer.

Private Lawsuits

The FMLA provides a private right of action for employees to file suit against an employer if that employer engages in any conduct prohibited by Section 105 of the Act. A private lawsuit must be filed within two years of the last FMLA violation, or within three years if the violation was willful. The filing of a complaint with the DOL is not required before an employee may bring suit.

Individual Liability under the FMLA

The regulations provide that individuals such as corporate officers "acting in the interest of an employer" are personally liable for FMLA violations (See 29 C.F.R. § 825.104(d)). The majority of courts have found that individual supervisors can be held personally liable for violations.

Factors that courts have used to find individual liability include:

- the supervisor's ability to control, in whole or in part;
- the employee's ability to take leave and return to his or her position;
- degree of control over an employee's ability to take leave;
- authority to hire and fire employees;
- position in the company and the degree of "operational control" of the company; and
- the degree to which the supervisor has exercised supervisory control over the employee.

Damages Available for FMLA Violations

Available damages for FMLA violations include:

1. Wages or benefits denied or lost because of the violation(s);
2. If wages or benefits were not actually lost because of the violation, then actual monetary losses because of the violation(s), up to a sum equal to 12 weeks of wages;

3. Interest on the lost wages, benefits or actual monetary losses; and

4. Liquidated damages equal to the sum of the lost wages, benefits or actual monetary losses and interest (29 U.S.C. § 2617(a)(1)(A)(i)–(iii)).

If the employer proves "to the satisfaction of the court" that the act or omission in violation of the FMLA was done "in good faith and the employer had reasonable grounds for believing that the act or omission was not a violation of the FMLA," then the court has the discretion to "reduce the amount of the liability" to the amount of the lost wages, benefit or actual damages, plus interest (29 U.S.C. § 2617(a)(1)(A)(iii)).

In some cases, the court may award equitable relief, such as hiring, reinstatement, promotion and front pay (29 U.S.C. § 2617(a)(1)(B)).

TERMS

health care provider
key employee
serious health condition

REVIEW QUESTIONS

1. Nancy, an independent contractor, requests an FMLA leave from the temporary agency through whom she is presently working at an employer's site. Is Nancy eligible for FMLA leave? Does the temporary agency have an obligation to grant an FMLA leave? Why or why not?

2. Mary Jane has been employed for 6 months by a small pharmaceutical company with 25 employees. She requests FMLA to care for her sick mother. Does she qualify for FMLA leave? If not, which criteria does she not meet?

3. David requests time off for his grandfather's "serious health condition." Does a grandparent qualify for granting David the requested leave? Would the employer be required to grant the leave if it were his father rather than grandfather who had the "serious health condition?"

4. Richard and Helen have lived together as "domestic partners" for ten years, but have never married. When Helen develops a serious health condition, is Richard's employer required to grant him a requested FMLA leave?

5. Would biweekly dialysis treatment qualify as a serious health condition? Would your answer be the same for biweekly chemotherapy treatments?

6. Does the FMLA classify a midwife as a "health care provider"?

7. If an employee has been replaced because of business necessity during the time that she has been off from work on an FMLA leave, does the employer have a duty to return the employee to her original position? Would your answer be the same if the employee is no longer capable of performing that job?

8. Assume that the employee in question 7 requested another position upon her return from FMLA leave because she believed that she would be able to perform that position easier than her original position. Does the employer have a duty to accommodate her request? If the change in position were the employer's idea, could the employer require that the employee take the other position if she did not want that position?

9. What is the time period within which a claim must be filed with the Secretary of Labor if the event that precipitated the filing was not willful? If the event was willful, what is the time period for filing?

10. What is the time period within which a private lawsuit must be filed if the event that precipitated the filing was not willful? What is the time period if the event was willful?

PROJECTS

1. Contact your regional Department of Labor Office, or research on the DOL Internet site, the number of claims filed last year that involved the FMLA. Draft a summary chart of the claims to show the reason for the filing and the disposition of the claims.

2. Search the legal Internet sites for cases involving a company's denial of FMLA leave because the plaintiff utilized a midwife or non-American physicians. Explain the court's position on the acceptability of a midwife or non-American physicians.

CHAPTER 15

The Employer's Rights versus the Employee's Right to Privacy

EMPLOYEE'S RIGHT TO PRIVACY

Overview

The advent of advanced computer and telecommunication technology has increased employers' ability to protect themselves from employee theft or fraud, monitor employee productivity, and evaluate the quality of an employee's work. While employee surveillance may protect employer interests, it has become a matter of great concern to employees. An increasing number of employees feel that their privacy rights are being invaded and are bringing lawsuits against employers for acts such as eavesdropping or recording conversations, reading private electronic mail messages, searching employees' offices, and requiring a polygraph test or drug test. The employer must balance the employee's right to privacy against the employer's need to evaluate or investigate.

An employee's rights to privacy are derived from four sources:

1. Constitution (state and federal);
2. Statutes (state and federal);
3. State common law; and
4. Contract.

Privacy Rights under Constitutional Law

The United States Constitution is the original source of privacy rights in the United States. The Bill of Rights protects citizens from any unwarranted intrusions by the federal government. In addition, the Fourteenth Amendment extends to all citizens those same protections against unwarranted intrusion by both state and local governments.

This protection is only protection from governmental action; private employees do not have federal constitutional protection from unwarranted intrusions of their privacy by their employers. However, private employees do have other sources for privacy rights. Some states also recognize a constitutional cause of action for invasion of privacy by private-sector employers or ordinary citizens. In addition, most states have common law actions regulating the invasion of an individual's privacy.

Privacy Rights under Statutory Law

The **Electronic Communications Privacy Act of 1986** (ECPA), 18 U.S.C. § 2510 et seq., is the only federal law governing the electronic monitoring of employees. ECPA prohibits the intentional interception of oral, wire, or electronic communication, with limited exceptions. Intentional disclosure or use of an electronic communication is also banned, provided the responsible person knows or has reason to know that it was intercepted illegally.

In many instances, ECPA's definition of an "electronic communication" includes e-mail and voice mail communication. The Act established both civil and criminal penalties for violations.

Although the ECPA and state wiretapping statutes restrict an employer's ability to intercept e-mail and voice mail messages, these statutes generally provide several exceptions under which employers may be allowed to monitor electronic communication in the workplace. These exceptions include:

- Readily accessible communications (bulletin board system with wide user access);
- Service-provider exception (telephone companies may intercept and disclose calls when necessary to protect their equipment and rights);
- Business Use Exception (telephone monitoring must be done to further a legitimate business interest; once the personal nature of a communication is discovered, the eavesdropping MUST stop).

Privacy Rights under Common Law

Employees are protected from intentional intrusions into their private affairs. For liability purposes, the manner of intrusion must be highly offensive to a reasonable person, and the employee must have had an expectation of privacy.

Common law rights accorded to employees include the right to avoid public disclosures regarding their private lives. The publicity must be highly offensive to a reasonable person and the subject matter must not be of a legitimate concern to the public.

An employee is protected from false or misleading public statements by the employer. Liability only ensues if the employer has passed on false or misleading information that was highly offensive or defamatory, and only if the employer's conduct was intentional or in reckless disregard for the truth.

Many states have introduced laws to protect employers who provide truthful employee references to prospective employers without fear of defamation lawsuits.

Privacy Rights under Contract Law

Employers create privacy rights through promises in employee manuals, collective bargaining agreements, and employment agreements.

GUIDELINES FOR MONITORING EMPLOYEES

Before an employer decides to monitor its employees, it should establish guidelines to minimize potential liability for such action, including:

- Review applicable state and federal laws;
- Provide employees with prior written notice of the nature and extent of the proposed monitoring;
- Provide employees with written notices of e-mail monitoring;
- Prohibit offensive and abusive communications by employees;
- Justify the monitoring;
- Limit the amount and forms of monitoring or surveillance to preserve the business use exception;
- Notify callers, such as customers, of the possibility that their phone calls may be monitored; and;
- Carefully control the use and disclosure of information gathered through monitoring.

CATEGORIES OF MONITORING

Personal Surveillance

Personal surveillance is observing or listening to employees without mechanical aids.

Electronic Mail (e-mail) Surveillance

Legal and ethical issues for employers have risen with the number of employees who now use electronic mail, and the ability of management to monitor such use. For example, employers should be aware of the possibility of **spoofing**—the construction of an electronic mail communication so that it appears to be from someone else. Employers investigating incidents of alleged harassment must consider the possibility that the actual harasser is not the person who supposedly sent the harassing message. Because of the relative ease of access to another employee's computer, employers should conduct a comprehensive investigation before firing an employee because of pornographic files on the employee's hard drive. Those files could have easily been downloaded by someone with a grudge against that employee.

In theory, the "header" for e-mail messages that identifies the route the message traveled, other recipients, the time, date, and location from which the message was sent, and the time, date, and location at which the message was received will reflect the name of the actual author of the e-mail. However, in practice that is not always the case. While the header identifies the name of the sender, the sender may not be the person who actually wrote the e-mail.

It is sometimes difficult to determine the true identity of the sender of a message, particularly if the sender wishes to hide his or her identity. This is due in part to the growth of anonymous "remailers." Remailers are relay stations on the Internet that protect the identity of their users who send messages through them. The remailer system is used by an individual to send an e-mail to a newsgroup run by the remailer. The remailer then strips the name and return address off the posting and replaces those entries with a new name and return address. The remailer system also adds a pseudonym, making responding to the message nearly impossible. E-mail sent through the system becomes almost untraceable. The greatest criticism of such services is that they allow individuals to send harassing or threatening messages without risk of identification.

ECPA does not normally protect the privacy of messages sent on *internal* company e-mail systems. However, management's act of accessing an employee's e-mail may violate common law privacy protections.

The uncertainty of this area of the law dictates that employers adopt a written policy concerning the use of e-mail. Some businesses have adopted a strict policy, allowing employees to use e-mail only for business-related messages. Other employers advise employees that they reserve the right to monitor the e-mail system for legitimate business reasons. Informing employees of policies and practices regarding e-mail will reduce the possibility that an employee has a claim for a privacy right in using the employer's e-mail system.

A developing concern in the use of e-mail is the employer's potential liability for "e-mail or voice mail harassment." Employees often use e-mail to disseminate inappropriate jokes or to play pranks on coworkers. Such conduct has the potential to offend or even create a "hostile work environment." The backup systems for e-mail and voice mail communications provide a real trail of evidence for the offended employee. Recent employment cases involving electronic communications have included claims for race, age, and other harassment and discrimination issues.

Employers should train employees on the appropriate use of electronic communications and prohibit employees from making offensive or harassing comments via e-mail or voice mail. In addition, employers must also initiate lawful monitoring procedures to identify potential harassing communications and take corrective action to halt such activities.

Video Camera Surveillance

Under certain circumstances, the use of a video camera to monitor employees while working could invade an employee's right to privacy. Video monitoring might also violate state common law or statutory protections of worker privacy. ECPA provides that videotaping with an accompanying audio signal constitutes "interception" of an oral communication.

An employee's right to privacy may be invaded by video monitoring when the monitoring occurs at times and in places where an employee has a reasonable expectation of privacy, including a bathroom or changing room. An employer who has a legitimate business purpose for video surveillance and who notifies employees of the monitoring may generally conduct reasonable video surveillance.

Video monitoring can violate federal and state statutes prohibiting the interception of wire, electronic, or oral communication. An employer should obtain written consent from employees for the interception of oral communications related to any video surveillance, or conduct such surveillance without audio recording.

Workplace Searches

Employer security problems have increased in recent years from concerns over theft to include safeguarding the workplace from alcohol and drugs and measuring workers' performance. These concerns have given rise to issues regarding the legality of searching desk and lockers provided by an employer, searching personal items such as purses, briefcases, and vehicles brought onto company property, and monitoring employees' productivity and substance abuse. The legality of a search will depend upon whether the employer is public or private, whether it has provided advance notice of the search, whether it has a good reason for the search, and whether the employer has conducted the search in a reasonable manner.

A public employer's ability to conduct workplace searches is limited by the Fourth Amendment's prohibition against unreasonable searches and seizures, as discussed in the following case.

O'Connor v. Ortega, 480 U.S. 709 (1987)

Facts:

Dr. Ortega had worked as a psychiatrist at a California state hospital for 17 years. Hospital officials searched his office and seized personal items from his desk and file cabinets. The search was conducted because of a concern about possible improprieties in his management of the psychiatric-residency program. The seized items were subsequently used in administrative proceedings that resulted in his discharge.

Opinion by Justice O'Connor:

This suit under 42 U.S.C. § 1983 presents two issues concerning the Fourth Amendment right of public employees. First, we must determine whether the respondent, a public employee, had a reasonable expectation of privacy in his office, desk and file cabinets at his place of work. Second, we must address the appropriate Fourth Amendment standard for a search conducted by a public employer in areas in which a public employee is found to have a reasonable expectation of privacy.

A search to secure state property is valid as long as petitioners had a reasonable belief that there was government property in Dr. Ortega's office which needed to be secured, and the scope of the intrusion was itself reasonable in light of this justification. Indeed, petitioners have put forward evidence that they had such a reasonable belief; at the time of the search, petitioners knew that Dr. Ortega had removed the computer from the Hospital. The removal of the computer-together with the allegations of mismanagement of the residency program and sexual harassment-may have made the search reasonable at its inception under the standard we have put forth in this case. As with the District Court order, therefore, the Court of Appeals conclusion that summary judgment was appropriate cannot stand.

On remand, therefore, the District Court must determine the justification for the search and seizure, and evaluate the reasonableness of both the inception of the search and its scope.

Accordingly, the judgment of the Court of Appeals is reversed, and the case is remanded to that court for further proceedings consistent with this opinion.

While the Court concluded that Dr. Ortega had a reasonable expectation of privacy in his office, the Court found that his privacy interest should be balanced against the hospital's right to conduct a search that was reasonable under the circumstances.

The two-step balancing test was based on whether there were reasonable grounds for suspecting that the search would turn up evidence that the employee was guilty of work-related misconduct, or the search was necessary for a noninvestigative work-related purpose, such as the retrieval of a needed file. Under this balancing test, the appellate court upheld the plaintiff's $450,000 jury award in *Ortega v. O'Connor*, 146 F.3d 1149 (9th Cir. 1998).

A public employer may lower its employees' expectations of privacy, and increase its ability to conduct searches, by notifying employees that the employees and their possessions may be subject to searches at work. As a result, many employers now require that employees sign waivers that permit their lockers to be subject to random inspection. Private employers are not subject to the Fourth Amendment, and therefore are generally less restricted than public employers in their ability to conduct searches. However, state constitutions, statutes, and common law may limit the nature and scope of permissible searches by private employers.

Because requirements for valid workplace searches vary from state to state, employers should minimize their liability searches for inappropriate searches by taking the precautions listed in Figure 15-1.

Litigation or possible liability may still arise from any workplace search, even if the employer takes all of the precautions listed in Figure 15-1.

Investigation

The process of investigation involves inquiries about the employee to persons other than the employee. Investigation may also include the review of documents pertaining to the employee, such as medical, school, and past employment records.

Testing

Testing involves direct inquiry of the employee, and may include physical tests, such as blood or urine tests, or psychological tests. The ADA prohibits certain pre-job-offer testing. Additionally, some psychological tests may have an adverse impact on minority applicants, and thus may raise an inference of discrimination.

DRUG AND ALCOHOL ABUSE

Abuse of alcohol and drugs costs employers billions of dollars every year. Recent studies show that substance abusers are generally absent more often, less productive, cause more accidents, and file more insurance claims. For example, one study reports

○ Retain a key or combination for each locker, desk, or vehicle on company property and notify the employees of this fact;

○ Make sure any lock on company property is owned and supplied by the employer, and forbid employees to use their own locks;

○ Expressly reserve the right to enter all lockers, desks, and vehicles at any time;

○ Provide formal notice to employees that lockers, desks, and vehicles may be searched without employee consent or knowledge and that refusal to permit such searches may result in discipline;

○ Notify employees that their purses, lunch boxes, or pockets may be searched and obtain employee consent prior to conducting such searches;

○ Prepare a written policy concerning searches and have each employee sign a written acknowledgment stating that the employee has received and read the written search policy;

○ Secure a valid search warrant prior to conducting a search at the request of police;

○ Conduct searches in an even-handed and nondiscriminatory manner;

○ Do not proceed with a search if an employee credibly denies knowledge of the search policy; and

○ If possible, obtain the employee's consent before conducting the search.

Figure 15-1
Employer's Checklist for Workplace Searches

that workers who illicitly use drugs are 2.5 times more likely to have absences of eight days or more; 3.6 times more likely to injury themselves or another person in a workplace accident; 5 times more often to be injured in an accident off the job that then affects attendance and job performance; 5 times more likely to file a workers' compensation claim; one-third less productive; and incur three times higher medical costs. ("What Every Employee Should Know About Drug Abuse" [1990, 2nd ed.], Institute for a Drug-Free Workplace, Washington, D.C.). In that same study Roger Smith, former chairman of General Motors, identified the cost of drug abuse to GM alone at an astonishing $1 billion per year. Another study conducted by the United States Postal Service estimated that drug users have up to 55% more industrial accidents, 85% more injuries, and 145% more absenteeism. (*Employee Relations Weekly* [BNA Dec. 1990], vol. 8, p. 1469).

Employers have a variety of options to control drug and alcohol abuse, including rules prohibiting employees from using, possessing, or selling drugs or alcohol or working under the influence of drugs or alcohol. Subject to compliance with applicable laws, employers have the right to require employees and applicants to cooperate in and pass tests for alcohol and drug use. Employers may adopt search policies, use undercover investigators, and require employees to seek treatment or face discipline.

Methods designed to counteract drug and alcohol abuse in the workplace are options for most employers, but they are requirements for some employers. Federal contractors and recipients of federal grants have drug-free workplace obligations. Transportation employers, including railroads, airlines, motor carriers, shipping companies, and pipeline operators must have drug and alcohol testing programs.

Options to control drug and alcohol abuse in the workplace are not entirely positive for employers, however. Federal law has limited employers' rights in numerous areas, discussed in this chapter. For example, federal law restricts what employers can discover and disclose about employees who abuse drugs or alcohol.

As discussed in Chapter 8, the ADA protects the following:

- Former illegal drug users who have successfully completed treatment;
- Former illegal drug users who are participating in treatment;
- Persons erroneously regarded as illegal drug users; and
- Disabled persons who are legally using prescription drugs.

ADA regulations permit the employer to conduct any testing required by Department of Transportation, Defense or Energy regulations.

Drug-Free Workplace Act of 1988

In November 1988, Congress passed the **Drug-Free Workplace Act of 1988**, authorizing the Small Business Administration (SBA) to give grants to organizations so that those organizations could help small businesses set up drug-free workplace programs. Direct recipients of federal grants, and many federal contractors holding contracts that exceed $25,000, must comply with the Drug-Free Workplace Act. Covered employers must adhere to the following requirements:

- To have clear, written policies that are available to all applicants and employees and that emphasize confidentiality;
- To use federally-certified labs;
- To collect specimens in secure private locations pursuant to a chain of custody;
- To provide training for at least two hours to all employees on alcohol and drug abuse prevention; and
- To advise persons who test positive of assistance programs.

Covered employers must have a policy statement and a drug-free awareness program. The policy statement must notify employees who are performing work under the contract or the grant:

- That they may not illegally manufacture, distribute, dispense, possess, or use controlled substances in the workplace;
- That they must report any criminal convictions for manufacturing, distributing, dispensing, possessing, or using controlled substances in the workplace to the employer within 5 days;
- The penalties for such criminal convictions; and
- These materials must be distributed to employees before drug and alcohol testing.

Once an employer has been notified of on-the-job convictions by employees directly engaged in contract/grant work, the employer has 30 days to take appropriate disciplinary action, up to and including discharge, or to require the employee's "satisfactory" participation in an assistance/rehabilitation program. Contractors and grantees have the discretion to decide what action to take for on-the-job convictions.

Convictions for workplace drug crimes by employees directly performing work under the contract/grant must be reported within 10 days to the contracting/granting agency. Convictions of other employees and for other crimes should not be reported.

The Act also requires contractors and grantees to establish drug-free awareness programs informing employees of the employer's drug-free workplace policy, the adverse effects of drug abuse, penalties for workplace drug violations, and available drug counseling, rehabilitation, or assistance programs.

Drug testing, employee assistance programs, and supervisor training are all optional under the Act. However, the majority of employers have exercised these options to ensure better and safer working conditions for employees. Figure 15–2 is a checklist for developing a drug testing policy.

Types of Employer Drug and Alcohol Testing Programs

Preemployment Testing

As a result of studies cited above showing that drug users, once hired, experience more job problems and increase business costs, employers have turned to preemployment techniques aimed at controlling the hiring of drug abusers. One such technique is preemployment drug and alcohol testing.

The courts have generally upheld the legality of preemployment drug testing to the extent that it is reasonable, accurate, confidential, and consistently applied. Figure 15-3 is a consent form for preemployment drug testing.

Random or Periodic Testing on the Job

On-the-job drug abuse presents the greatest legal obstacles in terms of detection and subsequent remedial action by the employer. To date, federal courts have rejected

	Yes	No

General

☐ Do you have a written drug and alcohol policy?
☐ Do you annually review your policy to update it?
☐ Do you have stated goals for your policy?
☐ Does your policy meet those goals?
☐ Do you communicate your policy to your employees?
☐ Is the policy contained in:

> Orientation sessions?
> Handbooks?
> Bulletin board notices?
> Supervisor training?
> Payroll envelope stuffers?

Policy

☐ Does your policy address both legal and illegal intoxicants?
☐ Does your policy address off-duty conduct?
☐ Does your policy address the issue of when you will test?
☐ Does it state who can require a drug or alcohol test?
☐ Does it require employees to cooperate with examinations?
☐ Does it ensure a chain of custody for the blood or urine sample?
☐ Does it permit retesting?
☐ Does it allow you to obtain medical records from a personal physician?
☐ Is it coordinated with your employee assistance program?
☐ Does it ensure confidentiality?
☐ Is it coordinated with your medical leave of absence policy?
☐ Do you pay for the drug or alcohol test?
☐ Do you address when the police will be informed of illegal activity?

Legal Issues

☐ Are you familiar with the Drug-Free Workplace Act of 1988?
☐ Are you regulated by any federal or state agencies that impose testing?
☐ Are you familiar with your state's drug testing laws?
☐ Has your policy been reviewed by legal counsel?

Figure 15-2
Checklist for Developing Drug and Alcohol Testing Policy

I, _____, have been fully informed by my potential employer of the reasons for this urine test for drug and/or alcohol. I understand what I am being tested for, the procedure involved, and do hereby freely give my consent. In addition, I understand that the results of this test will be forwarded to my potential employer and become part of my personnel record.

If this test result is positive and I am not hired for that reason, I understand that I will be given the opportunity to explain the results of this test.

I hereby authorize these test results to be released to:

.
_____

_____   _____
Signature   Date
_____   _____
Witness   Date

Figure 15-3
Consent for Drug/Alcohol Screen Testing (Preemployment)

random drug testing of broad categories of employees, and have imposed strict criteria before such testing can be legally justified.

Examples of employee categories that pose sufficient safety concerns to justify random drug testing include railroad employees, employees carrying firearms, air traffic controllers, pilots, and aviation mechanics.

Reasonable Suspicion Testing

The reasonable suspicion testing program calls for testing employees only upon an employer's subjective suspicion that a specific employee is under the influence of drugs while on the job. Following the issuance of Executive Order No. 12564 in 1986 and the enactment of the Drug-Free Workplace Act of 1988, this program of "testing for cause" was widely implemented. Courts generally have upheld this type of testing when the employer abides by certain limitations.

Postaccident Testing

Postaccident testing has been considered only in the context of jobs involving transportation or safety-sensitive positions, where accidents pose real risks to the health, safety, and welfare of others. Accidents in an office setting probably do not pose sufficient risks to justify this type of testing.

Department of Transportation Regulations

The Department of Transportation (DOT) was the first executive agency to implement drug-testing program following the enactment of President Ronald Reagan's Executive Order 12564. The DOT regulations require preemployment testing, postaccident testing, testing based on reasonable suspicion, testing after rehabilitation, and random testing of employees. These regulations affect transportation employees, including airline pilots, truck and bus drivers, gas and oil pipeline workers, railroad workers, and merchant seamen. As is true with all federal drug-testing programs, employers are to utilize only laboratories certified under the Department of Health and Human Services Mandatory Guidelines. A list of such laboratories is published and available to the public.

At least six agencies of the DOT have implemented drug-testing programs, including:

- Federal Aviation Administration
- Federal Highway Administration
- Federal Railroad Administration
- Coast Guard
- Urban Mass Transportation Administration
- Research and Special Programs Administration

The DOT rules require covered employers to have written policy materials that provide details of the following topics:

- Which employees are covered
- What kinds of drug and alcohol use are prohibited
- When the DOT drug and alcohol rules apply
- When testing is required
- Specimen collection procedures
- Drug and alcohol testing procedures
- Consequences of testing positive
- What a "refusal" to cooperate in testing is, and its consequences
- The adverse effects of alcohol and drugs
- How to intervene and help a coworker when a drug or alcohol problem is suspected

DOT Required Testing

Preemployment Testing

Applicants for employment in covered positions must successfully pass a drug test before performing a safety-sensitive function. Employees transferring from a noncovered position to a covered position, or employees who have been laid off for more than 30 days, may also have to be tested. Preemployment alcohol tests are optional.

Random Testing

Most DOT employers are required to conduct a number of random drug tests equal to 50% of the number of covered positions each year. The number of alcohol tests must equal 10% of the number of covered positions. Random tests must be spread throughout the year. Employees can have no advance warning of random tests. Tested employees stay in the selection pool for future tests.

Postaccident or Incident

Drug testing is required within 32 hours after serious accidents or rule violations, but should be conducted as soon as practicable. Alcohol testing must be done within eight hours of the accident, and should be done within two hours. Testing should occur after employees who may have caused or contributed to the accident have received any necessary medical attention.

Reasonable Cause

Reasonable cause testing must be based on documented observations by a trained supervisor. The supervisor's observations should be documented promptly, and should be made when the employee has safety-sensitive responsibilities, not when the employee is off the job.

Return to Duty

Employees who fail or refuse to cooperate in testing must take and pass a test before returning to a safety-sensitive job.

Follow-up

Employees are subject to follow-up testing after they return to duty. The follow-up tests for truck drivers must last at least a year, and may last up to five years.

Consequences of Positive Tests and Refusals of Testing

Applicants who refuse to take or fail to pass a required preemployment test cannot be hired for a safety-sensitive job unless and until they pass such a test.

Employees who have an alcohol test result of between.02 and.039 must immediately be removed from all sensitive duties and not allowed to resume work for 24 hours.

If an employee refuses to submit to a required drug or alcohol test, the DOT rules require that the employee be removed immediately from performing safety-sensitive duties, and advised of available resources for evaluating and resolving drug or alcohol problems.

Employers may exercise their independent authority to discipline or discharge employees who test positive. DOT rules do not regulate discipline; however, they do regulate the process of returning an employee who has tested positive to duty. Prior to returning to work, the employee generally must be evaluated by a substance abuse professional (SAP), successfully complete or participate in any counseling or treatment the SAP prescribes, pass a return-to-duty test, and be approved to return to work by a SAP. Once reinstated, such employees are subject to follow-up tests for one to five years. Under the DOT rules, the SAP schedules follow-up tests, and must schedule at least six during the first year.

Recordkeeping

The DOT rules require retention of virtually every record an employer might generate or receive in connection with its DOT program. Records relating to negative test results and cancelled tests should be kept for one year. Records relating to positive test results, refusals, SAP evaluations, and referrals should be kept for five years.

EMPLOYEE POLYGRAPH PROTECTION ACT OF 1988

The **Employee Polygraph Protection Act** (29 U.S.C. § 2001–2009) imposes severe restrictions on the use of lie-detector tests, and as a result has effectively eliminated the use of polygraph testing as a preemployment screening mechanism. This Act bars most private-sector employers from requiring, requesting, or suggesting that a job applicant or employee submit to a polygraph or lie-detector test, and from using or accepting the results of such tests. Employers are also prohibited from disciplining, discharging, or discriminating against any applicant or employee:

1. for refusing to take a lie-detector test;
2. based on the results of a lie-detector test; or
3. for taking any actions to preserve employee rights under the Act.

This Act only prohibits mechanical or electrical devices—paper and pencil tests, chemical tests, or other nonmechanical or nonelectrical means that purport to measure an individual's honesty are permitted. The fact that chemical testing is specifically excluded from the definition of lie detector permits the use of medical tests to determine the presence of drugs or alcohol in an individual's bodily fluids.

The Act contains several limited exceptions to the general ban on polygraph testing. One such exception permits the testing of prospective employees of security firms. This exception, however, is limited to a security service company. A security guard employed by a manufacturing company, for example, would not fall under this exemption. A second exemption to the Act is for employers who manufacture, distribute, or dispense controlled substances. The third exception is for any covered employer to test current employees who are reasonably suspected of involvement in a workplace incident that resulted in economic loss or injury to the employer's business.

Employers may lawfully require an employee to submit to a polygraph test only under the following conditions:

1. The employer is engaged in an ongoing investigation involving economic loss or injury to the employer's business;
2. The employee to be tested had access to the property in question; and
3. The employer has a reasonable suspicion that the employee was involved in the incident.

The only acceptable honesty test is the polygraph test (See *Long v. Mango's Tropical Café, Inc.*, 972 F. Supp. 655 (S.D. Fla. 1997)). Use of any other mechanical or electronic honesty testing device will be considered a violation of the Act, even if the employer fulfills all of the other requirements of the exemption.

Notice of Intent to Administer Polygraph Test

The employer must provide the employee to be examined with a statement at least 48 hours prior to the test, in a language understood by the examinee, that explains the specific incident being investigated and the basis for testing the particular employee. The employer must maintain statements for at least three years. Figure 15-4 is an example of a Notice of Intent to Administer Polygraph Test.

Administration of a Polygraph Test

Employers must adhere to certain procedural requirements, including:

1. Inform the examinee of his or her right to obtain and consult with counsel or an employee representative;
2. Provide the examinee with an explanation of the physical operation of the polygraph machine;
3. Explain to the examinee prior to the test that he or she need not submit to

Date:
To:

You are hereby notified that you are scheduled for a polygraph test to take place at
_____ [location] on _____ [month, day and year], at _____.m.

You have the right to consult with legal counsel or an employee representative before each phase
of the test. However, the legal counsel or representative will not be allowed to be present in the room
where the examination is administered during the actual test phase.

Attached to this notice is a complete list of questions that you will be asked during the polygraph
test. Please review it prior to attending the testing session. You have the right to terminate the test
at any time.

The characteristics of the test and the instruments involved are:

You will receive further written information, which will be read to you before the polygraph
examination.

_____
Supervisor

Figure 15-4
Notice of Intent to Administer Polygraph Test

the test as a condition of continued employment, that any statement made
during the examination can be used as evidence to support disciplinary action,
and the legal rights and remedies permitted by the Act if there are any violations of the Act;
4. Provide the examinee with all the questions to be asked on the exam; and
5. Inform the examinee of his or her right to terminate the examination at any
time.

Employers are prohibited from permitting anyone other than a qualified examiner to administer the test. The polygraph test must last at least 90 minutes to ensure
that there are a sufficient number and variety of questions and responses to accurately analyze the employee's response pattern.

After the conclusion of the polygraph test, the test results must be reviewed with the examinee. The employer must interview the employee about the test results prior to taking any adverse employment action based on the polygraph examination results. The examinee is entitled to receive a copy of the questions and his or her charted responses, along with the examiner's opinions regarding the test. The examiner is required to retain all data, interpretation, charts, and opinions relating to each polygraph test for a minimum of three years.

Use of Polygraph Test Results for Disciplinary Action

Neither an employee's refusal to submit to a polygraph examination administered as part of an ongoing investigation of economic loss to the company, nor polygraph test results, can provide the sole basis for discharge, discipline, refusal to promote, or any other form of adverse employment action. An employer is required to provide additional supporting evidence prior to taking such action. "Additional supporting evidence" is evidence indicating that the employee had access to the missing or damaged property that is the subject of the ongoing investigation, and evidence leading to the employer's reasonable suspicion that the employee was involved in the incident or activity under investigation, or admissions or statements by an employee before, during, or following a polygraph examination (29 U.S.C. § 2006(d)).

This Act prohibits employers or examiners from disclosing any information obtained through a polygraph test, with the following exceptions:

1. The examinee or any person designated in writing by the examinee;
2. The employer who requested the examination; or
3. A court, governmental agency, arbitrator, or mediator that obtains a court order.

The employer may disclose such information to an appropriate governmental agency, without court order, only when the information disclosed is an admission of criminal conduct.

ACCESS TO PERSONNEL INFORMATION

State statutes, and some federal laws, govern whether and to what extent employees are to be permitted access to their own personnel files. For example, the Occupational Safety & Health Act requires employers to permit employees to inspect their own medical records. The Federal Privacy Act requires federal agencies to allow individuals to examine, copy, and request the correction of information in the agency's records. Most laws governing personnel file access contain exceptions and limitations on such topics as the time and place of access, right to make copies, right to correct information, and right to insert explanations.

The **Federal Privacy Act** prohibits federal agencies from disclosing personnel records without first obtaining written consent (5 U.S.C. § 522a). For purposes of the Act, several courts have found that even employment applications are records (See *Sullivan v. U.S. Postal Serv.*, 944 F. Supp. 191 (W.D.N.Y. 1996)). In this case, the court found that a prospective postal-service employee had a claim under the Act when the postal service did not respect his request not to contact his current employer. In addition, this Act requires that the person who is in charge of maintaining the personnel information must ensure that the files are not falling into the wrong hands, and that the information contained within the files is accurate, reliable, and is used for the proper reasons.

The Federal Privacy Act offers two types of relief to employees: criminal penalties and civil remedies, including damages and injunctive relief. The Act also permits employees who are adversely affected by an agency's noncompliance with the Act to bring a civil suit against the agency in federal court.

INFORMATION RELATING TO REASON FOR DISCHARGE OR VOLUNTARY TERMINATION

In response to a request, an employer may generally furnish a truthful statement concerning the reason for a former employee's discharge or voluntary termination. Even when an employer responds truthfully to a prospective employer's appropriate request, the employer may be liable if its response is unfavorable and in retaliation against an employee for having filed a claim under certain employee-protection laws, such as the Fair Labor Standards Act or Title VII. In *Rutherford v. American Bank of Commerce* (565 F.2d 1162 (10th Cir. 1977)), the employer violated Title VII by voluntarily reporting to a prospective employer that a former employee had filed a sex discrimination charge.

DEFAMATION LIABILITY POTENTIAL

An employer may suffer civil liability for defamation by releasing inaccurate or misleading information about an employee or a former employee. Defamation is a tortious invasion of an individual's interest in maintaining a good reputation. **Defamation** includes any false communication, either oral or written, that has a tendency to injure a person in his or her occupation. Although many state statutes grant employers a privilege against liability for providing job references, employers should seek an employee's written consent before providing detailed job-reference information.

FEDERAL FAIR CREDIT REPORTING ACT

The **Federal Fair Credit Reporting Act** (FFCRA) was amended by the Consumer Credit Reporting Act of 1996. These changes impose new limitations on the use of consumer credit reports in making employment decisions.

Prior to the amendments, the FFCRA required that employers provide notice to applicants and/or employees regarding credit checks in only limited circumstances. More stringent notice requirements are now imposed on employers who use consumer reports for employment purposes.

Employers who utilize consumer reports for employment purposes must now:

1. make a written disclosure to the applicant or employee that a consumer report may be obtained; and obtain the written authorization of the applicant or employee; and
2. notify the applicant/employee if any adverse action is to be taken based upon the consumer report, and provide a copy of the report and a summary of the consumer's rights.

Compliance with the FFCRA may be enforced by state or federal actions and private lawsuits. To ensure compliance with the FFCRA as amended, employers should make certain that employment applications and other documentation used in the hiring process satisfy the new notice requirement.

TERMS

defamation
Drug-Free Workplace Act of 1988
Electronic Communications Privacy Act of 1986
Employee Polygraph Protection Act
Federal Fair Credit Reporting Act
Federal Privacy Act

personal surveillance
spoofing

REVIEW QUESTIONS

1. Allen Harrington is hospitalized for an unknown medical problem. Based on his recent weight loss and his known association with gays, his supervisor tells coworkers that Allen "probably has AIDS." Allen sues for invasion of privacy. Can he sustain such a claim?

2. An employer suspects that an employee has drugs stored in his locker. The employer had purchased and installed the lock. Can the employer remove the lock and search the locker? Would your answer be the same if the employee had purchased the lock?

3. Are drug and alcohol tests required for shipping companies such as Federal Express or UPS?

4. Do random drug tests of air traffic controllers constitute an invasion of privacy? Why or why not? Would the same be true for office personnel?

5. A security company requires that all applicants submit to a polygraph test. Is this an invasion of the applicants' right to privacy? If the same applicants apply for a security position at a department store, could they be required to submit to a polygraph test?

6. The district office of a federal agency discloses information from an employee's personnel file to a third party without the employee's knowledge or consent. Does this disclosure violate any federal rules or statutes? If so, which rule or statute?

7. An employer discloses to the potential employer of a former employee that the employee had filed two workers' compensation claims and one claim of sexual harassment. Does this action violate the former employee's right to privacy?

8. A bank requests a credit report on an applicant for a teller position. Does this violate the former employee's right to privacy?

9. If the bank had notified the applicant in question 8 that it would request a credit report, would your answer be the same?

10. A production worker in a clothing manufacturing plant is terminated for inflating her production numbers. The worker is paid by the number of pieces of

clothing she completes in a day. Her supervisor discloses to her coworkers the reason for her discharge in an attempt to discourage other employees from inflating production. Is this a violation of the discharged worker's right to privacy?

PROJECTS

1. Draft a drug testing policy for your company or firm.

2. Research recent cases in your state to determine the state courts' position on the use of polygraph tests in the workforce. Prepare an outline of the courts' findings in those cases.

CHAPTER 16

Immigration

OVERVIEW

Few restrictions were applied to U.S. employers who hired illegal aliens or other undocumented workers prior to the enactment of the **Immigration Reform and Control Act of 1986** (IRCA), later amended by the Immigration and Nationality Act of 1990. The IRCA and all subsequent amendments require that an employer inquire into the citizenship or residence status of all job applicants. Generally, every person born or naturalized in the U.S. and subject to its jurisdiction is a citizen. All other individuals are either resident or nonresident aliens. The IRCA, in conjunction with other statutes such as the Federal Migrant and Seasonal Agricultural Worker Protection Act, applies to all employers, including those that hire domestic help or farm laborers. The Federal Migrant Worker Act also requires employers to make a bona fide inquiry into the citizenship or residence status of every job applicant.

The **Immigration and Nationality Act of 1990** significantly expanded visa availability for persons seeking to enter the United States for employment. Under this Act, 40,000 visas are available for "priority workers." Forty thousand visas are available for professional aliens with advanced degrees, or aliens with exceptional abilities in the sciences, arts, or business. Forty thousand visas are available for "skilled workers, professionals and other workers" who are capable of performing skilled labor for which qualified workers are not available in the United States. The "professional" alien is one with a baccalaureate degree. A certification from the secretary of labor is required to indicate that employer demand is not satisfied by a sufficient number of qualified workers in the United States for the category of work the applicant desires.

Under the Immigration Act of 1990, ten thousand visas are available for aliens intending to invest at least $1 million in new commercial enterprise. The enterprise must create full-time employment for at least 10 U.S. citizens or lawfully admitted aliens who have work permits. Three thousand of those types of visas are targeted for areas of high unemployment.

Total immigration is limited to 675,000.

The **Illegal Immigration and Responsibility Act of 1996** significantly restricted immigration and increased penalties by granting incentives for individual states to develop counterfeit-resistant driver's licenses and birth certificates that could be used in employment verification systems. Congress also established voluntary pilot programs to enhance the ability of employers to confirm the employment eligibility of new workers.

The IRCA offers legal documented status to aliens who illegally entered the United States prior to January 1, 1982, and have continuously resided here since then. Any dishonest reporting of alien status may result in a $2,000 fine against the individual who made the dishonest reporting and a maximum of five years in prison.

ADMINISTRATION OF IMMIGRATION LAWS

The Immigration and Naturalization Service (INS), a component of the United States Department of Justice, administers immigration laws and has been delegated authority that was statutorily vested in the Attorney General. In many cases, the INS must consult with the United States Department of Labor or the United States Department of State before making decisions on admitting certain classes of aliens.

The INS is organized into district offices that are authorized to handle applications and petitions and commencement of exclusion and deportation hearings, regional offices and regional service centers. Administrative appeals are handled by the appeals unit in the INS central office in Washington D.C. and by the Board of Immigration Appeals (BIA), located in Falls Church, Virginia. The five members of the BIA sit in three-person panels to decide immigration appeals.

Three separate governmental entities oversee the immigration process. The Department of Labor conducts inspections during its standard visits to employers to ensure compliance with EEOC and wage and hour laws. The National Labor Relations Board is charged with investigating and prosecuting unfair labor practices. The Department of Justice, through the office of the Attorney General, decides controversies relating to legalization of alien workers and establishes the procedures that the INS and DOL enforce during their investigations. The secretary of labor deals with certifications of foreign seasonal agricultural workers

EMPLOYERS' DUTIES REGARDING ALIEN EMPLOYMENT

The IRCA makes it unlawful to "knowingly" hire, recruit, refer for a fee, or continue to employ any alien not authorized to work in the United States. An employer can be charged with "knowledge" on the basis of indirect and/or circumstantial evidence. An **authorized alien** is an alien either lawfully admitted for permanent residence or authorized for employment.

A "grandfather" clause in the IRCA eliminates the need to complete any paperwork for a certain class of employee if that person was already employed on November 6, 1986 and has remained "continuously" employed. This provision does not apply to independent contractors or domestic labor employed at home on an irregular or intermittent basis.

The Immigration and Nationality Act of 1990 contains six conditions that impact an employer:

1. Employers cannot request more or different documents than are required under the new antidiscrimination provision of the Act. An employer must see *only one of the documents* from List A or one document each from Lists B and C reflected on Figure 16-1. Note that birth certificates have been removed from the list of approved verification documents. The INS has developed a new employment authorization form (I-766) with better quality controls, such as holograms and specific information about the authorized alien. This new form should help employers determine if the document is genuine. The I-766 will eventually replace the I-688A and I-688B forms and may be used by employers for employment eligibility verification requirements on the I-9 form as a "List A" document.

2. Employers cannot knowingly use, attempt to use, possess, obtain, accept, or receive any forged, altered, counterfeit, or falsely made documents that are covered under the new fraud conditions.

3. Employers cannot backdate or otherwise falsely make a Form I-9 appear as if it meets the requirements of the IRCA.

4. Employers must require that all new employees complete section 1 of Form I-9 at the time the employee is hired by filling in the correct information, signing, and dating the form.

5. Employers are responsible for reviewing and ensuring that the employees fully and properly complete section 1 of Form I-9.

6. Employers must examine the original document(s) presented by the employee and then fully complete section 2 of I-9. Employers are required

Please read instructions carefully before completing this form. The instructions must be available during completion of this form. **ANTI-DISCRIMINATION NOTICE. It is illegal to discriminate against work eligible individuals.** Employers CANNOT specify which document(s) they will accept from an employee. The refusal to hire an individual because of a future expiration date may also constitute illegal discrimination.

Section 1. Employee Information and Verification. To be completed and signed by employee at the time employment begins

Print Name: Last	First	Middle Initial	Maiden Name
Address *(Street Name and Number)*		Apt. #	Date of Birth *(month/day/year)*
City	State	Zip Code	Social Security #

I am aware that federal law provides for imprisonment and/or fines for false statements or use of false documents in connection with the completion of this form.	I attest, under penalty of perjury, that I am (check one of the following): ❑ A citizen or national of the United States ❑ A Lawful Permanent Resident (Alien # A _____ ❑ An alien authorized to work until _____/_____/_____
Employee's Signature	Date *(month/day/year)*

Preparer and/or Translator Certification. *(To be completed and signed if Section 1 is prepared by a person other than the employee.) I attest, under penalty of perjury, that I have assisted in the completion of this form and that to the best of my knowledge the information is true and correct.*

Preparer's/Translator's Signature	Print Name
Address *(Street Name and Number, City, State, Zip Code)*	Date *(month/day/year)*

Section 2. Employer Review and Verification. To be completed and signed by employer. **Examine one document from List A OR examine one document from List B and one from List C** as listed on the reverse of this form and record the title, number and expiration date, if any, of the document(s)

List A	OR	List B	AND	List C
Document title: _____		_____		_____
Issuing authority: _____		_____		_____
Document #: _____		_____		_____
Expiration Date *(if any):* ___/___/___		___/___/___		___/___/___
Document #: _____				
Expiration Date *(if any):* ___/___/___				

CERTIFICATION - I attest, under penalty of perjury, that I have examined the document(s) presented by the above-named employee, that the above-listed document(s) appear to be genuine and to relate to the employee named, that the employee began employment on *(month/day/year)* ___/___/___ **and that to the best of my knowledge the employee is eligible to work in the United States.** (State employment agencies may omit the date the employee began employment).

Signature of Employer or Authorized Representative	Print Name	Title
Business or Organization	Address *(Street Name and Number, City, State , Zip Code)*	Date *(month/day/year)*

Section 3. Updating and Reverification. To be completed and signed by employer

A. New Name *(if applicable)*	B. Date of rehire *(month/day/year) (if applicable)*

C. If employee's previous grant of work authorization has expired, provide the information below for the document that establishes current employment eligibility.

Document Title: _____ Document #: _____ Expiration Date (if any):___/___/___

I attest, under penalty of perjury, that to the best of my knowledge, this employee is eligible to work in the United States, and if the employee presented **document(s)**, the **document(s)** I have examined appear to be genuine and to relate to the individual.

Signature of Employer or Authorized Representative	Date *(month/day/year)*

Form I-9 (Rev. 11-21-91) N

Figure 16-1
United States Department of Justice Immigration and Naturalization Service Employment Eligibility Verification (Source: United States Department of Justice)

LISTS OF ACCEPTABLE DOCUMENTS

LIST A		LIST B		LIST C
Documents that Establish Both Identity and Employment Eligibility	**OR**	**Documents that Establish Identity**	**AND**	**Documents that Establish Employment Eligibility**

LIST A — Documents that Establish Both Identity and Employment Eligibility

1. U.S. Passport (unexpired or expired)

2. Certificate of U.S. Citizenship *(INS Form N-560 or N-561)*

3. Certificate of Naturalization *(INS Form N-550 or N-570)*

4. Unexpired foreign passport, with *I-551 stamp or* attached *INS Form I-94* indicating unexpired employment authorization

5. Alien Registration Receipt Card with photograph *(INS Form I-151 or I-551)*

6. Unexpired Temporary Resident Card *(INS Form I-688)*

7. Unexpired Employment Authorization Card *(INS Form I-688A)*

8. Unexpired Reentry Permit *(INS Form I-327)*

9. Unexpired Refugee Travel Document *(INS Form I-571)*

10. Unexpired Employment Authorization Document issued by the INS which contains a photograph *(INS Form-688B)*

LIST B — Documents that Establish Identity

1. Driver's license or ID card issued by a state or outlying possession of the United States provided it contains a photograph or information such as name, date of birth, sex, height, eye color, and address

2. ID card issued by federal, state, or local government agencies or entities provided it contains a photograph or information such as name, date of birth, sex, height, eye color, and address

3. School ID card with a photograph

4. Voter's registration card

5. U.S. Military card or draft record

6. Military dependent's ID card

7. U.S. Coast Guard Merchant Mariner Card

8. Native American tribal document

9. Driver's license issued by a Canadian government authority

For persons under age 18 who are unable to present a document listed above:

10. School record or report card

11. Clinic, doctor, or hospital record

12. Day-care or nursery school record

LIST C — Documents that Establish Employment Eligibility

1. U.S. social security card issued by the Social Security Administration *(other than a card stating it is not valid for employment)*

2. Certification of Birth Abroad issued by the Department of State *(Form FS-545 or Form DS-1350)*

3. Original or certified copy of a birth certificate issued by a state, county, municipal authority or outlying possession of the United States bearing an official seal

4. Native American tribal document

5. U.S. Citizen ID Card *(INS Form I-197)*

6. ID Card for use of Resident Citizen in the United States *(INS Form I-179)*

7. Unexpired employment authorization document issued by the INS *(other than those listed under list A)*

Illustrations of many of these documents appear in Part 8 of the Handbook for Employers (M-274)

Figure 16-1 *(continued)*

to maintain I-9 forms for three years after the date the employment begins or one-year after the termination, whichever is later.

The Immigration and Nationality Act contains two conditions that affect an employee:

1. Employees must present original documents to establish their identity and employment eligibility within three business days of the date that employment begins. However, employees must present the documents at the time of hire if they are hired for less than three business days.
2. Employees must indicate, by checking an appropriate box in section 1 of I-9, that they are already eligible for employment in the U.S. and must present I-9 and acceptable documents within three business days of employment. If employees are unable to produce the required documents within three business days, they must produce a receipt showing that they have applied for the document and must present the original document within 90 days of hire. However, employees hired for less than three business days must produce the actual document at the time that employment begins.

The employer is not required to verify the *authenticity* of the documents presented. The 1990 amendments to the Act specifically state that an employer may be wrongfully discriminating against an applicant if it refuses to honor the documents presented, if those documents appear to be genuine on their face.

Employers may also use a telephone verification system to check out the applicant's alien registration number that is found on Form I-551, the alien registration receipt card, commonly referred to as a "Green Card." (See Figure 16-2) Forms I-551 issued between 1977 and 1989 are valid indefinitely. Green cards issued after August 1989 are valid for 10 years.

INDEPENDENT CONTRACTORS

Form I-9 is not required for individuals who are independent contractors. The INS has a more strict definition of independent contractor than the IRS definition. For example, an independent contractor for federal tax purposes may be considered an employee for employment eligibility verification purposes.

NORTH AMERICAN FREE TRADE AGREEMENT (NAFTA)

Public Law 103-182, enacted December 8, 1993, superseded the United States-Canada Trade Agreement as of January 1, 1994. NAFTA continues the special

OMB #1115-0004

Application to Replace Permanent Resident Card

START HERE - Please Type or Print

Part 1. Information about you.

Family Name	Given Name	Middle Initial

U.S. Mailing Address - C/O

Street Number and Name		Apt. #
City		

State	ZIP Code

Date of Birth (Month/Day/Year)	Country of Birth

Social Security #	A #

Part 2. Application type.

1. My status is: (check one)

  a. ☐ Permanent Resident - (Not a Commuter)

  b. ☐ Permanent Resident - (Commuter)

  c. ☐ Conditional Permanent Resident

2. Reason for application: (check one)

I am a Permanent Resident or Conditional Permanent Resident and:

  a. ☐ my card was lost, stolen, or destroyed. I have attached a copy of an identity document.

  b. ☐ my authorized card was never received. I have attached a copy of an identity document.

  c. ☐ my card is mutilated. I have attached the mutilated card.

  d. ☐ my card was issued with incorrect information because of INS administrative error. I have attached the incorrect card and evidence of the correct information.

  e. ☐ my name or other biographic information has changed since the card was issued. I have attached my present card and evidence of the new information.

I am a Permanent Resident and:

  f. ☐ my present card has an expiration date and it is expiring.

  g. ☐ I have reached my 14th birthday since my card was issued. I have attached my present card.

  h. 1. ☐ I have taken up Commuter status. I have attached my present card and evidence of my foreign residence.

  h. 2. ☐ I was a Commuter and am now taking up residence in the U.S. I have attached my present card and evidence of my residence in the U.S.

  i. ☐ my status has been automatically converted to permanent resident. I have attached my Temporary Status Document.

  j. ☐ I have an old edition of the card.

Part 3. Processing information.

Mother's First Name	Father's First Name
City of Residence where you applied for an Immigrant Visa or Adjustment of Status	Consulate where Immigrant Visa was issued or INS office where status was Adjusted
City/Town/Village of Birth	Date of Admission as an immigrant or Adjustment of Status

Continued on back.

FOR INS USE ONLY

Returned	Receipt

Resubmitted

Reloc Sent

Reloc Rec'd

☐ Applicant Interviewed

Status as _____ Verified by _____

Class _____ Initials _____

FD-258 forwarded on _____

I-89 forwarded on _____

I-551 seen and returned _____
                         (Initials)

Photocopy of I-551 verified _____
                         (Initials)

Name	Date

Sticker # _____
            (ten-digit number)

Action Block

To Be Completed by
***Attorney or Representative**, if any*

☐ Fill in box if G-28 is attached to represent the applicant

VOLAG#

ATTY State License #

Form I-90 (Rev. 10/08/99)N

Figure 16-2

United States Department of Justice Immigration and Naturalization Service Application to Replace Permanent Resident Card (Source: United States Department of Justice)

Part 3. Processing information (continued):

If you entered the U.S. with an Immigrant Visa, also complete the following:

Destination in U.S. at time of Admission	Port of Entry where Admitted to U.S.

Are you in deportation or exclusion proceedings? ☐ No ☐ Yes

Since you were granted permanent residence, have you ever filed Form I-407, Abandonment by Alien of Status as Lawful Permanent Resident, or otherwise been judged to have abandoned your status? ☐ No ☐ Yes

If you answer yes to any of the above questions, explain in detail on a separate piece of paper.

Part 4. Signature. *(Read the information on penalties in the instructions before completing this section. You must file this application while in the United States.)*

I certify under penalty of perjury under the laws of the United States of America that this application, and the evidence submitted with it, is all true and correct. I authorize the release of any information from my records which the Immigration and Naturalization Service needs to determine eligibility for the benefit I am seeking.

Signature	Date	Daytime Phone Number

Please Note: If you do not completely fill out this form, or fail to submit required documents listed in the instructions, you cannot be found eligible for the requested document and this application may be denied.

Part 5. Signature of person preparing form, if other than above. *(Sign below)*

I declare that I prepared this application at the request of the above person and it is based on all information of which I have knowledge.

Signature	Print Your Name	Date	Daytime Phone Number

Name and Address of Business/Organization (if applicable)

Figure 16-2 (*continued*)

reciprocal trading relationship between the United States and Canada and establishes a similar relationship with Mexico. NAFTA permits Canadians to enter the United States as visitors for business or pleasure without first obtaining a visa. Mexican applicants must still obtain a visa or use a Border Crossing Card. Individuals who are business visitors engaging in legitimate business activities of a commercial or professional nature are comparable to the business visitor (B-1) discussed in this chapter. The business activities must be necessary to international trade or commerce.

SANCTIONS

An employer must have *knowledge* that the employee is an illegal alien before the employer can be held liable under IRCA. Since the Act imposes on the employer the duty to verity the legal employment status of all employees, failure to correctly verify that status may subject the employer to liability. The rule that establishes this requirement of knowledge suggests that *knowing* "includes not only actual knowledge, but also knowledge which may be inferred through notice of certain facts and circumstances which would lead a person, through the exercise of reasonable care, to know about a certain condition."

Violations for "knowingly" employing an illegal alien result in three escalating levels of fines:

1. For a first violation, a civil fine of at least $250 and up to $2,000 for each unauthorized alien will be levied.
2. For a second violation, fines increase to a minimum of $2,000 and up to $5,000 for each unauthorized alien.
3. For any subsequent violation, fines increase to a minimum of $3,000 and up to $10,000 for each unauthorized alien.

The IRCA also provides for **criminal sanctions**. An employer found guilty of engaging in a "pattern or practice" of "knowingly" hiring illegal aliens is subject to a criminal penalty of up to $3,000 for each unauthorized alien employed and/or six months in prison.

Additional civil penalties from $100 to $1,000 may be assessed against employers who do not follow IRCA's document verification and recordkeeping requirements for each employee for whom the I-9 was not properly completed, retained, or made available for inspection, regardless of the employee's legal status. Additionally, the employee within the company who is responsible for checking and maintaining documentation may be liable.

RECORDKEEPING REQUIREMENTS

Completed and signed I-9 forms must be retained for three years after the date of hire or one year after termination of employment, whichever is later. An employer may use an employee's same I-9 for rehire purposes up to three years after the date of initial hire if that individual "remains authorized to work." That rule also applies to the rehiring of a former employee within one year of termination. Documents should be retained in separate files (NOT AS PART OF A PERSONNEL FILE) in order to avoid possible claims of discrimination or other legal problems.

Employers are not required to retain copies of employees' identification documents. However, if copies are kept, the retention should be done consistently for all employees and should be filed with the I-9 form.

ANTIDISCRIMINATION PROVISIONS

Section 102 of the IRCA prohibits employers of four or more employees from discriminating against employees on the basis of their "citizenship or intended citizenship," and from hiring those not legally authorized for employment in the United States. However, the IRCA permits a preference for U.S. citizens over legal aliens, and both citizens and legal aliens have an evident preference over "unauthorized" or illegal aliens.

Certain rights are available to citizens and legal aliens through the Fair Labor Standards Act and the National Labor Relations Act. However, government benefits, such as Medicare and Medicaid are available only to citizens.

Unlike Title VII, the Department of Justice's rules stipulate that *intent* to discriminate and knowledge are required to find liability for an employer's violation of section 102. Because of this intent requirement, IRCA claims are considered to be applicable to disparate treatment cases, but not disparate impact cases, discussed in Chapter 7.

Two complete defenses to discrimination claims under the IRCA are innocent or negligent discrimination.

In the case of a discrimination claim under the IRCA, the employer may identify a bona fide occupational qualification (BFOQ) that disqualified the employee or applicant from the employment benefit. Two statutory BFOQ defenses are granted by the IRCA:

1. English-language skill requirements that are reasonably necessary to the normal operation of the particular business or enterprise.
2. Citizenship requirements specified by law, regulation, executive order, or government contracts, along with citizenship requirements that the attorney general determines to be essential for doing business with the government.

Discrimination by employers in order to avoid sanctions is prohibited. Such prohibited discrimination includes the refusal to hire anyone who appears to be foreign. Civil penalties include:

- For a first violation, a civil fine of at least $250 and up to $2,000 for each individual who was discriminated against
- For a second violation, fines of a minimum of $2,000 and a maximum of $5,000 for each individual who was discriminated against
- For any subsequent violation, fines of a minimum of $3,000 and a maximum of $10,000 for each individual who was discriminated against

- Orders to hire or reinstate
- Posting of notices in the workplace stating that the employer will not engage in specified violations of IRCA in the future
- Back pay and additional paperwork requirements

The IRCA created the Office of Special Counsel (OSC) in the Department of Justice to receive, process, and investigate discrimination complaints of "unfair immigration-related employment practices."

NONIMMIGRANT BUSINESS VISAS

Aliens may be admitted to the United States as **nonimmigrants** under regulations prescribed by the attorney general. **Nonimmigrant business visas** allow foreign nationals to enter the United States to work, study and/or train on a nonimmigrant basis. Visas granted in the categories listed below are employer-sponsored and limit work authorizations only to the sponsoring employer.

B-CATEGORY VISAS

B-1 and B-2 visas are nonimmigrant visas available to aliens who have a residence in a foreign country that they have no intention of abandoning, and who are visiting the United States for either business (B-1) or for pleasure (B-2). The B-2 is generally referred to as a "tourist visa." Holders of the B-2 visa may not be employed by any employer under any circumstances. A B-1 business visitor may only perform work on behalf of his foreign employer, and must remain on that foreign payroll at all times.

E-CATEGORY VISAS

The E-1 ("international trader") and E-2 ("international treaty investor") categories of visas are available to companies seeking to trade with or invest in the United States. **E-category visas** permit those enterprises to transfer aliens to the United States for substantial periods of time to oversee trade or investments.

F- AND M-CATEGORY VISAS

F and **M visas** permit aliens to enter the United States as nonimmigrants to pursue academic studies. The F visa covers students in elementary, college, or graduate schools; the M category covers those students in nonacademic or vocational programs.

H-CATEGORY VISAS

An **H-1B visa** is available to professional individuals with baccalaureate or other advanced degrees, such as engineers, scientists, chemists, and registered nurses. The H-1 is normally valid for a period of up to three years, and may be extended up to a maximum of five years. A United States employer must sponsor the alien.

H-2B visas are available for skilled and unskilled temporary employees who do not qualify for an H-1 visa. This category of immigrant is coming to the United States to perform temporary services of labor "if unemployed persons capable of performing such services or labor cannot be found in this country." Generally H-2B visas are issued for a period of one year; one-year increment extensions may be granted, not to exceed a total of three years. This type of visa is also employer sponsored. In addition, H-2B visa holders must obtain a "labor certification" from the United States Department of Labor. Employers are liable for return transportation costs if H-1B or H-2B aliens are dismissed before the end of their period of authorization.

The **H-3B visa** is available to aliens who have a residence in a foreign country that they have no intention of abandoning and who come to the United States as a trainee. This employer-sponsored visa is normally approved for a maximum period of one year, with a single extension of six months upon showing good cause. H-3 visa holders must be in the United States for the sole purpose of training, and cannot have productive employment.

L-CATEGORY VISAS

The **L visa** is generally limited to high-level managers, executives, or persons with highly specialized knowledge of a company's product or manufacturing process. The holder of such a visa must have been continuously employed for one year by a company, an affiliate, or subsidiary, and must temporarily come to the United States to render his services to that same employer, subsidiary, or affiliate. L-visas are employer-sponsored and are generally granted initially for three years, with extensions between five and seven years. The L-1 visa holder may only work for the sponsoring company.

O-CATEGORY VISAS

An **O visa** is available to aliens with extraordinary ability in the sciences, arts, education, business, or athletes, or aliens seeking solely to participate in specialized artistic or athletic performances. The "event" for which O-1 and O-2 visas are granted might include lecture series, tours, business projects, or academic year.

P-CATEGORY VISAS

The **P visa** is available for artists and entertainers. P-1 and P-2 visas are available for athletes and artists who are coming to the United States to perform in a specific athletic competition, or for specific entertainment functions or as part of an exchange program. P-3 classifications are available for aliens coming to the United States for the purpose of developing, interpreting, representing, coaching, or teaching a unique or traditional ethnic, folk, cultural, musical, theatrical, or artistic performance or presentation.

Q-CATEGORY VISAS

The **Q visa** is available for international cultural exchange visitors for up to 15 months. The program for Q status visitors must include cultural components related to explaining to the American public the attitude, customs, heritage, history, philosophy, or traditions of the visitor's country of nationality.

TN-CATEGORY VISAS

The **TN visa** permits an expedited entry to the United States for professionals through an on-the-spot determination of eligibility at the border. This type of visa is issued under the North American Free Trade Agreement (NAFTA) between the alien's country (Mexico or Canada) and the United States. Persons in this category may be employed only by the sponsoring employer.

DERIVATIVE VISAS

Derivative visas are granted to the immediate family members (spouse and minor children) of aliens who have been classified as nonimmigrant visa holders in other categories of visas. Persons holding derivative visas are not permitted employment while in the United States until they have obtained employment visas of their own.

PERMANENT RESIDENT VISAS

Employers desiring to employ outstanding professors and researchers, certain multinational executives and managers, skilled workers, professionals, advanced-degree professionals, or aliens of exceptional ability may petition the Attorney General for a **permanent resident visa**. Any person, including the alien himself, may petition for (b)(1)(a) status (aliens with extraordinary ability) or (b)(4) status (special immigrants).

The attorney general must investigate the facts of the *Petition for Immigrant Worker* (Immigration Form I-140) and consult with the secretary of labor with respect to professional aliens who possess advanced degrees, aliens of exceptional ability, skilled workers, or professionals. Once the attorney general approves the petition, he or she forwards the approved petition to the Department of State, and the secretary of state is obligated to authorize the consular office to grant the preference status.

CITIZENSHIP APPLICATION

Applicants for naturalization must be at least 18 years old and must have been lawfully admitted to the United States for permanent residence. Individuals who have been lawfully admitted as permanent residents must be able to produce an I-551, *Alien Registration Receipt Card*, as proof of their status. In addition, an applicant must have resided continuously as a lawful, permanent resident in the United States for at least five years prior to filing, with absences from the United States totaling no more than one year; and have been physically present in the United States for at least 30 months out of the previous five years. Absences of more than six months but less than one year break the continuity of residence, unless the applicant can establish that he or she did not abandon his or her residence during such period. The applicant must also have resided within a state or district for at least three months.

Generally, an applicant must show that he or she has been a person of good moral character for the statutory period (five years, or three years if married to a U.S. citizen, or one year for armed forces personnel), prior to filing for naturalization. The INS is not limited to this statutory period in determining whether an applicant has established good moral character. An applicant is permanently barred from naturalization if he or she has ever been convicted of murder or an aggravated felony. A person cannot be found to be of good moral character if during the past five years he or she:

- Has committed and been convicted of one or more crimes involving moral turpitude.
- Has committed and been convicted of two or more offenses for which the total sentence imposed was five years or more.
- Has committed and been convicted of any controlled substance law, except for a single offense of simple possession of 30 grams or less of marijuana.

- Has been confined to a penal institution during the statutory period, as a result of a conviction, for an aggregate period of 180 days or more.
- Has committed and been convicted of two or more gambling offenses.
- Earns or has earned his or her principal income from illegal gambling.
- Is involved or has been involved in prostitution or commercial vice.
- Is or has been involved in smuggling illegal aliens into the United States.
- Is now or has been a habitual drunkard.
- Is now practicing or has practiced polygamy.
- Has willfully failed to or refused to support dependents.
- Has given false testimony under oath in order to receive a benefit under the Immigration and Naturalization Act.

IMMIGRATION FORMS AND INFORMATION

The Form I-9 may be obtained in limited quantities at the INS district offices, or ordered from the Superintendent of Documents, USGPO, Washington, DC 20402. Forms may also be requested by calling (800) 870–3676 or by accessing the Internet at http://www.ins.usdoj.gov/forms/I-9.htm.

For more information about immigration generally, contact an INS district office or call the INS employer information service at (800) 255-8155, (800) 755-0777, or (800) 375-5283. Employers may also wish to obtain booklet M-274, *Handbook for Employers*, which is available from the INS or the Superintendent of Documents at the address listed above. Further information can also be obtained from the INS Web site: www.ins.usdoj.gov/index.html.

TERMS

B-1 and B-2 visa
derivative visas
E-category visa
F and M visas
H-1B visa
H-2B visa
H-3B visa
Illegal Immigration and Responsibility Act of 1996
Immigration Act of 1965
Immigration Act of 1990
Immigration and Nationalization Act of 1952

Immigration Reform and Control Act of 1986
L visa
nonimmigrant business visa
O visa
P visa
permanent resident visa
Q visa
TN visa
Tourist visa

REVIEW QUESTIONS

1. Assume that a governmental agency has a regulation that prohibited the employment of temporary resident aliens. Is this a violation of the IRCA?

2. A large grocery store received a citation from the INS for over 100 instances of recordkeeping violations, mainly involving failure to maintain I-9s, and was fined. The company has made an attempt to correct those violations, but the INS found that, because of clerical errors, a large number of violations remained. The grocery store was given additional fines. Will the grocery store's opposition to the additional fines be successful? Explain.

3. Can an undocumented alien expect to receive the minimum wage provided by the FLSA? Why or why not?

4. An employer has heard rumors that a valued ranch employee is not authorized to work in the United States. He has no direct evidence that the rumor is true, and elects to allow the employee to continue to work. Is the employer susceptible to a penalty for his action (or inaction) based on no direct evidence about this employee?

5. Assume that an applicant does not present a Social Security card to his employer within the required three-day period after his employment. Can the employee continue to work? Under what circumstances, and for how long?

6. An employee who has completed an I-9 quits his job after eight months. A year later, the individual asks to return to his old position. Is the employer required to obtain another I-9?

7. An employer interviews both a U.S. citizen and a legal alien for a position, but hires the U.S. citizen because of his "preference" for hiring citizens over legal aliens. Is this preference a violation of the IRCA?

8. Discuss why IRCA claims are considered to be applicable to disparate treatment cases, but not disparate impact cases.

9. Explain the requirements for citizenship.

10. List five incidents that would prohibit an applicant for citizenship from obtaining citizenship, if those incidents occurred within five years prior to the citizenship application.

PROJECTS

1. Assume that a client has contacted your attorney for advice on the procedure that he or she must follow to enable a nanny from Sweden to work in the client's home for a year. Research the type of documents that will be needed, the type of visa that must be requested, and the steps that must be followed to obtain the visa. Draft a memorandum to your attorney detailing the results of your research.

2. Research through the Internet the background facts for President Clinton and President George W. Bush's recommendations for cabinet positions who withdrew prior to Senate confirmation because of personal issues relating to immigration laws. List the possible immigration violations for each of those designated appointees.

CHAPTER 17

Safety Regulations in Employment

OVERVIEW

Prior to 1970, when President Richard Nixon signed the Occupational Safety and Health Act (OSHA) into law, employers were required by common law to provide a safe place for employees to work. The requirement was weakened, however, by three strong common law defenses: contributory negligence, assumption of risk, and the fellow servant rule. Consequently, employers evaded liability in connection with the majority of industrial accidents. Employer responsibility generally was limited to the requirements of state workers' compensation regulations.

Contributory negligence is defined by *Oran's Law Dictionary* as "negligent (careless) conduct by a person who was harmed by another person's negligence; a plaintiff's failure to be careful that is a part of his or her injury when the defendant's failure to be careful is also part of the cause."

Assumption of risk is knowingly and willingly exposing yourself (or your property) to the possibility of harm. This defense prevents the employee from recovering when the employee knows of a risk in the workplace and chooses to take a chance on not being injured, but who is subsequently injured.

The **fellow servant rule** is a rule, abolished in most states by employers' liability acts, that an employer is not responsible for the injury one employee does to another employee if the employees were carefully chosen.

Most states' occupational safety and health laws prior to 1970 were not consistently and completely enforced. Workplace injury compensation was limited to recovery provided for by state workers' compensation statutes. Unfortunately, workers' compensation statutes, as discussed below, normally limit recovery to medical expenses and a portion of lost wages.

In an effort to assure consistently safe and healthy working conditions for all employees, section 5(a) of OSHA imposes the following duties for employers:

§ 654(§5) Duties
    (a) Each employer
        (1) shall furnish to each of his employees employment and a place of employment which are free from recognized hazards that are causing or are likely to cause death or serious physical harm to his employees;
        (2) shall comply with occupational safety and health standards promulgated under this Act.

The major focus of OSHA was to encourage a cooperative effort among employers, the government, and labor unions in identifying both the causes of illnesses and injuries and corrective means, and to achieve OSHA compliance through provisions for inspections and penalties.

In an attempt to determine what standards to apply in OSHA case, the Act provided for the creation of the National Institute for Occupational Safety and Health (NIOSH) to serve as a research arm of OSHA. NIOSH recommendations regarding workplace health and safety are forwarded to the secretary of labor. If NIOSH's recommendations are approved, those recommendations then may become the standards of conduct in connection with a particular industry.

Workers' compensation is regulated at the state level. The purpose of workers' compensation is to require the employer to provide coverage for compensation and medical expenses for employees, regardless of fault, for work-related injuries or illness. In return, the employer who has workers' compensation coverage cannot be sued under a negligence tort claim.

In the majority of states, workers' compensation is mandatory for employers, with the exception of very small employers, agricultural workers, and domestic employees. All states require that an employer have either workers' compensation insurance, be self-insured, or participate in a state fund. Failure to obtain insurance, or be qualified to obtain insurance, or be qualified as a self-insurer is a crime, and may result in penalties ranging from substantial fines to prison time, or both. In addition, an employee who is hurt on the job and whose employer does not have workers' compensation insurance may sue under common law. In that case, the typical defenses—assumption of risk, contributory negligence, reckless behavior, failure to use provided safety equipment or techniques—are not available to the employer. Also, the claims and awards under common law, such as negligent infliction of emotional distress and punitive damages, may go beyond the benefits that workers' compensation provides.

Self-insurance results in cost savings, generally, but there is an inherent risk involved. For example, a medium-size company might save $70,000 by being self-insured, but several large claims quickly eradicate the savings.

Independent contractors are not covered by the contractor's workers' compensation insurance. Merely labeling a worker as an "independent contractor" does not automatically disqualify that worker from employee status for workers' compensation purpose if the "employer" controls the individual's work and give direction to the worker. Additionally, a contractor can be liable for workers' compensation benefits for subcontractors' employees if the subcontractor fails to obtain workers' compensation insurance.

Appendix A is a listing of the state workers' compensation administrations and commissions. Each of these offices will answer questions and provide forms to facilitate the filing of workers' compensation claims.

OSHA COVERAGE

OSHA covers all nonpublic employers who employ one or more persons full or part-time, permanent or temporary. All employees, including executives and managers, are protected by OSHA.

EMPLOYEES' RIGHTS UNDER OSHA

The Act affords certain rights to employees, including requesting and participating in inspections, notice of an employer's violations or citations, access to monitoring procedures and results, and access to medical information. These rights are identified and summarized on OSHA Poster No. 2203. Employees must be informed of their OSHA rights by their employer, but the employer is not required to post OSHA Poster No. 2203.

EMPLOYER REQUIREMENTS UNDER OSHA

General OSHA requirements for employers include:

- Furnish employment and places of employment that are free of recognized hazards that are causing, or possibly might cause, death or serious injury, but are not covered by specific OSHA standards.
- Adhere to all standards and regulations set or adopted by the U.S. Department

of Labor Occupational Health and Safety Administration (DOL-OSHA) or its state counterparts.

- Maintain records of work-related injuries and illnesses and report to OSHA within eight hours any workplace death or events resulting in hospitalization of three or more employee.
- Permit employees to exercise their rights under the act, without coercion, harassment, or discrimination.
- Comply with hazard abatement orders issued by OSHA or a state agency.

GENERAL DUTY CLAUSE

The **general duty clause** of OSHA is a provision requiring that employer furnish to each employee employment and a place of employment free from recognized hazards that cause or are likely to cause death or serious physical harm to the employee. A key to this obligation is "hazard recognition," as a hazard may be recognized if the existence and means of correction are known in the employer's industry, even if the particular employer was not aware of that hazard.

REPORTING REQUIREMENTS

OSHA sets out the following requirements for each covered employer with 11 or fewer employees (with the exception of certain industries, including banking):

- Maintain a log (DOL-OSHA Form 200, Figure 17-1) of workplace injuries resulting in death, lost time, restrict work capability, and/or medical treatment or illness.
- Incidents must be reported on Form 200 as long as the incident involves an illness, a death, or an injury that involves medical treatment, loss of consciousness, restriction of work or motion, or transfer to a different position. The incident is considered to be work-related if it occurred on the employer's premises, occurred as a result of work-related activities, the employee was required to be there by the employer, or the employee was traveling to work or to a place he or she was required to be by the employer. While the use of Form 200 is not mandatory, posting the information contained in the form is mandatory. It is necessary to post the information contained in the 200 log even if there were no employee injuries or illnesses within the past year.
- Complete a supplement report (DOL-OSHA Form 101, Figure 17-2) of each such illness or injury within six days of an incident reported on Form 200.

OSHA Form 200

U.S. Department of Labor

For Calendar Year 20____					Page ____ of ____				
Company Name			Form Approved						
Establishment Name			O.M.B. No. 1220-0029						
Establishment Address									
Extent of and Outcome of INJURY			Type, Extent of, and Outcome of ILLNESS						
Fatalities	Nonfatal Injuries		Type of Illness			Fatalities	Nonfatal Illness		
Injury Related			Injuries With Lost Workdays			Injuries Without Lost Workdays			

CHECK Only One Column for Each Illness (*See other side of form for terminations or permanent transfers.*) — Illness Related Illnesses With Lost

Workdays   Illnesses Without Lost Workdays

Enter DATE of death. Mo./day/yr.	Enter a CHECK if injury involves days away from work, or days of restricted work activity, or both.	Enter a
CHECK if injury involves days away from work.	Enter number of DAYS *away from work.* Enter number of DAYS of *restricted work activity.*	Enter a

Columns (vertical headers):
- Occupational skin diseases or disorders
- Dust diseases of the lungs
- Respiratory conditions due to toxic agents
- Poisoning (systemic effects of toxic materials)
- Disorders due to physical agents

CHECK if no entry was made in columns 1 or 2 but the injury is re-cordable as defined above.

- All other occupational Illnesses

Enter DATE of death. Mo./day/yr.   Enter a CHECK if illness involves days away from work, or days of restricted work activity, or

both.   Enter a CHECK if illness involved days away from work.   Enter num-ber of DAYS *away from work.*   Enter number of DAYS of *re-stricted work*

activity.   Enter a CHECK if no entry was made in columns 8 or 9.

(1)	(2)	(3)	(4)	(5)	(6)	(7)								(8)	(9)	(10)		
	(11)	(12)	(13)															
						(a)	(b)	(c)	(d)	(e)	(f)	(g)						

Figure 17-1
OSHA Form 200

Certification of Annual Summary Totals By _____ Title _____

Date _____

OSHA No. 200   POST ONLY THIS PORTION OF THE LAST PAGE NO LATER THAN FEBRUARY 1.

Bureau of Labor Statistics Log and Summary of Occupational Injuries and Illnesses

NOTE: This form is required by Public Law 91-596 and must be kept in the establishment for *5 years.* Failure to maintain and post can result in the issuance of citations and assessments of penalties. *(See posting requirements on the other side of form.)* **RECORDABLE CASES:** You are required to record information about every occupational **death**, every nonfatal occupational **illness**, and those nonfatal occupational **injuries** which involve one or more of the following: loss of consciousness, restriction of work or motion, transfer to another job, or medical treatment (other than first aid). (*See definitions on the other side of form.*)

Case or File Number Enter a nondupli-cating number which will facilitate com-parisons with supple-mentary records. (A) **Date of Injury or Onset of Illness** Enter Mo./day. (B) **Employee's Name** Enter first name or initial, middle initial, last name. (C) **Occupation** Enter regular job title, not activity employee was performing when injured or at onset of illness. In the absence of a formal title, enter a brief description of the employee's duties. (D) **Department** Enter department in which the employee is regularly employed or a description of normal workplace to which employee is assigned, even thought temporarily working in another department at the time of the injury or illness (E) **Description of Injury or Illness** Enter a brief description of the injury or illness and indicate the part or parts of body affected. Typical entries for this column might be: Amputation of 1st joint right forefinger; Strain of lower back; Contact dermatitis on both hands; Electrocution-body. (F)

				PREVIOUS PAGE TOTALS
				TOTALS (Instructions on

other side of form)

Figure 17-1 (*continued*)

U.S. Department of Labor

Bureau of Labor Statistics

Supplementary Record of

Occupational Injuries and Illnesses

This form is required by Public Law 91-506 and must be kept in the establishment for *5 years*. Failure to maintain can result in the issuance of citations and assessment of penalties.

Approved O.M.B. No. 1220 0029

Case or File No. _____ Form _____

Employer

1. Name

2. Mail address (*No. and street, city or town, State, and zip code*)

3. Location, if different from mail address

Injured or Ill Employee

4. Name (*First, middle, and last*)   ·

Social Security No.

5. Home Address (*No. and street, city or town, State, and zip code*)

6. Age

7. Sex: (*Check one*)

Male ☐   Female ☐

8. Occupation (*Enter regular job title, not the specific activity he was performing at time of injury.*)

9. Department (*Enter name of department or division in which the injured person is regularly employed, even though he may have been temporarily working in another department at the time of injury.*)

The Accident or Exposure to Occupational Illness

If accident or exposure occurred on employer's premises, give address of plant or establishment in which it occurred. Do not indicate department or division within the plant or establishment. If accident occurred outside employer's premises at an identifiable address, give that address. If it occurred on a public highway or at any other place which cannot be identified by number and street, please provide place references locating the place of injury as accurately as possible.

10. Place of accident or exposure (*No. and street, city or town, State, and zip code*)

11. Was place of accident or exposure on employer's premises?

Yes ☐   No ☐

12. What was the employee doing when injured? (*Be specific. If he was using tools or equipment or handling material, name them and tell what he was doing with them.*)

13. How did the accident occur? (*Describe fully the events which resulted in the injury or occupational illness. Tell*) what happened. Name any objects or substances involved and tell how they were involved. Give full details on all

factors which led or contributed to the accident. Use separate sheet for additional space.)

Occupational Injury or Occupational Illness

14. Describe the injury or illness in detail and indicate the part of body affected. (*E.g., amputation of right index finger at second joint; fracture of ribs; lead poisoning; dermatitis of left hand, etc.*)

15. Name the object or substance which directly injured the employee. (*For example, the machine or thing he struck against or which struck him; the vapor or poison he inhaled or swallowed; the chemical or radiation which irritated his skin; or in cases or strains, hernias, etc., the thing he was lifting, pulling, etc.*)

16. Date of injury or initial diagnosis of occupational illness

17. Did employee die? (*Check one*)

Yes ☐   No ☐

Other

18. Name and address of physician

19. If hospitalized, name and address of hospital

Date of Report

Prepared by

Official position

OSHA No. 101 (Feb. 1981)

Figure 17-2
Department of Labor OSHA Form 101

OSHA requires that this form be maintained for five years. Failure to maintain the form can result in the issuance of citations and assessment of penalties.

- Publish an annual summary of the log. The OSHA log must be conspicuously posted during the month of February following the calendar year. The log and any supplemental reports must be available for review by OSHA, the National Institute for Occupational Safety and Health (NIOSH), and employees.

ENFORCEMENT PROCEDURES

OSHA, under the auspices of the Department of Labor (DOL), is responsible for enforcing the Act. Enforcement procedures include workplace inspections by OSHA compliance officers as a result of employee complaints, grievances filed, or reports of multiple or fatal injuries. The Act protects employees who file complaints against retaliation charges by prohibiting an employer from discharging or discriminating against an employee who exercises a right provided by the Act.

Citations for violations of OSHA must be issued within six months after OHSA personnel knew, or reasonably should have known, of the violation. The citation should describe the nature of the violation, including the standard, regulation, or obligation violated, the degree and particular circumstances of the violation, the proposed penalty for the violation, and a date for correction of the hazard created by the violation. Any protest of the citation must occur within 15 working days after receipt, or the citation and penalty will be deemed final and the employer will no longer be able to challenge the citation.

PENALTIES FOR OSHA VIOLATIONS

Penalties for violation of OSHA requirements may include up to $7,000 per violation in the case of serious violations that could lead to serious injury or death, up to $7,000 per violation per day in the event of failure to correct or abate previously cited violations, and up to $70,000 per violation in the cases of "willful" or "repeated" violations.

The amount of penalty levied depends upon the following four factors:

1. The size of the employer.
2. The gravity of the violation (number of employees exposed to harm, frequency and duration of exposures, and potential for serious injury or death created by the violation).
3. The employer's prior history of OSHA violations.
4. The employer's "good faith" attitude toward compliance, measured by such factors as the quality of its overall safety programs, cooperation with OSHA

personnel, and diligence in correcting hazards disclosed through OSHA inspections, discussed below.

Employers are also subject to criminal prosecution under federal law for willful violations of standards that result in the death of an employee, or for making false statements to OSHA. In some cases employers, as well as individual employees, have been prosecuted under state criminal manslaughter or reckless endangerment laws.

OSHA does not penalize *employees* for violating OSHA standards. Employee compliance with OSHA is to be secured through lawful disciplinary action by employers to ensure that compliance with OSHA rules is a condition of employment.

INSPECTIONS AND INVESTIGATIONS

DOL-OSHA is authorized to conduct on-site inspections without advance notice, and to issue subpoenas for records or testimony to determine whether employers are in compliance with specific OSHA standards. A maximum fine of $1,000 may be imposed on any individual who gives unauthorized advance notice of the inspection. However, an employer may refuse to allow an inspector to conduct on-site inspections, and may stop an inspection at any time. In that case, OSHA must obtain an administrative search warrant from a court.

Administrative search warrants are generally limited to 30 days after issuance. Any employer who continues to refuse an inspection after receiving a search warrant faces contempt-of-court proceedings.

There are three phases to an OSHA inspection:

1. The opening conference;
2. The actual inspection; and
3. The closing conference.

ABATEMENT CERTIFICATION

OSHA regulations require that an employer certify to OSHA in writing, by affidavit or signed statement accompanied by documentation, that safety or health hazard violations listed in citations have been abated or corrected. An employer is required to submit the abatement certification no later than 10 days after the abatement date contained in the citation. In cases where the citation contains lengthy abatement dates, the employer may be required to submit an abatement plan and progress reports in the interim.

Employees are entitled to notice of the employer's actions regarding abatement.

EMPLOYER DEFENSES TO OSHA CITATIONS

An employer's defenses to citation include the following:

1. **Physical Impossibility of Compliance.** There are some OSHA standards where the employees believe that the burden of complying is greater than the danger prevented by the compliance.

2. **No violation or no health or safety hazard.** This defense maintains that the employer has not violated the standard or regulation listed in the citation, or that no hazard actually resulted from the violation, or the employer reasonably had no knowledge of the violation.

3. **"Greater Hazard" Defense.** Employers may contend that compliance with a health or safety standard would subject the employees to a greater hazard than that prevented by the compliance.

4. **De minimis Violation.** This type of violation is one that did not create a hazard, or did not directly compromise safety health conditions in the workplace, or was violated only in minor, technical ways by the employer who provided alternative protections equal to or greater than those provided by the standard. A de minimis violation carries no penalty.

5. **Vague or Ambiguous Standard; Improperly Communicated Standard; or Non-Mandatory Standard.** A standard may have been violated, but the wording was so vague or ambiguous that a reasonable person would not know the exact conduct that was prohibited, or the standard was not enforceable because of improper issuance, or the standard was merely a suggestion and not a directive.

6. **Employee Misconduct.** Noncompliance resulted from reasonably unanticipated employee failure to follow previously established work rules, or an employee acted in unpredictable fashion. Employers bear the burden of proving this defense.

7. **Citation Untimely Issued.** The citation was not issued within 180 days.

OBTAINING INFORMATION ABOUT OSHA

OSHA information is available through OSHA's Web address (http://www.osha.gov), or by writing or calling its regional or state offices, listed on its Web site. (See Figure 17-3) In addition, a number of booklets relating to OSHA can be purchased for a nominal charge from the Government Printing Office. Telephone orders with the Government Printing Office (202) 512-1800 can be placed by using either a VISA or MasterCard.

Region	Address/Telephone	States Covered
1	JFK Federal Building, Room E340 Boston, MA 02203 (617) 565-9860 (617) 565-9827 (Fax)	Connecticut Massachusetts Maine New Hampshire Rhode Island Vermont
2	201 Varick Street, Room 670 New York, NY 10014 (212) 337-2378 (212) 337-2371 (Fax)	New Jersey New York Puerto Rico Virgin Islands
3	U.S. Department of Labor/OSHA The Curtis Center-Suite 740 West 170 S. Independence Mall West Philadelphia, PA 19106-3309 (215) 861-4990 (215) 861-4904 (Fax)	District of Columbia Delaware Maryland Pennsylvania Virginia West Virginia
4	61 Forsyth Street, SW Atlanta, GA 30303 (404) 562-2300 (404) 562-2295 (Fax)	Alabama Florida Georgia Kentucky Mississippi North Carolina South Carolina Tennessee
5	230 South Dearborn Street, Room 3244 Chicago, IL 60604 (312) 353-2220 (312) 353-7774 (Fax)	Illinois Indiana Michigan Minnesota Ohio Wisconsin
6	500 Griffin Street, Room 602 Dallas, TX 75202 (214) 767-4731 (214) 767-4137 (Fax)	Arkansas Louisiana New Mexico Oklahoma Texas
7	City Center Square 1100 Main street, Suite 800 Kansas City, MO 64105 (816) 426-5861 (816) 426-2750 (Fax)	Iowa Kansas Missouri Nebraska

Figure 17-3
OSHA Regional Offices

Region	Address/Telephone	States Covered
8	1999 Broadway, Suite 1690 P.O. Box 46550 Denver, CO 80201-6550 (303) 844-1600 (303) 844-1616 (Fax)	Colorado Montana North Dakota South Dakota Utah Wyoming
9	71 Stevenson Street, Room 420 San Francisco, CA 94105 (415) 975-4310 (415) 975-4319 (Fax)	Arizona California Guam Hawaii Nevada
10	1111 Third Avenue, Suite 715 Seattle, WA 98101-3212 (206) 553-5930 (206) 553-6499 (Fax)	Alaska Idaho Oregon Washington

Figure 17-3 (*continued*)

COMPENSABLE INJURY UNDER WORKERS' COMPENSATION LAWS

A **compensable injury or illness** "must arise out of or in the course of employment." Simply because an injury occurs at the place of employment does not make the incident a compensable injury.

The compensable injury must occur within the time of employment, within the physical boundaries of the workplace, and must be work-related.

Examples of compensable injuries include:

- Injuries sustained by an employee while entering or exiting a employer's premises
- Changing clothes or cleaning up before or after work in the employer's locker room
- Injuries that occur during lunch hour or while going to the bathroom
- Injuries sustained by the nonparticipating victim of horseplay
- Injuries during required recreational or social activities or during permitted physical activities on the company's premises (companywide volleyball game, for example)
- Injuries from unexplained falls (if the work activity increases the risk of a fall)
- Some workers' compensation awards have been made for mental conditions either related to a physical injury or resulting from the stress of the employment.

NONCOMPENSABLE INJURY UNDER WORKERS' COMPENSATION LAWS

Examples of noncompensable injuries include:

1. Injuries sustained by employees while traveling to and from their place of employment (with the exception of those required to travel in their job, such as salesmen)
2. Injuries that occur as a result of horseplay, intoxication, or violation of safety rules.

OCCUPATIONAL DISEASES

All states provide workers' compensation coverage for occupational diseases that occur as a result of exposure to harmful conditions of employment. However, most states require that the exposure be greater than the exposure to the general public before compensation is permitted.

INFECTIOUS DISEASES

Infectious diseases are compensable when employment increases the risk of contracting such diseases. For example, a nurse's risk for contracting infectious disease is greater than the risk for the general public.

HEARING LOSS

A worker's loss of hearing is compensable if it is caused by either direct trauma or as an occupational disease when it is caused by exposure to excessive workplace noise. Each state has a guideline for determining whether the hearing loss is work-related and the degree of the hearing loss.

Compensable losses can be reduced or eliminated by an effective and enforced hearing loss program. Manufacturing plants, automotive repair shops, and other businesses associated with noise should conduct hearing tests frequently to make certain that their business is doing everything possible to reduce the possibility of hearing loss by its employees.

PREEXISTING DISEASES

Preexisting diseases, including heart disease, which are precipitated or aggravated by physical exertion at work, are compensable if the work activities aggravated or accelerated the underlying medical condition.

NOTICE OF INJURY

Employees are obligated to report all work-related injuries to their employer, regardless of how minor the injury might be. Mere knowledge that an employee is suffering from symptoms of an injury is not sufficient to meet notice requirements unless it is accompanied by facts regarding the specific work-related injury or illness.

An employee's failure to timely provide a notice of injury may not be a defense, unless the employer's investigation of the accident was hampered because of the late notice, or the employee's condition became worse because of the employer's inability to provide early diagnosis and treatment.

FILING OF CLAIMS

Each state has very specific rules regarding the time by which a claimant must file for workers' compensation benefits. The employer's voluntary payment of compensation may extend the filing period. The statute of limitations may also be affected by the employer's payment of medical bills, the employer's assurances to the employee that it will take care of the claim, and the mental or physical incompetence of the claimant.

BENEFITS

Most workers' compensation systems provide benefits to the injured worker depending on whether the disability is temporary or permanent and partial or total in nature. A **temporary disability** occurs when a worker is still receiving medical care and has not reached **maximum medical improvement** (the best the worker will ever be). If maximum medical improvement has been reached, the disability is permanent. The disability is total if the employee cannot work at any employment. If the worker can still work, but at reduced wages, the worker has a **partial disability**. There is a scheduled award based on medical impairment for certain parts of the body, such as the extremities, hands, arms, legs, and hearing and sight. Compensation is generally available for serious and permanent disfigurement.

Injured workers receive lost-time benefits or **temporary total disability benefits** for the period of time he or she is incapable of doing any type of employment and he or she is still recovering from injuries. **Temporary partial disability benefits** are paid when an employee is recovering from an injury and is capable of returning to some type of work but not full duty and, therefore, sustains an actual wage loss. **Permanent partial disability benefits** are paid based on any residual medical impairment after maximum improvement. **Permanent total disability** is the compensation award to an employee who, because of injuries, can perform no service for which any reasonable job market exists.

Benefits are calculated normally by using one-half to two-thirds of the injured worker's actual wages during the year preceding the injury. Each state sets a maximum rate for benefits, which is normally based on 100% to 200% of the state's average weekly wage. The minimum rate is usually a fixed dollar amount.

If an employee dies as a result of a work injury, the employee's dependents are entitled to death benefits. Other individuals possibly eligible for dependent's death benefits include parents, brothers, sisters, grandchildren, and grandparents. Most states determine the benefits paid to dependents based on a percentage of the employee's average weekly wage. Multiple dependents may share equally, or in proportions fixed by statute.

All state statutes specify that the employer must pay for medical and hospital benefits. The majority of statutes stipulate that the employer is to provide all reasonable and necessary medical services. Some states permit the employees to choose their own medical providers, but place a limit on the number of choices, reasonableness, and necessity of the care provided.

Injured employees may be entitled to rehabilitation services if the injury prevents them from returning to their former employment, and if they are retrainable. Rehabilitation costs include the cost of the program, physical maintenance, and lost-time compensation during the rehabilitation program.

ADMINISTRATIVE HEARINGS

All state statutes provide for an administrative body to administer the workers' compensation statute. Any evidence relied on for an administrative finding must be in the record or identified in the record. A hearing officer's initial decision may be administratively reviewed in most workers' compensation systems. An appeal to the courts can be made after the final administrative ruling but that appeal is usually confined to questions of law.

COORDINATION OF BENEFITS

The purpose of workers' compensation benefits is to restore to the worker a portion of his or her lost wages, normally one-half to two-thirds. There are several other potential sources of benefits for injured employees, including:

1. **Social Security.** Workers' compensation benefits are coordinated with the Social Security system so that duplicate payments are avoided. The Social Security system reduces the amount of the injured worker's benefit so that the combined Social Security and periodic workers' compensation benefit does not exceed 80% of the injured worker's average weekly earnings. Some states reduce the amount paid in workers' compensation by a percentage of the Social Security benefits received by the injured worker.

2. **Unemployment Compensation.** Some states permit the injured worker to simultaneously receive both unemployment and workers' compensation benefits, while other states require an offset for unemployment insurance benefits received against workers' compensation payments.

RETALIATION FOR WORKERS' COMPENSATION CLAIMS

State workers' compensation statutes prohibit retaliation by an employer against an employee because he or she filed a workers' compensation claim or testified or participated in an investigation or proceeding under the statute. Employers who terminate an employee shortly after the employee has sustained an on-the-job injury must carefully document the reasons for the discharge. For example, an employee who is absent from work for a number of days without a doctor's excuse stating that the absence was due to the workers' compensation accident may be terminated for violation of the employer's attendance policy. However, a termination for poor production quality might result in a retaliation charge if the injured worker is able to prove that the poor production quality is a result of the workers' compensation accident.

Documentation of production prior to the accident becomes critical. If the worker has had good quality and quantity production before the accident, but both declined following the accident, the employer will face a difficult defense of its termination decision.

MINIMIZING ON-THE-JOB INJURIES

Safety Programs

On-the-job injuries are often unavoidable. Some jobs result in injuries because of the repetitive nature of the employment. For example, a line worker who uses the same movements to perform the same tasks for a period of eight hours a day is often prone to carpal tunnel syndrome.

Employee orientation, particularly in a manufacturing or plant environment, should include a program on safety awareness. Films are available to educate an employee on how to lift or bend correctly to reduce the possibility of an on-the-job injury. Back and arm braces may be utilized to permit an employee in certain jobs to work relatively pain-free. Safety equipment such as safety shoes, protective eye-wear, and ear plugs should be mandatory in all areas where there is a known potential for injuries. Periodic reinforcement of the company's safety program should be instituted, with a mandatory attendance by all employees.

Accident Investigation

The company's safety program must require that all employees report an accident on a timely basis, no matter how minor the accident may seem at the time. A written accident report should be required for *all* incidents on the job. This report should include information on how and where the accident occurred, the time and date of the accident, witnesses to the accident, the employee's injuries, and the doctor or hospital who provided medical care for the employee following the accident. Figure 17-4 is a sample accident report.

Many companies offer a safety bonus for a certain number of hours worked without a lost-time accident. However, companies providing such a safety incentive have the additional responsibility of ensuring that the incentive does not prevent the reporting of accident because of pressure from the injured worker's supervisors or coworkers.

Figure 17-5 is a Supervisor's Investigation of Accident Report. An important part of this report is the corrective action to be undertaken following an accident.

Proper discipline of employees for unsafe work acts, including discharge where appropriate, should be uniformly followed by management.

Medical Care

Industrial companies face a difficult balancing process in providing medical care to injured employees. From an economic standpoint, the company needs all of its employees to be well and capable of producing at their maximum abilities. However, the employee's health cannot be jeopardized in order to achieve that production. The company and the employee must work as a team to ensure that the injured worker receives the best medical care possible and returns to his/her job as quickly as possible, without incurring the possibility of reinjury.

TERMS

assumption of risk
compensable injury or illness
contributory negligence

Employee: _____ Age: _____ Sex: _____

Department: _____ Supervisor: _____

Date of Accident: _____ Time of Accident: _____

Location of Accident: _____

Witnesses: _____

Cause of Accident: _____

Nature of Injuries: _____

If employee left work, time of leaving: _____

If employed returned to work, time of return: _____

Name and address of physician seen by employee: _____

_____

If hospitalized, name and address of hospital: _____

_____

Comments: _____

_____   _____
                Supervisor   Date

Figure 17-4
Accident Report

> fellow servant rule
> general duty clause
> maximum medical improvement
> partial disability
> permanent partial disability benefits
> permanent total disability
> temporary disability
> temporary partial disability benefits
> temporary total disability benefits

Employee: _____ Age: _____ Sex: _____

Department: _____ Supervisor: _____

Date of Accident: _____ Time of Accident: _____

Location of Accident: _____

Witnesses: _____

Date OSHA Report Filed: _____

Employee Interviewed: _____

Summary of Witness' Statement: _____

_____

_____

_____

_____

_____

Supervisor's Conclusion Regarding Reason for Accident: _____

_____

_____

Corrective Action to be Taken: _____

_____

_____   _____
            Supervisor   Date

_____   _____
            Witness   Date

Figure 17-5
Supervisor's Report of Accident Investigation

REVIEW QUESTIONS

1. What is required to prove a section 5(a) violation of the general duty clause of OSHA?

2. List three examples of *willful* acts of an employer that could result in penalties up to $10,000.

3. Maria and Nancy begin fighting while working on a sewing assembly line. Nancy suffers a broken arm. If Nancy files a workers' compensation claim, will she be able to collect benefits?

4. Jack Davidson has worked in the maintenance department of Morrison Aircraft Manufacturing for twelve years. During that time, he has been subjected to constant verbal abuse and pressure by his supervisor. Will Jack be able to collect workers' compensation benefits for mental injury caused by his supervisor's treatment of him?

5. Lane Building Products' management has verbally admonished employees about riding on the tractor lifts it uses to move heavy products from one part of the store to another. Jerry, a supervisor, has ridden on a tractor lift operated by William several times. William has never objected because of Jerry's position with the company. Jerry is injured when William hits a pile of lumber. Is Lane Building Products guilty of OSHA violations? Is Jerry guilty of OSHA violations?

6. Alma slips in the company parking lot and severely injures her back. Will she be eligible for workers' compensation benefits since the accident did not occur in the building?

7. Linda contracts tuberculosis while working in a ward where three patients have been diagnosed with tuberculosis. Is Linda eligible for any type of compensation for her illness?

8. A fire at a recycling plant results in the hospitalization of four employees. The plant files a report with OSHA a week later. Has the plant violated OSHA regulations?

9. Assume that an employee who is required to lift seventy-five pounds as an airline baggage handler is injured on the job. His physician has declared him unable to return to his position. Is the employee eligible for retraining services in an area such as ticket agent? Will the employee be entitled to compensation while he is retraining?

10. Terri Blackstone suffers from carpal tunnel syndrome. However, she has never advised her employer of any particular time when the pain became so severe that she could not perform her job duties. Does the employer have a responsibility to Blackstone under the workers' compensation laws?

PROJECTS

1. Draft a sample workers' compensation retaliation complaint using the facts in review question 4 above, assuming that Jack Davidson was terminated after filing a workers' compensation claim for mental damages as a result of harassment by his supervisor.

2. Search the internet to determine the number and types of OSHA violations in your state. Prepare a summary of the results.

APPENDIX A

EMPLOYEE HANDBOOK ACKNOWLEDGMENT

This employee handbook and the personnel policy manual highlight the company policies, procedures, and benefits. In all instances the official benefit plan text, trust agreements, and master contracts are the governing documents. The employee handbook is not to be interpreted as a legal document or an employment contract. Employment with the company is at the sole discretion of the company and may be terminated with or without cause at any time and for any reason. Nothing in this handbook or in the personnel policy manual constitutes an express or implied contract or assurance of continued employment, or implies that just cause is required for termination.

AGREEED TO:

_____
Employee

_____
Date

APPENDIX B

U.S. DEPARTMENT OF LABOR REGIONAL OFFICES

Location	Phone Number	Area Served
Region I 11th Floor 1 Congress Street Boston, MA 02114 OSHA; 1st Floor 13 Portland Street Boston, MA 02114	Wage and Hour: (617) 565-2066 Contract Compliance: (617) 565-2055 Workers' Compensation: (617) 565-2102 OSHA: (617) 565-7164	Connecticut, Maine, Massachusetts, New Hampshire, Rhode Island, and Vermont
Region II 201 Varick Street New York, NY 10014 OSHA: 1 Main Street Brooklyn, NY 11201	Wage and Hour: (212) 337-2000 Contract Compliance: (212) 337-2010 Workers' Compensation: (212) 337-2075 OSHA: (212) 337-2325 or (718) 797-7671	New Jersey, Puerto Rico, New York, and Virgin Islands
Region III Gateway Building 3535 Market Street Philadelphia, PA 19104	Wage and Hour: (215) 596-1185 Contract Compliance: (215) 596-6168 Workers' Compensation: (215) 596-1180 OSHA: (215) 596-1201	Delaware, Virginia, Maryland, West Virginia, and Pennsylvania
Region IV 1375 Peachtree Street, NE Atlanta, GA 30367 Room 1026 214 North Hogan Street Jacksonville, FL 33202	Wage and Hour: (404) 347-4801 Contract Compliance: (404) 347-4211 OSHA: (404) 347-3573 Workers' Compensation: (904) 791–2569	Alabama, Florida, Georgia, Kentucky, Mississippi, North Carolina, South Carolina, and Tennessee
Region V 230 South Dearborn Chicago, IL 60604-1591	Wage and Hour: (312) 353-8290 Contract Compliance: (312) 353-0335 Workers' Compensation: (312) 353-5656 OSHA: (312) 353-2220	Illinois, Indiana, Michigan, Minnesota, Ohio, and Wisconsin

Location	Phone Number	Area Served
Region VI Federal Office Building 525 Griffin Street Dallas, TX 75202	Wage and Hour: (214) 767-6294 Contract Compliance: (214) 767-4717 Workers' Compensation: (214) 757-4712 OSHA: (214) 767-4731	Arkansas, Louisiana, New Mexico, Oklahoma, and Texas
Region VII 1100 Main Street Kansas City, MO 64105	Wage and Hour: (816) 426-5381 Contract Compliance: (816) 426-5386 Workers' Compensation: (816) 426-2195 OSHA: (816) 426-5861	Iowa, Kansas, Missouri, and Nebraska
Region VIII 1801 California Street Denver, CO 80202	Wage and Hour: (303) 844-4405 Contract Compliance: (303) 391-6082 Workers' Compensation: (303) 391-6000 OSHA: (303) 391-5858	Colorado, Montana, North Dakota, South Dakota, Utah, and Wyoming
Region IX 71 Stevenson Street San Francisco, CA 94105	Wage and Hour: (415) 744-5590 Contract Compliance: (415) 975-4040 Workers' Compensation: (415) 975-4090 OSHA: (415) 975-4310	Arizona, California, Guam, Hawaii, Nevada, and Philippines
Region X Federal Office Building 1111 Third Avenue Seattle, WA 98101-3212	Wage and Hour: (206) 553-4482 Contract Compliance: (206) 553-7182 Workers' Compensation: (206) 553-5508 OSHA: (206) 553-5930	Alaska, Idaho, Oregon, and Washington

APPENDIX C

RECORD RETENTION REQUIREMENTS

Federal recordkeeping requirements are quite extensive. The following table explains some of the requirements that apply to most employers. All employers, especially those that perform public contracts or do any work for the federal government, should review the latest edition of the federal *Guide to Record Retention Requirements*, available from the Superintendent of Documents, U.S. Government Printing Office, Washington, DC 20402.

Statute	Records to be Kept	Time Requirements
Age Discrimination in Employment Act	Job applications, resumes, other forms of job inquiries; promotions, demotions, transfers, training selection, layoff, recall, or discharge; job orders submitted to employment agencies; candidate test papers for any position; physical exam results if used in employment decisions; ads or notices relating to job openings, training opportunities, or opportunities for overtime; employee benefit plans. (**Note:** for employee benefit plans, records must be kept for one year from *termination* of plan.)	One year from date of action; see note
	Payroll or other records containing employee name, address, date of birth, occupation, rate of pay, and compensation earned each week.	Three years
Americans with Disabilities Act	Same as for Civil Rights Act Title VII. Information from medical exams is confidential, must be maintained separately, access limited to employee's supervisors, managers, safety workers, workers' compensation, employer's insurance carrier.	Same as CRA Title VII
Civil Rights Act of 1964 (Title VII)	No record creation required, but if made, must be retained. Includes application forms, promotion, demotion, transfer, layoff, termination, rate of pay, or other compensation, selection for	One year; see note

Statute	Records to be Kept	Time Requirements
	training or apprenticeship records. (**Note:** Employers with 100 plus employees must keep Form EEO-1 at each unit or company head-quarters. If bias charge, records re: charging party and other similarly employee employees, test papers from rejected applicants and candidates for same position must be retained.)	
Employee Polygraph Protection Act	Copy of statement provided employees telling specific incident under investigation, basis for testing, records identifying loss, nature of employee's access to person/property being investigated; notice given examiner identifying person(s) to be examined; reports, questions, lists, all records relating to testing, other records given employer by examiner.	Three years from date of test
Fair Labor Standards Act and Equal Pay Act of 1963	Employee information (name, address, occupation, birthdate if under 19, sex), complete payroll records, certificates, union agreements, and notices, written training agreements (kept for training period), notices of wage-hour department, sales and purchase records, certificate of age until termination.	Three years
	Basic employment and earnings records, wage rate tables, actual work completed, additions to/deductions from wages, wage differential payments to employees of the opposite sex/same job, evaluations, job descriptions, merit or seniority systems.	Two years
Family and Medical Leave Act	Payroll data, dates/hours of FMLA leave taken, employer notices describing leave benefits and policies, premium payments, records of disputes with employees about FMLA. Employee medical records must be kept separately, confidentially.	Three years
Immigration Reform and Control Act	Form I-9. **Note:** form must be kept for three years after the employee is hired or one year after termination, whichever is later. Also, keep copies of supporting identification and work authorization documents.	Three years; see note
Rehabilitation Act of 1973	Employment records, including vacancy, training, promotions, demotions. Positions for which workers and applicants were considered, reasons for rejection, accommodations considered, rejected, or made. Records of complaints.	One year

APPENDIX D

NOTICES (POSTING) REQUIRED
(UNDER FEDERAL EMPLOYMENT LAW)

Virtually all federal and most state employment laws have some notice posting requirement. Such notices must be posted conspicuously and in enough places so that employees are able to see the notices as they enter and exit the workplace.
The federal government has consolidated some of its posters to simplify posting problems. Some of the official posters are available in Spanish as well as English, but regulations require only the English-language poster.

Penalties for violating posting requirements may be quite high. Displaying posters can be helpful in defending discrimination charges also.

Statute	Coverage	Basic Requirements	Official Form
Age Discrimination in Employment Act	Employers engaged in interstate commerce with 20 or more employees	Prohibits employment discrimination on the basis of age 40 or over	"Consolidated EEO Poster" 29 USCS § 627
Americans with Disabilities Act	Employers with 15 or more employees engaged in interstate commerce; also employment agencies	Prohibits employment discrimination on the basis of disability	"Consolidated EEO Poster" 42 USCS § 12115
Civil Rights Act of 1964 (Title VII)	Employers engaged in interstate commerce with 15 or more employees	Prohibits employment discrimination on the basis of race, color, religion, sex, or national origin	"Consolidated EEO Poster" 29 USCS § 2000e-10
Employee Polygraph Protection act	All employers engaged in commerce or in production of goods for commerce	Bars lie detector tests to screen job applicants; limits employers' use of lie detector tests for current employees	"Notice of Protection" 29 USCS § 2003

Statute	Coverage	Basic Requirements	Official Form
Equal Pay Act of 1963	Employers engaged in interstate commerce	Requires equal pay for substantially equal work regardless of sex	"Consolidated EEO Poster"
Fair Labor Standards Act	Employers engaged in interstate commerce	Sets minimum hourly wage, training wage, and overtime hours and rate; age limits for child labor	"Your Rights Under the Fair Labor Standards Act"; also "Consolidated EEO Poster" 29 CFR § 516.4
Family and Medical Leave Act	Employers with 50 or more employees	Allows leave for certain medical reasons and compelling family reasons	As provided by U.S. Department of Labor (WH Publication 1420) 29 USCS § 2619
Rehabilitation Act of 1973	Federal government contractors and subcontractors with a contract of $2,500 or more.	Prohibits employment discrimination on the basis of disability; requires affirmative action to employ and advance the disabled.	"Consolidated EEO Poster"

The majority of the posters referenced above may be obtained from the EEOC, Publishing and Information, (800) 669-4000.

The FLSA and FMLA posters may be obtained from the Department of Labor, Wage and Hour/Employment Standard Division, 200 Constitution Avenue NW, Washington, DC 20210, (202) 219-8151.

APPENDIX E

RECORD RETENTION REQUIREMENTS UNDER ADEA

The following types of records are to be retained for one year from the date of action:

Job Applications
Resumes
Promotion Forms
Demotion Forms
Transfer Records
Training Selection
Layoff Records
Recall Records
Discharge Documentation
Job Orders to Employment Agencies
Tests of Applicants
Advertisements or Notices Relating to Job Openings
Training Opportunity Documents
Documents Reflecting Opportunities for Overtime
Employee Benefit Plan Documentation—Note: One-year period is based on *termination from plan*.

The following types of records are to be retained for three years:

Payroll or other records containing employee name, address, date of birth, occupation, rate of pay, and compensation earned each week

APPENDIX F

INTERNET SITES RELATING TO GENERAL LEGAL TOPICS

Subject	Site
American Bar Association	http://www.abanet.org
Americans with Disabilities Act	http://www.usdoj.gov/rt/ada/pubs/ada.txt
Bureau of Labor Statistics	http://www.stats.bls.gov
Civil Rights Division, U.S. Department of Justice	http://www.usdoj.gov/crt
Code of Federal Regulations	http://www.gsa.ogv/far/
Congressional Telephone, Fax and E-Mail Information	http://geopages.com/Capitol-Hill/1007/
Employment law central	http://www.employmentlawcentral.com
ERISA	http://www.benefitslink.com/?erisa/index.html
Federal Rules of Evidence	http://www.law.cornell.edu/rules/fre/overview.html
FINDLAW	http://www.findlaw.com
Freedom of Information Regulations	http://ww.law.cornell.edu/copyright/relations/regs.overview.html
'LECTRIC LAW LIBRARY	http://www.lectlaw.com
Occupational Safety and Health Administration	http://www.osha.gov
Social Security Administration	http://www/ssa.gov
Supreme Court Cases	http://wwwlaw.cornell.edu/supct/supct.table.html
The White House	http://lcweb.loc.gov/global/executive/white house.html
U.S. Census Bureau	http://www.census.gov/
U.S. Constitution	http://wwwlaw.cornell.edu/constitution
U. S. Department of Labor	http://www.dol.gov

APPENDIX G

STATE WORKERS' COMPENSATION AGENCIES

Alabama
Workers' Compensation Division
Department of Industrial Relations
Industrial Relations Building
649 Monroe Street
Montgomery, Alabama 36131
(334) 242-2868

Alaska
Division of Workers' Compensation
Department of Labor
P.O. Box 25512
Juneau, Alaska 99802-5512
(907) 465-2790

Arizona
Industrial Commission
800 West Washington
P.O. Box 19070
Phoenix, Arizona 85005-9070
(602) 542-4661

Arkansas
Workers' Compensation Commission
Fourth & Spring Streets
P.O. Box 950
Little Rock, Arkansas 72203-6905
(501) 682-3930

California
Department of Industrial Relations
Division of Workers' Compensation
45 Fremont Street, Suite 3160
San Francisco, California 94105
(415) 972-8846

Colorado
Division of Workers' Compensation
1515 Arapahoe Street
Denver, Colorado 80202
(303 575-8700

Connecticut
Workers' Compensation Commission
700 State Street
New Haven, Connecticut 06510
(203) 789-7512

Delaware
Division of Industrial of Industrial
4425 N. Market Street, 3rd Floor
Carvel State Office Building
Wilmington, Delaware 19802
(302) 761-8200

District of Columbia
Department of Employment Services
Office of Workers' Compensation
1200 Upshur Street, N.W.
Washington, D.C. 20011
(202) 576-6265

Florida
Division of Workers' Compensation
Department of Labor and Employment Security
103 Forrest Building
2728 Centerview Drive
Tallahassee, Florida 3399-0684
(850) 488-5201

Georgia
Board of Workers' Compensation
270 Peachstreet Street NW
Atlanta, Georgia 30303-1299
(404) 656–3875

Hawaii
Disability Compensation Division
Department of Labor and Industrial Relations
P.O. Box 3769
Honolulu, Hawaii 96812
(808) 586-9151

Idaho
Industrial Commission
317 Main Street
P.O. Box 83702
Boise, Idaho 83702
(208) 334-6000

Illinois
Industrial Commission
100 West Randolph Street
Suite 8-200
Chicago, Illinois 60601
(312) 814-6555

Indiana
Workers' Compensation Board
402 West Washington Street
Room W196
Indianapolis, Indiana 46204
(317) 232-3808

Iowa
Division of Industrial Services
Workforce Development
1000 E. Grand Avenue
Des Moines, Iowa 50319
(515) 281-5934

Kansas
Division of Workers' Compensation
Department of Human Resources
800 SW Jackson Street, Suite 600
Topeka, Kansas 66612-1227
(913) 296-4000

Kentucky
Department of Workers' Claims
Perimeter Park West
1270 Louisville Road, Building C
Frankfort, Kentucky 40601
(502) 564-5550

Louisiana
Department of Labor
Office of Workers' Compensation
    Administration
P.O. Box 94040
Baton Rouge, Louisiana 70804-9040
(504) 342-7555

Maine
Workers' Compensation Board
Deering Building
27 State House Station
Augusta, Maine 04333-0027
(207) 287-3751

Maryland
Workers' Compensation Commission
6 North Liberty Street
Baltimore, Maryland 21201
(410) 767-0900

Massachusetts
Department of Industrial Accidents
600 Washington Street, 7th Floor
Boston, Massachusetts 02111
(617) 727-4300

Michigan
Bureau of Workers' Disability Compensation
Department of Consumer and Industry Services
7150 Harris Drive
P.O. Box 30016
Lansing, Michigan 48909
(517) 322-1296

Minnesota
Workers' Compensation Division
Department of Labor and Industry
443 Lafayette Road
St. Paul, Minnesota 55155

Mississippi
Workers' Compensation Commission
1428 Lakeland Drive
P.O. Box 5300
Jackson, Mississippi 39296-5300
(601) 987-4200

Missouri
Division of Workers' Compensation
Department of Labor and Industrial Relations
3315 West Truman Boulevard
P.O. Box 58
Jefferson City, Missouri 65102
(573) 751-4231

Montana
Montana State Compensation Insurance Fund
P.O. Box 4759
Helena, Montana 59604-4759
(406) 444-6518

Nebraska
Workers' Compensation Court
P.O. Box 98908
Lincoln, Nebraska 68509-8908
(402) 471-2568

Nevada
State Industrial Insurance System
515 East Musser Street
Carson City, Nevada 89714
(702) 687-5284

New Hampshire
Department of Labor
Division of Workers' Compensation
State Office Park South
95 Pleasant Street
Concord, New Hampshire 03301
(603) 271-3171

New Jersey
Department of Labor
Division of Workers' Compensation
P.O. Box 381
Trenton, New Jersey 08625-0381
(609) 292-2414

New Mexico
Workers' Compensation Administration
2410 Center Avenue SE
Albuquerque, New Mexico 87106
(505) 841-6000

New York
Workers' Compensation Board
180 Livingston Street
Brooklyn, New York 11248
(718) 802-666

North Carolina
Industrial Commission
Dobbs Building
430 North Salisbury Street
Raleigh, North Carolina 27611
(919) 733-4820

North Dakota
Workers' Compensation Bureau
500 East Front Avenue
Bismarck, North Dakota 58504-5685

Ohio
Bureau of Workers' Compensation
30 West Spring Street
Columbus, Ohio 43215-2256
(614) 466-2950

Oklahoma
Oklahoma Workers' Compensation Court
1915 N. Stiles
Oklahoma City, Oklahoma 73105
(405) 522-8600

Oregon
Workers' Compensation Division
Department of Consumer and Business Services
350 Winter Street NE
Salem, Oregon 97310
(503) 378-4100

Pennsylvania
Bureau of Workers' Compensation
Department of Labor and Industry
1171 South Cameron Street, Room 324
Harrisburg, Pennsylvania 17104-2501
(717) 783-5421

Puerto Rico
Industrial Commission
G.P.O. Box 364466
San Juan, PR 00936-4466
(787) 781-0545

Rhode Island
Department of Labor
Division of Workers' Compensation
610 Manton Avenue
P.O. Box 3500
Providence, Rhode Island 02909
(401) 457-1800

South Carolina
Workers' Compensation Commission
1612 Marion Street
P.O. Box 1715
Columbia, South Carolina 29202
(803) 737-5700

South Dakota
Division of Labor and Management
Department of Labor
Kneip Building, Third Floor
700 Governors Drive
Pierre, South Dakota 57501-2291
(605) 773-3681

Tennessee
Workers' Compensation Division
Department of Labor
710 James Robertson Parkway
Andrew Johnson Tower, Second Floor
Nashville, Tennessee 37243-0661
(615) 741-2395

Texas
Workers' Compensation Commission
Southfield Building
4000 South IH 35
Austin, Texas 78704-7491
(512) 448-7900

Utah
Labor Commission
P.O. Box 146600
Salt Lake City, Utah 84114-6600
(801) 530-6800

Vermont
Department of Labor and Industry
National Life Bldg. Drawer 20
Montpelier, VT 05620-3401
(802) 828-2286 or 1-800-734-2286

Virginia
Workers' Compensation Commission
1000 DMV Drive
Richmond, VA 23220
(804) 367-8600

Virgin Islands
Workers Compensation Division
Department of Labor
3012 Vitraco Mall-Golden Rock
St. Croix, VI 00820-4666
(80) 692-9390 or (809) 773-1994, Ext. 238

Washington
Department of Labor and Industries
Headquarters Building
7273 Linderson Way, SW, 5th Floor
Olympia, Washington 98504
(360) 902-4200

West Virginia
Workers' Compensation Division
4700 McCorkal Avenue SE
Charleston, West Virginia 25304
(304) 926-5000

Wisconsin
Workers' Compensation Division
Department of Workforce Development
201 E. Washington Ave., Room 161
P.O. Box 7901
Madison, Wisconsin 53707
(608) 266-1340

Wyoming
Workers' Safety and Compensation Division
Department of Employment
122 West 25th Street, 2nd Floor
East Wing, Herschler Building
Cheyenne, Wyoming 82002-0700
(307) 777-7159

APPENDIX H

EEOC DOCUMENT REQUEST UNDER FOIA

_____
[Date]

_____
[Name]
Regional Attorney
U. S. Equal Employment Opportunity Commission
_____District Office
Re:[Cause No. _____]; In the [court]
EEOC Charge No. _____

Dear [Name of Regional Attorney]:

Pursuant to the Freedom of Information Act, 5 U.S.C. § 552 (1988), and as the representative of the Defendant in the above-captioned case, we request the disclosure of the Equal Employment Opportunity Commission's investigative files on [name of plaintiff], Charge No. _____.

I have attached a copy of the plaintiff's lawsuit, a copy of our answer on behalf of the Defendant, and a Non-Disclosure Statement for your file. If you take the position that some of the documents requested are not discoverable, please set forth a complete list of such items and the reasons for declining to produce those documents.

Please send a certified copy of the file to my attention, [name of firm], at the address noted above. I agree to pay any reasonable copying charges [up to $_____].

If you have any questions about this request, please do not hesitate to contact me at [area code and phone number]. Thank you for your assistance in this matter.

Very truly yours,

[typed name of legal assistant]
Legal Assistant to
[name of attorney]

Enclosures:
Certificate of Non-Disclosure
Copy of Plaintiff's Complaint
Copy of Defendant's Answer

APPENDIX I

EQUAL EMPLOYMENT OPPORTUNITY COMMISSION AGREEMENT OF NONDISCLOSURE

Pursuant to Section 706(g) of Title VII, the EEOC shall have power to cooperate with private individuals in order to accomplish the purposes of Title VII. The Commission requires that the following procedures be adhered to when a party makes a request for copies of or to review documents in a charge file(s):

PERSON REQUESTING DISCLOSURE (Check the Appropriate Party)
_____ **CHARGING PARTY** _____ **RESPONDENT'S ATTORNEY**

CHARGE NAME/NUMBER TO BE DISCLOSED:

_____

STATEMENT

I, _____, request the disclosure of Commission file(s) in connection with contemplated or pending litigation. I agree that the information disclosed to me will not be made public or used except in the normal course of a civil action or other proceedings instituted under Title VII involving such information.

The Commission's regulations provide that the first two hours of search time and the first hundred pages of duplication shall be provided without charge. Charges for time or pages in excess of these amounts are set out in 29 CFR Section 1610.15.

In witness thereof, this agreement is entered into as of this _____ day of _____, _____ by the Equal Employment Opportunity Commission representative(s) named below and the person requesting disclosure.

_____
Person requesting disclosure (Signature and telephone number/area code)

_____
Address

_____
EEOC Representative (Signature and title)

APPENDIX J

AUTHORIZATION TO OBTAIN MEDICAL RECORDS

TO: Dr. [name]
    [address]

    I hereby authorize you to provide to [law firm or company], or their authorized representatives, any and all information relevant to my physical condition, and all treatment [and billing] records which may be requested, including, but not limited to, reports, evaluations, x-rays or other diagnostic tools, prescriptions, progress notes, order sheets, admission forms, laboratory reports, HIV or AIDS-related information, nurses' notes, incident reports, and consultation records.

    I agree that a photocopy of this authorization has the same force and effect as the original.

    This authorization is not limited in time or medical subject area.

    This authorization shall act as a revocation of any and all other authorizations that I may have signed prior to the effective date of this authorization.

_____[signature]
          [typed or printed name of authorizing person]

WITNESS:

_____
[signature of witness]

SWORN AND SUBSCRIBED TO before me this _____ day of _____, _____.

_____ [signature of notary]
    [typed or printed name of notary]

    Notary Public in and for the State of _____.

    My commission expires: [date]

APPENDIX K

STATE FAIR EMPLOYMENT PRACTICE OFFICES

Office Location and Number	FEP Statute
Alabama	**Alabama has no FEP laws.**
Alaska Alaska State Commission for Human Rights 800 A Street, Suite 202 Anchorage, AK 99501-3669 (07) 276-7474	**Alaska Stat. § 18.80.010 to 3300 and § 22.10.020**
ARIZONA Arizona Civil Rights Division 1275 West Washington Street Phoenix, AZ 85007 (602) 542-5263	**AZ Rev. Stat. § 41-14461 to 1465, § 1481 to 1484**
ARKANSAS No state office. Contact the EEOC	**Arkansas Stat. Ann. § 16-123-101 to 108**
CALIFORNIA California Dept. of Fair Employment and Housing 2014 T Street, Suite 210 Sacramento, CA 95814 (916) 227-0551	**Ca. Gov't Code § 12900 to 12996**
COLORADO Colorado Civil Right Commission 1560 Broadway, Suite 1050 Denver, CO 80202 (303) 894-2997	**Colorado Rev. Stat. § 24-34-301 to 406**
CONNECTICUT Connecticut Commission on Human Rights and Opportunities 1229 Albany Avenue Hartford, CT 06112 (860) 566-7710	**Conn. Gen. Stat. § 46a-51 to 99**

Office Location and Number	Fep Statute
DELAWARE Delaware Department of Labor Anti-Discrimination Section 4425 North Market Street Wilmington, DE 19802 (302) 761-8200	Del. Code Ann. tit. 19, § 710 to 718
DISTRICT OF COLUMBIA D.C. Department of Human Rights 441 4th Street NW, Suite 970N Washington, DC 20001 (202) 724-1385	D.C. Code § 1-2501 to 2557
FLORIDA Florida Commission on Human Relations 3255 John Knox Road Suite 240, Building F Tallahassee, FL 32303-4149 (904) 488-7082	Fla. Stat. Ann. § 760.0 to.11
GEORGIA* Georgia Commission on Equal Employment Opportunity 710 International Tower 229 Peachtree Street, NE Atlanta, GA 30303-1605 (404) 656-1736	Ga. Code Ann. § 45-19-20 to 45 *Only applies to state employees
HAWAII Hawaii Civil Rights Commission 830 Punch Bowl Street, Suite 411 Honolulu, HI 96813 (808) 586-8636	Hawaii Rev. Stat. § 368-1 to 17, § 378-1 to 9
IDAHO Idaho Human Rights Commission 1109 Main Street Boise, ID 83720 (208) 334-2873	Idaho Code Ann. § 67-5901 to 5912
ILLINOIS Illinois Department of Human Rights 100 West Randolph Street Chicago, IL 60601 (312) 814-6245	Ill. Ann. stat. Ch. 68, § 1-101 to 2-1055, § 7A-101 to 104, § 8-101 to 105, § 8A-101 to 104; or Ill. Comp. Stat. Ann. Chapter 775 § 5/1-101 to 5/2-105, § 5/7A-101 to 104, § 5/8A-101 to 104
INDIANA Indiana Civil Rights Commission 100 North Senate Ave., Room E 103 Indianapolis, IN 46204 (317) 232-2600	Indiana Stat. Ann. § 22-9-1-1 to 18

Office Location and Number	Fep Statute
IOWA Iowa Civil Rights Commission Grimes State Office Building 211 East Maple Street, 2d Floor Des Moines, IA 50319 (515) 282-4121	Iowa Code Ann. § 601A.1 to.19 or Iowa Code § 216.1 to.20
KANSAS Kansas Commission on Human Rights Landon State Office Building 300 SW 10th Street Topeka, KS 66612 (913) 296-3206	Kan. Stat. Ann. § 44-1001 to 1013 and § 44-1044
KENTUCKY Kentucky Commission on Human Rights 332 West Broadway, Site 700 P.O. Box 69 Louisville, KY 40202 (502) 595-4024	Ky. Rev. Stat. § 344.010 to.450
LOUISIANA No state office. Contact the EEOC	La. Rev. Stat. Ann. § 23:1006
MAINE Maine Human Rights Commission Statehouse Station 51 Augusta, ME 04333 (207) 624-6050	Maine Rev. Stat. Ann., tit. 5, § 4551 to 4633
MARYLAND Maryland Commission on Human Relations 6 St. Paul Street, Suite 900 Baltimore, MD 21202 (410) 767-8600	Md. Ann. Code, art. 49B, § 9 to 39
MASSACHUSETTS Massachusetts Commission Against Discrimination One Ashburton Place, Room 601 Boston, MA 02108 (617) 727-3990	Mass. Ann. Laws ch. 151B, § 1 to 10
MICHIGAN Michigan Department of Civil Rights 303 West Kalamazoo Lansing, MI 48913 (517) 335-3164	Mich. Comp. Laws Ann. § 37.2101 to.2804; Mich. Stat. Ann. § 3548(101) to (804)
MINNESOTA Minnesota Department of Human Rights Bremer Tower Seventh Place and Minnesota Street St. Paul, MN 55101 (612) 926-5665	Minn. Stat. Ann. § 363.01 to.15

Office Location and Number	Fep Statute
MISSISSIPPI No state office. Contact the EEOC.	**Miss. Code Ann. § 25-9149*** **(Although there is a state law prohibiting discrimination against state employee, there are no damages, exclusions or other specifics mentioned in the statute).**
MISSOURI Missouri Commission on Human Rights 3315 West Truman Boulevard P.O. Box 1129 Jefferson City, MO 65102 (314) 751-3325	**Mo. Ann. Stat. § 213.010 to.137**
MONTANA Montana Human Rights Division Department of Labor and Industry P.O. Box 1728 1236 6th Avenue Helena, MT 59624 (406) 444-2884	**Mont. Code Ann. § 492-101 to 49-2-601**
NEBRASKA Nebraska Equal Employment Opportunity Commission 301 Centennial Mall South, 5th Floor P.O. Box 94934 Lincoln, NE 68509 (402) 471-2024	**Neb. Rev. Stat. § 48-1101 to 1126**
NEVADA Nevada Equal Rights Commission 1515 East Tropicana, Suite 590 Las Vegas, NV 89158 (702) 486-7161	**Nev. Rev. Stat. Ann. § 613310 to.430, § 233.160 to.210**
NEW HAMPSHIRE New Hampshire Commission for Human Rights 163 Loudon Road Concord, NH 03301 (603) 271-2767	**N.H. Rev. Stat. Ann. § 354-A:1 to A:14**
NEW JERSEY New Jersey Division on Civil Rights P.O. Box 46001 Newark, NJ 07101 (609) 984-3100	**N.J. Stat. Ann. § 10:5-1 to 28**
NEW MEXICO New Mexico Human Rights Division Aspen Plaza 1596 Pacheco Street Santa Fe, NM 87505 (505) 827-6838	**N.M. Stat. Ann. § 28-1-1 to 15**

Office Location and Number	Fep Statute
NEW YORK New York State Division of Human Rights 55 West 125 Street, 13th Floor New York, NY 10027 (212) 961-8400	N.Y. Exec. Law § 290 to 30
NORTH CAROLINA (For private employees) North Carolina Human Relations Commission 217 West Jones Street Raleigh, NC 27603 (919) 733-7996 and (For state and county employees and employees of the University of North Carolina) North Carolina Office of Administrative Hearings 1203 Front Street, Room 240 Post Office Drawer 27447 Raleigh, NC 27611-7447 (919) 733-0431	N.C. Gen. Stat. § 143-422.1 to.3
NORTH DAKOTA North Dakota Department of Labor 600 East Boulevard 13th Floor, State Capitol Building Bismarck, ND 58505 (701) 328-2660	N.D. Cent. Code Ann. § 14-02.4-01 to.4-21
OHIO Ohio Civil Rights Commission 220 Parsons Avenue Columbus, OH 43215 (614) 466-2785	Page's Ohio Rev. Code Ann. § 4112.01 to 99
OKLAHOMA Oklahoma Human Rights Commission 2101 North Lincoln Boulevard, Room 481 Oklahoma City, OK 73105 (405) 521-3441	Oklahoma Stat. Tit. 25 § 1101 to 1706
OREGON Oregon Bureau of Labor and Industry Civil Rights Division 800 NE Oregon, Suite 1070 Portland, OR 97232 (503) 731-4075	Or. Rev. Stat. § 659.010 to.990
PENNSYLVANIA Pennsylvania Human Relations Commission 101 South 2nd Street, Suite 300 Harrisburg, PA 17101 (717) 787-4412	43 Pa. Stat. Ann. § 951 to 962.2

Office Location and Number	Fep Statute
RHODE ISLAND Rhode Island Commission for Human Rights 10 Abbott Park Place Providence, RI 02903 (401) 277-2661	R.I. Gen. Laws § 28-5-1 to 40
SOUTH CAROLINA South Carolina Human Affairs Commission P.O. Box 4490 Columbia, SC 29240 (803) 253-6336	S.C. Code tit. 1, § 1-13-10 to 110
SOUTH DAKOTA South Dakota Division of Human Rights 18 West Capitol Street Pierre, SD 57501 (605) 773-4493	S.D. Codified Laws, § 20-13-1 to 56
TENNESSEE Tennessee Human Rights Commission 530 Church Street, Site 400 Nashville, TN 3724 (615) 741-5825	Tenn. Code Ann. § 4-21-101 to 408
TEXAS Texas Commission on Human Rights 8100 Cameron Road, #525 P.O. Box 13493 Austin, TX 78753 (512) 837-8534	Tex. Lab. Code 21.001 to.259
UTAH Utah Labor Commission/Anti-Discrimination Div.160 East 300 South, 3rd Floor Salt Lake City, UT 84114 (801) 530-6801	Utah Code Ann. § 34A-5-101 to 108
VERMONT Vermont Attorney General's Office Civil Rights Division 109 State Street Montpelier, VT 05609 (802) 828-3171	21 Vt. Stat. Ann. § 495
VIRGINIA Virginia Council on Human Rights 1100 Bank Street Washington Building, 12th Floor Richmond, VA 23219 (804) 225-2292	Va. Code Ann. § 2.1-714 to 725

Office Location and Number	Fep Statute
WASHINGTON Washington State Human Rights Commission Evergreen Plaza Building 711 South Capitol Way, Suite 402 Olympia, WA 98504-2490 (360) 753-6770	**Wash. Rev. Code Ann. § 49.60.010 to.330**
WEST VIRGINIA West Virginia Human Rights Commission 1321 Plaza East, Room 106 Charleston, WV 25301 (304) 558-2616	**W. Va. Code § 5-11-1 to 19**
WISCONSIN Wisconsin Equal Rights Division Department of Industry, Labor and Human Relations P.O. Box 898 201 East Washington Avenue Madison, WI 53708 (608) 266-6860	**Wis. Stat. Ann. § 11.31 to 39**
WYOMING Wyoming Fair Employment Commission Herschler Building 6101 Yellowstone Ave., Suite 259C Cheyenne, WY 82002 (307) 777-7261	**Wyo. Stat. Ann. § 27-9-101 to 108**

APPENDIX L

STATE LAWS PROHIBITING DISCRIMINATION ON THE BASIS OF AIDS OR HIV

State	Statute or Regulation
California	Cal. Gov't Code § 12940
Colorado	Colo. Stat. 24-34-402.5
Connecticut	Conn. Gen. Stat. Ann. § 46a-60
Delaware	Del. Code Ann. Tit. 19, § 724(a)
Florida	Fla. Stat. Ann. § 760.50
Georgia	Ga. Code Ann. § 34-6a-4(a)
Illinois	Ill. Comp. Stat. Ann. Ch. 775, § 5/2-102
Iowa	Iowa Code § 216.6
Kentucky	Ky. Rev. Stat. § 207.150, 207.160
Massachusetts	Mass. Gen. L. ch. 151B, § 4(16)
Michigan	Mich. Comp. Laws § 37.1202(1)(a)
Minnesota	Minn. Stat. Ann. § 363.03(2)
Missouri	Mo. Ann. Stat. § 213.055(1)
Nebraska	Neb. Rev. Stat. §§ 20-168
New Jersey	N.J. Stat. Ann. § 10:5-12
New York	N.Y. Exec. Law § 296(1)(a)
North Carolina	N.C. Gen. Stat. Para. 130-A-148(I)
Ohio	Ohio Rev. Code Ann. § 4112.02
Oregon	Or. Rev. Stat. § 659.436
Pennsylvania	Pa. Sta. Ann. tit. 43 § 955
Rhode Island	R.I Gen. Laws 23-6-22
Tennessee	Tenn. Code Ann. § 8-50-103
Texas	Tex. Lab. Code Ann. § 21.051
Vermont	Vt. Stat. Ann. tit. 3 § 961; tit. 21, 495
Washington	Wash. Rev. Code § 49.60.172
Washington, D.C.	D.C. Code § 1-2512(a)(1)
West Virginia	W. Va. Code § 5-11-9(1)
Wisconsin	Wis. Stat. Ann. § 111.321

GLOSSARY

401(k) plan   A profit-sharing plan that permits employees to make salary deferral contributions to the profit-sharing plan on a before-tax basis.

absolute privilege   Freedom from all claims of defamation.

adverse impact   Employment practices which are neutral on their face in the treatment of different groups, but which fall more heavily on one group than another and cannot be justified by business necessity.

affinity orientation   A person attracted to those of her or his own gender.

affirmative action   Steps to remedy past discrimination in hiring and promotion, for example, by recruiting more minorities and women.

Affirmative Action Plan   A plan that is designed to remedy racially discriminatory practices suffered in the past by members of certain minority groups within 120 days of the beginning of the contract.

after-acquired evidence doctrine   A rule that if an employer discharges an employee for an unlawful reason and later discovers misconduct sufficient to justify a lawful discharge, the employee cannot win on a claim for reinstatement.

Age Discrimination Act of 1975   An Act passed to specifically address age discrimination in employment.

agent   A person who has the legal authority to act on behalf of the principal and to bind the principal to third persons by contract

Americans with Disabilities Act of 1990   An Act to address discrimination involving Americans who suffer from some type of physical or mental disability.

association with an individual with a disability   A relationship with an individual known to have a disability.

assumption of risk   Knowingly and willingly exposing yourself (or your property) to the possibility of harm.

Atheism   The absence of a belief in a supreme being or other religious tenets.

B-1 and B-2 visa   A nonimmigrant visa available to aliens who have a residence in a foreign country that they have no intention of abandoning, and who are visiting the United States for either business (B-1) or for pleasure (B-2).

back pay   The present value of wages and benefits the employee would have earned for the remainder of the employment term, less any wages and benefits the employee earned or could have earned in the interim, exercising reasonable diligence.

Belo contracts   A guaranteed weekly compensation to employees who work irregular hours.

bona fide occupational qualification   An employer's legitimate need to discriminate in hiring.

cafeteria plan   A plan that offers the employee a choice between cash and certain statutory nontaxable benefits provided under either insured or self-funded plans.

checklist system   Evaluation of each employee through the use of a list of behaviors found to be related to job performance.

civil servants   Government employees.

430

COBRA   An acronym used to refer to the health care continuation coverage provisions contained in ERISA and the Internal Revenue Code.

collective bargaining agreement   A contract between a union and an employer's union members that serves as a specialized employment agreement for unions and union workers.

compensable injury or illness   An injury or illness that arises out of or in the course of employment.

compensatory damages   Damages awarded for the actual loss suffered by a plaintiff.

construct validation   A test that considers the psychological makeup of the applicant and compares it with the traits necessary for adequate job performance.

constructive discharge   The employer makes working conditions so intolerable that a reasonable person in the employee's position would have felt compelled to resign.

content validation   A test that specifically examines applicants for the skills required by the specific position that the applicant seeks.

contributory negligence   Negligent (careless) conduct by a person who was harmed by another person's negligence; a plaintiff's failure to be careful that is a part of his or her injury when the defendant's failure to be careful is also part of the cause.

creditable coverage   Health coverage arrangements that count toward reducing preexisting condition exclusion under a new employer's group health plan, and includes coverage under an employer-provided group health plan, an individual insurance policy, Medicare, or an HMO.

criterion-related validation   A test that accurately predicts job performance, as evidenced by the applicant's ability to do the job.

defamation   Transmission to others of false statements that harm the reputation, business, or property rights of a person.

defined benefit pension plan   A plan established by an employer to systematically provide a pension to employees over a period of years after retirement, based on factors such as years of service, the participant's age, compensation and possibly other variables.

derivative visas   A visa that is granted to the immediate family members (spouse and minor children) of aliens who have been classified as nonimmigrant visa holders in other categories of visas. Persons holding derivative visas are not permitted employment while in the United States until they have obtained employment visas of their own.

direct threat   A "significant risk of substantial harm to the health or safety of the individual or others that cannot be eliminated or reduced by reasonable accommodation."

disability   A physical or mental impairment that substantially limits one or more major life activities, a record of such an impairment, or being regarded as having such impairment.

disparate impact   Employment practices that are neutral on their face in the treatment of different groups, but that fall more heavily on one group than another and cannot be justified by business necessity.

disparate treatment   Intentional discrimination based on a person's race, color, religion, sex, national origin, age, or disability.

Drug-Free Workplace Act of 1988   An Act authorizing the Small Business Administration (SBA) to give grants to organizations so that those organizations could help small businesses set up drug-free workplace programs.

duty to reasonably accommodate   A legal obligation to try to find a way to avoid a conflict between workplace policies and an employee's religious practices or beliefs.

E category visa   The E-1 ("international trader") and E-2 ("international treaty investor") categories of visas are available to companies seeking to trade with or invest in the United States and permit those enterprises to transfer aliens to the United States for substantial periods of time to oversee trade or investments.

economic realities test   A test that focuses upon whether the alleged employee is dependent upon the business for which he or she is working.

Electronic Communications Privacy Act of 1986   A law that prohibits the intentional interception of oral, wire or electronic communication, with limited exceptions.

eligibility testing   Testing to ensure that the applicant is capable of performing and qualified for the position.

employee   A person in the service of another under any contract of hire, express or implied, oral or written, where the employer has the power or right to control and direct the employee in the material details of how the work is to be performed.

employee benefit plans   Any plan, fund, or program established or maintained for the purpose of providing medical, surgical or hospital care or benefits, or benefits in the event of sickness, accident, disability, death or unemployment, or vacation benefits.

Employee Polygraph Protection Act   An Act that bars most private-sector employers from requiring, requesting or suggesting that a job applicant or employee submit to a polygraph or lie detector test, and from using or accepting the results of such tests.

employee welfare benefit plan   A plan, fund, or program established by an employer for the purpose of providing certain types of benefits through the purchase of insurance or other types of benefits for participants and their beneficiaries.

employer   Someone who hires another to perform work on his or her behalf, and who has the right to control the details of how the work is performed.

employment at will   The employer's ability to select an employee, control the hours and rates of pay for the employee, and to discharge the employee with or without cause.

English-only rules   Rules that require that employees not communicate in the workplace in any language other than English.

English-proficiency rules   Rules that require that employees or job applicants have the ability to write, speak, and understand English at a given level of proficiency.

ERISA   An act that applies to employee benefit plans.

essential functions of the job   The *fundamental* job duties of the position, but not the *marginal* functions of the position.

estoppel   The theory under which an individual is stopped by his or her own prior acts from claiming a right against another person who has legitimately relied on those acts.

F and M visa   A visa that permits aliens to enter the United States as non-immigrants to pursue academic studies. The F visa covers students in elementary, college, or graduate schools and the M category covers those students in non-academic or vocational programs.

Fair Labor Standards Act   An Act that established the federal minimum wage, maximum hours of work, overtime pay, and the regulation of child labor for employers engaged in interstate or foreign commerce and employees of state and local government.

Federal Child Labor Law   An Act establishing the minimum age for employment as sixteen years.

Federal Fair Credit Reporting Act   An Act that imposed new limitations on the use of consumer credit reports in making employment decisions.

Federal Privacy Act   An Act that requires federal agencies to allow individuals to examine, copy, and request the correction of information in the agency's records.

fellow servant rule   A rule, abolished in most states by employers' liability acts, that an employer is not responsible for the injury one employee does to another employee if the employees were carefully chosen.

fetal protection policies   Policies adopted by an employer that limit or prohibit employees from performing certain jobs or working in certain areas of the workplace because of the potential harm presented to pregnant employees, their fetuses, or the reproductive system or capacity of employee.

fiduciary   Acting for another in a position of trust.

fiduciary duty   A duty to act with the highest degree of honesty and loyalty toward another person and in the best interests of the other person, to the employer.

front pay   The amount of money that the employee would have earned from the date of trial to the conclusion of the employment contract.

general duty clause   An OSHA provision requiring that an employer furnish to each employee employment and a place of employment free from recognized hazards that cause or are likely to cause death or serious physical harm to the employee.

good faith and fair dealing   Honest dealing.

H-1B visa   A visa that is available to professional individuals with baccalaureate or other advanced degrees, such as engineers, scientists, chemists, and registered nurses.

H-2B visa   A visa that is available for skilled and unskilled temporary employees who do not qualify for an H-1 visa.

H-3B visa   A visa that is available to aliens who have a residence in a foreign country that they have no intention of abandoning, and who come to the United States as a trainee.

health care provider   Doctors of medicine or osteopathy who are licensed to practice medicine or surgery by the state in which the doctor practices, or any other person determined by the secretary of labor to be capable of providing health care services.

Health Insurance Portability and Accountability Act of 1996 (HIPAA)   An act that made health care coverage more widely available.

hostile work environment   Conduct that "has the purpose or effect of unreasonably interfering with an individual's work performance, creating an intimidating, hostile or offensive work environment."

hybrid test   A test that combines the right to control and economic realities tests to determine whether an individual is an employee or independent contractor.

Illegal Immigration and Responsibility Act of 1996   An Act that significantly restricted immigration and increased penalties by granting incentives for individual states to develop counterfeit-resistant driver's licenses and birth certificates that could be used in employment verification systems.

Immigration and Nationality Act of 1990   An Act that significantly expanded visa availability for persons seeking to enter the United States for employment.

Immigration Reform and Control Act of 1986   An Act that was amended by the Immigration and Nationality Act of 1990.

implied contract   A contract that is not expressed but is created by other words or the conduct of the parties, from the circumstances of the relationship.

incentive stock options   Options that are granted only to employees and that meet requirements of Section 422 of the Internal Revenue Code.

independent contractors   Persons who contract with an "employer" to do a particular piece of work by his or her own methods and under his or her own control.

individual disparate treatment   The employer deliberately treated an employee differently from other employees because of his or her membership in a protected class (age, sex, race, disability, for example).

ineligibility testing   Testing for disqualifying employment factors, that include drug and alcohol tests, HIV testing, and polygraphs.

injunction   A court order requiring violators of antidiscrimination laws to cease their discriminatory conduct and to refrain from committing future violations.

integration test A test that requires that the employment relationship not only meet the standards for the mutual control test, but that a certain degree of integration must exist between the two employers.

intentional infliction of emotional distress Allegations that the discharge of an employee was carried out in a manner that was intentionally and extremely abusive, degrading or humiliating.

joint employment A job in which the essential terms and conditions of the employee's work are controlled by two or more entities.

key employee A salaried, FMLA-eligible employee who is among the highest paid 10% of all of the employees within 75 miles of the employee's work site at the time the employee gives notice of the need for leave.

known disability A disability of which an employer is aware.

leased employees Workers who are assigned to projects of relatively longer duration, require greater technical expertise, and may, in some cases, involve relatively less direct control and supervision by the employer who is leasing the employee.

libel Written statements to others of false statements that harm the reputation, business, or property rights of a person.

liquidated damages An amount equal to lost wages and benefits.

lodestar A figure of attorneys' fees derived by multiplying the number of hours reasonably expended by a reasonable hourly rate.

L visa A visa that is generally limited to high-level managers, executives or persons with highly-specialized knowledge of a company's product, manufacturing process, etc. The holder of such a visa must have been continuously employed for one year by a company or an affiliate or subsidiary, and must temporarily come to the United States to render his services to that same employer or subsidiary or affiliate.

major life activity Activities that an average person performs with little or no difficulty, including: walking, sitting, working, speaking, seeing, caring for self, learning, lifting, breathing, hearing, or performing manual labor.

malice Ill will, intentionally harming someone, having no moral or legal justification for harming someone.

managed care program A purchaser of health care that controls or influences the utilization of health care services in an attempt to achieve high quality and cost-effective health care services.

management by objective Measurement of an employee's performance on the basis of objectives set by the manger and employee to be met by a specified time limit

master A person who employees another person.

maximum medical improvement The best that an employee will ever be.

mental impairment Any mental or psychological disorder, such as mental retardation, organic brain syndrome, emotional or mental illness, and specific learning disabilities.

Minimum Wage Increase Act of 1996 An act that dictates that an employee covered by the FLSA must be paid a minimum hourly wage of $5.15.

mitigate damages Reasonable diligence to seek other employment substantially equivalent to his or her previous position.

mixed motives case A situation where an employer offers both a legitimate and an illegitimate reason for the adverse action.

money purchase plan An individual account plan that requires that an employer commit to a specific contribution formula.

mutual control A test that is based on the joint control over labor relations or working conditions of the employee.

national origin discrimination   Discrimination on the basis of the country from which an employee or his or her relatives descended.

negligent hiring   The master's careless hiring of someone who was likely to injure third parties.

nonimmigrant business visa   A visa that allows foreign nationals to enter the United States to work, study and/or train on a nonimmigrant basis.

non-pecuniary damages   Noneconomic losses for the intangible injuries of emotional harm, such as emotional pain, suffering, inconvenience, mental anguish, loss of enjoyment of life, injury to professional standing, injury to character and reputation, and loss of harm.

Notice of Right to Sue   A form from the EEOC stating that the employee has a right to sue for an ADA violation.

offer of judgment   The offer of a specified amount that the plaintiff could obtain if the case went to trial.

Older Workers' Benefit Protection Act   An Act that amended requirements for employee benefit plans.

O visa   A visa that is available to aliens with extraordinary ability in the sciences, arts, education, business, or athletes, or aliens seeking solely to participate in specialized artistic or athletic performances.

partial disability   A worker who can still work, but at reduced wages

permanent partial disability benefits   Benefits that are paid based on any residual medical impairment after maximum improvement.

permanent resident visa   A permanent visa granted to outstanding professors and researchers, certain multinational executives and managers, skilled workers, professionals, advanced-degree professionals, or aliens of exceptional ability

permanent total disability   The compensation awarded to an employee who, because of injuries, can perform no service for which any reasonable job market exists.

personal surveillance   Observing or listening to employees without mechanical aids.

physical impairment   Any physiological disorder or condition, cosmetic disfigurement, or anatomical loss affecting one or more of the following body systems: neurological; musculoskeletal; special sense organ; respiratory, including speech organs; cardiovascular; reproductive; digestive; genito-urinary; hemic and lymphatic; skin; and endocrine.

polygraph   Lie detector test.

preemployment testing   Testing that occurs before hiring, or sometimes after hiring, but before employment, in connection with such qualities as integrity, honesty, drug and alcohol use, HIV, or other such characteristics.

principal   An employer or anyone else who has another person (an agent) do things for him.

profit sharing plan   An individual account plan that contains a contribution formula.

promissory estoppel   The principle that when Person A makes a promise and expects Person B to do something in **reliance** upon that promise, then Person B does act in reliance upon that promise, the law will usually help Person B enforce the promise because Person B has *relied* upon the promise to his or her *detriment*. Person A is "stopped" from breaking the promise even when there is no **consideration** to make the promise binding as part of a contract, may prevent the employer from denying an alleged promise.

public policy   Broadly, principles and standards regarded by the legislature or by the courts as being of fundamental concern to the state and the whole of society," and "more narrowly, the principle that a person should not be allowed to do anything that would tend to injure the public at large."

punitive damages   An award to discourage defendants from acting maliciously or in reckless disregard of the law.

punitive/exemplary damages   Damages awarded in addition to actual damages when the defendant acted with recklessness, malice, or deceit and intended to punish and thereby deter blameworthy conduct.

P visa   A visa that is available for artists and entertainers.

qualified   Offering those individuals who were actually covered under the plan on the day before the qualifying even an opportunity to purchase continued coverage under the plan at a cost of up to 102% of the group rate for periods up to 18 or 36 months.

qualified beneficiaries   Individuals who are eligible for COBRA rights only if they were actually covered under the plan on the day before the qualifying event.

qualified individual with a disability   One who, with or without reasonable accommodation, has the requisite education, skill, experience, and other job-related requirements necessary to perform the primary job functions of a position.

qualified privilege   Otherwise defamatory statements are made under circumstances where the person making the statement has a legitimate and reasonable justification to communicate.

qualified retirement plan   A written plan established by an employer to provide retirement benefits for its employees.

qualifying event   An action that results in the loss of coverage of an employee, former employee, spouse or dependent child under a group health plan subject to COBRA.

quid pro quo **harassment**   A manager or supervisor engages in unwelcome sexual conduct in a manner that, expressly or implicitly, makes submission to that conduct a term or condition of employment, or uses the employee's response as a basis for employment decisions affecting that person

quid pro quo **religious harassment**   The conditioning of an economic or other job benefit upon an employee's submission to the employer's religious observances or practices in the workplace, or punishing the employee for failure to comply with those religious observances or practices.

quotas   The strict numbers of women or minorities that must be hired to comply with affirmative action requirements.

Q visa   A visa that is available for international cultural exchange visitors for up to 15 months.

race   Any identifiable class of persons.

racial discrimination   Discrimination against an individual because of his or her race.

ratification   The confirmation and acceptance of a previous act done by another person.

reasonable accommodation   Any modification or adjustment to the job or work environment to enable a qualified applicant or employee with a disability to participate either in the application process or to perform essential job functions.

reasonable factor other than age   Uniformly required credentials such as education, prior experience, and systems that measure merit or the quality or quantity of performance that when applied do not reflect discrimination in employment decisions.

reasonable person standard   Conduct that is severe or pervasive enough to create an objectively hostile or abusive work environment that a "reasonable person" would find hostile or abusive.

reasonable woman standard   A standard that is subjective in nature, and allows the complainant to decide what is unacceptable conduct.

record of impairment   History of a disability.

red circle rate   Temporarily paying a worker at a higher-than-normal rate for a reason that is not based on gender.

regarded as having such an impairment   Individuals perceived as having a disability.

religion   All aspects of religious observance and practice, as well as belief.

religious belief   A sincere and meaningful belief that is not confined in either source or content to traditional or parochial concepts of religion.

respondeat superior   The doctrine of the master's liability for a servant's action within the scope of employment.

retaliation   An employee alleges he or she suffered an adverse employment action because he or she filed a charge of discrimination, made a complaint of discrimination, participated in a discrimination investigation, or otherwise opposed sex discrimination by the employer.

reverse discrimination   Situations in which the employee feels discriminated against specifically because of a remedy applied by the court to redress wrongs found to have existed or by an employer under an affirmative action plan.

self-compelled publication   An employee is compelled to repeat the reason for his discharge (allegedly defamatory) to other persons in searching for a new job.

serious health condition   A condition that prevents an employee from performing the functions of his or her job.

servant   A person employed by another person.

severance pay   Payment intended to provide financial security for employees whose jobs have been eliminated.

sexual harassment   Unwelcome sexual advances, requests for sexual favors and other verbal or physical conduct of a sexual nature.

single employer   A theory that distinct entities may be exposed to liability upon a finding that they represent a single, integrated enterprise

slander   Oral statements to others of false statements that harm the reputation, business, or property rights of a person.

spoofing   The construction of an electronic mail communication so that it appears to be from someone else.

statute of frauds   A statute that provides that any contract that cannot be performed within one year is not enforceable unless it is in writing and signed by the person against whom the agreement is to be enforced.

substantially limit   A situation where an individual is unable to perform a major life activity that the average person in the general population can perform; or is significantly restricted as to the condition, manner, or duration under which an individual can perform a particular major life activity as compared with the condition, manner, or duration under which the average person in the general population can perform that same major life activity.

summated scale   A measurement that requires supervisors to indicate how often the employee satisfies each of several behavior-based statements, including desirable and undesirable performance.

systemic disparate impact   Employment practices that are neutral on their face in the treatment of different groups, but which fall more heavily on one group than another and cannot be justified by business necessity.

systemic disparate treatment   A pattern of discrimination against one general protected group.

temporary disability   A worker who is still receiving medical care and has not reached maximum medical improvement.

temporary employees   Workers of one employer who are assigned to relatively short projects of another employer, the "client company."

temporary partial disability benefits   Benefits that are paid when an employee is recovering from an injury and is capable of returning to some type of work but not full duty and, therefore, sustains an actual wage loss.

temporary total disability benefits   Benefits that a worker receives for the period of time he or she is incapable of doing any type of employment and he or she is still recovering from injuries.

TN-visa   A visa that permits an expedited entry to the United States for professionals through an on-the-spot determination of eligibility at the border.

tort   A civil (as opposed to a criminal) wrong, other than a breach of contract, that results in injury to another person.

tourist visa   The B-2 visa that is available to aliens who have a residence in a foreign country that they have no intention of abandoning, and who are visiting the United States for pleasure.

unconditional offer of reinstatement   An offer by an employer to reemploy the discharged employee under comparable working conditions.

underrepresentation   Fewer minorities or women in a particular job group than would reasonably be expected by their availability.

undue hardship   Any accommodation that would be unduly costly, disruptive, or substantial, or that would fundamentally alter the nature or operation of the business.

undue hardship   A burden imposed on an employer by accommodating an employee's religious conflict that would be too onerous for the employer to bear.

validated   Evidence that the test evaluates what it says it evaluates.

vesting   Absolute, accrued, complete right to benefits

vicarious liability   Indirect legal responsibility for the acts of an employee.

whistleblower   An employee who brings organizational wrongdoing to the attention of government authorities.

white-collar exemptions   Exemptions to FLSA, including executive, administrative, professional, and outside salesmen.

workplace assessment   An assessment that measures the workplace for the representation of women and minorities in each of seven employment categories, ranging from unskilled workers to management employees.

wrongful discharge   Alleged termination in breach of either an express or implied employment contract.

INDEX